ANCIENT WARFARE

ANCIENT WARFARE

Archaeological Perspectives

Edited by

John Carman and Anthony Harding

SUTTON PUBLISHING

First published in the United Kingdom in 1999 by
Sutton Publishing Limited · Phoenix Mill
Thrupp · Stroud · Gloucestershire · GL5 2BU

British Library Cataloguing in Publication Data
A catalogue record for this book is available from the British Library.

ISBN 0-7509-1795-4

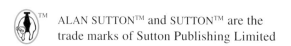

ALAN SUTTON™ and SUTTON™ are the
trade marks of Sutton Publishing Limited

Typeset in 10/13 pt Sabon.
Typesetting and origination by
Sutton Publishing Limited.
Printed in Great Britain by
Redwood Books, Trowbridge, Wiltshire.

CONTENTS

LIST OF CONTRIBUTORS

Don Brothwell is Professor of Human Palaeoecology in the University of York. He has had a lifetime interest in the nature of human conflict and the anthropology of warfare. Prior to his University studies, his 'national service' was in Lincoln Prison, and he has remained a committed pacifist, though not a naïve one.

John Carman gained his PhD in Archaeology from Cambridge University in 1993. He is an Affiliated Lecturer in the Department of Archaeology, University of Cambridge, and a Research Fellow at Clare Hall, Cambridge. His specialisations include archaeological heritage management and archaeological theory as well as archaeologies of violence and war. He published his first book *Valuing Ancient Things: archaeology and law* in 1996. He has edited *Material Harm: archaeological studies of war and violence* and is co-Director with Patricia Carman of the 'Bloody Meadows' Project on historic battlefields world-wide.

John Chapman is Reader in Archaeology at the University of Durham. He has specialised in the prehistoric archaeology of the Balkans, notably the Neolithic, and published his doctoral work on the Vinča Culture in 1981. A major survey of prehistoric Dalmatia in the 1980s was published in 1996 as *The Changing Face of Dalmatia* (with R. Shiel and Š. Batovič). Since 1991 he has been working in north-east Hungary on the Upper Tisza Project, now nearing completion. He is also a writer on theoretical archaeology, and edits *The European Journal of Archaeology*.

Pavel M. Dolukhanov is Reader in East European Archaeology at the University of Newcastle upon Tyne. He is the author of *Ecology and Economy in Neolithic Eastern Europe*, *Environment and Ethnicity in the Ancient Near East*, and *The Early Slavs, Eastern Europe from the initial settlement to the Kievan Rus*. He is co-editor (with J.C. Chapman) and contributor to *Cultural Transformations and Interactions in Eastern Europe* and *Landscapes in Flux, Central and Eastern Europe in antiquity*. He has also written many articles on the environment and ethnicity of prehistoric Eastern Europe.

Jonathan Haas is the MacArthur curator of Anthropology at the Field Museum in Chicago and an External Professor with the Santa Fe Institute. He has researched and published widely on the development of complex cultural systems, the origins of warfare, and the rise of early states. Among his publications are *The Evolution of the Prehistoric*

State and *The Anthropology of War*. He has conducted fieldwork in the eastern and south-western United States as well as in Peru.

Victor Davis Hanson is Professor of Greek and Classics at California State University, Fresno. He is the author of *Warfare and Agriculture in Classical Greece, The Western Way of War, The Other Greeks, The Wars of the Ancient Greeks* and *The Soul of Battle* in addition to other books and articles on ancient Greek military and agrarian history.

Anthony Harding is Professor of Archaeology at the University of Durham. A specialist on the Bronze Age archaeology of Europe, he has published a number of books on the subject including *The Bronze Age in Europe* (with J.M. Coles) and *The Mycenaeans in Europe*. He has conducted excavations in Britain, Poland and the Czech Republic on a variety of Bronze and Iron Age sites, and is currently working on the application of landscape archaeology techniques to eastern Europe.

Dimitra Kokkinidou gained her degree in archaeology and art history from the Aristotle University of Thessaloniki, Greece, and her M.Phil and PhD in prehistoric archaeology from Birmingham University, UK. Her publications concern the Greek Neolithic and Bronze Ages, gender interpretations of material culture and educational implications of cultural heritage. She has taught at secondary and tertiary level in Greece and is currently Teaching Associate at the School of European Languages and Cultures, Monash University, Melbourne, Australia.

Kristian Kristiansen is Professor of Archaeology at the University of Gothenburg in Sweden. His most recent books are *Europe Before History* and, with Michael Rowlands, *Social Transformations in Archaeology: global and local perspectives*. He has edited several books and the *Journal of Danish Archaeology*. He was the first President of the European Association of Archaeologists between 1994 and 1998. His research interests include archaeological history and heritage management as well as the Bronze Age.

Roger Mercer obtained an MA in Archaeology at the University of Edinburgh (1963–67). In 1969 he became an Inspector of Ancient Monuments for the Department of the Environment (now English Heritage) where his responsibilities included the whole of south-west England as well as excavations on a number of sites in state care. In 1974 he became lecturer in prehistory in the Department of Archaeology, University of Edinburgh, and Reader in 1982. His specialism was in Neolithic and Bronze Age prehistory in Britain and Europe. In 1990 he became Secretary (Chief Executive) of the Royal Commission on the Ancient and Historical Monuments of Scotland.

Marianna Nikolaidou graduated from the Department of History and Archaeology, Aristotle University of Thessaloniki, Greece, and did her graduate studies in Thessaloniki and Cambridge, UK. Her PhD on Minoan religious symbolism was completed in 1994 and she is co-author of *Archaeology and Gender, approaches to Aegean prehistory* (published in Greek). Based at the Institute of Archaeology, University of California in Los Angeles, and the Getty Museum in Malibu, she specialises in the Neolithic and Bronze Age of the Aegean and her research interests include pottery studies, religion and symbolism, and gender issues.

Klavs Randsborg is Professor at the Archaeological Institute, University of Copenhagen. He has written several books and many articles on the European and Scandinavian Bronze and Iron Ages, Classical and Roman periods, and the Early Middle Ages in the fields of archaeological chronology, culture and social history, settlement, burial and archaeological interpretation. He has current fieldwork projects in Greece, Russia, Ukraine and West Africa.

Deborah Shepherd is Visiting Scholar in Interdisciplinary Archaeological Studies at the University of Minnesota, Minneapolis, USA. Her dissertation, *Funerary Ritual and Symbolism: an inter-disciplinary interpretation of burial practices in Late Iron Age Finland*, will be published in 1999 as a British Archaeological Report. She is currently involved in long-term field excavation of a Norse settlement area in northern England.

Slavomil Vencl is a researcher at the Archaeological Institute of the Czech Academy of Sciences in Prague. He also teaches Stone Age Archaeology at the Universities in Prague and Plzeň. He has written monographs which include *Les instruments lithiques des premiers agriculteurs en Europe centrale* and *Hostim – Magdalenian in Bohemia*, as well as numerous articles on the Palaeolithic and Mesolithic, and on the methodology of prehistoric archaeology.

ONE

INTRODUCTION

John Carman and Anthony Harding

This book is about warfare in the ancient past. More specifically, it is about how archaeologists can address issues that are of contemporary interest and concern to students of mass violence as a part of human existence.

The book derives in part from a conference on the theme of ancient warfare held in Durham, England, in 1996, at which some of the contributions had their origins.[1] Other contributors were specifically invited to address issues not otherwise covered. The contributions as a whole attempt to provide the most complete coverage of the archaeological study of ancient warfare (excluding other forms of human violence) currently available.

We are concerned with five principal themes, each of which can be expressed in the form of questions:

• What general lessons applicable to archaeology are to be learnt from a study of warfare in ethnographic and historical situations? Why do so many societies engage in warfare? What advantages does it bring, and what risks does it involve?

• In what ways can archaeological evidence be used to tell us about warfare in the past, before (or without) writing? Is artefactual material with warlike associations (weaponry, defensive structures) necessarily to be seen in itself as evidence for warfare? If not, what is?

• In what ways was warfare a structural part of the development of early Europe? How did it relate to social and political development – for instance, the emergence of chiefdoms or state-formation?

• Can general statements be made cross-culturally about ancient warfare in archaeological terms? Can the study of, for instance, Egyptian or Roman warfare contribute to the study of prehistoric or early Medieval warfare?

• What can archaeology contribute to studies of warfare? Is a distinctively archaeological contribution to the study of warfare a valid objective?

Anyone who has considered the nature and importance of ancient warfare will have come across a number of key texts. All students of war realise the pervasive importance of the great work of Carl von Clausewitz, *On War* (1976 [1832]), which sets out many of the fundamental concepts that underlie the modern study of the subject. Von Clausewitz's concerns were partly with warfare as he knew it (see Keegan 1993, 12ff. for an account of von Clausewitz's career in so far as it affected his thought) and partly with what he saw as the universals of warfare. At the time, neither archaeology nor anthropology existed as recognised disciplines with a body of theory and data of their own, and as a consequence von Clausewitz could not know much about forms of warfare outside his direct experience, or beyond available texts.

For writers of the present day, a couple of works are key – one might say required – reading. The first is H.H. Turney-High's compellingly written *Primitive War: Its Practice and Concepts* (1949).[2] Though much has changed since then, and current ethnographers would not today adopt (or even accept as valid) his cross-cultural approach, this remains one of the most far-reaching, and certainly the best-written, anthropological texts on the subject, reaching also into archaeology – at least into the archaeology that was being written before the Second World War. Especially for present-day students, the first couple of chapters are crucial, the first dealing with weapons, and the second with the general practices of war. It is salutary, on reading Chapter 1 of *Primitive War*, to find how many of the statements in this present volume are foreshadowed there.

The second work is more recent: John Keegan's *A History of Warfare* (1993). Keegan is a military historian, and neither an anthropologist nor an archaeologist, but his panoramic knowledge of the theoretical as well as the historical literature means that he can range across these as well as his home disciplines. The book is not really a history of warfare at all, but a review of most aspects of the study of warfare, illustrated with historical examples.

More recently still, Lawrence H. Keeley has published his *War Before Civilization* (1996) which has a particular message to press home: that the past was not a peaceful place. According to Keeley, the past has been 'pacified': that is to say, scholars have allegedly not attributed to it the warlike qualities he believes it possessed. War in the ancient past was, in his view, frequent and deadly: even if particular periods do not appear to possess many weapons, fortifications or much evidence of slaughter, that does not mean they were not prone to constant wars. We have read Keeley's work with interest and profit, which is not to say we agree with everything he says, as the contents of this book will make clear.[3]

Other recent authors who have dealt with war in the anthropological literature include Robert L. Carneiro, R. Brian Ferguson and Jonathan Haas. We are glad to acknowledge here their many insights. An archaeologist who has brought the study of warfare into many of his writings is Timothy Earle, well known for his studies of chiefdoms. His most recent book on this subject, *How Chiefs Come to Power* (1997), explicitly devotes a chapter to 'Military Power: The Strategic Use of Naked Force' in his consideration of the long-term development of 'chiefdoms' in Denmark, Hawaii and the Andes. Among the issues Earle raises are the ways warfare relates to the establishment and maintenance of political power, comparing approaches such as the cultural-ecological or political-ecological (e.g., the 'circumscription' theory of Carneiro) with those placing greater importance on economic or ideological factors. Earle concludes that 'warfare was critical in all three cases', though it differed greatly in its nature and effectiveness in each.

Several authors have pointed out – though until now, perhaps not clearly enough – that for an archaeologist, what is crucial is a conjunction between observed archaeological data (artefacts in the wide sense) and the material remains of known violent encounters in the historical or ethnographic record. Archaeologically, what survive are three potential categories of data (cf. Chapter 5): artefacts used with aggressive intent ('weapons'), damage inflicted on other humans in the form of pathological marks on human skeletons (or rarely, soft tissue) and site evidence in the form of constructions for defence or, more rarely, offence.[4] What do not survive are the motives, causes, courses and outcomes of the aggression, at least not in directly observable form. On the other hand, it is a reasonable presumption that at least some weapons – perhaps the majority – and at least some fortifications were the result of the causes and courses of ancient wars. Archaeologists seeking to understand the nature of the societies they are studying want to be able to specify how and why these evidences of conflict occurred, and how they affected the development of the societies in question. But in warfare as in so many other things, recent practice may be a poor guide to what happened in ancient times, so help is needed from other sources.

DEFINING ANCIENT WARFARE: ANTHROPOLOGICAL INFLUENCE

The theme of warfare has been much debated by anthropologists since Malinowski (1941) and before. In recent times, Fried et al. (1968), Ferguson (1984; 1990; Ferguson & Whitehead 1992), Haas (1990b) and Carneiro (1990) have made notable contributions, as have historians, sociologists, psychologists and (bringing up the rear) archaeologists (cf. other chapters in this volume; Escalon de Fonton 1964; Behrens 1978; Vencl 1983; 1984a; 1984b; 1984c; Goldberg & Findlow 1984).

Almost inevitably, archaeologists of warfare are bound to notions about war derived from the sister-disciplines of history and anthropology (especially Keeley 1996; Carman 1997a), while others (e.g., Haas 1990b; Goldberg & Findlow 1984) locate themselves within the anthropological discourse about war. From these associations come a confusing number of terms applied to periods and types of warfare. In general, the term 'ancient warfare' as used in this book, means warfare in the past, from the first (unrecorded) instance of war up to the first millennium AD. Some references which derive from anthropological sources may apply to the kind of warfare we generally expect to have been experienced over a thousand years ago, even though they were learned from societies contemporary with our own. Terms for this kind of low-technology, limited war fought by traditional societies may include 'ritual war' (Chaliand 1994, 7) or (although we very much prefer to avoid these terms' pejorative overtones) 'wars by primitive societies' (Chaliand 1994, 7) and 'primitive war' (Turney-High 1949; Keegan 1993).

Conventional military history chooses to define warfare by a mixture of Western historical periods ('Ancient', 'Medieval', 'Modern'), geographical region ('Eastern') and description of the style of war ('Total' or 'Nuclear') (Montgomery 1968). A newer breed of military historian (especially Keegan 1993) chooses to use terms applicable universally to define types of warfare: 'primitive' for occasional small-scale wars fought by traditional societies, 'determined by subsistence and demography and . . . not very costly in lives' (Chaliand 1994, 7); 'Oriental' for wars distinguished by 'evasion, delay and indirectness' (Keegan 1993, 387), often by the application of defensive strategies, and deemed to be the kind of wars fought by the complex cultures of Asia (Chaliand 1994, 21), and finally, 'Western' for the fierce wars of annihilation in battle we inflict upon ourselves (cf. Hanson 1989; Keegan 1993). The majority of the authors in this book are concerned with the earliest kind of war fought by anatomically modern humans – the kinds still fought by some societies which are dubbed by some writers as 'primitive'. Others cross the 'military horizon' (Turney-High 1949; Keegan 1993) to consider the violence of more 'civilised' warfare.

Confusion of terminology can arise where a term is appropriated as part of a different scheme from our own. Thus, Gray (1997) locates 'ancient' warfare in a continuum with modern war and postmodern war, as part of a discourse whereby war became an activity subject to 'rules, order, and form' (Gray 1997, 107) akin to Turney-High's non-'primitive' 'true war' (Turney-High 1949). This organised war is intended to be clearly distinguished from 'primitive, heroic, unorganised, ritual war' (Gray 1997, 106), which is a form of ongoing discourse between the human and 'the other' in which the conservation of the enemy is as important as, or even more so than their destruction (Gray 1997, 97). Gray's ancient, modern and postmodern wars fall into Chaliand's rationally ordered categories of 'wars with limited objectives', 'conventional wars of conquest' and 'mass wars' (Chaliand 1994, 7). Unorganised wars are designated by him as either 'ritual wars', defined as those which are 'not to the death. Generally they are the mark of societies that are still archaic or traditional' (Chaliand 1994, 7), or they may fall into the category of 'wars without quarter' – either wars of ideas (about religion or identity) or wars against those seen as radically different (Chaliand 1994, 7–8). In general, the kind of warfare indulged in by early societies has been held to be limited, having 'recourse to all sorts of devices which spare [combatant and non-combatant alike] from the worst of what might be inflicted' (Keegan 1993, 387). This is the view put forward by Turney-High: 'Many of the slayers of consanguine society were [natural] . . . But there is certainly one which has been consistently neglected. This is the rise of the army with officers' (Turney-High 1949, 253). This view has been taken up by his successors. For Ferguson & Whitehead and their contributors, it is the contact zone between civilisation and indigenous peoples which is the location of the most violent forms of warfare: 'a tribal zone can be a very violent place. At its worst it can consume a population' (Ferguson & Whitehead 1992, 27).

The work of those such as Turney-High (1949) and Ferguson & Whitehead (1992), and the results they have achieved, derive from efforts to understand how and why the kinds of traditional societies studied by anthropologists fight, putting the focus on the formal aspects of their warfare. Keeley (1996) challenges archaeologists and anthropologists to look again at their evidence and he is concerned to understand how what he considers to be the conventional view of a 'pacified past' came about. Like Carman (1997a), he locates this in a review of the history of anthropologies of war. Carman (1993; 1997a, 6–10) links the concerns of anthropologists in this area with events beyond academic anthropology, in an effort to explain how and why certain styles of approach were adopted in anthropology at particular times since the end of the Second World War. By contrast, Keeley – perhaps more fairly to anthropological students of warfare – considers anthropological developments independently from broader social and political ones (Keeley 1996, 5–17, 164–70).

Keeley's work owes much to Turney-High (1949) and Keegan (1976), not least because he chooses to structure the book in terms of the kinds of evidence they each consider, and he shares with them a preparedness not to be squeamish. Where he differs from both is in the conclusion reached: 'civilised' warfare is not more terrible than other forms, for after 'exploring war before civilisation in search of something less terrible than the wars we know, we merely arrive where we started with an all-too familiar catalog [sic] of deaths, rapes, pillage, destruction, and terror' (Keeley 1996, 174):

> Primitive war was not a puerile or deficient form of warfare, but war reduced to its essentials: killing enemies with a minimum of risk, denying them the means of life via vandalism and theft . . . terrorising them into either yielding territory or desisting from their encroachments and aggressions . . . It is civilised war that is stylised, ritualised and relatively less dangerous. When soldiers clash with warriors . . . it is precisely these 'decorative' civilised tactics and paraphernalia that must be abandoned. (Keeley 1996, 175)

Keeley draws very largely on surveys of the anthropological literature to provide quantified cross-cultural comparisons which support his contention that 'The facts recovered . . . indicate unequivocally that primitive and prehistoric warfare was just as terrible and effective as the historic and civilised version' (Keeley 1996, 174). Moreover, whereas 'the modern nation-state goes to war once in a generation . . . [and after adjusting for the duration of such wars, being] at war only about one year in every five . . . 65 percent [of a sample of non-state societies were] at war continuously' (Keeley 1996, 33). In addition, 'by the measure of . . . mobilisation . . . war is no less important to tribes than to nations' (Keeley 1996, 35–6). A valuable insight of Keeley's is that there is more to warfare than the formal battle. In a battle between warriors and other warriors, formal limiting rules apply (cf. Chapters 4, 12 and 13, this volume), 'but unrestricted warfare, without rules and aimed at annihilation, was practised against outsiders' (Keeley 1996, 65). Here he turns the anthropological and archaeological focus away from mutually-agreed modes of combat towards rather less 'honourable' kinds: the raid, the ambush and particularly the massacre of non-combatants. Keeley finds all war – 'civilised', 'tribal', 'primitive' or 'prehistoric' – to be always total and unlimited war.

Keeley's argument forces anthropologists and archaeologists to rethink their approach to warfare. In particular, it presents us with a challenge: either to continue to believe – despite the presence of arguments and evidence to the contrary – that the distant past was relatively peaceful and such warfare as took place was characterised by restraint and ritual controls on violence, or to face the possibility that the concept of 'limited' war (at least in the past) is an oxymoron. The idea that war is either 'real' and unlimited in its violence or 'ritual' and thus limited is rooted deep in our thinking: Turney-High (1949) drew the distinction between 'primitive' war and 'true' war, which his successors have followed. But even before anthropologists began to study the warfare of non-literate traditional societies, the great philosopher of war, von Clausewitz (1976 [1832]), had pointed out that war is inevitably a province of violence, and the limitation of that violence is only the product of other factors external to the combatants – what he terms 'friction' (von Clausewitz 1976 [1832], 119–21):

> Kind hearted people might of course think there was some . . . way to disarm or defeat an enemy without too much bloodshed . . . [But] it is a fallacy that must be

exposed . . . If one side uses force without compunction, undeterred by the bloodshed it involves, while the other side refrains . . . [t]hat [first] side will force the other to follow suit; each will drive its opponent toward extremes . . . This is how [war] must be seen. It would be futile – even wrong – to try and shut one's eyes to what war really is from sheer distress at its brutality. (von Clausewitz 1976 [1832], 75–6)

Von Clausewitz's words – although denying the possibility of 'limited' war – nevertheless open up the conceptual space for such an idea to develop. Drawing on the distinction thus opened up, Halsall (1989) was able to distinguish between small-scale 'ritual' and large-scale 'non-ritual' warfare in Anglo-Saxon England. Keeley is also inevitably beguiled by it: he rejects the notion of large-scale prehistoric palisades and ditches as purely 'symbolic' features, 'the Neolithic equivalent of . . . elaborate symbols bearing the message Keep Out!' (Keeley 1996, 18), and instead argues for a defensive function. The idea that such features may be primarily symbolic and also functionally defensive is not considered, just as Halsall (1989) does not consider the idea that 'ritual' war is as 'real' as 'non-ritual', the difference – if any – lying simply in scale. The idea of a distinction between 'ritual', 'primitive' warfare and 'real', 'true' war thus remains a powerful one in anthropology and archaeology, as it is for military historians. But 'ritual' behaviour is not the only means of limiting the violence in war, which depends also on technological and other capabilities. Perhaps Keeley's (1996) alternative idea that all war is total does have some merit: if violence is restrained in formal battlefield encounters, then maybe it is not so restrained in other forms of related violence; where battlefield violence is unrestrained, then violence against non-combatants is limited. Such distinctions between the 'battlefield' and 'non-combatant' are as 'ritual' as any other ideological limitation placed upon war-making: in this sense, both 'primitive' and 'modern' warfare can be simultaneously limited and total.

MATERIAL REMAINS: THE ARCHAEOLOGICAL CONTRIBUTION

The terms and understandings archaeologists use for the study of warfare inevitably derive from other fields where such terms and understandings are already available: these are usually either history or ethnography. But archaeologists study the past – especially the most distant and prehistoric past – without access to the witness testimony available to the historian and the ethnographer. All we have is the mute material remains of that distant and inevitably different past which we must make speak.

For all his concern to convince us of the violence of the distant past, Keeley (1996) relies upon very few compelling archaeological examples (see Chapman, Chapter 8, this volume). There is, of course, nothing wrong with attempting to understand the violence of the past: it is the purpose of this book to contribute something to that understanding, and to do so, it is not unreasonable to seek out evidence and to suggest interpretations of that evidence. Archaeologists in general place a close reliance on skeletal evidence, ethnographic data, monuments and artefact analysis. This can be augmented with a close concern for contextual issues and the use of other sources of information – such as iconography or text – to support or challenge an interpretation of violent activity (Carman 1997a, 224). The evidence carried by human remains can tell us that violence existed in the past (cf. Wakely 1997; Filer 1997, as well as several chapters in this volume), but it offers little in the way of a firm indication of the prevalence of such violence. The interpretations offered of other evidence – 'defensive' structures, 'buffer zones', the suitability of axes for use as weapons – are predicated upon beliefs about past violence, and do not of themselves constitute evidence for it. More serious than this is Keeley's failure to make any meaningful linkage between archaeological evidence and that from other disciplines. As archaeologists, we want to know if weapons, skeletal trauma and fortifications really do tell us about the nature and existence of prehistoric warfare. Keeley, having boxed himself into a corner on the issue of the warlike past, in effect assumes that they must, and do, whereas they may, or they may not.

Keeley (1996) and this volume's editors and contributors are among a number of archaeologists, recent and not so recent, to have shown interest in warfare – that is to say, in the weapons of war, and the sites where remains indicative of supposedly warlike practices occur. Often, that interest has shown itself as part of a concern with a specific period or area (such as Classical Greece: Lawrence 1979; Snodgrass 1964; Hanson 1989, 1991), or as part of a particular theoretical approach to understanding the past, such as Marxism (Spriggs 1984) or 'peer-polity interaction' (Renfrew & Cherry 1986). One reason for its current popularity as a subject is simply the revived interest in war as a phenomenon shared with other disciplines: in particular, the works edited by Ferguson (1984), Haas (1990a) and Ferguson & Whitehead (1992) all testify to a revived interest among anthropologists of all areas and theoretical persuasion. Military history – spurred on by Keegan (1976, 1993), Weigley (1991) and others such as Nordstrom (1992, 1995) – has shown a new vitality, and the newly discovered threats of the post-Cold War world have helped to encourage students of politics and international relations to reconsider the possibilities of war in a new light (e.g., Gray 1997). In particular, traditional theories of strategy and war are of little help when faced with the complexities and apparent irrationality of ethnic or religious conflict, which would seem (at least on the surface) to share some of the attributes of war prior to the emergence of the nation-state, and certainly the modern superpower. Here, a deeper insight into the warfare of societies other than states may prove valuable, and the long time-depth that archaeology can offer may help.

The chapters in this book are mostly concerned with early warfare in Europe: the exceptions are Haas (Chapter 2), who draws upon his work in the prehistoric southwest of the United States, and Carman (Chapter 4), who goes beyond battles in Europe to those in north Africa and Asia. Chronologically, the book moves from the Upper Palaeolithic (Dolukhanov, Chapter 6), through the main periods of later European prehistory, into the Medieval. Vencl (Chapter 5), Kokkinidou & Nikolaidou (Chapter 7), Chapman (Chapter 8) and Mercer (Chapter 9) cover the emergence of warfare in different areas of Europe during the Neolithic period. Harding (Chapter 10), Kristiansen (Chapter 11) and Randsborg (Chapter 12) are concerned with the developed warfare of the Bronze and Iron Ages, and Hanson (Chapter 13) concentrates on the approximately contemporary – and indeed in some respects similar – warfare of the Greek *polis*. Shepherd (Chapter 14) stops just short of the Medieval, to focus on Anglo-Saxon warrior society. All apart from Carman avoid an engagement with the warfare of the civilisations of Egypt, Babylon, Assyria, Carthage and Rome. Like Keeley (1996), some contributors see warfare as endemic to the periods they study, or at least as a practice that occurred regularly within them. Some take a more 'neutral' stance (eg. Brothwell, Chapter 3).

To some extent, one's stance on ancient warfare depends on one's theoretical perspective and specific focus of study. Haas, for instance, is very much concerned with the role of warfare in the process of 'tribalisation' (Haas 1990a) and its connection with environmental stress, which is an approach shared with others, such as Zimmerman (1997). At the same time, it reflects a concern for a 'social-evolutionary' approach, shared by Keeley (1996), and in this book by Dolukhanov, Vencl and Kristiansen. At variance with these types of approach is a concern for the possibility of an innate aggression in the human species, reflected as an interest in socio-biological and bio-social understandings in the sources of human violence. A third approach is represented by a concern not for the causes of violence, but for understanding its manifestation and consequences, in this book especially reflected in the chapters by Carman, Hanson, and Kokkinidou & Nikolaidou: this 'social' understanding of warfare extends also to Harding, Randsborg and Shepherd, and their concern to delineate the social roles of specific categories of people in warfare (see also Treherne 1995). For Haas, Harding, Kokkinidou & Nikolaidou and Carman (1997a), warfare and violence are not 'natural' responses of human beings, but the product of particular social contexts: it therefore has to be proven to exist before it can be studied. In the cases of Hanson, Carman and Shepherd, well-established instances of warfare provide the starting place for study, not its end; for them, warfare is not an explanatory medium, but the object of study itself. For Harding and Kokkinidou & Nikolaidou, it is the material evidence for warfare itself that comes under scrutiny: the former tries to elucidate the nature of Bronze Age warfare on the basis of the artefactual finds and thus evaluate how widespread a phenomenon it was (see also Bridgford 1997), and the latter attempts to find alternative meanings for Neolithic 'defensive' structures in the Aegean (for Iberia, see also Oosterbeek 1997).

These differences in interpretation, style and approach – as well as chronological spread – form the basis around which this book has been structured. The opening chapters cover the three main strands of theory represented: the social-evolutionary and ecological, the bio-social and socio-biological, and 'warfare as cultural expression'. The questions asked concern how we consider warfare, and how we as archaeologists can or should approach it meaningfully. After Chapter 4, the contributors focus very strongly on the interpretation of material remains: Vencl (Chapter 5), Dolukhanov (Chapter 6) and Mercer (Chapter 9) all find clear evidence for past warfare; Kokkinidou & Nikolaidou (Chapter 7) and Harding (Chapter 10) question the meaning of evidence which could be interpreted as indicating the presence of warfare. Chapter 11 and those that follow look at the role of warfare in society: Kristiansen (Chapter 11), Randsborg (Chapter 12) and Shepherd (Chapter 14) all outline the implications for understanding society which can be found in the available evidence for the organisation of warfare; Hanson (Chapter 13) – one of only two authors who have the benefit of historical texts as their main source – looks at warfare from the other end, examining the consequences of styles of warfare for the societies that make them. Overall, the authors reflect the range of current interests in the study of warfare in the distant – and not so distant – human past.

In the end, much boils down to personal preferences in the interpretation of ancient material remains, but this is not to say that archaeological perspectives on ancient warfare should be a matter of some nebulous relativism, espoused as some form of anti-scientific posturing. Unlike Ember & Ember (e.g., 1992), we would not go so far as to seek through statistical manipulation of ethnographic data in numerical form some kind of scientific basis for supposing that warfare is correlated with particular social, economic or ideological manifestations in human societies. However, we do believe that ancient warfare can be susceptible to rational and stimulating treatment of a kind that depends on the detailed study of material data and its correlation with what is known from other sources about humankind at various stages of the past.

NOTES

1. The conference was held under the auspices of the Centre for the Archaeology of Central and Eastern Europe, University of Durham. Of those who spoke at that conference, Haas, Carman, Dolukhanov, Chapman, Vencl, Kristiansen and Randsborg are represented here. Many other interesting papers presented at the conference could not be accommodated in the present volume, which has been adapted to present a balanced selection of material that deals with core issues of warfare rather than highly specific manifestations of warlike material.
2. Keeley (1996, 10ff.) gives an informative account of Turney-High's career and major work.
3. Several of the authors in this volume quote Keeley with approval, Kristiansen regarding his book as 'inspirational' (see Chapter 11). As a counterbalance to this view, we would advise readers to consult R. Brian Ferguson's review of the work (Ferguson 1997) while bearing in mind that Ferguson is one of those criticised by Keeley as promoting the 'pacific' view of pre-industrial war.
4. Such as earthworks believed to have been constructed by the Roman legions for siege warfare at sites such as Masada (Israel) or Woden Law (Scottish Borders).

Two

The Origins of War and Ethnic Violence

Jonathan Haas

From the perspective of those of us living at present, it might seem that war is an inevitable part of human existence. Warfare and ethnic violence presses around us at every turn. We see its tragic face today in Northern Ireland, Bosnia, Rwanda, the Middle East, and reflecting back from our near and distant pasts. In the minds of the general public, there is a pervasive belief that organised, mortal conflict is somehow inherent to the human species. This seemingly inescapable conclusion can be based on almost any perusal of recorded history, where we find a continuous stream of warfare and violence between nations, states, ethnic groups and religions. Indeed, much of human history is written using such markers as wars, battles, heroic warriors and peace treaties to delineate the major eras of a particular culture or world area. Even in simpler, non-western types of community-based society, anthropologists have found war to be relatively ubiquitous in the contemporary ethnographic record (Ember & Ember 1992; Carneiro 1994).

Since both history and ethnography point to the apparent inevitability of war, it is a relatively easy leap to assume that the causes of war are inherent or natural to humanity. The evidence here, however, is a little more ambiguous. For example, it has been argued that there are biological foundations for aggression in humans, particularly among males (Lorenz 1966). While such arguments are intriguing and perhaps intuitively compelling, they are all short on the substantive data needed to confirm them empirically. No one has yet discovered a warfare gene or complex of genes, nor have they been able to show that some mix of hormones leads inexorably to combat and organised violence. Where biological models *may* prove helpful in the study of warfare is in understanding the possible relationships between the participation of men in combat and the reproductive 'fitness' of those men (Chagnon 1990).

Another argument, developed inductively and again based largely on intuition, maintains that people who are culturally or ethnically different from one another have a fundamental fear and dislike of one another. It is pertinent (and perhaps risky) here to look to the devastating situation today in Bosnia. Many media accounts of the events maintain that the ethnic violence and hatred was there before the break-up of the state of Yugoslavia, but it was suppressed by the iron-fisted rule of communism. Released from the rule of communism, the inherent violence was allowed to flourish, growing into ethnic warfare. As the media then search for the causes of the conflict, it is depicted as a power struggle between ethnic groups who have always hated one another. *Why* they hate one another is either attributed to historic reasons (e.g. the relationship between the Croats and Serbs during the Second World War) or to the in-born boundary of distrust and conflict between ethnically different groups. The reasoning is that their religions, their values, their cultures are all *so* different that they cannot live side by side in peace. Ethnic diversity in this and many other cases around the world is seen as a reasonable explanation by itself for hostile and combative relationships between groups of people (see Horowitz 1985 for a discussion of ethnic diversity and conflict).

The problem with making inferences about the inevitability of war or the inherent quality of warfare in human existence on the basis of historic or even ethnographic records is that all those records date from very late in the sequence of human development. They also come from a time when all human society has been dominated by the presence of large state polities intimately involved in regional or global systems of economic competition. Even the simplest band societies of South Africa or the Amazonian rainforest have suffered significant impact from the aggressive dominance of western colonialism for at least three or four hundred years (Ferguson & Whitehead 1994). The pervasive warfare we see today throughout the world, whether in simple or in complex societies, all takes place within the context of the political, economic, environmental and demographic relationships characteristic of the modern world system. Any inferences we can draw from the historic and ethnographic record about the inevitability of warfare only pertain to the relatively recent circumstances brought about by the evolution and global spread of the nation state. Warfare may be ubiquitous in the modern and historic worlds, but humanity has been around a lot longer than the nation state. If we want to look at whether warfare and the hatred of enemies is an inherent characteristic of the human species, we must look back prior to the rise of the nation state.

The historical record around the world is only a few thousand years old. We have written records from Mesopotamia several thousand years before Christ, and within a thousand years or so these are followed by systems of writing in the classic civilizations of the Old World, namely Egypt, India and China. For the New World, the first writing system, that of the Maya, does not really develop until the first millennium AD. In all these cases, the development of writing went hand in hand with the evolution of highly complex state-level societies, with centralised government, organised religion, and, significantly, a standing army. In most cases, writing first developed primarily as a means of keeping records for the government and bureaucracy. But every early writing system quickly expanded to recount historical events, glorify the rulers and pronounce the outcomes of wars. So even from the very beginning of the historic era, war is an integral part of the political relationships between the earliest state-level societies (Haas 1982). However, what if we go back prior to the written record – back into the prehistoric past?

Five or six thousand years may seem like a long time to those of us living our lives in the present, but five or six thousand years is but a tiny slice in the very long sequence of human development. The first human-like creatures diverged from their primate relatives in Africa several million years ago. The first modern *Homo sapiens* in turn also emerged in Africa several hundred thousand years ago, and soon migrated across most of Africa, Europe and Asia. Looked at from the perspective of several hundred thousand years of humans wandering across the planet, the last five thousand years of complex nation states begins to lose its stature as a marker of what is natural or inherent in the human species. What has happened in the past five thousand years demonstrates the *capacity* of humans for certain kinds of behaviour, not the *predisposition* of humans towards certain kinds of behaviour.

The sequence of human prehistory prior to the development of writing then assumes enormous importance in any effort to understand the fundamental causes of warfare within the human species. Furthermore, the only scientific medium we have for looking back to the origins and evolution of patterns of warfare in the human species is archaeology. Within this context, archaeological research comes to assume a critical role in helping to understand the causes of warfare and ethnic conflict across cultures and across time. It is archaeology and the archaeological record that hold the most appropriate intellectual resources to answer broad, pressing questions about the inevitable or intrinsic qualities of human warfare.

When we do turn to the archaeological record prior to the beginnings of writing, it is immediately interesting to note that we find that warfare is not nearly so ubiquitous as we see today. With some exceptions, it appears that warfare tends to go hand in hand with increasing political complexity and rising levels of population density. There is also growing evidence that in virtually every part of the world where we have explicitly looked into the question, we can determine when and why warfare starts in a specific prehistoric sequence. Furthermore, archaeologists have found that as long as the circumstances that led to warfare persist, the warfare also persists. At the same time, there are bodies of archaeological evidence showing that when circumstances change over a long period, warfare can also dissipate, and eventually disappear. It should be noted here that Keeley, in his recent book, *War Before Civilization* (1996), makes the point that war is much more pervasive in the archaeological record than has previously been recognised. However, Keeley's analysis, rather than leading to the conclusion that war was a universal in the past, forces us to examine the critical question of why warfare appears and disappears at different times and places (see Ferguson 1984; 1990; 1997).

Although this is the first in a series of chapters on patterns of warfare in Europe, it will nevertheless focus on the New World, to illustrate some of the kinds of insights that can be gained from looking at the archaeology of warfare. The examples cited relate to both the rise and fall of warfare, and give some perspective on the relationship between warfare and the existence of ethnically different people who might be labelled and attacked as 'enemies.'

For a number of reasons, the North American continent provides an ideal laboratory for examining patterns of prehistoric war and the relationship between war and ethnicity. First, North America was not significantly affected by the advanced nation states of Latin America or the Old World until the arrival of Europeans in the fifteenth and sixteenth centuries. Its evolutionary sequence is thus indigenous, and relatively 'pristine' (Fried 1967) in the sense of not being influenced by more complex outside societies. Second, the sequence is fairly short, given that humans did not enter North America much before 15,000 years ago (only archaeologists would think of 15,000 years as a 'short' time.) We therefore have a reasonably well-defined 'experiment' through which to examine the origins of warfare. Finally, there has been more than a century of research by literally thousands of archaeologists working on widely disparate ancient cultures in highly diverse environments. The result of this research is that for large areas of prehistoric North America, there are marvellously rich excavation and survey records, coupled with detailed chronological charts and palaeo-climatological reconstructions. My point here is not just Yankee bragging about the great American archaeological record, but to emphasise that a comprehensive prehistoric database provides a critical foundation for understanding the complexity and detail of evolving patterns of warfare.

Looking at North America as a laboratory for studying the origins and evolution of warfare in a prehistoric context, there are a number of insights to be gained when we look at different times and different places. If we start right at the beginning of human occupation on the continent, we find that warfare does not seem to be part of the cultural picture. Although the exact date of the first humans in the New World is the subject of much dispute, the first identifiable and abundant cultural assemblages are those of the big-game-hunting Palaeoindians of roughly 13,000 to 7,000 years ago (plus or minus a millennium). These first nomads would have crossed over the Bering Straits from Siberia and entered into a hunter's paradise. North America was a land of abundant game, including mammoth, mastodon, horses, large bison and other Pleistocene animals. Never before had these animals seen human beings or been exposed to human predation.

From a modern perspective, this might seem to be an entrepreneur's paradise – what a perfect opportunity to go in and stake out the best plots of land to be fully exploited and defended against all-comers. We might expect to see the rapid emergence of discrete, territorially based social units centred on optimal resource zones. This is not what happened, however. These first pioneering nomads, finding a land of plenty with ample resources for all, did not stake out territorial claims, but rather spread far and wide in very small, mobile, nomadic bands. The archaeological record gives no evidence of territorial behaviour on the part of any of these first hunters and gatherers. Rather, they seem to have developed a very open network of communication and interaction that spread across the continent.

Starting with the first recognisable Palaeoindian archaeological assemblage, the Clovis, we find what is truly a remarkable pattern: virtually identical artefacts – specifically, a very distinctive type of fluted spearpoint (Fig. 1) – are found distributed throughout the North American continent, from Maine to Mexico, and from the East Coast to the West, a total area of about 15,000,000 km². Other types of Clovis artefacts, although made of locally available stone materials, are also very similar across the entire continental region. The widespread distribution of the Clovis stone tools across North America is indicative that there was free and open interaction between the small, nomadic bands of hunters and gatherers spread across the entire continent. There were no cultural boundaries separating one band or group of bands from any of the others, and there is no evidence of competition or ethnic differences of any kind setting one group apart from any of the others.

In the earliest stages of human occupation in North America, then, with low population densities and an abundance of resources for all, everyone looks basically alike. Most importantly for the focus of the present discussion, we find no sign anywhere in the archaeological record of even a *hint* of conflict or warfare. There are no skeletal remains with markers of violence such as parry fractures, broken heads or spearpoints embedded in the body, nor is there any indication that the Clovis people selected camp-sites that were in any way strategically or defensively located. This negative evidence is not in and of itself convincing proof of the absence of warfare, since relatively few Clovis sites and even fewer human remains have been excavated. However, the Clovis data does provide one empirical case that does not openly support the argument that warfare is a ubiquitous and 'natural' component of human affairs. In fact, it is difficult to see how or why the Clovis people could have been in conflict with one another, given both the abundance of resources and the marked similarities of their cultural assemblages.

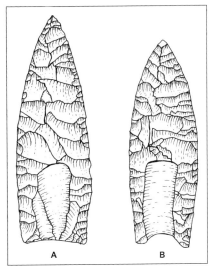

Fig. 1. *Two Clovis fluted points showing similar human occupations across North America: A. Blackwater Draw, New Mexico; B. Vail site, Maine, dating to 11,500–11,000 BP.*

As we move forward in time in North America, the environmental and demographic circumstances change, as do the patterns of interaction among the people. Across the continent, the time from approximately 11,000 years ago to the start of the first millennium AD is marked by gradual growth in the size and density of population, and by environmental changes that began to impinge on the abundant qualities of the New World paradise. The big-game animals of the late Pleistocene mostly became extinct, and environmentally, the continent came to look more and more like it does today. Archaeologically, we see that after the Palaeoindian period, the open, continent-wide network of communication and interaction begins to break into somewhat smaller regional cultures. These regional cultures, still mostly characterised by a nomadic hunting and gathering form of subsistence, are only loosely defined on the basis of types of spearpoints and other kinds of artefacts (Bettinger 1991). While the overall similarities of tool types within these regional cultures are indicative of close interaction and communication, there are no sharp lines clearly separating one region from its neighbours; instead, there tends to be an intermingling and blurring of artefacts and artefact types at the loose boundaries between the regions. Within these broad regional cultures, we find that there are distinct differences in the emergence and evolution of warfare. Rather than try to relate the full range of complexity across the continent, I will focus on the South-western United States, and compare it briefly to a very different pattern found in the Eastern US.

The south-west, an area of about 700,000 km² occupying the present states of Arizona, New Mexico, Utah and Colorado, has been both the training ground and the proving ground for much of American archaeology for over a century. As a result, the archaeological record for the south-west is filled with detail on chronology, settlement, economics and social organisation. A combination of variables makes this an optimal area for studying prehistoric warfare. First, the chronometrics for the area are unparalleled for a prehistoric context. There is a highly refined tree-ring record for the area, stretching back thousands of years, and this record enables us to date the construction and abandonment of sites with considerable accuracy. In some areas, it is possible to determine within a decade, if not to a specific year, when a site was founded and when it was abandoned.

Researchers have also been able to correlate the dendrochronological record with palaeo-environmental data to develop detailed reconstructions of past patterns of annual precipitation, erosion/aggradation, fluctuating water table and changing botanical communities. Thus, it is not only possible to determine when a site was occupied, but also to measure the prevailing weather patterns, availability of fuel-wood, and the potential productivity of the surrounding soils and biological zones (Van West 1994; Gumerman 1988).

Complementing the chronometrics and palaeo-environmental records is a rich body of excavation and survey data from more than a century of concerted archaeological research. The environment of the south-west is dry and warm, and as a result, preservation of architecture and material culture is good. Archaeological sites, from lithic scatters to large villages, are visible on the surface, and much detail can be recorded, even without excavation. Furthermore, because of a relatively sparse modern population and limited farming, the destruction of sites has been substantially less than in many other areas.

Taken together, the chronological, palaeo-environmental and archaeological records from the south-west provide a level of detail that allows us to see both the presence and absence of prehistoric warfare, and to examine closely the causes, nature and evolution of warfare on local and regional levels.

Looking across the south-west in the time following the Clovis and the era of the big-game hunters, the region was occupied by generalised hunters and gatherers who pursued a relatively stable annual round. Population densities were relatively low, and there were no significant concentrations of people in specific locales. Across the region, there are few material manifestations of cultural differences within the resident population. Tool assemblages and styles of projectile points are similar, as are settlement and subsistence strategies. In looking for signs of conflict, violence or warfare in this nomadic population, we find that there is a period of more than 5,000 years when there continues to be not a single manifestation in the archaeological record. Here, the negative evidence begins to carry more weight, since the record for this long period is much richer than for the early Palaeoindian period. Again, there are no signs of violence in the skeletal population in terms of broken heads, scalp marks, parry fractures or projectile points embedded in bodies, nor do we find villages or camp-sites being located with an eye to defence or the guarding of territory.

Beginning in the first millennium BC, this long period of peaceful hunting and gathering started to change, and the rate of change accelerated for the next 2,000 years. Gradual population growth filled in most of the environmental niches, and we begin to see the first experiments with sedentism and intensification of production, either through specialised procurement or simple horticulture. The nomadic bands began to stay in one area more consistently as they either exploited specialised resources or tended occasional crops. With population on the rise, nomadic bands were also encountering more and more neighbours searching for the same food resources.

Looking then across the region in the first millennium BC, we begin to see the end of the pattern of undifferentiated hunters and gatherers. Across the region, people began to adopt corn-based agriculture and settle into permanent or semi-permanent communities. Although basic patterns of architecture and material culture are similar across the region, the different parts of the south-west quickly became distinct from each other in terms of the details of material culture, subsistence strategies and settlement. Specifically, archaeologists are able to distinguish the Hohokam culture area in the desert south, the Mogollon culture area in the mountainous region, and the Anasazi culture area in the plateau and canyon region to the north. Each of these groups had distinctive pottery designs, lithic artefacts, housing styles (Fig. 2), subsistence strategies, religious practices, and so on. These groups were clearly different from one another culturally and ethnically. We will focus here on the Anasazi, who were the ancestors of the modern Pueblo people widely known in the South-west today, to examine the origins of enmities and warfare.

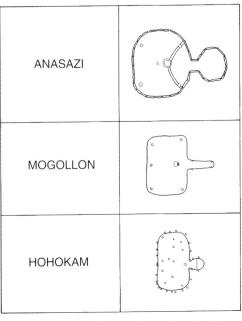

Fig. 2. American south-west pithouses from the three major culture groups – Anasazi, Mogollon and Hohokam – dating to c. AD 500–900. Small circles represent posts, and the central larger circle the fire pit.

Among the Anasazi, the transition from a nomadic hunting and gathering lifestyle to one of settled village agriculture was a gradual one, extending over more than a thousand years (Plog 1997; Cordell 1997). As in other parts of the world, the development of agriculture in the South-west resulted from a combination of growing population and climatic changes that affected the availability of the resources that could be obtained through hunting and gathering. Without enough wild food resources to feed a growing population, the Anasazi began to devote an increasing amount of time to growing their own food resources. The increased time spent on cultivating such crops as corn, beans and squash led in turn to an increasingly sedentary lifestyle, and to corresponding changes in material culture. They constructed permanent houses, adopted ceramics, and largely gave up the throwing-spear in favour of the bow and arrow. The sedentary life also brought with it profound changes in the nature of social relations within the Anasazi culture area. Instead of a relatively open network of nomadic bands interacting with each other off and on throughout the year, the bands settled down into communities, and the communities were faced with each other as permanent neighbours.

The presence of neighbours, even semi-permanent ones, requires the forging of new kinds of social and political ties. If for no other reason, neighbouring communities must have some political means of settling inter-group disagreements over land, water and the like, since the option of moving away to new encampments is no longer so simple. In addition to finding means to settle disagreements, it can be expected that most neighbouring communities will be linked by common language, kinship ties, exchange, religious activities and general socialising. Archaeologically, we begin to see the increased patterns of interaction among the Anasazi by AD 500. It can be seen in such things as communal religious facilities and localised, subregional variation in ceramic design styles, arrowhead types and some architectural features (Plog 1984).

Over the course of the next five hundred years, the population of the Anasazi grew significantly, and the people became increasingly reliant on domesticated crops, principally corn. During this same period, we also see the process of increasing regional differentiation. As the people became permanently sedentary in year-round villages, they interacted more frequently with their neighbours, and less with people outside the immediate area. They then became more like their immediate neighbours, and less like the people outside their sphere of neighbourly interaction. By AD 700, this pattern was well developed, and becomes evident in the appearance of distinctive subgroups or 'branches' within the Anasazi area. In the archaeological record, the pattern is manifested in about six different branches of the Anasazi, such as the Mesa Verde, Kayenta and Cibola. Each of these had its own distinctive cultural assemblage of artefacts, design styles, architecture, religion, burial practices and patterns of community interaction (Haas 1989).

These different branches of the Anasazi then lived side by side with each other in the northern south-west for the next six hundred years. All the evidence we have indicates that this was a peaceful co-existence for the first five hundred years. There is active exchange of resources and exotic goods across the tribal boundaries, and there continue to be no signs of either intra-tribal or inter-tribal warfare. It should be noted that there are isolated signs of violence in Anasazi culture during this time. For example, physical anthropologists have, documented a number of instances of aggressive cannibalism where it appears that people were not only eaten, but their facial bones were deliberately smashed into small fragments (Fig. 3) (Turner 1989; 1993; Turner & Turner 1992; 1995; White 1992). These occasional manifestations of violence all appear to be internal conflict within communities, however, apparently aimed at social control.

Similar kinds of internal homicide are expressed in the ethnographic record of the Pueblos in the execution of people accused of being witches. Signs of inter-group conflict,

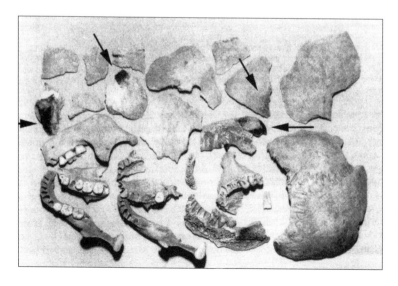

Fig. 3. Cannibalised human remains from the Canyon Butte Ruin 3 site in Arizona, dating to AD 1000–1200, and showing violent fracture and burning (arrows) of cranial remains. Photo: courtesy of C.G. Turner.

behaviour patterns that could be interpreted as warfare, continue to be absent in the Anasazi region from the eighth century through to the twelfth century. Indeed, as we sweep back across more than 10,000 years of human prehistory in the Anasazi area, through periods of great change in the development of agriculture, sedentism, major population growth and environmental fluctuations, there are no indications of organized inter-group conflict developing until the thirteenth century AD. The peace of the south-west is only broken when a complex of environmental and demographic variables finally lead to the violent appearance of warfare.

Beginning at about AD 1150, the environment of the northern south-west began to change. This was not particularly unusual, as the south-west witnessed environmental cycles about every three hundred years (Dean et al. 1985). In the century prior to AD 1150, the environment was characterised by winter-dominant precipitation, soils were building up, and the water table was relatively high. Then, beginning in the middle of the twelfth century, there was a switch to a summer-dominant precipitation pattern, soils began to erode away, and the water table dropped. The region witnessed cyclical droughts and the progressive loss of arable land. Areas that were marginal for agriculture at the beginning of the twelfth century were uninhabitable by the end of the century. In the mean time, the sharp upward population growth curve, which started with the development of agriculture, had reached a maximum. The result of high population coupled with a deteriorating environment led to severe economic stress among the Anasazi. This stress was most clearly manifested in the skeletal population. Human remains through the twelfth and thirteenth centuries show a significant rise in the markers of malnutrition, such as hypoplasias or Harris lines, among adults, and greatly increased infant and child mortality (Ryan 1977).

By the middle of the thirteenth century, the conditions were finally sufficiently harsh for a major outbreak of warfare in the Anasazi region. The initial signs of conflict appear in the 1240s, when a few small, isolated villages were constructed in strategically defensive locations. Over the course of the next ten to fifteen years, the material markers of warfare multiplied dramatically. By 1260, clear and unequivocal signs of warfare were ubiquitous across the entire region. We find burned houses, wrecked villages, bodies pierced by arrows, headless skeletons and skeletonless heads (Figs 4–5). People living out in the open began to build palisades around their villages, and other people took extraordinary measures to move their homes into protected and highly defensible locations (Wilcox & Haas 1994; Haas & Creamer 1993, 1996). The well-known cliff dwellings of the south-west, while romantic and mysterious today, were the defensive redoubts of people at war seven hundred years ago (Fig. 6). Aside from moving into defensible locations in the middle 1200s, the people were also aggregating together into much larger and more defensible towns and villages. In the first half of the thirteenth century, there were few villages of more than 2–25 rooms, whereas in the second half of the century, almost the entire population was living in communities of 75–400. Clearly, the Anasazi people found safety in numbers.

Altogether, the archaeological data provides a record of serious, endemic warfare all across the northern south-west, lasting for a period of about fifty years. Then, at AD 1300, the heartland of the most intensive Anasazi occupation was completely abandoned. Warfare does not appear to have been the immediate cause of this regional abandonment, in that there is little evidence of wholesale slaughter of people or destruction of large numbers of villages.

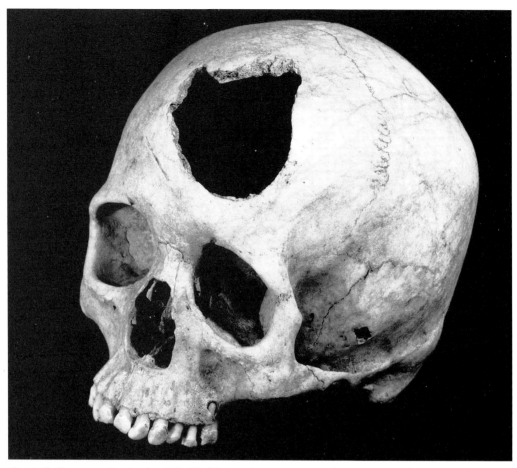

Fig. 4. Skull uncovered at the site of Kin Klethla (AD 1250–1300) in north-east Arizona, showing manifestations of violence with bashed-in forehead and one of two cut marks. Photo: author.

Fig. 5. Massacred remains of eight adults, two male youths (15–18 years old) and a 12-year-old individual of unknown sex. All these individuals were uncovered on a pithouse floor at the Largo-Gallina site in New Mexico, dating to AD 1100–1300. Photo: courtesy of C.G. Turner.

Rather, warfare played an indirect role in tipping the balance in a fragile ecosystem. In earlier, more peaceful times, local mobility was a preferred strategy in responding to environmental problems, such as erosion or a lowered water table. With the advent of warfare and much larger villages, however, the options for moving around locally and exploiting viable micro-environments were greatly reduced. By 1300, the combination of environmental stress and social conflict drove the inhabitants completely from the region.

If we look at the south-west after 1300, we find that environmental conditions improved significantly, with increased annual precipitation, soil erosion being reversed, and rising water tables. We are also able to follow the Anasazi as they moved into other parts of the south-west, and find that the level of warfare was greatly reduced as the environmental conditions improved. However, it is of interest to note that warfare remained a part of Anasazi life for the next five hundred years. The people stayed in large villages, they took basic steps to defend those villages, and there are occasional signs of violence in the skeletal population (Haas & Creamer 1997).

Fig. 6. Defensive cliff dwelling in north-east Arizona, dating to AD 1250–1300, showing climbing posts. The author is climbing the in situ aboriginal poles that provided access into the site. Photo: author.

The pattern seen in the prehistoric south-west has interesting implications in terms of both the causes of warfare and the social context of warfare in pre-state societies. Ultimately, the archaeological record of the Anasazi, extending back for thousands of years, makes it impossible to argue that warfare and fear of 'the other' is somehow natural to the human species. Warfare among the Anasazi was not an inevitable response to either ethnic diversification or to environmental stress and resource shortages. There are marked cultural differences between groups in the south-west well before the time of Christ and ethnically discrete branches of the Anasazi arising by AD 700. Yet the first signs of inter-group violence do not appear until AD 1250 – more than five hundred years later. Anasazi co-existed peacefully with culturally different groups around their borders for more than a thousand years, and within the Anasazi culture area, ethnically distinct groups lived side by side for centuries, generation after generation, with absolutely no signs of organised conflict or war. The violent markers of raiding, killing and burning appear only very late in Anasazi culture, as a complex response to changing demographic patterns and a prolonged period of severe environmental stress.

We will now turn briefly from the south-western United States to look at a second and very different pattern of warfare in eastern North America. Eastern North America is

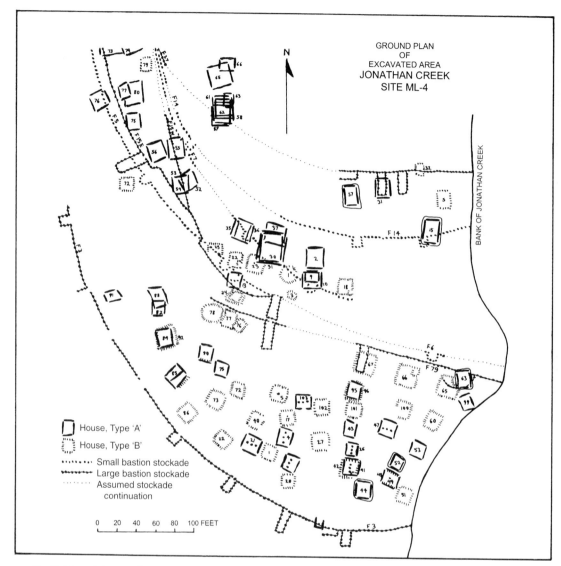

Fig. 7. Map of the Jonathan Creek site (AD 1400–1600) in Marshall County, Kentucky, showing typical houses surrounded by defensive bastion stockades (rectangular structures protruding from the stockade).

strikingly different from the south-west in terms of both environment and the evolution of war. The east is much wetter overall, and has a much greater abundance of natural resources. In adapting to these environmental circumstances, some early inhabitants in the area, particularly in the central south, moved fairly quickly from nomadic hunting and gathering to a more sedentary lifestyle. Their settled communities were centred on rich resource zones, and there was little reason to move seasonally or annually (Streuver & Holton 1979). However, the area was not an unlimited paradise. As population grew, all the best resource locations were quickly occupied, and people were gradually pushed into less favourable zones. These more marginal zones may have provided adequate resources in good years, but may not have been able to meet the needs of the resident population in bad years. This combination of environment and demography then set the stage for the early appearance of pre-agricultural warfare in the east.

Fully within the context of settled hunting and gathering, we then see the appearance of warfare and systematic violence by 5000 BC, several thousand years before it occurred in the south-west. Archaeologically, the warfare in this early period is manifested primarily in the form of human casualties – bodies found with scalp marks, decapitation, and projectile points stuck in bones (Milner 1995; 1998; Smith 1995). The sites in the period between 5000 and 2000 BC are mostly shell middens, with few signs of formal residential architecture and no indications of defensive features such as palisades. It is also important to note that there are no material manifestations to indicate any ethnic or cultural differences between the people engaged in the fighting. Styles of projectile points and other artefacts are relatively uniform across the areas of conflict. Whereas in the south-west we saw warfare arising only after the development of ethnic and cultural differences, in the east we see warfare arising prior to the appearance of such differences in the archaeological record.

Between 2000 BC and the time of Christ, the East witnessed a gradual transition towards less reliance on gathered resources, and increased dependence on cultivation of a variety of food crops (Smith 1989). The pattern of settled communities did not change qualitatively during this transition, but the nature of social and ecological relationships changed. The development of horticulture meant that there were many more 'good' zones, and fewer 'bad' ones. As a result, continued population growth did not require some people to move into marginal zones while others monopolised a limited amount of prime productive land. There was adequate arable land to meet the needs of a growing population for more than 2,000 years. So what happens to the signs of warfare in the prehistoric record for this period? They largely disappear (Milner 1998). Although there are occasional skeletons with indications of violence, they are quite rare in the overall skeletal population. There is also an absence of conflict or defensive posturing among the many sites and settlements known from this time.

Thus, following a 3,000-year period during which conflict was relatively common among settled hunters and gatherers, we see a period of more than 2,000 years of peace among settled village horticulturalists. This pattern of peaceful relations is broken by the beginning of the second millennium AD, when warfare again appears across the eastern United States – and it does so with a vengeance. Villages are fortified (Fig. 7), massacres and war deaths are common (Fig. 8), and warfare iconography and symbolism are prevalent (Milner 1998; Peregrine 1992; 1993; Anderson 1994). Warfare continues and intensifies in the region again until the intrusion of the English, Spanish and French in the sixteenth and seventeenth centuries. Unfortunately, there is not as much environmental and chronological detail in the archaeological record of the East as there is for the south-west, and at the moment we cannot explore possible short-term exceptions to these millennial patterns. The eastern data, however, do provide another excellent case for the valuable insights to be gained through the study of the archaeology of warfare.

As the other chapters in this volume attest, archaeologists and their laboratories of time can provide an important perspective on both the science and history of warfare across the

Fig. 8. Crow Creek, South Dakota – massacre site of nearly five hundred men, women and children, dating to AD 1325, and showing signs of warfare through the mutilation and scalping of the dead. Photo: courtesy of P. Willey.

globe. However, to realise the potential strength of the archaeological record, we must occasionally look up from our stones, bones and ancient sites and bring the record of the ancient past to bear on the issues of the contemporary world. By looking at the distant past of prehistory, we may be able to extract a somewhat more optimistic view of human nature than we might derive solely from reading news accounts of the modern world. There is good, solid evidence from North America to affirm that humans are not inherently warlike animals just looking for opportunities to attack and conquer one another. The peaceful record in the south-west shows that warfare is not a first, second or even third resort of people faced with stress, uncertainty and growing population densities. It is indeed the *last* resort of people faced with dying children and the threat of imminent extinction. The record from eastern North America also shows that a cycle of war lasting for thousands of years can be broken and replaced by a cycle of peace under the right set of environmental and economic conditions. As we look for answers to the ever-present problem of warfare in the modern era, we must look beyond human nature and search for the root causes of warfare that are to be found in demography, the environment and the economic conditions of the many different societies struggling to co-exist on the face of our planet.

THREE

BIOSOCIAL AND BIO-ARCHAEOLOGICAL ASPECTS OF CONFLICT AND WARFARE[*]

DON BROTHWELL

There is no doubt that a major theme within archaeological studies should be the history of violence and the development of warfare. Yet the term 'war' is used so loosely that the complex nature of conflict – extending from individual aggression and small-group violence to large-scale warfare – is obscured. The anger and violent aggression of one person towards another does not equal war. A few people fighting does not equal war. Raiding for wives or trophy heads, or to settle old grievances does not equal war. While at a small-scale level violent conflict is probably associated with feelings of personal involvement and aggression, large-scale warfare is likely to include many who do not feel personally aggressive, do not feel anger towards the 'enemy', and perhaps do not even know in detail the reasons they are being drawn into the conflict. There is clearly a need to clarify the situation, in archaeology and other studies, and in particular, we need to consider the possibility of constructing a critical classification of all grades of violence up to and including warfare.

Why should archaeology be concerned with war? A first obvious answer is that there is plenty of evidence in the past of weapons and direct evidence of human trauma indicative of some form of conflict. But more importantly, human aggression, conflict and warfare have a history, and archaeology demonstrates that the temporal dimension is long and deserves detailed study, as it is certainly a major and recurring theme in ancient human society. During the last century and into the Nazi era, perverted social Darwinism has been used to justify war and struggles for ethnic supremacy (Oldroyd 1980). The German historian Heinrich von Treitschke (1916) articulated this sentiment when he wrote: 'Brave peoples alone have "an evolution or a future" . . . The grandeur of history lies in the perpetual conflict of nations.' The literature on the history of war is vast, and is surrounded by such romanticism and mythology. While definitions of war have been given and discussed by many (see especially Giner 1975; Ferguson 1984; 1990; Keeley 1996), there is no clear consensus about what should be included. 'War as politics', Harris (1978)

---

[*] To the memory of William Brothwell, who died on the Somme, not understanding the nature of militarism, nor knowing of Gandhian *ahimsa*.

says, makes 'good sense in relation to the wars of history', but he sees band and village conflicts as a different dimension, as they 'do not conquer territories or subjugate their enemies', and are 'lacking the bureaucratic, military and legal apparatus of statehood'. At a pre-state level, land and other resources, as well as women, may initiate raiding. Feuding and revenge can precipitate smaller-group conflict. Power and prestige may also act as driving forces at the leadership level, as well as ideologies and religions.

The lumping together of all aspects of conflict and violence under the term 'war' is a common practice, but is certainly erroneous. As the ethologist Robert Hinde says: 'War has causes quite different from those of aggression between individuals, and even the behaviour of many of those who take part would not fall within some definitions of aggression' (Hinde 1974, 250). The aim of this chapter is to consider some of the more biosocial/bio-archaeological aspects of the archaeology of conflict and war, and to emphasise that a broad scientific approach is needed.

HUMAN AGGRESSION

Whatever has been carried through during our evolution from earlier primates in terms of selected aggression traits, overall brain size increase has transformed our capacity to control our behaviour at an individual and group level. In human societies, potential aggressive behaviour will be influenced both by individual values and influences of society as a whole. Xenophobic or paranoid 'misreading' of a social situation, or feelings of denigration, may unjustifiably stimulate an aggressive response. The response can be both offensive and defensive. It is also worth considering the extent to which earlier societies, by accident or design, have evolved cathartic measures to divert aggressive energies (in games or other endeavours) away from destructiveness in their own societies. The ultimate diversion is surely to redirect attention to a real or imagined 'enemy' of the society.

One certainty in terms of studies on human aggression is that true to the general mammalian pattern, young and adult males behave more aggressively than females (Frodi et al. 1977; Maccoby & Jacklin 1980). While this may be partly related to endocrine differences between the sexes (Turner 1995), it may well also be influenced by social-learning factors, boys being more likely to imitate dominant and more aggressive adult males.

Can aggression, then, be described as an instinct – driving males in particular? Is it really an inherent compulsion? Lorenz (1966) certainly believed that human aggressiveness amounted to a 'fighting instinct' under certain circumstances. Indeed, as a result of biosocial pressures, he suggested that the instinct hypertrophied during prehistory, but with later urban development of more complex societies, this fighting energy was redirected and sublimated in other activities (e.g., games). This simplistic view has come under critical evaluation (Schneirla 1973; Jacobi et al. 1975), and demonstrates how even attractive hypotheses must be viewed critically. From the evidence of child psychology, an alternative view – that aggressive behaviour is largely learned, and not innate behaviour – must certainly be seriously considered (Belschner 1975).

Is there a difference between 'physical aggression' and 'violence'? The terms have been used as alternatives, but Archer (1995) argues that they should be used to emphasise differences in degree, with 'violence' being used to indicate behaviour which can or may lead to injury or death.

Can we subdivide aggression? Moyer (1976) and Weisfeld (1995) suggest that there is value in identifying different types, which seem to have distinctive functions. The main differences may be briefly listed as follows:

fear-induced aggression leading to defensive action may be threatening or as a counter-attack;

maternal aggression is in defence of offspring;

predatory aggression is concerned with feeding;

territorial aggression is for the defence or expansion of territory;

dominance aggression is concerned with attaining rank (rank ordering can help to maintain stability and peace in a group);

angry aggression is perhaps equivalent to the original frustration-aggression hypothesis, and the violation of a norm may produce a 'rage reaction'.

These forms of aggression can be seen more clearly in non-human species, the complex nature of human behaviour in society somewhat obscuring these precise categories. This is not to deny their existence in influencing human societies, however.

Aggression and Frustration

The possible relationships between frustration, depression and aggression have been much debated. While too much emphasis has probably been placed on these potential links, evidence of an association can be provided. Lyons (1972) has demonstrated an inverse relation between the occurrence of depression in Northern Ireland and 'the opportunity to externalise aggressive behaviour'. With the increase in rioting, homicide and other crimes of violence, the suicide rate declined by nearly 50 per cent. Factors causing the social frustrations and individual depressions included bad housing and crowding, with generally high unemployment. Social frustrations are clearly extremely important factors in causing instability in a population, but it is nevertheless debatable whether 'aggression is always a consequence of frustration', as Dollard et al. (1944) have argued.

While 'frustration' can be simply defined as a state of mind, a feeling of dissatisfaction as a result of being thwarted, rendered ineffectual or discouraged, H.G. Wells (1936), in his over-lengthy consideration of frustration, also points to the powerful force of sexual frustration. However, both at an individual and community level, it is surely a more complex phenomenon. Maier (1949) suggests that aggressive behaviour in adults might be related to childhood frustrations, as well as those met with in adulthood. The violence can be directed at the source of the frustrations, but alternatively it can be aimed at scapegoats (Hovland & Sears 1940). While there is a range of evidence suggesting that, whatever the culture, frustrations are significant precipitating factors in producing aggression and conflict (Yates 1962), there are clearly various other factors involved.

CHIMPANZEE ETHOLOGY

It is an established fact that other animals can engage in battles (Lorenz 1966). For example, ant colonies can be extremely aggressive towards each other (Wilson 1971, 1978). But such animal conflicts are simple compared to human conflict, which in more advanced society demands 'an intellectual, social and economic sophistication to which animals do not aspire' (Passingham 1982, 329). However, it would seem relevant here to consider conflict in our closest cousins, the chimpanzees, particularly as their behaviour may hold clues to the behaviour of the earliest hominids. Indeed, as Hamburg says: 'chimpanzees live in societies that are very complex by non-human primate standards, possibly similar to the societies of Australopithecus' (Hamburg 1991, 427).

Chimpanzee communities may contain fifteen to eighty individuals, and conflict may occur within or between groups. Threatening and submissive behaviour may occur, as well as less common open attack. Goodall (1990) has noted that there can be considerable aggression and violence between wild chimpanzee groups, and the violence can extend to females and infants. When numbers reach a critical level, the groups may divide, and there may then be animosity between the two subgroups. Attacks between groups can lead to cannibalism, perhaps especially of babies. Fighting can be brutal, with severe twisting of limbs, biting and the hurling of rocks. The need to expand territory seems to be one factor leading to the males in an adjoining group being attacked and even killed. Studies on zoo chimpanzees seem to confirm Goodall's studies of wild groups (de Waal 1989; 1996). Males can take part in fierce fighting, causing severe injuries. One interesting fact revealed by these studies was that groups with a formalised dominance relationship were far less likely to fight. If male dominance relationships were lost during early hominid evolution, could this indicate that male competition became more open, and thus more conflict occurred?

ECOLOGICAL ASPECTS

A number of ecological factors have been discussed in the past in relation to human inter-group conflicts and warfare (Ferguson 1990). Resources, especially food, have clearly been a core theme in strategies for survival in all hominids. The group successful in 'resource competition' would be at an advantage (Durham 1979), at least at a reproductive level, provided the costs were not too great. But resource-driven competition and conflict is not usually a one-off phenomenon, thus conflict becomes self-perpetuating (Bates & Lees 1979). Indeed, Vayda (1974) argues that inter-group conflict can be viewed in some circumstances as a 'continuous ecological process'.

The frequency of violence depends on the proximity of groups, as Hallpike (1977) found in his study of the Tauade of Papua. Mobility of the groups, also influenced by ecological factors, similarly had an effect on conflict frequencies (Fig. 1). Seasonal fluctuations in resources may also influence the pattern of human predation on other areas, as Lewis (1985) found in his study of Somali groups. In agricultural societies, perhaps with variable harvests and increasing population, territorial conquest is a recurring possibility (Vayda 1961). With the development of agriculture in different world centres, conflicts probably became more frequent (Harris 1978), and with the development of weaponry through into the Bronze Age, more wounded and more dead in relation to population size may have been sustained.

Demographic factors have clearly been a background influence of significance, especially pressure from increasing population (Carneiro 1970; Sanderson 1992). Strategies to cope with the problem of too many people included further land clearance, irrigation and raiding for additional resources. During the past few centuries, population increase has been considerable, so some tribal leaders could call on considerable forces to go plundering. In the latter half of the nineteenth century, for instance, King Mutesa I of Buganda could call on 125,000 warriors to go in search of cattle, slaves and wives (Lewis 1985). Tainter (1990) suggests that the major Mayan fortifications constructed by AD 150–300 may have been associated with increasing population, and thus increased resource needs.

DEMOGRAPHIC ASPECTS OF CONFLICT

Human conflict and violence can be viewed from various perspectives: social organisation, demography, nature of weaponry, political systems, and so on. In the case of demographic factors, these have an influence on all groups, at all levels of cultural complexity. Other species are similarly affected by factors of population: crowding, for instance, is known to consistently increase the amount of aggressive behaviour (Jolly 1972). Sex differences in aggressive and violent behaviour also occur in various species, and in ourselves some of the differences may be influenced by social learning (Hoffmann et al. 1995).

Within and also between communities, recognition of family links – real but also symbolic – may be important in influencing the extent of potential conflict. In the case of the Jie, a warlike tribe on the Kenyan border, raiding and counter-raiding regularly occurred with neighbours except for the Turkana, who were regarded as 'cousins', linked by peaceful trading (Gulliver 1966). Population increase among the Busama gave rise to new settlements, but peaceful links remained with the parent group, unless quarrels developed which transformed them into 'enemies' (Hogbin 1963). Similarly, marriage against the wishes of their kindred could give rise to conflict and feuding. In contrast, within-group factional differences may be submerged by the need for greater social cohesion in the face of a greater common enemy (Tylor 1881; Wright 1942; Murphy 1957).

Conflict and violence between family, hamlet and tribal individuals is clearly complex and variable. Within-family conflict can be linked to emotions of jealousy, envy, incest, petty theft, adultery and rivalry. Such undercurrents may spill out and affect the hamlet in general, or other settlements with family links. While any serious violence may lead to long-term bitterness and even feuding, conflict at a tribal level is likely to be of a different order of complexity. In the case of the Papuan Tauade society (Hallpike 1977), conflict is seen to be linked to a web of variables (Fig. 1). Studies on the Chimbu people of New Guinea (Brown 1979) and the Dobu Islanders of Melanesia (Benedict 1934) again show much conflict within tribal groups, though not necessarily with the same aetiology. There is no value in expanding here on the causes of within-group violence, except to emphasise that there are numerous variables – food-sharing, land competition, stealing, sexual needs – and such factors will be seen to have different emphasis in different communities. In the case of

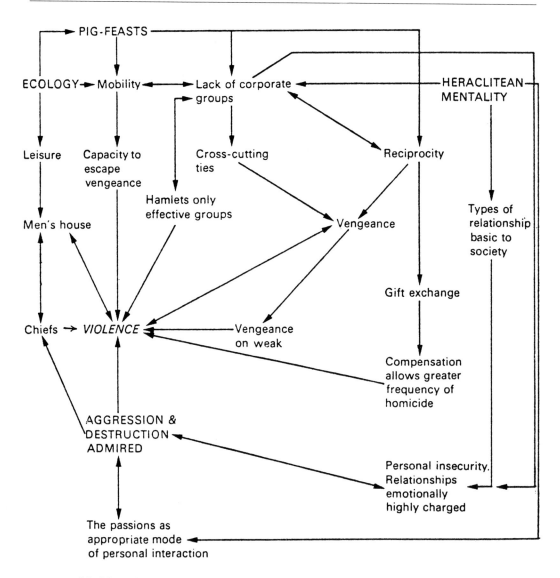

Fig. 1. Model of the web of factors associated with the generation of conflict in Tauade (Papuan) society (after Hallpike 1977).

Yanomamö of Venezuela, conflict is nearly always about women (Chagnon 1968), and it is impressive that a quarter of the males die in what are really sexually related skirmishes.

At an inter-tribal level, we are generally viewing a different order of informed behaviour and conflict. Confrontation may involve vastly greater numbers of individuals, bonded by shared ethnocentrism, and at times with an 'irrationally exaggerated allegiance of individuals to their kin and fellow tribesmen' (Wilson 1978, 110). The conflicting groups are primed with appropriate cultural information – distorted or otherwise. Darwin (1890) was interested in inter-tribal competition from the point of view of the extinction of groups, but it is difficult to find information of this kind. Tribal groups have certainly disappeared – Tasmanian communities, for instance – but as a result of disease rather than violence.

Violence at this level may be triggered by an inter-tribal killing between hostile groups, or the capture of slaves, or land acquisition, or other economic reasons. Modern ethnographic explanations may not fully reflect the reasons for violence in past societies, although the regular common denominators in recent societies suggests that some continuity extends back in time.

HOMINIDS AND CONFLICT TRAUMA

It is always tempting to ponder the changing behavioural patterns which must have occurred during hominid evolution, even though it is pure speculation. Bigelow (1969) argues that with increasing brain size, the Australopithecines would have had the ability to engage in little fights. Alexander (1971) sees it as quite a critical factor in human evolution, but its importance has been doubted by Caspari (1972). Surprisingly, to my knowledge, no one has reflected on the advantage (compared to chimpanzee posture) of being bipedal and thus being far more capable of using sticks as clubs or hurling stones more accurately.

A major argument against more than localised outbreaks of violence, perhaps concerned with territory, is the fact that early hominid regional population density is unlikely to have been much greater than maximum chimpanzee densities. Moreover, although cultural elaboration, especially of language and tool technology, is associated with the evolution of *Homo erectus*, these Pleistocene hominids were expanding over time into the vast territory of the habitable Old World, from Britain to Indonesia. It is thus highly debatable whether there was an increase in population in any area sufficient to precipitate any major long-term conflicts at territorial boundaries. But that is not to deny the possibility of some clashes.

From studies of the cranial injuries to *Homo erectus* skulls from China, Weidenreich (1943) and Courville (1967) both considered that the damage was not simply post-mortem (Fig. 2). The most difficult problem with skeletal injuries which do not show healing, whether Pleistocene or more recent, is the differentiation of trauma which causes or occurs at the time of death from damage which occurs later. More conclusive evidence is in the form of healing or healed injury, and fortunately there is cranial vault scarring in this *Homo erectus* series. Three parietal depressions, which again seem to indicate scarring, also occur on the Middle Pleistocene Swanscombe skull from southern England (Brothwell 1964) (Fig. 3).

While samples of Pleistocene fossil hominids are not large, there is sufficient evidence of possible trauma to make this a problem worthy of further investigation. By the time of the appearance of the Neanderthalers in late Middle Pleistocene times, healed injury is becoming more impressive. In the Shanidar series from Iraq, four individuals clearly display trauma, and in Nos 1 (Fig. 4) and 4 there had been serious head injury (Trinkaus 1983). It would be difficult to explain the various Neanderthal injuries (including those in the original Neander Valley male) as simply accidents, and it seems more likely that conflict was the cause. Such injuries are very unlikely to be the result of family squabbles, but rather of serious, hard-hitting conflict, perhaps linked to territory or hunting rights over game or other resources.

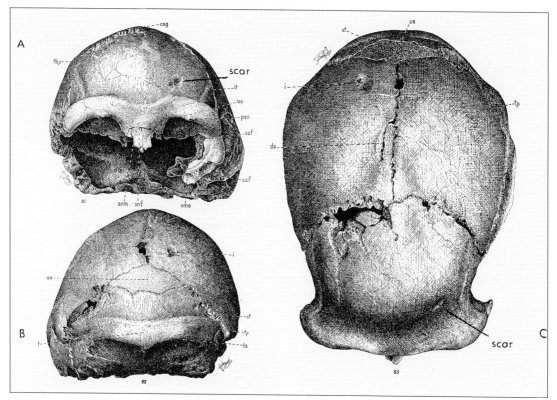

Fig. 2. Frontal (a), posterior (b) and vertical (c) views of one of the Homo erectus *skulls from Zhoukoudian, China (after Weidenreich 1943). There appears to be healed trauma to the frontal area (seen as a well-defined crater).*

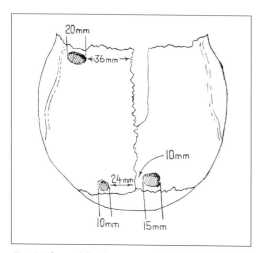

Fig. 3. The Middle Pleistocene Swanscombe skull (vertical view), showing the extent and positions of the parietal depressions, possibly indicating old injuries (from Brothwell 1964).

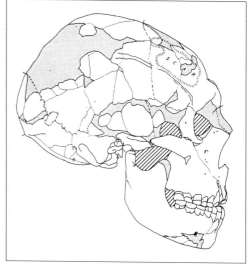

Fig. 4. The right lateral view of the Shanidar I Neanderthaler, showing the large scar on the frontal bone (after Stewart 1959).

By the Holocene, with the increasing numbers of skeletons available for study, there is more and more evidence of conflict injuries of the kind discussed by Wakely (1997), Filer (1997) and Arnold (1995). However, there are still major problems of interpretation, unless the injuries are clearly axe or sword wounds, as in the skeletons from the War Cemetery at Maiden Castle (Wheeler 1943). In this latter case, there is no doubt from the number and range of head wounds that some of the Iron Age occupants were ferociously cut down – a scenario that is fully compatible with Roman standards of fighting.

MILITARISM AND THE STATE

This discussion will not seek to split hairs over the possible distinctions between chiefdoms and states. When considering the past, it is not easy to separate levels of social complexity to the extent that social anthropologists might wish to do on recent populations. But at least past communities can be considered in terms of their probable overall size, the differentiation of their urban centres, their degree of social stratification, the extent of protective walls or other fortifications (Fig. 5), and the extent to which there was a distinctive military organisation. In these respects, there is some contrast with tribal peoples, having smaller populations, less social variation and no permanent warrior class.

There is a case to be made for conflict at a chiefdom/state level being truly 'warfare', with bands and tribes being distinguished by the quality of the inter-group conflicts and fighting. This distinction has relevance to an understanding of the evolution of warfare, as well as how one views it in human behavioural terms. To include all levels of inter-group (not intra-group) fighting under the single heading of 'warfare' seems to simplify a more complex pattern of conflict and fighting. For Cohen (1984) too, 'warfare and statehood invariably are linked'. Goody (1971) also indicates that the most impressive differences between state and non-state are in the means of destruction. Carlton (1977) suggests that there are links between warfare and urbanism, fortifications and the rise of military elites. McCauley (1990) further makes an important point in saying that the interests of state leaders could be very different to those of the general population (e.g., in power and status rather than in basic resources). Moreover, ordinary individuals are no longer able to influence the elite's decisions about battles, their views being subordinated to the state

Fig. 5. The prehistoric town walls of Jericho. Photo: Courtesy of the late K.M. Kenyon.

dictates of the elite. Coercion, intimidation and drafting may be the techniques for gathering armies (Sanderson 1992; McCauley 1990).

The Near East provides one of the best early examples of the links between developing states and warfare. In particular, Assyrian conquests and social developments between *c.* 800 BC and *c.* 650 BC established the first major empire, clearly supported by an advanced army (Ferrill 1985). But over time, military adaptations were needed, and chariots gave way to infantry (Drews 1993). Siege warfare was developed, and propaganda was used to intimidate other groups. Atrocities were publicised to inspire fear and damage morale (von Soden 1994). Assyrian military power could not in any case dominate in a socio-economic vacuum. What caused eventual Assyrian collapse was not outdated warfare, but political instability, economic chaos and major depopulation (Toynbee 1951). The Assyrian case of state-supported warfare is thus a good example of the early development of the military machine in all its complexity. Even before the Greek and Roman empires, a well-defined military class had separated in the Near East, disciplined and at times barbaric in conduct. Gone was tribal conflict, where each warrior could feel a personal commitment and justification in the face of the enemy. 'Depersonalised' warfare had arrived.

LEVELS OF VIOLENCE AS PATHOLOGY

Is all violence best considered as abnormal for humans, even if the behaviour is acute and transient? If violence is pathological, is it possible to detect variants? There are clearly levels of violence in two respects: it may be mild, or extremely ferocious; it may affect an individual, or involve a number or many people.

In the early stages of the tropical infection trypanosomiasis, the majority of individuals display altered mental states, with irritability and aggressiveness (Mayer-Gross et al. 1977). Similarly, in the epidemic of encephalitis lethargica in 1920, children recovering from the condition displayed mental changes, including greater destructiveness (Hill 1964). Of a different order of mental disease, the relatively common condition of paranoid schizophrenia can also give rise to hostility and abuse. Such instances are, of course, marginal to a consideration of group conflict and warfare, except to establish one end of the range of human conflict and hostility. Having said that, it can certainly be debated how often those in a position of leadership have influenced the violent course of history when they were in an abnormal mental state. Was Hitler mentally normal in the late stages of the Second World War (Fromm 1973)? There is little doubt that Anthony Eden was in poor health – mental and physical – at the time of the Suez Crisis, and it is probable that the stresses and strains of leadership in the past have also resulted in abnormal mental states, leading to hostilities.

But my concern here is not to debate the psychopathology of individuals, whether precipitated by genetic susceptibility, infection, stress or even 'shell shock', but the broader issue of how inter-group fighting – and ultimately state warfare – should be viewed in terms of normality or abnormality. In their review of male violence, Daly & Wilson (1995) consider whether it is maladaptive in terms of evolutionary psychology, and conclude that it is not. Hamilton (1975, 148) is also of the opinion that warfare is not 'a pathological development in man', and does not believe that 'mortal intraspecific fighting must always endanger the survival of a species'. The distinguished ethologist Tinbergen (1976) disagrees, and sees 'intra-specific killing' in the later hominids as entering a state of 'disadaptation'. But whether human behaviour in groups is abnormal is not simply related to a consideration of survival in evolutionary terms. The concern in this chapter is to view conflict behaviour in epidemiological terms. In general, most of us would agree that the enormous pandemic of killing in wars this century – causing perhaps some 100,000,000 deaths – is 'plain madness' (Lonsdale 1951). Lionel Penrose (1952, 49), a geneticist with a special interest in mental abnormality, viewed war as an 'abnormal state of society . . . that human beings frequently organise themselves for the purpose of intraspecific conflict must be accepted as fact. But it is as reasonable to treat the fact as material for the study of crowd psychopathology.' The author would argue that archaeology has a commitment to extend this study back in time, and that it is important to have the right perspective on conflict when doing so.

Brown (1973) points out that psychopathology is associated with a blunting of conscience. Individual psychopaths ignore the moral codes of their societies. The psychopathology of warfare and group violence ignores the fact that it infringes normal respect for other humans on a larger scale. Acceptance into a culture often demands the adoption of an uncritical attitude towards its make-up, especially in relation to other societies (Henry 1966). Social pressures can sustain xenophobic fears and aggressive propaganda which take the individual beyond reason. The 'group mind' (Brown 1939), influenced by a leadership with conflict inclinations, may be very different to the reflections of the individuals concerned. No wonder this contrast and potential conflict between the group and individual 'mind' is now seen to give rise to a spectrum of 'psycho-neuroses' (Rivers 1924).

These mental conditions must have a long history. Gustave Le Bon, writing during the First World War, critically describes a situation which in various respects must be as applicable to conflicts in early Greece or the Roman Empire. He writes: 'The present war is a contest between psychological forces. Irreconcilable ideals are grappling with one another. Individual liberty is drawn up against collective servitude' (Le Bon 1916, 18). He continues: 'The mentality of man in crowds is absolutely unlike that which [people] possess when isolated . . . Reason has very little influence upon the collective mind, which is governed by collective logic, a form strictly peculiar to it' (Le Bon 1916, 31). While the mass infantry warfare of classical Greece (Hanson 1989) is modest in scale compared to that of the First World War, it is correct to look for some behavioural similarities through time. Contrary to the various doubts expressed about using the term 'pathology' when considering the evolution of warfare, the author believes it is not only correct but essential to view all human violence in epidemiological terms, as erroneous behaviour which has swelled over the millennia into the nuclear madness of this century. Archaeology must accept a commitment to view human societies through time, not judgementally, but at least with a clinical and scientific eye to hominid limitations and aberrations.

ADAPTATIONS FOR PEACE

It is not usual in studies on human conflict and war to also discuss strategies for peace, yet this is an aspect of behaviour which is the polar opposite of conflict, and probably has an equal antiquity. In mammals, it is viewed as submissive behaviour, usually related to younger males placating the dominant male. In humans, however, although there is a popular literature on our hierarchical societies and the 'pecking order' which can be seen in some aspects of society, this behaviour is quite foreign to the philosophies of non-violence. These have evolved during at least three millennia, and have probably been tried by numerous tribal societies over a much longer period.

In more advanced agricultural societies, the birth of Gautama (Buddha) in about 560 BC brought a creative new idea of reverence for life. While concerned only with humans, not animals in general, early Christianity was also opposed to military service, war and killing (Ferguson 1977). While Christianity as a whole has faltered and adopted militarism, some groups, such as the Quakers, remain committed to the original pacifism. The ethnographic evidence from tribal societies suggests that perhaps 12 per cent can be regarded as pacifistic (Keeley 1996). Some communities clearly hover between the two poles, and Loudon (1972, 312) notes that in Tristan da Cunha, 'the open display of aggressive impulses . . . is successfully discouraged by socialisation processes in childhood'. Similarly, the Batek of Malaysia teach their children the values of sharing and non-violence (Endicott 1988; Barnard & Woodburn 1988). Similarly, it was mass education, assisted by the frustrations of colonial rule, which enabled Gandhi to bring non-violent tactics so successfully to India. 'Ahimsa expresses an ancient Hindu, Jain and Buddhist ethical precept' (Bondurant 1965), and not only means non-violence, but the refusal to do harm generally. This, if anything, is a new order of thinking in human society. It acknowledges the potential for conflict and violence, and proposes a positive philosophy to counteract and disarm this potential.

Two decades ago, Ashley Montagu (1978) contributed to this important question, gathering together contributions from various scholars, and further investigating degrees of non-aggression among the Fore of New Guinea, the !Kung of the Kalahari, two Canadian Inuit groups, the Semai of Malaysia, the Mbuti of Zaire and Tahitians. Different societies have clearly arrived at non-violence as a behavioural strategy by different routes, influenced by the nature of the culture. Whether they could have survived in the face of an aggressive, territory-expanding society in their proximity is of course debatable. Gandhi believed that *ahimsa*, if practised by European societies, could have defeated the Nazi movement – lives would have been lost, but would the cost have been as high as the Second World War's 30,000,000 dead? The ultimate problem with *ahimsa* is not the philosophy, but the practice. It is 'easier' to fight than stand non-violently. The next step in human cultural evolution is to determine how to eliminate the fearfulness and uncertainty which prevents societies from embracing *ahimsa* in one of its various forms – Gandhian *satyagraha* (or non-violent activism: Woodcock 1974), Buddhism, and Quaker-style Christianity. Education in childhood is the main way, but Eibl-Eibesfeldt (1979) points out that strains of laboratory mammals can display aggressive or non-aggressive forms, clearly influenced by genetic factors. In the new millennium of genetic engineering, will this be the ultimate hope for the future?

CONCLUSIONS

Human conflict and violence are major themes for study, not only today, but extending back into prehistory. We have just come through a period of nuclear brinkmanship, and there are still countries in the world spending vast resources on joining the nuclear club. Surely, there must be more to three million years of hominid evolution than these current perverse power struggles and the inability of people to behave perceptively and wisely? There is no doubt that archaeology should contribute to an understanding of war-history; it has an ideal time scale on which to do so.

While the early hominids have yet to provide evidence of their potential aggressiveness (although chimpanzees give clues as to what could have happened), there is certainly a case for *Homo erectus* fighting, and by Neanderthal times, the skeletal evidence suggests fighting with some ferocity. But this level of conflict cannot sensibly be called 'warfare' – a term which deserves special reservation for urban armies. True warfare depends on increasing population density, as well as the development of social hierarchies, with the differentiation of a professional military class. The military elite could, of course, have other social positions, and in the case of the Aztecs, the nobility were also linked to military actions, and with the elaborate rituals associated with the mass sacrifice of war captives and slaves (Adams 1966). This is not to argue that early armies were all disciplined and tactically advanced, but they represent the socio-political evolution of a separately resourced group, who promoted their own interests and those of the ruling elite. In times of military success, the army could have popular support, but it was a separate unit of power which could be equally repressive to its own community as it was to the 'enemy'.

Sadly for human society, once the military machine had evolved, with large numbers under arms, controlled by training and a command hierarchy, with special weaponry and an organised supply system, it was difficult to rethink the resolution of conflict (and be rid of the megalomania which is so often associated with it). As Keeley rightly points out, what 'makes civilised men easier to reduce to strict subordination and military discipline . . . is their habituation to hierarchy and obedience as a result of being raised in a state' (Keeley 1996, 43). Kurtz (1978) points out that fear was injected into Aztec citizenry as a means of ensuring conformity to imposed social values and norms. Fear similarly kept many quiet in Nazi Germany.

While conflict is understandable in this, the most emotional of any species, is killing a suitable way of resolving the problem? It could be argued that killing is a part of Darwinian natural selection – survival of the 'fittest'. But the extent of human intelligence and the extra, non-Darwinian dimension of culture renders killing an unacceptable answer to the problem of conflict. Armed fighting may have been an immediate, pragmatic answer to the problem, but it is no ultimate solution for our species.

This chapter has tried to indicate that there are different levels of violence, from that of the individual psychopath, to the squabbles within families or hamlets, to larger disputes involving different communities, tribes or states. At some point in this sequence, personal outrage and special commitment may fade, and participation may be more an act of duty to the group or an act of solidarity. Beyond this level of dispute and fighting, we move to armed and organised conflict – true warfare. While the simpler forms of violence are perhaps more understandable – and may be considered 'normal', in that they are linked to personal frustrations or anger – with the emergence of armies, society moved into the realm of maladaption and social pathology. This point is laboured because it is important to classify militarism and warfare correctly, and to view critically the transformation of human violence through time.

Archaeology should question whether it can contribute to a balanced understanding of human violence and war. The author believes it can, provided it establishes a reasoned perspective first, with a detailed scientific analysis of the material evidence, from skeletal trauma to fortifications and weaponry. The dimension of time may provide a unique opportunity to see something of the increasingly complex nature of violence and war. As Groebel & Hinde (1989, 228) eloquently conclude, we need to expose the myths which surround individual aggression, group violence and war. As they say: 'The abolition of violence and war demands a systematic analysis of their causes, a falsification of the myths surrounding them and especially an efficient search for non-violent alternatives to conflict resolution.'

FOUR

BEYOND THE WESTERN WAY OF WAR: ANCIENT BATTLEFIELDS IN COMPARATIVE PERSPECTIVE

JOHN CARMAN

The approach of scholars to the study of war can be peculiarly bloodless. It is as if, in recognising the stupidity and destructiveness of war, any concern for people's actual experience of it becomes unworthy of attention, so we try instead to seek out its 'origins'. These may be held to lie in society, in which case we draw on sociological and anthropological insights (Haas, Chapter 2, Chapman, Chapter 8 this volume), or they may be held to lie within the individual, encouraging us to draw upon the insights of psychology, biology and socio-biology into human behaviour (Brothwell, Chapter 3 this volume).

As an alternative to this search for origins, this chapter will offer one way of studying war as a realm of actual human experience. It will do so by focusing on what may be considered (and many do consider) the definitive form of war-making in the western world – the battle. It will approach battle as a way of acting in the world, and from a perspective that treats that way of acting as an aspect of cultural choice and as a performed 'ritual' rather than a rationally organised procedure designed to meet functional ends. It aims to highlight the non-functional – and even dysfunctional – choices made as part of this style of war-making and the highly ritualised actions it requires.

Such a concern with ideas about functional reason and ritual is not entirely new in archaeology, or indeed elsewhere. What may be somewhat new is to apply the ideas to a field of activity where a functional logic is deemed to hold powerful sway. In the conventional approach of military historians, war-making decisions and actions are explained as either designed to perform a particular (often strategic or tactical) function successfully, or as a failure to identify correctly an opportunity or a threat. Instead, this chapter will focus upon some of the cultural assumptions which guide war-making – ideas about what is 'proper' or 'appropriate' or 'right', ideas about what can be done and what cannot, ideas about what war is for, and ideas about what is legitimate and what is illegitimate. It will focus in particular on decisions about where it is appropriate to conduct war, and the cultural significance of places where war-making reaches its climax to become the actual violence of battle. In doing so, it puts the experience of the physical at the forefront of this particular approach to the problem of war.

VIOLENT ENCOUNTERS: THE WESTERN WAY OF WAR

Fighting battles is the way western societies conduct their wars. Our histories are dotted with such encounters, a few capable of being considered significant or 'decisive' (Creasy 1908, Fuller 1970), or more commonly dismissed as 'indecisive' (Weigley 1991). Battles are the usual focus – and certainly the main punctuation points – of military history (cf. Keegan 1976; Nosworthy 1992; 1995; Weigley 1991) to the almost complete exclusion of other aspects of military organisation and activity. Weigley explains interest in military history as the 'thirst to experience vicariously the intense emotions of battle' (Weigley 1991, xi), a thirst capable of being assuaged because the 'element in which the [kind of war represented by battles] exists is [that of] danger' (von Clausewitz 1976 [1832], 85). The Western way of war is 'an act of force to compel our enemy to do our will', and accordingly, primarily a political instrument (von Clausewitz 1976 [1832], 87). This model of how to conduct warfare is the legacy to us of our claimed cultural descent from the Ancient Greek city-state and its wars (Hanson 1989), transferred to modern times by the addition of elements from other cultures (Keegan 1993). This ideal of battle is: 'a paradox of the highest order, a deliberate attempt to harness, to modulate, and hence to amplify the wild human desire for violence through . . . order and discipline' (Hanson 1989, 16). Battle in the Western tradition is at heart held to be the starkly simple infliction of mass violence, 'bereft of heroics and romanticism' (Hanson 1989, 17), to achieve a particular aim.

The historical study of battle can take a long-term perspective: for Keegan (1976, 298), 'battle is a historical subject whose nature . . . can only be understood down a long historical perspective'. His excellent and highly influential book covers battles fought by English soldiers from the fifteenth century AD to the twentieth, and it is possible to take a longer perspective still, spanning almost 3,500 years. The earliest battle recorded was that outside the walled city of Megiddo, fought in what is now Syria in 1469 BC; the most recent is the battle fought yesterday, or last week, or last month and reported on TV or in the newspapers. A survey of recorded encounters over a period of about 2,000 years (Dupuy & Dupuy 1970; Perrett 1992; Laffin 1995) makes clear two things: first, that in the period from the mid-second millennium BC to the mid-first millennium AD, battle was a comparatively rare event, and second, that it is a phenomenon apparently geographically limited in scope.

Over this entire 2,000-year period, history records only 288 battles worthy of note: an overall average of a mere one every seven years. Of these, 138 (48 per cent) were fought in the Mediterranean lands of Europe, and a further 63 (21 per cent) were fought in the Near East; 73 battles (25 per cent) were fought in Greek or Roman internecine or civil wars, and if one excludes these, the number for all other peoples across the globe drops to a total of 215, or one battle every nine years. Total exclusion of all battles involving Greek and Roman forces – against others of the same kind, against each other and against all others – leaves a mere 50 recorded battles (17 per cent of the total) fought by all other peoples, or only one every forty-one years; those recorded for China consist of two only, 138 years apart, and both relatively late in our study period. Military historians such as

Chaliand (1994, xxx–xxxi) emphasise the limitation of 'conflict' during a period covering the third century BC to the fourteenth century AD to a relatively narrow strip of territory reaching from eastern Asia to northern Europe, and the area in which battles were fought is narrower still. One reason for this is evident: we are reliant for our information on written records, so battles fought by peoples who did not mark or commemorate them will go unrecorded. On the other hand, a willingness to remember one's battles is likely to indicate a cultural acceptance of battle as a way of making war. Battle is thus not an inevitable component of war-making: it is a matter of cultural choice.

The phrase 'battles worthy of note' used in the above statistics is significant. It is quite likely that cultures other than those of the western world have engaged in organised mass violence. It seems that what they are less likely to have done is to celebrate them in collective memory, which may explain why images of actual fighting are comparatively rare in the ancient world (Montgomery 1968, 37). A review of the literature of the 'art' of war in the ancient world shows that it is predominately writers from Greece and Rome who celebrate the battle as the epitome of war. In China and India, the works of such important and influential thinkers as Sun Zi (China) and Kautilya (India), both ascribed to the fourth century BC, focus much more upon alternatives to battle – such as stratagem, delay, the use of spies, and alternatives to war itself – the making and keeping of alliances, the uses of deceit, and a willingness to submit, at least temporarily, to more powerful foes (Chaliand 1994).

Battle as a distinct form of war-making spread initially from the Near East to the lands of the Mediterranean (second millennium BC–later first millennium BC). It was taken up in a major way by the Greek city-states (a phenomenon explained and elaborated upon by Hanson 1989; 1990). From Greece, it was also taken to Italy and perfected as a tool of conquest by Rome. It was thereafter re-exported by the Greek and Roman Empires to the Near East, and introduced by the Roman Empire to western and northern Europe (first millennium BC–first millennium AD). The warrior cultures of northern and western Europe subsequently continued to see battle as the appropriate form of war (cf. Kristiansen, Chapter 11, Randsborg, Chapter 12, this volume): and this myth of the appropriateness of making war by the decisive single clash of arms continues to our own day (Keegan 1993).

Adoption of battle as 'the way of war' has resulted in the study of military history being predominately that of the study of battles as events. This includes the selection of those considered 'significant' or 'decisive' for placing in historical context (Creasy 1908; Fuller 1970), or their inclusion in gazetteers and reference texts (e.g., Perrett 1992; Laffin 1995). Keegan (1976, 36–78) goes further by highlighting and criticising the dominant position of the 'battle piece' in military literature, seeking to replace it with a 'search for the face of battle' (Keegan 1976, 78) in terms of what actually happened at such places, knowledge of which could be useful to modern soldiers – by delineating what happens, for instance, when men are struck by metal spikes or fragments, how bodies of troops break and flee, how they are made to stand and fight, or what happens when horses or men are made to charge home. Weigley (1991) points to the failure of the European belief in decisive battle to produce its expected results while charting the rise of military professionalisation from the mid-seventeenth to early nineteenth centuries AD, a period he dubs 'The Age of Battles'; Nosworthy (1992; 1995), by contrast, is more concerned to understand changes in 'doctrine' as they developed over a similar period, rather narrowly defined in terms of troop dispositions and movements in battle. In more recent times, strategic theorists and military planners have focused their attention on how to win current and future wars in terms of increased battlefield effectiveness (Gray 1994).

The archaeological study of battle is a comparatively rare thing, except for more modern periods. Brooke's (1854) 'visits' to some of the battlefields of the English Wars of the Roses (fifteenth century AD) possibly rank as some of the earliest examples of such research. The battlefields of nineteenth-century America have come under some scrutiny, especially as they represent officially designated monuments to American history (e.g., Scott et al. 1989), and in England, the seventeenth-century AD battlefields of Naseby (Foard 1995) and Marston Moor (Newman 1981) have been investigated using archaeological techniques. Hanson acknowledges the value of various types of archaeological evidence for ancient Greek warfare (Hanson 1989, 48–50), although he relies most heavily on literary sources.

BATTLE AS CULTURE

The violence of battle takes the form of 'institutionalised combat', something which needs to be clearly distinguished from 'an impromptu scrap' (Jones 1980, 98). The difference is that the former 'has rules, and the rules must be followed, otherwise the participants lose, rather than gain, prestige' (Jones 1980, 98). Types of violence which for Jones have no rules include murder, assassination, ambush, street brawl (although on the rule-bound Brazilian *briga* see Linger 1992), terrorist activities, and spectator violence at sports events (Jones 1980, 100). He suggests that the roots of rule-bound violence lie in the 'need, forced on participants by society, to maintain, and preferably to enhance their reputations' (Jones 1980, 101). While Jones's explanation for the existence of forms of rule-bound violence – and indeed, his list of violence which has no rules – can be questioned, his point about rule-bound behaviour is very important in respect of the study of battles. Battles – in order to be battles, rather than ambushes, skirmishes, riots, massacres or other dishonourable events – have to be intensely rule-directed. The purpose of the line of research outlined here is to identify those rules as they apply in particular times and places, and how they change through time and across space.

This idea is very similar to the charge made by Gray (1997) and others, that war represents a kind of discourse – a way of speaking about and acting towards things. Discourses also have rules that must be followed and an appropriate language in which to 'speak'. The language of war is that of blood and flesh (cf. von Clausewitz 1976 [1832], 149). Sun Zi (fourth century BC; Chaliand 1994, 221–38) identified five factors of importance in war of which only three were under human control: from the beginning of the study of war the crucial distinction was always between what was inevitably 'natural' and what was 'rational' or controllable (Gray 1997, 94).

One way this has been converted into archaeology is in terms of study of the regular patterning of human behaviours in particular sets of circumstances and contexts, called after Schiffer (1977) 'behavioural archaeology' (Scott et al. 1989). At the nineteenth-century Custer site, where the Battle of the Little Big Horn was fought in 1876, Scott and his colleagues undertook research to determine the positions and movements of combatants during the fight, to find the disposition of twenty-eight missing soldiers, and to ascertain the relationship between markers representing the fallen and actual burial locations (Scott et al. 1989, 7). Overall, they sought to reconstruct 'the events of the . . . fight as they are represented in the archaeological record' (Scott et al. 1989, 8). Evidence sought included artefacts which could be identified as either that of soldiers, or that of those against whom the soldiers fought, and their movement on the day. These then allowed the researchers to develop an idea of events, especially the movements of forces (Scott et al. 1989, 89–145). This in turn allowed them to construct models of the patterning of material remains at the site using this data: a static model of patterning at the gross scale (Scott et al. 1989, 147), and dynamic models of patterning at the level of the movements of individuals or of units (Scott et al. 1989, 148–9). These models are expected to contribute to the development of further models representing the common or expected behaviour patterns for American nineteenth-century warfare (Scott et al. 1989, 150) which can be of use in the study of other such sites. These common or expected behaviour patterns would themselves represent part of 'the discourse of war' for that place and period of history.

In describing European warfare of the High Middle Ages, Prestwich (1996) makes clear how exceptional battle was in this period. Part of the reason lies in the kind of enemy being faced: certain types of enemy were simply not of the kind to fight battles (Prestwich 1996, 306–7). Enough examples exist, however, to be able to ascertain the particular kind of discourse represented by Medieval battle. It was perceived as 'a trial before God . . . [a matter of] pride, a sense of honour and perhaps obstinacy' (Prestwich 1996, 308). Where battles were fought by prior agreement – a not uncommon arrangement – complex preparations were part of the procedure. Prayers were offered on the eve of battle, speeches would be made by commanders to the troops, and 'the display of standards . . . [was] a symbol of all-out war, in which no quarter would be given' (Prestwich 1996, 314). While there appears to have been little dishonour in avoiding battle (Prestwich 1996, 307), once battle was joined, it was joined with ferocity: the repeated battle-cry was used 'in part as a means of recognition, in part to frighten the enemy, and perhaps also in part as a means of reinforcing a collective identity, and supporting friends in the fight' (Prestwich 1996, 324); long-range weapons were used only to allow men-at-arms to close on the same terms as an advancing enemy rather than as an intentional battle-winner, although the English longbow proved to be just such a weapon (Prestwich 1996, 324); actual fighting took the form of 'butcher's blows' (Keegan 1976, 103). The discourse of Medieval warfare thus included much that was very violent, but also much that was highly ritualised, as does modern warfare: it is these rule-bound 'ritual' aspects which change over time.

Much of this ritual – in the present as in the past – both derives from and simultaneously determines the very definition of 'battle' itself. A battle is held to be not the same as a *skirmish*, which is a mobile encounter between forces who never become fully engaged (English Heritage 1994, 3). Nor is a battle a *siege*, which involves cutting off a fortified castle or settlement from outside help in order to force its surrender: for Weigley (1991, 55) the drawn-out formal siege of the seventeenth century AD is 'ritualistic' in form, while the battle is simply 'bloodshed'. But there are sufficient ritual aspects to battle for this particular distinction to be considered unnecessary.

English Heritage (1995) has determined that to be included in its official register, a battle must not represent a 'lesser form of engagement', such as a skirmish; it must have involved recognised military units, and thus not riotous crowds or other disorganised groups; it must have had political, military historical or 'biographical' significance, and it must have been fought over a definable geographical space. Similarly, the functions of battle are closely defined: 'the purpose of the engagement [is] the destruction of the enemy' (von Clausewitz 1976 [1832], 230); it is 'a moral conflict . . . [requiring] the moral collapse of one of the two contending parties' (Keegan 1976, 296); it is also thereby designed to curb 'the horrors of war [by] achieving decisiveness in the conduct of war' (Weigley 1991, 73). Battles are also always mutually agreed: 'There can be no engagement unless both sides are willing' (von Clausewitz 1976 [1832], 245); '*all* battles take place by mutual agreement, although such agreement is usually informal in the modern era' (Keeley 1996, 60); battle 'requires . . . a mutual and sustained act of will by two contending parties' (Keegan 1996, 296). Keeley (1996) in particular points to the highly ritualised elements of modern battle: the complex 'choreography' required in acts of surrender by individuals and units, such as white flags, raised hands, proffered or cast-away weapons, the use of certain key words, and sometimes carefully arranged cease-fires (Keeley 1996, 61); legal and other limitations upon who may be killed by what weapons and under what conditions, rendering the slaughter of prisoners illegal (Keeley 1996, 62), and the obsession of soldiers throughout recorded time with the capture of enemy standards, and correctly worn regalia (Keeley 1996, 62–3). Von Clausewitz was highly aware of the ritualised and dance-like movements of early modern warfare:

> The troops move calmly into position in great masses deployed in line and depth . . . [and are] left to conduct a firefight for several hours, interrupted now and then by minor blows – charges, bayonet assaults, and cavalry attacks. . . . Gradually, the units engaged are burned out, and when nothing is left but cinders, they are withdrawn and others take their place. (Von Clausewitz 1976 [1832], 226)

With a historian's hindsight, Weigley sees the same: 'Battles [of the eighteenth century AD] were tournaments between serried ranks of colorfully [*sic*] uniformed toy soldiers come to life, advancing toward each either to the beating of drums . . . [so] the notion of battlefields as paradegrounds is not altogether deceptive' (Weigley 1991, 168).

These aspects of battle – mutual agreement to fight, closely ordered movement, formalities of surrender and cease-fire – may seem to us to be grounded in an obvious rationality. But this is much more the effect of an accumulated historical focus on the battle as the epitome of war, and even of philosophical attention in coming to terms with war, than with the objective reasonableness of battle's practices for all times and places. Battle does not emerge onto the historical stage until the Bronze Age of Egypt. It becomes something relatively common only as written history develops: indeed, battle is the subject of much early history. The normality of battle depends upon its familiarity to us. How reasonable is it really for closely organised and heavily controlled groups of specific individuals to come together at a specific place at a specific time, to stand under what may be a long and lethal bombardment, not to run away and hide, but at a determined time to approach close to others who share the intention of mass slaughter? If Weigley (1991, 73) is right, and violent battles of annihilation serve to curb the other horrors of war, then they do so by a form of magic which has little to do with reason. Instead, they are to do with common understandings about what is appropriate and right. These rules – frequently unwritten, but in modern times transposed into actual laws – concern and determine the nature of battle in any particular period, and indeed the appropriateness of battle itself as a mode of behaviour. The rules concern when it is appropriate to fight: for what reason, over what dispute, and after which declarations of animosity and intent. Garlan (1975, 41–3) emphasises the 'sacral rhythm' evident in the Greek and Roman approach to warfare, the importance of a legitimate cause for war (Garlan 1975, 47–8), and the formalities of declaration (Garlan 1975, 48–50). The rules concern whom it is appropriate to fight: certain categories of foe are not worthy of meeting in battle; these must represent at least one's equals in some sense. The rules concern who *may* be involved in the fighting, who *must* be involved in the fighting, and who must remain a non-combatant (Garlan 1975, 78–117). They concern how to fight – which weapons may be used, and whether one attacks or defends, stands or moves – and these rules relate to those concerning who may or must fight, and extend beyond mere functionality to questions of social status (Garlan 1975, 117–29). In particular, the rules concern where it is appropriate to fight: at what kind of place, on what type of ground, or even that it shall be at a specific location sanctioned by law or custom.

BATTLEFIELD LANDSCAPE AND ARCHITECTURE

The ground over which battles on land are fought is conventionally treated by military historians as an inconvenience to be overcome or a resource to be used – a phenomenon generally called 'terrain'. The idea has begun to extend beyond history to the emerging field of 'military geography' (Doyle & Bennett 1997), but this way of thinking about the land on which soldiers fight has an ancient pedigree. Kautilya (India, fourth century BC) emphasises the importance of possessing the advantage of strength, time and place: '[space] means the earth . . . there are such varieties of land as forests, villages, mountains, level plains, and uneven grounds . . . That part of the country in which [our] army finds a convenient place for its manoeuvre . . . is the best; that part [convenient to the enemy] is the worst' (Chaliand 1994, 322). For Sun Zi (China, fourth century BC), 'earth' is the third of the five constant factors to be taken into account in war, and comprises 'distances, great and small; danger and security; open ground and narrow passes; the chances of life and death' (Chaliand 1994, 222); his practical advice covers how to manoeuvre in mountains, how to cross rivers and marshes, and the use of high ground (Chaliand 1994, 233–4). The General Maxims of Flavius Vegetius (Rome, fourth century AD) include the belief that 'The nature of the ground is often of more consequence than courage.' Recommendations include advice to 'cover one of your flanks either with an eminence, a city, the sea, a river or some protection of that kind', and always to 'choose the proper ground for [cavalry]' (Chaliand 1994, 216). Leo VI (Byzantium, ninth century AD) exhorts commanders not to 'go near the foothills of mountains' in case the enemy occupies them (Chaliand 1994, 356), while Al-Rawandi (Persia, thirteenth century AD) advises that 'if the enemy has more horsemen, a narrow terrain . . . must be chosen' (Chaliand 1994, 442). Under this influence, von Clausewitz (1976 [1832], 348–54) thought terrain an important enough factor to be accorded two entire chapters, indicating how 'geography and the character of the ground . . . have a decisive influence on the engagement':

> Geography and ground can influence military operations in three ways: as an obstacle to the approach, as an impediment to visibility, and as cover from fire. . . . We shall find . . . that there are three distinct ways in which an area may differ from the concept of a flat and open plain: first in the contours of the countryside, such as its hills and valleys; second in such natural phenomena as forests, swamps and lakes; and third in the factors produced by agriculture. . . . It is . . . easiest to wage war in flat and only moderately cultivated areas. But this holds true only in general and altogether disregards the value of natural obstacles to defence. (von Clausewitz 1976 [1832], 348–9)

He nevertheless concludes that the 'only thing that really counts' is *victory in battle . . . [determined by] the relative quality of the two armies and their commanders. Terrain can only play a minor role*' (Clausewitz 1976 [1832], 354). Keegan takes a wider perspective, pointing out that:

> about seventy per cent of the world's . . . dry land is either too high, too cold or too waterless for the conduct of military operations . . . [Intense] military activity has been concentrated into a fraction even of that space where conditions do favour the movement and maintenance of armed forces. Battles not only tend to recur on sites close to each other . . . but have also frequently been fought on exactly the same spot over a very long period of history. (Keegan 1993, 68–70)

For all these students of war – ancient and modern – topography generally represents one of the naturally occurring limitations upon the capacity to make war successfully.

There are hints of a possible alternative approach in Garlan's (1975, 58) discussion of the immunity given to certain types of place in Ancient Greek warfare, especially temples and religious shrines. The phenomenon of 'ritual wars', 'rather like long-term tournaments or competitions . . . [taking] place periodically within a religious context of a mythical or cultural nature, according to rules which restrict the object and the extent of the conflict' (Garlan 1975, 26) also suggests the periodic return to a designated 'battle site', a place of deliberate cultural choice rather than one determined by external environmental factors. This idea is given further support by:

> repeated engagements, generation after generation, in the identical Argive, Corinthian, and Mantinean plains . . . [and] the striking proximity of battle-sites in Boiotia – a veritable 'blood alley' of sorts – over a 200-year period; there, only a very few miles separate Plataia, Tanagra, Oinophylia, Delion, Haliatos, Koroneia, Leuktra, and Chaironeia. (Hanson 1991, 254)

Ober (1991, 188) sees in Greek hoplite warfare 'a system of war that was more ritualistic than rational in its set forms'. There are also hints in Sun Zi of a more 'metaphorical' and rather less functionalist understanding of natural features in the colourful use of imagery:

'The general who is skilled in defence hides in the deepest recesses of the earth; he who is skilled in attack flashes forth from the heavens' (Chaliand 1994, 226); 'just as water retains no constant shape, so in warfare there are no constant conditions' (Chaliand 1994, 230); 'Let your rapidity be that of the wind, your compactness that of the forest. In raiding and plundering be like fire, in immovability like a mountain' (Chaliand 1994, 231). Ancient Greek immunities and rituals, and ancient Chinese metaphors all imply the cultural importance of places and natural features in warfare: rather than these things acting as impediments to action, useful resources or simply topographical background, they are capable of being invested with a kind of meaning. It is this meaning that research into historic battlefields of all periods aims to understand.

Elsewhere (Carman 1999), the author has argued that battles from the earliest to the late Medieval periods were generally fought on relatively flat and unfeatured ground: 'unfeatured' meaning ground that contains no major natural features or built structures which play a significant part in the action of the battle. This does not mean that such features do not exist at the battle site: lines of stream, linear embankments or ditches, or rising ground, and even buildings may well be present. But it does not automatically follow that soldiers fighting battles at that place will necessarily take notice of them or use them to allow or impede movement, for concealment or as cover. It is clear that the Greeks as far as possible always made the deliberate 'choice of level battlefields' (Hanson 1991, 6), comprising 'usually a flat terrain' to accommodate up to 50,000 fighters (Lazenby 1991, 88). This was because 'hoplites could do battle properly only in a wide, clear, flat space that was free of even minor obstacles' (Ober 1991, 173):

> the essentially agonistic nature of hoplite conflict [was] a form of warfare that could only be engaged in by men who had agreed (formally or informally) on the nature of weapons, armour and formations that would be permitted to the field of honour. This agreement did not make the ensuing battle any less fierce or more 'civilised' – but it did permit the battle to take place. (Ober 1991, 179)

'The set forms of hoplite battle . . . [thus] defy geomorphic logic' (Ober 1991, 173), and one can expect the practical advice of commentators as to the 'proper' use of terrain to have been lost on them. However, from the point of view of a modern scholar of ancient warfare, the type of landscape over which battles were fought can perhaps give insights into the attitudes of those fighting the battle to the landscape.

It is a prerequisite of such research, of course, that the location of battle be securely known. This in itself is problematic: many such sites are known or inferred only from the sparest of descriptions, and the precise spot where this or that body of troops met may not be at all evident. The idea of marking such sites permanently was not widespread among the ancients. Garlan (1975) reports the Greek origin of the battlefield monument in the practice of hanging pieces of enemy armour from tree branches. Later, such 'trophies' took the form of standing columns, as at Marathon *c*. 460 BC, some thirty years after the battle itself. The first permanent monument was built at Leuktra in 371 BC, and by 319 BC it took proper architectural form, becoming 'a stereotype for the minor arts' (Garlan 1975, 62–3). The Romans and others, unlike the Greeks, 'were content to burn the enemy spoils on the spot, dedicating them to' the gods (Garlan 1975, 63). By the third century BC they preferred 'trophies which they could carry' or set up in the Capitol, and by the first century BC they became 'a symbol of [the person of the conqueror]' and so had 'even less connection with the battlefield than in the past' (Garlan 1975, 63).

Rodwell (1993a) nicely sums up the problems of such sites in his search for the battlefield of Assandun (England, AD 1016). The written descriptions from near-contemporary sources of troop movements prior to the battle are suggestive but by no means conclusive (Rodwell 1993a, 133). The search for archaeological evidence reveals earthworks at the two most likely locations, but it is by no means clear that these in any way relate to the fighting (Rodwell 1993a, 139–40), and at neither site is there any evidence of a battlefield cemetery (Rodwell 1993a, 145). Hanson (1989, 48), in reconstructing the form of hoplite battle, also calls upon archaeology in the form of evidence from excavations of battlefield tumuli and the evidence from sculpture and vase paintings, along with topographical studies. The latter are inevitably very valuable, for over time the shape of the battlefield may change very significantly. The near-contemporary poetic description of the Battle of Maldon (England, AD 991) does not represent the site as it is seen in the late twentieth century: geological research in 1973 aimed to help recreate the appearance of the site in the latter part of the tenth century AD, which found the sea level to have been some two metres lower than it is today (Petty & Petty 1993, 168). Accordingly, action inserted by more recent historians to make sense of the site – such as a supposed withdrawal by the defending Saxons from the shoreline, to allow the invading Norsemen to land and form in battle array – no longer becomes necessary (Petty & Petty 1993, 168). Where one is investigating battles of a millennium or more ago, an appreciation of what the landscape looked like then is of crucial importance.

We are hampered, however, by the fact already mentioned: that ancient depictions of battle do not usually include a representation of the local topography (Montgomery 1968, 37). Instead, we have images of groups of fighting men: anonymous, often closely packed, but highly mobile. Clearly, the emphasis is being placed upon these formations composed of human beings, dressed and equipped alike, and all moving in unison. These formations are people as part of a machine: what Haraway (1995) calls 'cyborgs'. If the topography of a battlefield, including any built structures it contains, can be seen as the static architecture of that space, then the linear or rectangular forms composed of mass humanity which traverse that space may be seen also as a kind of architecture: not static architecture, but mobile. In moving there, three things come together in the battlefield space: groups of people organised in various ways; things these people carry with them in the form of equipment and weapons, and the physical form of the battlefield space itself. In making the thing called 'battle', these three things – people, technology and landscape – interact. The forms of interaction which take place on any particular battle site can give us a means of understanding the attitudes and ways of thinking of the people involved.

The technology of war – the specifics of weapon types – is, if not determinate, then at least reflective of the way in which bodies of fighters will move on the ground, and of the kind of attitude they have towards killing. Aztec warfare, as reported by Keegan (1993, 110), was dominated by swords whose blades were made of chipped stone, designed not to kill, but to wound: captives taken in war were not to die on the battlefield, but as sacrifices.

The dominant weapon in ancient India (Dupuy & Dupuy 1970, 35) and ancient China (Dupuy & Dupuy 1970, 15) was the bow, designed to allow their typical low-casualty warfare of manoeuvre and avoidance. The Assyrians, known for their chariots (Keegan 1993, 169–77), and the cavalry of the Scythians (Keegan 1993, 177–8) were typically armed with the bow. Keegan (1993, 160) provides a chilling account of how such peoples drew on a knowledge of animal herding, husbandry and slaughter to control and overcome enemy formations. Infantry armies were armed more variously. The Egyptians used stone maces and flint-tipped spears until relatively late in the Bronze Age (Keegan 1993, 131), and later adopted the bronze battle-axe and sword against iron-wielding enemies (Filer 1997, 68). The weapons of late Bronze Age Minoan soldiers included swords, daggers and spears of bronze, with bronze helmets for protection (Nikolaidou & Kokkinidou 1997, 185). This combination of mixed weapons for hand-to-hand combat requires a degree of free movement on the part of individuals, with light armour if any, and a certain amount of space around each fighter. By contrast, the phalanx of heavily armoured, shielded and spear-wielding soldiers of Babylon (Montgomery 1968, 37) or Greece (Keegan 1993, 249–50) implies determined shock action and close manoeuvre in formation: the form of hoplite warfare (Hanson 1989). Different again was the Classical Roman: heavily armoured and shielded, armed with a sword of iron, standing shoulder-to-shoulder in disciplined formation, these troops made the most effective killing machine of the ancient world.

Dupuy & Dupuy offer a likely description of early battle involving relatively unformed bodies of infantry and chariots or cavalry:

> [The] objective was to reach a suitable place of battle in order to overwhelm the enemy before he was able to prevail . . . [since a] campaign was [no more than] a huge raid . . . Maneuver [*sic*] in battle was largely accidental . . . Sometimes the initial charge of chariots and horsemen would strike terror into the opposite side, in which case battle quickly became a chase, with only the fleetest men . . . escaping the slaughter. More often, the two masses simply converged to carry on the butchery. (Dupuy & Dupuy 1970, 3–4)

This kind of relatively disorganised warfare – which perhaps can be described as a 'swarming' of the enemy – contrasts with the tight discipline representative of other infantry forces. Babylonians (third to second millennium BC) and Greeks (later first millennium BC) both fought in tight formations of heavy infantry armed with spears up to sixteen ranks deep (Dupuy & Dupuy 1970, 17). While the Babylonians combined such formations with chariots, the Greeks largely ignored the possibilities of the horse for warfare. Battle for Greek formations was a simple process: an advance leading to a charge to close with the enemy; a collision followed by a mutual 'push'; tears and gaps in the lines forcing one side to give ground and collapse (Hanson 1989, 135–93; Lazenby 1991, 90–7). The Greek style came to dominate western Asia and the Mediterranean: Kristiansen and Randsborg (Chapters 11 and 12 this volume) make a strong case for its dissemination throughout Europe too, while Hanson (1989) and Keegan (1993) argue that its fundamental ideology still dominates western thinking about war. Roman republican and imperial armies were similarly disciplined and similarly ruthless, although differently armed. Their formation was thinner – ten ranks deep – and thus more 'linear' in appearance, but just as lethal, if not more so. Battles by Roman armies and against them are often more complex than those of the Greeks and their followers, involving the use of terrain and more sophisticated systems of movement, command and control. Vegetius (Rome, fourth century AD) outlines seven different styles of formation and movement appropriate for late Roman armies: the 'oblong square' phalanx standing firm; advancing the 'right wing obliquely against the enemy's left'; attacking the enemy's right wing if your left is stronger; attacking both enemy wings at once; covering one's centre with light infantry and charging both enemy wings; beginning the action with one's right and extending the rest of the army 'perpendicular to the front and extended to the rear like a javelin', and covering one's flanks with a natural feature (Chaliand 1994, 216). Leo VI (Byzantium, ninth century AD) offers advice similar to Vegetius concerning appropriate troop dispositions and forces against various foes, including Persians, Turks, Scythians, Bulgarians, Franks, Lombards, Slavs and Saracens, each of whom fought in a different manner (Chaliand 1994, 362–8). The weapons and methods of fighting of particular peoples were not mere responses to their enemies: they maintained a home-grown style for long periods, both in victory and defeat. The style of warfare adopted by a particular people are also reflections of their culture and their cultural attitudes (cf. Hanson 1989 and Chapter 13 this volume; Kristiansen, Randsborg, Shepherd, Chapters 11, 12 and 14 this volume). Those attitudes are reflected in – and more importantly acted out at – the place of battle.

The Place of Battle

These theoretical considerations are designed to provide a framework within which individual battle-sites can be considered as places of cultural significance. The purpose of this approach is to find out what they may be able to tell us about the people who went there in the past, and those peoples' attitudes to each other and that place. The discussion so far has outlined a number of different aspects of battle-sites that may be questioned and drawn upon as a means to greater understanding of ancient warfare, summarised in Table 1. These can then be applied to individual battles in an attempt to gain a deeper insight into them. Here, three examples have been chosen: the first well-recorded battle in history, a decisive clash from the Greek Wars, and a third example from the closing years of Roman rule in the west.

Table 1 Parameters for studying battlefields

Rules of war	*Battlefield architecture*
Agreement to fight: Y/N	Features present
Mutual recognition as 'legitimate' enemies: Y/N	Type of feature used
Level of violence: High, medium, low	Type of feature not used
Marking of battle-site	Use of terrain:
	as cover;
	to impede visibility;
	to impede movement
Participants	Structured formations: Y/N
Functional aspects	
Dysfunctional aspects	

Kadesh, 1294 BC

The sources for this section are:
Montgomery (1968, 45–8), Perrett (1992, 149), Dupuy & Dupuy (1970, 6) and Chaliand (1994, 49–58).

In marching to restore Egyptian rule in Syria, Ramesses II divided his army of chariots and infantry into three contingents, well spread out along the road, with a flank guard some distance away to the west. The first contingent, led by Ramesses himself, encamped to the north of Kadesh prior to a siege of that city. The forces of the Hittite king used the city as cover to hide their movements, and launched a surprise attack with chariots on the second contingent a little south of Kadesh. Both Ramesses' first two contingents were defeated and ran from the field, leaving Ramesses alone with his bodyguard. After fierce fighting, the flank guard contingent came to Ramesses' aid, the first and second contingents returned, and the third main contingent arrived to complete defeat of the Hittites.

Table 2 Kadesh

Rules of war	*Battlefield architecture*
Agreement to fight: N	Features present: rivers hills city fortified camp
Mutual recognition: possibly N	Type of feature used: city fortified camp
Level of violence: Medium	Type of feature not used: rivers hills
Marking of battle-site: by neither side. Battle was unexpected and opportunistic.	Use of terrain: as cover; to impede visibility; Y to impede movement
Participants: chariots only on both sides; no infantry	Structured formations: Y

Functional aspects: Surprise attack; use of city to hide movement
Dysfunctional aspects: Gaps between Egyptian forces, which were spread out over several miles; non-use of infantry by either side; failure of either side to use natural landscape features for advantage; failure to reconnoitre in advance of movement; use by Egyptians of 'outmoded' weapons of bronze versus Hittite iron; reliance of Hittites on spears for chariots, versus Egyptian reliance on the bow

From the available evidence, it is clear that the Hittites had a sophisticated approach to using features as impediments to visibility: but this sophistication, at least as demonstrated here, only extended towards built features rather than natural ones. There was no effort by either side to use rising ground or watercourses to their advantage, especially to impede enemy movement. They used flat ground on which to deploy chariots only, leaving infantry standing idly by, except for those caught by the Hittite attack. Defeated troops seem to have fled rather than being pursued and killed, which may suggest a lower incidence of violence than among other peoples, and perhaps an aversion to killing. A surprising feature is the return of defeated Egyptian units to the fight, which suggests systems of command and control among the Egyptians worthy of further investigation. The battle-site itself was not expressly chosen except as the site of an attack by the Hittites: monuments to the battle are elsewhere, glorifying Ramesses rather than Egypt or Egyptian soldiers, and they are scathing of the Hittites as enemies (Chaliand 1994, 49–58). Overall, battle was more accidental than deliberate, with little notice being taken of the natural terrain. The nearby presence of a city (Kadesh) may reflect the expectation that such a feature stands near to a battle-site, or simply the strategic situation.

Leuktra, 371 BC

The sources for this section are:
Dupuy & Dupuy (1970, 42), Perrett (1992, 172) and Montgomery (1968, 70).

An army of Thebans and their allies formed on a flat plain opposite a similarly equipped and organised army from Sparta. The Thebans strengthened their left flank by making their formation much deeper, withholding their weaker centre and right. Attacking by the left, they defeated the Spartans, who ran from the field.

Table 3 Leuktra	
Rules of war	*Battlefield architecture*
Agreement to fight: Y	Features present: none
Mutual recognition: Y	Type of feature used: none (irrelevant)
Level of violence: High	Type of feature not used: (irrelevant)
Marking of battle-site: Site chosen by mutual agreement. A permanent trophy (monument) subsequently raised on the site.	Use of terrain: none (irrelevant)
Participants: hoplite citizen-soldiers only	Structured formations: Y

Functional aspects: Solid formations to make effective use of weaponry; tactical innovation by Thebans

Dysfunctional aspects: Extreme violence (typical of Greek warfare); non-use of any landscape features for advantage; no use of manoeuvre (e.g. flanking movement) for advantage; complete moral collapse of Spartans – ineffective command and control?

The Greeks avoided any kind of featured landscape: if any features existed, they were ignored. Battle was mutually agreed, and the site of battle was both carefully selected and subsequently recognised by the erection of a permanent marker, making it a special place. Levels of violence were high, but apart from Theban alterations to the standard formations, there was little sophistication in movement. Command and control systems once battle was joined were rudimentary. The focus in war was nevertheless very much upon the human architecture of the battlefield, and upon inflicting harm to the enemy. Battle was deliberate, and the place of battle was very significant.

Châlons, AD 451

The sources for this section are:
Dupuy & Dupuy (1970, 174–5), Perrett (1992, 71–2) and Fuller (1970, 195–214).

An army of Romans and their allies formed on a plain against a similarly armed and organised army of Huns and their allies, recently expelled from Orléans. An attempt to seize prominent high ground by one of the Roman allies led to general engagement and heavy but confused fighting. Fighting ceased upon nightfall. Negotiations the following day led to the retreat of the Huns and their allies.

Table 4 Châlons

Rules of war	*Battlefield architecture*
Agreement to fight: Y	Features present: city river hill
Mutual recognition: Y	Type of feature used: hill
Level of violence: High	Type of feature not used: city river
Marking of battle-site: Site chosen by mutual agreement.	Use of terrain: as cover; to impede visibility; to impede movement Y
Participants: 'warriors' of various peoples	Structured formations: Some

Functional aspects: Awareness by both sides of strengths and weaknesses; use of natural feature to gain advantage; sophisticated arrangements for disposition of troops
Dysfunctional aspects: Full advantage of terrain not taken by either side; battle probably avoidable by Huns; the outbreak of actual fighting and its continuation into darkness suggests a breakdown of systems of command and control: fighting itself may not have been of a particularly organised or disciplined kind, but more akin to a large-scale and violent affray or a 'swarming' of nearby enemies.

This battle shows many of the attributes we would expect to find in a modern approach to war: an awareness of the relative risks and advantages of battle; sophisticated dispositions; relatively effective systems of command and control; a use of terrain to advantage, and the concentration and use of appropriate forces by both sides. Use of terrain is limited to one low hill, however, ignoring other alternatives. Also, given their relative disadvantage, the Huns could initially have retreated to more difficult terrain. Battle may not have been necessary for them, and their ability to extricate themselves by negotiation the following day suggests that offering and giving battle may have been more a matter of 'honour' than a functionally strategic necessity. The style of preparation for battle reflects the increased theoretical sophistication of strategic commentary of its time (e.g., Vegetius), while the phenomenon of battle itself may have been more of a 'ritual' than a solution to a real strategic problem. However, battles were still largely fought on flat ground with a minimal use of landscape features, and once actual fighting had started, systems of command broke down, leading to a confused and violent series of mêlées. We see here a possible mixing of systems – the relatively loosely organised 'swarming' of an enemy, combined with the violence of Greek warfare – if so, the effect of previous traditions is being felt in war. The presence nearby of a city (Châlons) may reflect the expectation that such a feature stands near to a battle-site, the strategic situation, or simply geographic accident.

CONCLUSION

The first battles of history may have been rather haphazard and ad hoc events, limited in their violence, in which levels of pre-combat organisation may not have been very different from post-combat disorganisation – this may have been what allowed the Egyptian troops to rally and return at Kadesh. The Greeks adopted battle as a formal ritual of bloody violence, with little or no regard for the use of other than human resources. The closing years of the Roman Empire present us with battles that can be interpreted meaningfully in the functionalist terms of our own age, and the weight of military tradition may be affecting styles of warfare, but some odd features remain.

The brief review of three ancient battles suggests that the actions of battles are imbued with cultural meanings. It suggests that sets of rules were in operation which determined whether battle could or should take place, and if so, the form it should take. These rules included sets of culturally determined attitudes towards the purpose of battle, towards participants, and towards the place of battle itself. The latter included attitudes towards features present at the battle-site: the deliberate seeking or avoidance of certain types of features, the recognition or non-recognition of certain types of features as relevant to battle, and if recognised as relevant, the uses to which they could be put. A significant number of battles in Antiquity were fought near or beside cities, from the earliest onwards. If battles were meant to be 'seen' and noted as well as simply fought, it is possible that this placing is not accidental, and tells us something about attitudes towards and expectations about battle in the ancient world.

This chapter has sought to outline an approach to the study of historic battle which overcomes the assumptions of modern military theory. The doctrine of the modern era – largely derived from von Clausewitz (1976 [1832]) – emphasises the practical, the functional and the power of reason in conducting war. All resources present on the battlefield – living, built and natural – are deemed to be equally available to the soldier for use in gaining advantage over the enemy; accordingly, the value of terrain is particularly emphasised. The trend in military history (Montgomery 1968; Fuller 1970; Perrett 1992) is to interpret ancient battles in the style of modern ones – as responses to strategic necessity. Failure in battle is ascribed to a failure to use resources appropriately, or to bad luck; success in battle is ascribed to the 'proper' use of available resources. In contrast, this chapter emphasises the cultural specificity of styles of warfare. These, it is argued, are revealed by a focus not on the aspects of a battle deemed to be successful when judged through modern eyes, but by an emphasis on the apparently 'dysfunctional', which should not be dismissed merely as failure to operate as a successful soldier.

The period covered by this chapter saw the invention of battle as the 'western way of war'. In the course of its invention, battle developed as a particular style of conducting war, with associated attitudes and expectations about participants, non-combatants, time and place. In studying and researching this, the focus is placed upon the material aspects of making war, and especially upon the consequences of fighting battles. These include the effects on human beings. In approaching war from this perspective, it becomes impossible to ignore what war is ultimately always about: the breaking of flesh, the spillage of blood, and the making of death. Archaeologists and others are turning once again to the study of warfare as a human activity. It is the purpose of this particular line of research to identify and investigate historic battles of all periods to understand them – and through them, the phenomenon of warfare across time and space – more effectively.

FIVE

STONE AGE WARFARE

SLAVOMIL VENCL

INTRODUCTION

The study of the emergence of any phenomenon in archaeology is faced by the limitations that are inherent in material remains, and by an inadequate understanding of that phenomenon. Research into the origins of war and warfare through archaeological sources focuses mainly on the following issues: evidence of injuries inflicted by weapons; weapons, which are a basic requirement of war, and warriors, who represent the institutionalisation of warfare; and fortifications, which are the material reflection of a passive strategy.

The components of warfare are not all recorded archaeologically from the start – they only appear gradually. Specialised equipment used in warfare (such as weapons and fortifications) seems to have been developed as a result of long-term standardisation processes of violent behaviour where, to begin with, tools and devices serving primarily for economic purposes were used. The individual components of warfare, as parts of a single system, confirm and complement each other's testimony, thus defining and enriching our knowledge of the whole phenomenon of Stone Age warfare.

INJURIES INFLICTED BY WEAPONS

Physical injuries inflicted by weapons are the earliest recognisable evidence of warfare, and provide an appropriate starting point for the study of the beginnings of military behaviour (Vencl 1984c, 1991; Constandse-Westermann & Newell 1984; Nuzhnyj 1989; Cordier 1990). Unfortunately, their identification is hindered by the fact that some unhealed (i.e., fatal) injuries are difficult to distinguish from secondary, post-mortem damage to the skeletal remains (Kunter 1981, 225). Physical anthropology also fails to distinguish injuries sustained during combat from those acquired accidentally or as result of violence not connected with warfare (Koenig 1982, 89ff.). The study of these injuries is further hampered by the fact that most wounds to soft body tissue are beyond archaeological recognition (those found on bog bodies are not only unique, but difficult to date; Dieck 1965, catalogue Nos 76, 83–90, 125, 199, 222, 266, etc.). Another complication arises from the periods when cremation was the prevalent burial practice, as this evidence is irretrievable. Arrowheads found embedded in calcified vertebrae are extremely rare (Buck 1979, 107; Unverzagt & Herrmann 1958, 109).

Moreover, archaeological sources fail to provide evidence of the large number of men lost in battle, and of the other war casualties that could not be buried. This has considerably reduced the number of weapon injuries which have survived in the archaeological record, while making indistinguishable the motives behind the killing, whether religious (Numbers 25, 9, Deuteronomy 13, 13–18, 2 Kings 18, 27), political (2 Kings 10, 7, 1 Samuel 22, 18), inflicted as criminal punishment (executions of defectors, slaves, war prisoners) or for other reasons (only written records can attest to mass acts of suicide committed by defeated soldiers: Tacitus, *Annals* 4, 50, 73). Consequently, injuries which are archaeologically recognisable as having been inflicted by a weapon are but a fraction of all the injuries that may have resulted from military actions, and these must also include an undetectable (probably relatively small) proportion of injuries which were not inflicted in fighting. Although not all these injuries are unambiguously interpretable, the archaeological context of most of them is distinctly military.

Palaeolithic

The relatively small number of surviving skeletal remains from the Palaeolithic have invariably been exposed to intense post-depositional processes, so great care is required when assessing the nature of their damage. Identification of the type of injury is further hampered by the non-specific or multi-purpose character of objects and artefacts used only incidentally as weapons, as they would produce similar effects to those sustained in accidents. Fractured skulls have been discovered as far back as the Australopithecines and Pithecanthropus (Roper 1969; Mohr 1971), and in 40 per cent of Neanderthalers, according to Kunter (1981, 226). Indeed, the earliest injury that can conclusively be identified as inflicted by a weapon was that caused by a wooden javelin blow in the femur of one of the Neanderthalers from Mugharet-es-Skhul (Cordier 1990, 463). Fractured skulls have been less frequently found among *Homo sapiens sapiens*, although the Upper Palaeolithic provides the earliest iconographic evidence of manslaughter (Roper 1969, 447; Sallé 1990, 38). However, the totality of evidence from the Upper Palaeolithic is not sufficient to indicate conclusively the existence of warfare at this time (Ullrich 1982; Wendorf, Schild & Close 1986; Klíma 1987, 243; Berger & Trinkhaus 1995).

Mesolithic

Indisputable evidence of the general prevalence of armed aggression has been proven thanks to the survival of stone and bone projectiles found embedded in human bones from early Holocene burials throughout the Old World (sometimes as early as the Late Glacial in Africa; Vencl 1991).[1] Bone and stone projectiles found in the thorax (rib-cage) and abdomen areas of skeletal remains in some graves may be considered potential evidence of the same phenomenon. Such artefacts need not belong to grave-goods, but might be projectiles which delivered a lethal blow to the soft tissues of the dead individuals.[2]

Further, though inconclusive, evidence suggestive of warfare is provided by the fractured skulls found in cemeteries, especially if projectiles are embedded in other bones (Fig. 1),[3]

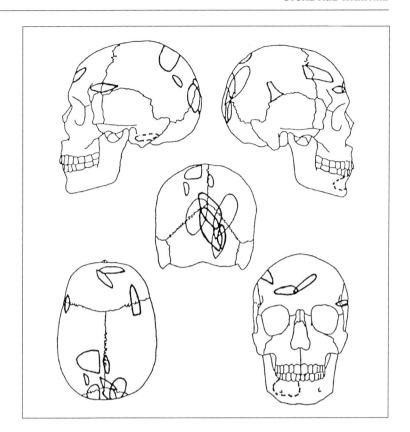

Fig. 1. Grosse Ofnet, Germany. The position of fatal injuries on late Mesolithic skulls. Source: Orschiedt 1998.

and likewise in isolated burials.[4] Decapitation represents a non-specific form of violence,[5] which may of course be related to non-military behaviour, such as ritual or cult practices.

This evidence of Mesolithic armed violence is regarded as a sign of inter-group conflict (this interpretation is rarely questioned: Price 1985, 359; Neeley & Clark 1990, 129). The relatively sudden and geographically widespread occurrence of injuries inflicted by weapons appears more likely to be a result of the diffusion of a successful pattern of special social behaviour rather than the reflection of a series of incidental and unrelated local events.

The find contexts of injuries in Mesolithic cemeteries provide more information about their character. This is especially true of multiple burials, where evidence would suggest mass violence rather than accidents or epidemics.[6] The involvement of females and children as victims in the violence (at Jebel Sahaba, Columnata, El Bachir, Popovo?, Colombres?), as well as the existence of multiple burials along with fatally wounded individuals (e.g., Burial 19 at Vedbaek), does not encourage an interpretation based on internal conflict, as these would hardly affect those of different ages and both sexes.

These details of the recorded injuries from burials in the Mesolithic are the reason this is regarded as the formative period of warfare (Telegin 1961, 8; Müller-Karpe 1968, 258; Dvoryaninov 1978, 13; Boroneanț 1981, 292). Indeed, the increased frequency of weapon injuries in the later phase of this period corroborates this picture (Constandse-Westermann

& Newell 1984). The recorded injuries from the Mesolithic point to the use of non-specific tools used as weapons, particularly bows, maces and stones.

Neolithic

The quantity of recorded injuries from skeletal remains increases in this period, which is perhaps a reflection on the rapid population growth and the widespread adoption of inhumation (Mohr 1971, 140; Gladykowska-Rzeczycka 1989, 13). The types of injuries generally remain the same as in the Mesolithic, with frequent evidence of stone or bone projectiles found embedded in human bones, and fractured skulls (arrowheads have been recorded by Cordier 1990; Edmonds & Thomas 1987, 192ff.; Bennike 1985; Bouville 1995; fractures by Angel 1974; for a general review, see Vencl 1984c, 533 with bibliography). There are also multiple burials attesting to mass violence at this time. What is new is evidence of extensive massacres and skeletons bearing traces of violence that have been found in the ditches of enclosures; both phenomena increased considerably in the later prehistoric and early historic periods.

Examples from central Europe illustrate the types of injuries in the Neolithic: the Linear Pottery people, representing the earliest Neolithic within this area, have until recently been regarded as a peaceful farming population. As no evidence of specialised weapons had been recorded (with the possible exception of double-edged and disc-shaped mace-heads where the obtuse edges indicate a purpose other than work: Vencl 1960, pl. VII–XI), one would not expect to find warrior burials in the context of this culture. This has resulted in a general hesitation in interpreting the function of the enclosures that appear on some Linear Pottery settlements.

Substantial evidence of mass violence has recently been uncovered in the context of the later phases of the Linear Pottery culture. One of the most conspicuous examples comes from the settlement site at Talheim, Kr. Heilbronn (Wahl & König 1987), where a multiple burial was discovered (Fig. 2) containing the remains of at least 34 people of various ages (16 were children and adolescents, and 18 belonged to adults, 9 of whom were male, 7 female, and 2 unidentified), and at least 18–20 skulls (59 per cent of the total assemblage, in which not all skulls have survived) bear signs of fatal injuries. As no evidence remains of the injuries to soft tissues, it can only be presumed that as with the remaining skeletons buried in the same pit, the entire group had been killed and deposited at one time, the corpses probably being thrown into the pit without proper burial ceremonies or personal belongings, as if cleared away rather than buried. Most of the skeletons had had the rear part of their skulls hit by the edges of stone polished tools, probably while trying to escape. The shapes of the skull injuries correspond to the shapes of the edges of flat shoe-last adzes, and there must have been at least five to six such artefacts used as killing weapons. Apart from 22 blows delivered probably by these woodworking tools, there were 4 injuries inflicted by the edges of massive shoe-last adzes (*Schuhleistenkeile*), and another 14 injuries were caused by blunt objects, or the sides of adzes (Wahl & König 1987, Abb. 47–50). Three individuals (two males, Nos 83/8 and 83/12, and an adult person No. 83/23) show traces of having been shot by arrowheads from behind, and this might indicate that the killing took place in daylight. As neither the

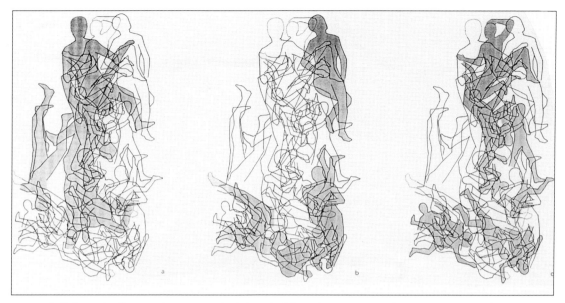

Fig. 2. Talheim (Heilbronn), Germany. Multiple burial of thirty-four persons on the Linear Pottery settlement site. Reconstruction of the position of nine men (a), seven women (b) and sixteen children with adolescents (c). Source: Wahl & König 1987.

faces, shoulders or arms of most of the victims bear traces of injuries, there does not seem to have been much resistance on their part. The skull of a 50–60-year-old man (No. 83/3A) showed, apart from an unhealed lethal wound, an earlier healed injury, which might suggest repeated participation in armed clashes (Wahl & König 1987, 139, abb. 29, 177, 185 with bibliography). The character of the injuries and the age categories of the Talheim victims would suggest that the village was raided and its inhabitants massacred. The attackers probably overwhelmed the village, but their motives remain uncertain (population pressure, family vengeance, irrational anxiety? – the demographic data obtained does not support the idea of revenge for the abduction of women, and it is unlikely that such a large number of people would have been sacrificed together in a cult ritual). Wahl and König (1987, 172) are probably correct in interpreting the evidence as being the result of a military conflict, even though no specialised weapons have been found and almost all the injuries seem to have been inflicted by woodworking tools.

At Schletz (Asparn an der Zaya) in Austria, on a long-lived settlement site of the Linear Pottery culture, a double oval enclosure (330 m in diameter) belonging to the final settlement phase with influence from the Želiezovce culture was discovered. Tens of human skeletons haphazardly thrown – largely lying face down, sometimes incomplete – were found in the bottom layer of the ditch (4 m wide, up to 2 m deep) (Fig. 3). Anthropological analyses of the sixty-seven skeletons recovered to date have revealed that with one exception, all were victims of violence, and none shows signs of a standard burial ceremony. Skulls bear traces of the edges of both flat and massive shoe-last adzes, and maybe also of mace-heads, which appear to have been used as killing weapons. If the

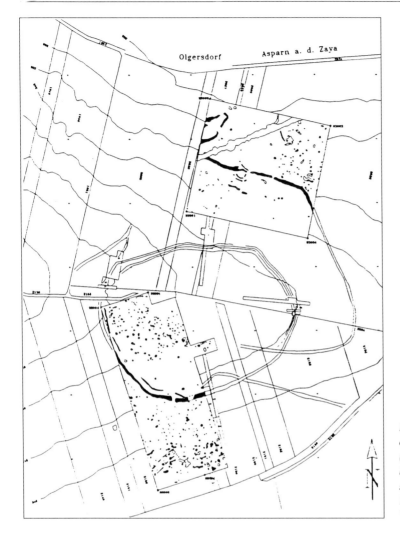

Fig. 3. Schletz, Austria. Plan of a double oval enclosure (330 m in diameter), belonging to the final settlement phase (Linear Pottery culture). Source: Windl 1994.

density of skeletons along the whole ditch was the same as that in the investigated area near the gate, the massacre would have involved several hundreds of individuals (Windl 1994, 11; 1996). As the long human bones bear traces of gnawing by animals, it is probable that the dead were left lying on the ground for some time (Teschler-Nicola et al. 1995). Human skeletons were even found in the well which had been dug inside the enclosure. Windl (1995) proposes that the ditch had a defensive function, and that the latest settlement phase at the site had been wiped out as a result of this massacre. This situation, too, does not seem to reflect ritual practices.

At Herxheim, Rheinland-Pfalz, a Late Linear Pottery enclosure was investigated recently (preliminary report: Spatz 1998). Most of the 334 whole or partial skeletons found up to late 1997 were buried in two deep ditches without the proper or normal care for the dead; the existence of armed conflicts on the site is proven by healed injuries on some skulls. Fragments of skulls and other human bones dispersed in numerous refuse

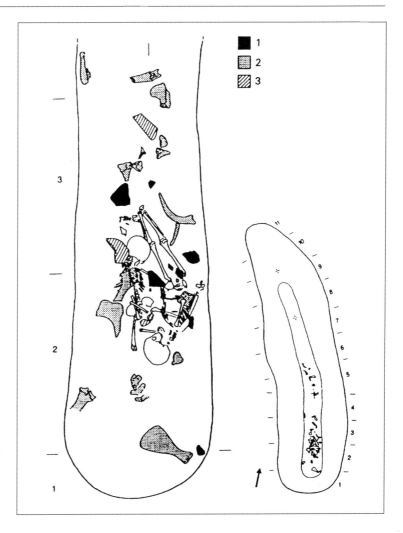

Fig. 4. Menneville (Aisne),
France. Children's
skeletons in the ditch of the
Linear Pottery culture.
1. Potsherds; 2. Animal
bones; 3. Stones. Source:
Farruggia et al. 1996.

pits on this settlement site attest to the common use of strange practices that are not
intelligible to us. At Menneville (Aisne, France) the skeletons of eleven childern were
discovered on the bottom of a Late Linear Pottery ditch (Veit 1993; Farruggia et al.
1996) (Fig. 4).

Evidence of violence within the Linear Pottery culture has only recently been brought to
light, perhaps suggesting that Neolithic agricultural communities were afraid of being
attacked by other groups. Enclosures were built, perhaps to reduce this fear. Ditches were
occasionally present in the earlier phases (Bicske, Eisleben), and became even more frequent
in later phases. Some enclosure ditches, or parts of them, contain human skeletons, either
complete or fragmentary (Eisleben, Kr. Wanzleben: Höckmann 1990; Kaufmann 1990a;
Langweiler, Aldenhovener Platte: Spatz 1998, 13). The isolated evidence of killed
individuals recovered from the limited sections of those Linear Pottery ditches that have
been investigated does not enable a conclusive interpretation (e.g., fragments of a skull of a

young man found in Ditch I/5 at Heilbronn-Neckargartach indicate that he died of repeated blows to the skull inflicted by a blunt object: Schmidgen-Hager 1992, 217).

The skeletal remains of forty-one individuals found at the Jungfernhöhle Cave (Tiefenellern, Upper Franconia) also belong to the later phase of the Linear Pottery culture; most of them were women and children not exceeding fourteen years of age, which until recently was sufficient reason for an explanation based on a cult ritual (Kunkel 1955). Orschiedt (1997), however, interprets this find as evidence of secondary funeral practices. In my opinion other interpretations are also possible: could it be evidence for the massacre of the defenceless remnants of a defeated community trying to escape and shelter in the cave? Isolated instances of injuries by weapons contribute to the wider characteristics of the situation in the Linear Pottery culture (e.g., a healed wound on the skull of a man from Burial 22 at the Stuttgart-Mühlhausen Cemetery, a fatal skull defect of a man from Waiblingen, and shattered skulls of three men and an unidentified person from Stetten ob Lontal: Wahl & König 1987, 180 with refs).

Evidence of mass violence is also known from later Neolithic cultures – for example, the skeletal remains of six killed people thrown into a ditch of the later phase of the Stroke-ornamented Pottery culture were found at Barleben, Kr. Wolmirstedt, Germany (Lies 1963, Abb. 1); skeletons of about ten people who died as a result of violence, both children and adults, were found thrown into a ditch of an unfinished circular enclosure (roundel) belonging to Lengyel culture at Ružindol-Borov, Slovakia. Němejcová-Pavúková (1995; 1997) assumes that the ditch, so far only partially examined, might contain the remains of another 60–70 people, though not all victims may have been given a place at the bottom of this unfinished ditch. Evidence of injuries found at Bisamberg and Langelois, Austria, also come from Lengyel culture contexts. Jungwirth (1977, 252) maintains they were cult-motivated, as more women and children were involved, but this may well be evidence of a massacre committed in the absence of men from the village or following their defeat at another place. Other finds follow a similar pattern (Friebritz: Neugebauer et al. 1984).

Eneolithic

In the Eneolithic, the frequency of injuries did not diminish. Besides massacres (Camps 1992, 13), there are arrowheads found embedded in human bones (Cordier 1990), axe injuries (Hanáková & Vyhnánek 1981, 19, 24 with refs), and skulls fractured as a result of crushing blows delivered to the head; this corresponds with the hammer-axes and maces which enjoyed a leading role among weapons at this time. Evidence of injuries also comes from contexts of the Ludanice culture,[7] the Michelsberg and Altheim cultures,[8] the Funnel Beaker culture (Bach & Bach 1972, 103, Feustel & Ullrich 1965, Grimm 1976), the Globular Amphora culture,[9] and the Corded Ware.[10]

A potentially helpful source of data could be the study of male mortality rate in each culture. Neustupný, for example (1983, 127), found by demographic analysis of the Corded Ware culture cemetery at Vikletice that men aged 15–30 died 15 per cent more frequently than would be their natural rate of death, which is interpreted as a consequence of their participation in fighting.

WEAPONS

Weapons generally mean the devices used for fighting (Vencl 1979; 1984a, 264–349). Although they seem to be the most reliable indicators of warfare, unfortunately this does not apply to archaeology. What the archaeological record presents as undoubted evidence of weapons is the product of a long evolution. Advanced and specialised artefacts often represent, first of all, the prestigious parts of weapons. This statement is confirmed by ethnohistorical sources, which present a wide variety of weapons, basically classifiable as: occasional – any tool used in emergency (such as the sickle, or even a non-artefact such as a pebble); non-specialised – all artefacts combining both tool and weapon functions (such as the bow, knife or axe), and specialised – made primarily for the purpose of fighting, such as swords (Vencl 1984a, 270). Specialised weapon forms appeared after a delay – in association with defensive armour – only as the result of a long and slow standardisation process in warlike behaviour. By contrast, the first two categories mentioned above were characteristic for the beginnings of warfare, although in some instances they outlived the Stone Age, and in some parts of the world they were used until modern times, particularly for defence, but also for offensive activities.

Typical examples of the tool-weapon are the polished adzes of the Linear Pottery culture, primarily woodworking implements used for wood-clearing and house construction (as proved by microwear traces on their edges: Vencl 1960), but at the same time status symbols for men (according to their presence in graves: Keeley 1992), and also occasional weapons, as demonstrated by injuries to skulls in the Talheim grave (Wahl & König 1987). Polished stone artefacts in the highlands of New Guinea retained identical functions into this century. Another ethno-archaeological case study, that carried out by Pétrequin & Pétrequin (1990) in New Guinea, illustrates perfectly the functional duality of the bow in recent times as being similarly unstable: they demonstrated the locally variable use of morphologically identical arrows within a linguistically homogeneous region. The possibility of a morphologically based use determination of archaeological arrow finds must therefore be questioned.

These three categories of weapons differ quite markedly in their degree of visibility within the archaeological record. Occasional weapons generally have the lowest degree of visibility, because they are rarely present in explicit contexts (such as a sling pebble embedded in a human skull); non-specialised weapons also suffer from rather limited visibility, so that their use can only be detected by their effects on human skeletal remains (e.g., skull wounds corresponding to the edge shape of stone adzes for woodworking). Consequently, it is only specialised weapons that generally tend to be recognisable in the archaeological record because of their morphological identifiability (provided they are made of materials resistant to both post-depositional processes and secondary use). The image of Stone Age warfare therefore hinges on the fact that a considerable part of the weaponry of that time is not archaeologically visible (such as stones thrown by hand, wooden javelins and clubs, or sling projectiles).

The sling, for example, a weapon spreading with the Neolithic, is marked by a low visibility due to the archaeological absence of corresponding injuries and its mostly inconspicuous ammunition. It was not demonstrably present until lead projectiles of the Bronze Age were found in the Mediterranean, and written records documented its place among the weaponry used by ancient armies (Korfmann 1972; Vutiropulos 1991; Völling 1990 with refs).

The study of the origins of weapons is complicated by the occurrence of artefacts of an unidentifiable function. These include firstly crushing weapons, such as the archaeologically visible stone mace heads with drilled shaft-holes, known from the Early Mesolithic onwards (Gramsch & Kloss 1989, 318, fig. 6.2; discussion in Broadbent 1978). From the Early Neolithic on, there is evidence in central Europe of disc-shaped, less frequently double-edged stone mace heads with drilled shaft-holes and blunt edges unsuitable for woodwork (these appear to be the only polished stone artefacts with drilled shaft-holes in the Linear Pottery culture: Vencl 1960, 31–6, pl. VII–XI). Microwear analysis produced no data about their function, and no information could be gained from the find context (are they a part of clubs, which may have been made mostly of organic material that has not survived?) It was only maceheads of the Eneolithic that undoubtedly acquired the character of weapons, and probably also became status symbols carried by warriors (Beková-Berounská 1989).

The function of antler mattocks presents a similar problem. Antler tools with drilled shaft-holes are a large heterogeneous category of axe-, adze- or hammer-shaped artefacts; their wide diffusion over a large area of Eurasia from the Mesolithic to the Bronze Age (they were present both in hunter-gatherer and in agricultural economies) makes it functionally a very diversified conglomerate of artefacts of relatively simple forms, which are all included under one archaeological category on the basis of the coincidentally similar raw material from which they were made. Find contexts suggest that some were used in mining, or processing the carcasses of whales, while others bear traces of earth digging, but they might equally have been used as weapons, since they were also found deposited with Late Neolithic male burials instead of stone hammer-axes; but antler mattocks were until recently also used in North America in hunting caribou and other reindeer while herds were crossing rivers (Bonsall & Smith 1990; Zápotocký 1992, etc.).

Hammer-axes, which were widespread throughout central Europe from the end of the Neolithic (from the Lengyel culture horizon), are a specialised type of crushing weapon which stands out from the category of maces: they do not have a sharp edge suitable for work, and they are more elaborate than tools, often symmetrical or decorated, also showing regional style trends. They also served as status symbols, and in the area of cult behaviour, they were probably regarded as godly attributes (Zápotocký 1992 with refs).

The knowledge of the earliest means of protection against the effects of weaponry, which evolved gradually into defensive armour, will probably remain beyond archaeological cognisance. The earliest unspecific forms of defensive armour arose as a result of reinforcing the components of dress – here, it is difficult to distinguish between clothing and armour. Relevant and convincing examples were given by Herodotus (*Histories* VII, 61–95) when describing the Persian army en route to Greece in 480 BC. Archaeological evidence of defensive armour earlier than the Bronze Age is either rare (e.g., the wooden shield from the Globular Amphora tumulus at Langeneichstädt, Kr. Querfurt: Priebe 1938, 77; Vencl 1984a, 323ff.) or the evidence is inconclusive. On the other hand, Bronze Age helmets, armour and shields already demonstrate a fully developed phase in the evolution of defensive armour.

On the whole, the Mesolithic weapons belong to the tool-weapon category (perhaps with the exception of antler mattocks and stone maceheads with drilled shaft-holes, the function of which remains uncertain). The majority of Neolithic weapons also do not belong to specialised artefacts, but to the dual tool-weapon category. From the end of the Neolithic a separation of weapons (such as maceheads, hammer-axes, daggers, etc.) took place, and during the Eneolithic a diversification, and consequently, these specialised weapons acquired a symbolic function.

FORTIFICATIONS

Fortifications are above all the materialised expression of the human fear of being attacked, and of losing life, freedom or property, which, in conditions of settled life and of accumulation of property, led to the development of defensive fighting tactics. Feeling safe is a basic and permanent human need, and fortifications are the manifestation of one possible answer to that need, an isolated aspect of the complex life functions of a human community. As a highly heterogeneous component of prehistoric warfare, fortifications enter the archaeological record as palisades, ditches, ramparts or other earthworks, walls, or as multiples or combinations of all these features. Ethnohistorical sources, including ancient written records about barbarian tribes, remove any doubts about the existence of prehistoric defensive structures, ranging from unfortified settlements situated in inaccessible places, through simple fortified villages, to elaborate stone-built forts.

However, evidence provided by archaeological sources is problematic due to the unspecific character of these features, which may be very inconclusive because they were also used in other types of constructions. For example, a palisade was sometimes used as a fortification element, but it might as well be a cattle fence; a ditch might indicate a fortified site as well as a sacred area (e.g., 1 Kings 18, 32). Neither dimensional analysis nor topographical characteristics can help to determine convincingly whether a feature is a functional part of a fortification. Prehistoric and ancient peoples built large monuments both for defence and religious purposes. A very slight ditch might also have a significant defensive function because the defensibility of a fortification is always dependent on the sum of two factors: the 'passive resistibility' – the strength, dimensions or solidness of the construction – and the 'active force' of the defenders. For example, the American defensive position in their victorious battle near Saratoga, which was decisive for the fate of the American Revolution, has archaeologically survived in the form of dwarf trenches, 40–50 cm deep and some 50 cm wide (Ehrich 1975). Some interpretative suppositions in archaeology based on the dimensions of fortification elements (such as 'this ditch is too narrow or too shallow to have defensive value') are simply false. Moreover, these dimensions have frequently been altered by erosion and other post-depositional processes.

The first (passive) factor is represented by features that are relatively visible archaeologically, for instance the topographical advantage of a place in relation to the dimensions and material resistibility of fortification constructions. These defensive values are not absolutely constant, as a consequence of climate (e.g., changes brought about through ice or mud) or of social effects (e.g., the maintenance of the ditches and walls). Because of its ready visibility, this factor is usually overestimated or absolutised in archaeology. By contrast, the second (active) component of fortification value tends to change quickly and profoundly. This active factor is brought about by the quantity as well as the quality of the defenders, their spirit and motivation, and not just by their fighting experience, their ability to use their equipment efficiently, or the quality of command. Unfortunately, this factor produces no durable material remains, and because of poor archaeological visibility, it is generally neglected or undervalued in explanation. The presence or absence of defenders changes the value of fortification absolutely and immediately, but with no trace in the archaeological record. Ethnohistorical sources offer numerous examples of the successful defence of weak or provisional fortifications by the resistance of resolute defenders, as well as contrary cases of the easy capture of mighty and impressive strongholds as a consequence of the poor spirit of those defending them.

The dimensions of fortifications varied not only in proportion to the fear which drove the builders to deter potential attackers by displaying their own technical, economic and managerial skills – additional, complementary or occasional functions of forts were also taken into account, such as their role as attractive places for gatherings of people who could satisfy all their needs there (production, marketplace, cult centre, customs-house, safe-haven, etc.). Also taken into account was the size and productivity of the labour force available, and the urgency, stress, or need to erect protection in a limited time. The final result was also affected by unpredictable circumstances – historical events – and that is why some fortifications have remained unfinished and unexploited, and have therefore lain idle. Fortifications of strategic value naturally displayed different characteristics from those of tactical value. For all these reasons, fortifications are also extremely heterogeneous from the topographical point of view. They are located on vantage places, either outside or inside settlement areas, on slight elevations or in flat countryside (both on wetland and near streams or rivers serving as natural obstacles for defence, but also lacking any topographically advantageous features). The last group, although quite abundant, had a very low visibility before the advent of aerial photography. It includes most of the tactical fortifications, such as temporary camps or garrison stations. The practice of warfare in culturally specific ways was another source of diversity. Populations preferring offensive warfare (e.g., Classical Sparta), or migrating peoples (German tribes in protohistory), did not build fortifications, so the occurrence of the phenomenon in archaeology is intermittent.

The earliest fortifications in particular show an extreme lack of distinctive features. Leaving aside barriers formed by felled trees, wagons or shields, and other archaeologically unattestable phenomena known from ethnology, history or linguistics (Němec et al. 1986, 223ff.; Vencl 1984a, 123ff.), these simplest defensive works will generally elude the archaeological record (Vencl 1983). Despite these exceptions and uncertainties, features indicating that a structure could have a military purpose can be summarised as follows: the presence and differentiation of various types of entrances (gates) restricting or controlling approach; the presence of traces of fighting (weapons, destruction, fire); multiplication of defence-works, especially at spots with easier access, revealing a concept of in-depth defence; proliferation of walls by the insertion of additional elements such as bastions and flanking towers; and the choice of inaccessible locations uncomfortable for daily living but possessing good views that offered greater safety and easier defence. No one of these indicators, if present, is in itself conclusive evidence of a military structure, but neither does their absence mean the contrary (for example, some quite simple entrances could have been defended effectively by archaeologically undetectable obstacles, such as features made of wood).

Another uncertainty in interpreting prehistoric fortifications stems from the low visibility of most of the defensive means or weapons (such as stones thrown from defence-works, wooden spears, ammunition used for slings, hot water or pitch, etc.), not to mention the low visibility of the fight itself (because of the usual practice of gathering up the *spolia*, the arms and armour stripped from the defeated party, or ambiguous evidence such as the traces of fire or destruction of defence-works, as well as the relatively rare evidence of siege). Not all hillforts were targeted for siege: the absence of military activities may then indicate that the decisive battle took place at a different venue. The last but substantial complication affecting the archaeological interpretation of this matter is the additional functions (economic, social, ritual, etc.) that a fortified site acquires through being a place of safety. This feature may even submerge its primary military purpose because of the different archeological visibility of particular activities.

In Europe, fortification features begin to appear in the Neolithic. According to Höckmann (1990), Neolithic enclosures occur in the area stretching from Anatolia and Aegean as far as central Europe, and also in the Impresso/Cardial culture contexts in Italy. Interpretations include a fortified site, refuge, sanctuary, meeting or marketplace, social centre, status symbol, and an animal stockade. In central Europe, they appear sporadically from the early Linear Pottery culture, more frequently from its later phase (Lüning 1988; Keeley & Cahen 1989; Steuer 1989; Höckmann 1990; Kaufmann 1990). Linear Pottery culture enclosures can be interpreted as fortified villages (this is indirectly supported at the close of this culture by the higher frequency of villages located at naturally protected elevated sites). A relatively short-lived fashion in the development of enclosures in central Europe occurred at the beginning of the Middle Neolithic with the standardised circular structures (called roundels), sometimes double or triple, with impressive ditches and gateways (Podborský 1988; Pavúk 1991; Petrasch 1991; Trnka 1991; Němejcová-Pavúková 1997 with refs), and their function has also been a matter of controversy (they have been interpreted as ceremonial and administrative centres, or as forts). Only at the end of the Lengyel period were forts erected at higher locations with strategic advantages (Hrádek near Kramolín in Moravia, Topol and Chrudim in Eastern Bohemia: Vávra 1990), which were fortified again in later prehistoric periods as sites naturally providing optimal defensive conditions. During the Eneolithic (with the exception of the latest phase of that period, where offensive warfare prevailed in the Beaker cultures), fortifications developed further through the differentiation of the defence systems of the gateways – the most vulnerable points – and through the multiplication of the fortification elements to form several lines for defensive fighting in depth, as well as by adding flanking towers to the walls, thus protecting their approaches by means of flanking fire (Vencl 1983; Burgess et al. 1988; Matuschik 1991; Camps 1992, etc.). Some Late Neolithic Mediterranean fortifications are real stone fortresses.

The uncertainties that persist in the interpretation of the function of early enclosures reflect the lack of convincing evidence provided by archaeological sources. This is due not only to the undistinctive character of the fortification features in the early phase of their development, and the low archaeological visibility of weapons and sieges, but also to the fact that every fortified site would involve a multitude of people, and therefore additional functions (social, economic, ritual, etc.) resulting from the everyday needs of both its inhabitants and those of the surrounding countryside. An interpretation of early enclosures as fortified sites is based for the most part on indirect evidence: the traces of group massacres from the Neolithic onwards suggest that the fear of being attacked probably played a role in defensive efforts, and resulted in fortified settlements; hillforts built at the end of the Neolithic on naturally protected sites that were more or less inaccessible correspond to the beginnings of specialised weapons (hammer-axes) – in other words, to the period of standardisation of warfare behaviour – and the widespread use and improvement of fortifications in the Eneolithic corresponds to the time when the diversification of specialised (i.e., proper) weapons took place. Attempts at a symbolic interpretation of early enclosures not only totally disregard these correlations,[11] but also create a new problem: they do not explain when and why the symbolic function of the early enclosures may have been lost, as their later counterparts served first and foremost as forts, according to the written records. The existence of prehistoric ceremonial centres, or a parallel use of some defensive sites for ritual, cannot be questioned, but the theory explaining prehistoric fortifications as having primarily a symbolic function contradicts the need for self-defence that is in evidence from the Neolithic. Arguments based on bodies found in ditches, apparently non-ritual burials, or the deposition of hoards are not convincing, as the evidence is ambiguous: the bodies need not be interpreted as sacrifices, but as war casualties, and the hoards as valuables deposited in advance of chaotic periods of war.

CONCLUSION

The asynchronous emergence of individual components of Stone Age warfare in the archaeological record does not permit a very distinct or conclusive picture of its earliest phase. Nevertheless, the following must be noted: this is typical of any emerging phenomenon; while it is underrepresented in the material remains (because of low visibility in general), this area is overrepresented in written records, and by the end of the Stone Age, the material remains in this area had reached a level comparable to that of the historic period, where the unambiguous existence of warfare is proven through written sources.

Three phases of aggression may be tentatively identified during the Stone Age, each characterized by a differing socio-economic background and qualities:

1 Palaeolithic injuries seem to indicate wounds resulting from everyday activities, partly ensuing from the hunter–prey relation; injuries on female skeletons predominate (Grimm 1976).

2 During the Late Palaeolithic and Mesolithic, basic socio-economic and ecological changes led in the Old World to demographic growth and the territorial economy and behaviour of hunter-gatherer groups. The territorial organisation of Mesolithic populations is evident in the continental distribution of cemeteries. The series of injuries attested at Mesolithic cemeteries seems to mirror the extreme forms of conflict waged in defence of the boundaries of individual territories.[12] The wide geographical distribution of Mesolithic injuries shows that what is involved is not a local phenomenon, but a widespread trend in social development.

3 The Neolithic brought about fundamental changes in the conditions and reasons for aggression. From the Neolithic onwards, a series of war symptoms developed, ranging from slight initial manifestations to well defined and clear-cut conflicts that were motivated mostly by the desire for enrichment through robbery, and for securing economic advantages through violence, the origins of which are to be sought in the rise of stable settlements and the resultant hoarding of supplies. These much-feared assaults seem to have instigated the earliest defensive architecture and the 'passive' mode of combat. From the Neolithic on, male injuries predominate. In the course of the Late Neolithic and Eneolithic, a complete and definitive set of archaeological war attributes developed, fully corresponding to the evidence from later periods when war and warfare are attested by written sources.

NOTES

1. African examples of such burials are Nos 21, 23, 31 and 103 at the Djebel Sahaba cemetery, Nubia (Qadan culture) (Wendorf 1968, 990, fig. 36), burials Nos 10 and 33a at Columnata and a find at El Bachir, Algeria (Chamla et al. 1970, 123, Pl. XVI), and burial No. 7 at Lothagam, Kenya (Robbins & Lynch 1978). European evidence of this type is known from Moita do Sebastião, Portugal (Lubell et al. 1985, 639), from burial K6-16 at Téviec, France (Péquart & Péquart 1931), triple burial No. 19 at Vedbaek, Denmark (Albrethsen & Brinch Petersen 1976, 14, fig. 15), from burials 13 and 34 of Cemetery I at Skateholm, Sweden (Larsson 1984), from burials at Bäckaskog and Stora Bjers, Sweden (Albrethsen & Brinch Petersen 1976, 24 with bibliography), from burial No. IV at Popovo, by Onega Lake (Oshibkina 1982, 128; 1983, 183), from burials 3 and 16 at Volos'ke on the Dnepr (Danilenko 1955; Alekshin 1994), from burials Nos 12, 34 and 37 at Cemetery III at Vasylivka in the Dnepr area (Telegin 1961, figs. 5, 1–2, 8 and 8, 1–2), and from two burials (No. 2/1968) at Schela Cladovei, Romania (Nicolăescu-Plopșor 1976, pl. I–II; Radovanović 1994). Similar finds are also known from Asia: stone projectiles were embedded in human bones deposited in Graves V, X and XII at Sriganar in the Ganges Valley (Cordier 1990, 473 with bibliography) and at a PPN A cemetery at Nemrik 9, Iraq (Kozłowski 1989, 27).
2. For example, a number of burials at the Jebel Sahaba Cemetery, burials Nos 10 and 17 at Cemetery I in Vasylivka: Stoljar (1959, 116, fig. 15:5); also burials 5, 12, 33 and 36 at the Vasylivka III cemetery: Telegin (1961).
3. For example, Burial 49 at Columnata, Burial 3 at Volos'ke.
4. For example, Burial 1 from the Franchthi Cave, Greece: Cullen (1995, 275); Argus, Denmark: Fischer (1987); Bennike (1987); Gøngehusvej 7, Denmark: (Brinch Petersen et al. 1993); Korsør Nor on Zealand and Tybrind Vig in Fyn, both in Denmark: Newell et al. (1979, 61ff., 95); Gough's Cave, England: Newell et al. (1979, 95); Mannlefelsen I, Culoz-sous-Balme, Le Trou Violet, France: Newell et al. (1979, 126, 113, 139); Birsmatten-Basisgrotte, Switzerland: Newell et al. (1979, 104); Colombres, Spain: Newell et al. (1979, 104); Ofnet, Germany: Wahl & König (1987, 180), Baum (1991), Orschiedt (1998); Langhnaj, India: Erhardt 1960.
5. Burials 35/1987 and 40/1989 at Schela Cladovei, Romania: Boroneanț 1993, 511; Ofnet, Germany: Baum (1991); Hohlenstein-Stadel, Germany: Orschiedt 1998, 155.
6. For example, male burials Nos 12-37-38 and 34-35-36 at Cemetery III in Vasylivka, where skeletal remains 34, 37 and 38 had fatal injuries; the Jebel Sahaba Cemetery with the triple burial of a child (No. l0l), an adult woman (No. 102) and a fatally wounded adolescent (No. 103), also a double male burial (Nos 20 and 21), the second of which shows evidence of a fatal injury, and a double burial of a ten-year-old child (No. 24) and a fatally wounded adult woman (No. 23) and a triple burial (No. 19) from the Vedbaek-Bøgebakken Cemetery containing the remains of a child, an older female, and a fatally wounded young man.
7. One-third of the persons buried at Jelšovce died as a result of violence: Pavúk & Bátora (1995).
8. About thirty skeletons, mainly children, at a ditch of enclosure at Heidelsheim skeletons and human bones at a ditch at Bour-en-Vexin: Bertemes (1991, 449, 456); multiple burial of six people, killed as a result of blows delivered by blunt objects to the skulls at Heidelberg-Handschuhheim: Wahl & Höhn 1988; another 6 persons from pit II at Inningen, killed in the same manner, and also evidence from other sites as Michelsberg, Bruchsal-Aue, Goldberg, etc.: Wahl & Höhn (1988, 172 with refs); about fifteen skeletons in the excavated part of the inner ditch at Altheim, enclosed by three ditches: Driehaus (1960 with refs).

9. At Ketzin, Kr. Nauen, 6 skull injuries, of 1 woman and 5 men, killed by crushing blows to the head were detected by Ullrich (1971, 52) among the remains of 15 individuals.
10. The cemetery at Vikletice, district of Chomutov, yielded six male skulls with traces of blows to the left side of the frontal bone as recorded by Chochol (1970, 276), which might indicate that the hammer-axes were predominantly struck by warriors holding the weapon in their right hands during face-to-face combat: Hanáková & Vyhnánek (1981, 17 with refs).
11. For example, Neustupný (1995, 199) believes that 'most fortifications can be assumed to be devoid of any practical function'.
12. The well-known drawings of combatant archer groups from North Africa or East Spain may well support such an interpretation if correctly attributed to the pre-Neolithic period; the Spanish drawings are contemporary with the Early Neolithic Cardial culture of the fifth millennium BC, according to M.S. Hernandez Pérez (1987).

Six

WAR AND PEACE IN PREHISTORIC EASTERN EUROPE

P.M. DOLUKHANOV

INTRODUCTION

Anthropological theory envisages three main groups of factors which are likely to lead to armed conflicts (Haas 1990): sociobiological, where aggression is instinctively antagonistic behaviour; cultural, where the motives are dominance and kin welfare; and materialistic, which involve group competition for material resources. Group competition is the most important for the present study, sociobiological factors being of a universal character and hardly detectable in the archaeological record, and cultural factors normally being realised under the conditions stipulated by competition for resources.

Armed conflicts arise between social interest groups when their relationships, under certain circumstances, acquire an antagonistic character. Social aggregations of various rank and character are perceptible at all stages of human prehistory. This was noted by Marx and Engels as early as 1846, when they wrote in *The German Ideology* (the first recognisable 'Marxist' text) that human beings 'become distinguishable from animals as soon as they begin to produce their means of subsistence, which defines the intercourse [*Verkehr*] of individuals with one another. The division of labour subsequently leads to 'various divisions among the individuals and the emergence of individual groups' (Marx & Engels 1985 [1846]).

The long-established European cultural-historical tradition, both in its Marxist-oriented and romantic-nationalist varieties, argued that the '[social] groups . . . constituted structured wholes and produced bounded material assemblages ("archaeological cultures") which directly and indirectly reflected their identity' (Thomas 1996, 21). The post-processualist school increasingly questions this simplistic equation, starting with Hodder (1982), who, on the basis of ethnographic observations in Kenya, proclaimed the polysemantic nature of material culture, of which elements were actively manipulated 'in the negotiation of group identities'.

In contrast to the cultural-historical discourse, post-modernist thought concentrates on understanding 'human identity as being stretched across time' (Thomas 1996, 51). Difficulties in the archaeological recognition of social entities lie in their dynamism and relativity. In contrast to the nineteenth-century European romanticist vision, social groups (including ethnic ones) are now viewed as a 'consciousness of difference reproduced in the context of ongoing social interaction' (Jones 1996, 71). Hence the pessimistic view that 'archaeologists may not be able to find a reflection of "past ethnicities" in the material record' (Jones 1996, 72).

This scepticism was further enhanced by analysis of spatial variability of archaeological artefacts, both at the extra- and intra-site levels. Scholars often fail to recognise any correspondence between the deposits of artefacts and past human activities (Rigaud & Simek 1989, 218). One may envisage at least one promising avenue for solving this problem in the recognition of symbols embedded in archaeological deposits. A person's group identity is signalled by means of symbols and symbolic behaviour (Durkheim 1947), which may take various forms, from land tenure and rituals to words and gestures (Fishman 1977). Symbols of group identity, as well as the interest groups themselves, do not remain intransigent. At each stage individuals negotiates and renegotiates own position within a group, and either accept or reject its norms and values, becoming 'enmeshed in a structure of meaning' (Thomas 1996, 17).

But how may the transient symbols of group identity be conceived in fossilised material culture? This is a feasible, albeit difficult, task: the relationship of the symbol to reality is often indirect and distant. The symbol is metaphorical – it operates within its own world, to which an archaeologist has little or no access. One may hardly doubt that 'archaeological culture', this 'homogeneous populations of artefacts', is an instrument hardly suitable for this task. In each particular case, the archaeologist's assignment would consist in the reconstruction of physical, cultural and social contexts within which the symbols operate, the assessment of their structural opposition, attaching to them a meaning, and testing meaningful propositions.

PALAEOLITHIC

Palaeolithic 'Mousterian facies' groups are the earliest distinct spatio-temporal cultural entities acknowledgeable in the archaeological record. These facies were first identified by Bordes & Borgon (1951) in France, who based their conclusion on the variations of sixty-three implement types presented in the form of cumulative diagrams. Originally, the number of groupings was five, and they were restricted to south-western France. In later publications, the number increased to seven, and they encompassed the whole of Europe and the Near East.

Considerable variability of Mousterian industries was also identified in eastern Europe. Stemming from the size of implements and their elements of secondary modification (notching, in particular), Ukrainian archaeologists (Gladilin 1976; Stanko 1997a) have identified seven 'Mousterian variants' in the Ukraine: 1 bifacial; 2 typical; 3 typical denticulate; 4 micro-bifacial; 5 micro-typical; 6 micro-denticulate; 7 micro-denticulate-bifacial. Each 'variant' had several local 'facies' and 'types'.

The interpretation of Mousterian industrial variability has caused considerable controversy. Bordes considered the Mousterian 'facies' as artefactual expressions of separate and coexisting ethnic communities. In Bordes' view, the Middle Palaeolithic universe consisted of low-density, small-sized, territorially bounded, semi- or fully sedentary, identity-conscious, nucleated social entities (Rolland 1990) – an approach presently shared by the great majority of east European archaeologists. Alternative explanations were suggested by Binford (1973), who viewed Mousterian 'stylistic variability' as reflecting functional differences, and by Mellars (1986) who attached much greater importance to chronological distinctions.

More recent publications (Praslov 1984; Rolland 1990) make the point that the observed Mousterian variability was attributable to environmental and technological factors. Thus, the parsimony of the lithic raw material may have affected the secondary transformation of cutting tools.

In the author's view, the Mousterian 'facies' originally resulted from the peculiarities in the functional use of lithic tools, the availability of raw material, and the territorial division of labour, primarily dictated by environmental constraints. At a later stage, these technical peculiarities developed into cultural symbols of distinct social entities.

The Mousterian–Upper Palaeolithic transition which occurred in the Near East and Europe between 45 and 35 thousand years (Kyr) ago is usually associated with the proliferation of *Homo sapiens sapiens*. This transition was manifested primarily by technological innovations: the core-and-blade technique, the wider use of bone, ivory and antler, and the greater variability of tools. One equally notes an increased social complexity and the change in subsistence activities, with an increased reliance on single species combined with the broadening of the subsistence base. This went together with a general increase in population density. The observed technical innovations are often seen as reflecting a major behavioural change, implying transformations in social organisation, specialisation in social roles, and the enhanced transmission of social information (Reynolds 1990). All these modifications were gradual in character with numerous Mousterian cultural elements persisting in the Upper Palaeolithic (Grigor'ev 1968; Simek & Price 1990). This was further emphasised by the discovery of 'transitional' cultural entities now recognisable throughout Europe. These entities (Châtelperronian in France, Szeletian in Hungary and Sreletskian in Russia) combined in their inventories Mousterian elements with Upper Palaeolithic technology. Several writers (e.g., Allsworth-Jones 1990) ascribe these units to surviving groups of Neanderthals.

Further studies have shown the 'Upper Palaeolithic package' to be much more complex than the simplistic model outlined above. The Upper Palaeolithic population density in Europe was prone to significant fluctuations. It has been noted that the density of Aurignacian groups was much less than that estimated for Gravettian ones (Rolland 1990). Considerable spatial differences were observable during the Last Glacial maximum (c. 25–15 Kyr). Judging by reliable radiocarbon measurements, at that time large areas of western and central Europe (including the British Isles, southern Germany, Austria and Moravia, Britain, and western Germany) became virtually depopulated (Housley et al. 1997), whereas the population in the east European plain increased markedly (Dolukhanov forthcoming).

Yet the most important feature of the east European Upper Palaeolithic was its social complexity. The Palaeolithic burials at Sungir form the most blatant example of this complexity. One of the graves included the skeleton of a senior male with numerous adornments and an unusually long spear made of mammoth tusk. Similar spears and other prestige items were found in another grave which contained the skeletons of two

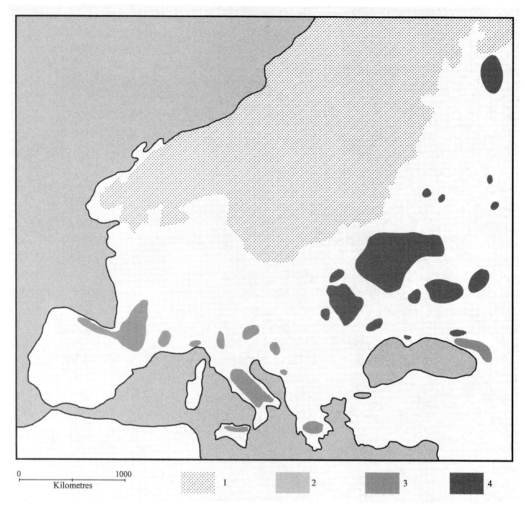

Fig. 1. Upper Palaeolithic 'provinces' in Europe (after Dolukhanov 1996).

adolescents of both sexes. These finds suggest an advanced stage of social hierarchy in a male-dominated society, and the hereditary character of social power. The internal hierarchy of Upper Palaeolithic society is further indicated in the occurrence of 'complex base-camps', with structures interpreted as residential loci of 'high-status individuals' (Soffer 1985). This, as well as clear evidence for long-distance trade in prestige items, suggests the existence of close-knit social entities with a male at the helm. According to Russian estimates (Kabo 1986) an average Upper Palaeolithic group included 100–200 members forming several nuclear families, each including six or seven individuals.

Cultural variability in the European Upper Palaeolithic remains a highly debatable topic. Statistical processing of Upper Palaeolithic lithic assemblages by means of multivariate techniques have led the author (Dolukhanov et al. 1980; Dolukhanov 1982) to the conclusion that stylistic distinctions became more articulate during the milder climatic period, becoming blurred in a harsh environment. During the colder stage of LGM Europe, only two major provinces are distinguishable in the Upper Palaeolithic: the Periglacial province, comprising the greater part of central and eastern Europe, and the Mediterranean one including Atlantic Europe, the entire Mediterranean basin and the Caucasus (Fig. 1). The occurrence of minor-scale cultural units is much more problematic. The applicability of west European typological schemes and related terminology raises serious doubts. In contrast to earlier times, Russian archaeologists (Sinitsyn et al. 1997) discussing the Upper Palaeolithic now avoid the use of the concept of 'archaeological culture'. The sites of a later Kostenki group (Kostenki 1/1) and typologically related settlements (Avdeyevo, Khotylevo and Berdyzh) are viewed as belonging to the 'Gravettian circle', which also includes the sites in Upper Austria and Moravia, arguably resulting from a major east-bound migration (Grigor'ev 1993; Soffer 1993). The sites with complex 'dwellings' of Anosovo-Mezin type, which also include Mezhirich and possibly Kostenki 11/ 1a, form a distinct entity. Other sites (Yurovichi, Pushkari, Peny and numerous sites in the Kostenki area) fail to fit any recognisable pattern.

There are anthropological data suggesting the racial diversity of the Upper Palaeolithic population of Europe (Gokhman 1966a). The main differences are noted between the dolichocephalic, moderately broad- and long-headed (Solutrean), and the brachycephalic, broad-faced and broad-nosed varieties. The skull from Markina Gora in Kostenki shows characteristics similar to the so-called 'Negroids' from the Grimaldi cave in southern France, while the skeletons from the Sungir and Kostenki 2 sites in central Russia reveal broad-faced features typical of the archaic Cro-Magnon type.

Thus, archaeological, environmental and anthropological data point to the occurrence of distinct groupings in Upper Palaeolithic Europe, often displaying considerable variability on genetic and cultural levels. Yet in no case could one find any evidence of inter-group conflicts, either in Mousterian or in Upper Palaeolithic eastern Europe. A relatively low of population density combined with the abundance and diversity of available resources enabled Palaeolithic groups to find peaceful strategies for coexistence even during the harshest periods of the Last Ice Age.

MESOLITHIC

The earliest evidence for warfare in eastern Europe comes from Early Mesolithic sites, corresponding to the early stages of the Holocene, between 10 and 7 Kyr ago (uncalibrated). With the beginning of the Holocene, the relatively homogenous periglacial zone which encompassed the entire east European plain at the time of the LGM disintegrated. In the early Mesolithic, two major ecological zones were already in place: the boreal zone in the northern and central parts of the plain, and the steppe in the south. The landscape structure and the pattern of Mesolithic settlement in these two major ecological zones were essentially different. In the boreal zone, the sites were located within river floors or near lakes and estuaries (Dolukhanov 1997). In the first case, a seasonally circulating settlement pattern included ephemeral summer sites close to waterways and more substantial winter camps further afield. The sites located in the lake-estuary landscapes were of sedentary or semi-sedentary nature, with broad-spectrum economies based on round-the-year exploitation of marine, lake and terrestrial resources.

In the south, the Early Holocene landscape consisted mostly of bunchgrass steppe. Later, in the early Atlantic, a moister grassland developed, with thickets of pine, birch and alder restricted to river floors and ravines. Natural resources were already depleted in the Late Palaeolithic groups: herd animals (mainly the bison) became extinct, and were substituted by the non-herd aurochs, roe deer and wild boar. This led to a deep ecological and socio-cultural crisis (Stanko 1997b). According to Stanko, no major settlements occurred in the Pontic steppe in the early Mesolithic. Faunal remains are either totally absent or consist of small numbers of fragmented bones. The tarpan was the most numerous, supplemented by the auroch in the north-west Pontic area, with wild boar and roe deer becoming more common further to the north. The small community was the basic socio-economic unit; it numbered 20–25 persons and comprised three or four nuclear families with four to six individuals in each (Bibikov 1971; Bibikov & Tolochko 1988). These communities, scattered over considerable areas, formed cultural entities recognisable in the material culture. Larger settlements start to appear only at a later stage of the steppe Mesolithic – Mirnoe and Ghirzhevo being the obvious examples. At this stage, the critical situation was at least partly overcome through the introduction of selective hunting, the regulation of hunting grounds, and a management of resources. The faunal records of Mirnoe show that killed animals consisted almost entirely of mature individuals, which implies conscious selection (Bibikova 1982). Stanko (1982, 1997a, 1997b) asserts that at this stage the entire steppe was controlled by several tribal groups. The tribal area in the Danube-Dniestr interfluve included a large central place – Mirnoe, with a population of over 150 – surrounded by a constellation of several smaller communities within a radius of 90 km, each consisting of two or three nuclear families. These smaller communities of auroch hunters were periodically connected in a central place, circulating seasonally within the tribal area limited by natural boundaries: the Black Sea in the south, the Danube in the west and the Dniestr in the east. The contact zone along these boundaries was open for interaction (not necessarily peaceful) with neighbouring groups.

An important feature of Mesolithic subsistence, particularly notable in the later stages, was the widening of its resource base, with an increased reliance on vegetable food. This was initially identified by sickles with use-wear resulting from the harvesting of grasses. One can hardly doubt that the grinders and pestles found at this site were used for processing vegetable food. Bibikov (1977) has suggested that some kinds of primitive vessels should have been in use for cooking and storing the food; these could be turtle shells, which were found in the immediate vicinity of the hearths at Mirnoe. An increased use of vegetable foods was further corroborated by the palaeobotanic evidence (Pashkevich 1982): the spectrum of edible plants identified in archaeological deposits included several edible plants, namely white goosefoot, black bindweed and hairy vetch. The measurements of 'postcranial variation' in the skeletons of Mesolithic cemeteries Vassil'ievka 3 and 2 led Jacobs (1993) to a similar conclusion: an increased postcranial robustity noticeable in the later specimen was a result of a 'major dietary change' – a reduction in the consumption of meat, compensated by a rise in the consumption of plant matter.

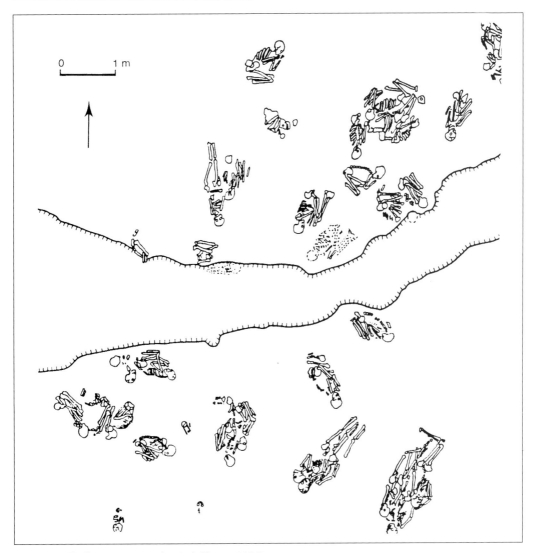

Fig. 2. Vassil'evka 3 cemetery (after Dolukhanov 1996).

It was in this environment of growing scarcity of food resources that the local groups resorted to warfare. Burials bearing traces of violent death were documented at the cemeteries at the Middle Dniepr Rapids (Stolyar 1959; Telegin 1982). The Mesolithic cemetery Vassil'evka 3 (radiocarbon dated to *c.* 10,000 BP) presents the earliest undisputable evidence of warfare: skeletons with arrowheads in the ribs and spine (Fig. 2). The Dniepr cemeteries provide important data on the gender structure of Mesolithic society. Vassil'evka 3 includes both male and female burials located in various sections of the cemetery: females in the middle, and males along the periphery. The Vassil'evka 1 Cemetery contained exclusively burials of mature males in small, compact groups, each consisting of two to four individuals. The impression is that in the both cases we are dealing with a male-dominated, military-oriented groups. No less significant is physical anthropological evidence suggesting the occurrence of at least three distinct race varieties.

Numerous Mesolithic cemeteries are known to occur in the northern boreal zone of the east European plain. The Oleneostovskii Mogil'nik on the Reindeer Island of the Onega Lake, dated to 7,700–7,300 BP, was the largest in Europe. The cemetery, excavated in the late 1930s (Gurina 1956), included more than 400 graves. The analysis of the burial rite and the material culture (O'Shea & Zvelebil 1984) suggests on the one hand a degree of internal status differentiation, and on the other the occurrence of an active exchange network, mostly in raw materials (flint) and exotic goods. There were recognisable signs of gender differentiation, yet no evidence of either male or female dominance. Male graves contained predominantly hunting equipment: bone daggers, slate knives, harpoons, fishhooks and quivers. Female grave inventories included flint blades, awls, polishers, burins, scrapers, perforated beaver incisors and snake-like effigies. In several cases, females in multiple graves were found buried together with either males or a child. Three 'shaft graves', where the skeletons were found in a vertical posture facing the west, stood apart from the rest. These graves can plausibly be seen as having belonged to religious leaders or shamans. Jacobs's odontometric analysis shows considerable dental differences from Scandinavian specimens of a comparable age. Based on these observations, Jacobs (1992) suggests that the Mesolithic population of northern Europe consisted of distinct mating networks with a large degree of closure. Using classical craniological criteria, Gokhman (1966b) has identified among the Oleneostrovski skeletons a racial type with broad and flattened faces, basically similar to a group recognised at the Dniepr Rapids (Vassil'evka 1, 'contracted' skeletons at Vassil'evka 3) as well as several Mesolithic burials in Denmark. This anthropological type, according to Gokhman, belongs to the oldest population of Eastern and Northern Europe, presumably inherited from the Upper Palaeolithic.

If one compares the boreal Mesolithic with that of the steppe, common elements and differences are both apparent. In both cases, the Mesolithic groups formed semi-closed aggregates or 'mating networks'. The nuclear family, the structure apparently inherited from the Upper Palaeolithic, remained the basic social unit in each case. In the boreal zone, in an environment of relative abundance and greater predictability of resources, these aggregates developed into shaman-dominated, comparatively harmonious social units. By contrast, in the steppe, where resources were scarce and less predictable, group competition among male-dominated groups led to hostilities and warfare. It is highly significant that both scenarios developed among genetically (and, very likely, linguistically) homogeneous populations.

NEOLITHIC TO EARLY BRONZE AGE

During the course of the climatic optimum, starting *c.* 8,000 BP, the entire continent of Europe was affected by profound socio-economic changes. It is generally accepted that Europe at that time initially became divided into two unequal parts: agricultural and non-agricultural. This distinction was highlighted most spectacularly by Hodder (1990) as that between '*domus*' and '*agrios*' – tamed and wild. Although new data indicate that this distinction was not as clear-cut as had previously been argued, the articulated differences are evident in various aspects of social existence. Notable distinctions are recognisable even in the rate of proliferation of cultural and technological novelties. Judging from the statistical analysis of the corpus of radiocarbon measurements (Dolukhanov in press), the spread of agricultural Linear Pottery (LBK) settlements on the European loess plains was accomplished within ten to twenty generations (average date: 5,270 ± 200 BC). This does not rule out the active involvement of indigenous non-agricultural groups recognisable in local variations of subsistence and material culture (Whittle 1996).

The spread of agricultural settlements was essentially peaceful. In most cases, LBK settlements were open, lacking defended perimeters. Whittle (1996, 174–5) has convincingly demonstrated that enclosures and shallow ditches recognisable at several LBK sites, particularly in the north-west, were not of a defensive character.

The longhouse, allegedly identifiable with the extended family, formed the focal point of the social landscape. Longhouses were usually found in clusters, several contemporary houses sharing a common orientation, thus suggesting kin relations between the inhabitants. The clusters of houses formed larger aggregations of various size, from 'hamlets' to 'villages'. These aggregations are seen as elementary agricultural communities sharing common property on land and other resources (Kabo 1986). Several communities formed a mating network, extending their control over considerable areas. Early agricultural settlements provide some evidence for social power and gender structure, the spread of the shell of *Spondylus gaedoropus*, the Mediterranean mollusc, in Linear pottery complexes of central Europe being one of the few examples. This was clearly a prestige item, and its expansion suggests the occurrence of an established distribution network targeted at 'powerful individuals' (Séfériadès 1995). Child burials were found at several sites within the settled areas, and Whittle (1996, 169) views them as a metaphor for regeneration. In the few cases when burial grounds were found, the grave goods of older males were often rich, and included exotics, suggesting social prominence. The female graves included smaller tools and pottery.

The spread of early Tripolye sites in the forest-steppe Ukraine, Moldavia and Romania was essentially similar to that of the LBK: the ready-made cultural-economic package, without any discernible ancestry, rapidly spread over a large area of the forest-steppe (4,500–4,350, BC calibrated; Wechler 1994). As with the LBK, the impact of indigenous groups was recognisable in the location of sites and the composition of the lithic inventory. Early Tripolye sites were relatively small and located in close proximity to or within river valleys, in most cases on natural elevations. Initially, Tripolye settlements included several one- or two-storeyed dwellings, each supposedly inhabited by a single family. The population of an average settlement (200–500 individuals) formed an elementary community sharing common property in terms of land and other resources. So far, no burial grounds have been identified at Tripolye sites of the early and middle stages. Within the settlement of Luka Vrublevetskaya, a child burial was found (Bibikov 1953), and a burial of a young man was discovered beneath the house floor at the Soloncheny II site (Chernysh 1982, 188). From the earliest stage on, female effigies were predominant among the portable figurines. One can hardly doubt that these figurines were a metaphor of fecundity – a suggestion substantiated by the finds of wheat and barley grains inside the fabric of several figurines at Luka-Vrublevetskaya (Bibikov 1953).

As with early agricultural settlements in central and western Europe, the impression is that the spread of early Tripolye communities in the East European forest-steppe was essentially peaceful. The resulting social units were balanced and harmonious, with clear symbols of fecundity and continuity.

Considerable modifications in the steppe became apparent at the Middle Tripolye stage (4,440–3,810, BC calibrated; Wechler 1994). The socio-ethnic situation at the time grew significantly more complex, with at least two more distinct socio-cultural entities developing further east: Sredni Stog and Mikhailovka. Each of these entities featured marked differences in subsistence, social pattern and material culture. Considerable changes are noticeable within Tripolye society itself. In the middle stage, settlements expanded far to the east and grew in size, particularly in the south. The largest sites were Vesely Kut (150 ha), Talyanki (450 ha and 2,800 houses) and Maydanetskoe (200 ha and more than 2,000 houses). Around these settlements, artificial fortifications were erected in the form of impressive ramparts and ditches. Significantly, these large fortified settlements emerged predominantly in the areas adjacent to alien cultural entities, mostly the Sredni Stog. At the same sites, commercial contacts with the Sredni Stog are noticeable in the form of imported ware (Videiko 1994). At this stage, one notes the growing social inequality, the material manifestations of social power, and even evidence for inter-group hostilities. Social inequality is evidenced, first and foremost, in the occurrence of rich graves. The only known kurgan-type barrow belonging to this stage occurs in Moldavia (Kainari). It contained a female with a rich inventory of ceramic vessels and copper adornments (Movsha 1985). On several occasions, Middle Tripolye sites included stone anthropomorphic sceptres and maceheads – direct symbols of power. Yet the most spectacular discovery was made within the settled area at the Middle Tripolye site of Nezvizko 3: a burial of a senior male in an oval-shaped, flat grave with a rich inventory. His forehead and jaw bore witness to three separate injuries, apparently inflicted by a stone axe when the individual was at least fifty years of age (he survived these injuries. living a further ten to fifteen years) (Fig. 3). It is significant that both the burial rite and the anthropological type find analogies in the Sredni Stog culture (Masson & Merpert 1982, 207–8).

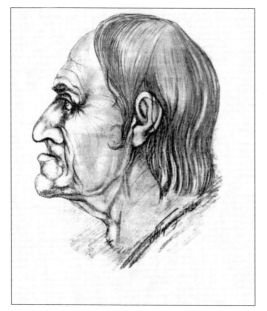

Fig. 3. Individual from Nezvizko 3 burial, reconstruction by M.M. Gerasimov (after Masson and Merpert 1982).

Still deeper transformations in Tripolye society occurred at its latest stage (3,780–3,320, BC calibrated; Wechler 1994). This period saw a considerable deterioration in environmental conditions as the climate grew increasingly arid. At this stage, the Tripolye settlement area became fragmented. One of the local groups (Vykhvatintsy) spread from the Middle Dniestr into the north-western Pontic Lowland. Later, it developed into the Usatovo variant of Late Tripolye. Subsequently, Usatovo sites spread over a vast area of Prut-Dniestr-Southern Bug interfluve, and further west into the lower Danube valley and into Romanian Moldovia. Simultaneously, another Tripolye group, Brynzeny, spread to the north, to eastern Volhynia, where the Troyan variant emerged. A subsequent movement led to the establishment of the Sofievka variant on the Middle Dniepr. Considerable differences became apparent in subsistence. The economy of Usatovo was largely dependent on stock-breeding, especially the horse and sheep/goat. Cattle-breeding was dominant among the groups settled in the Middle Prut and Dniestr area. This type of mixed agriculture was equally typical of Volhynia and the Middle Dniepr. Defensive structures became more common. Thus, the settled area at the Kosteshti 4 site in Moldavia, located on a natural hill, was protected by a triple system of walls and ditches, and the walls, strengthened by stone ramparts, were at least 6 m wide.

Deep transformations in social structure may particularly be recognised in the burial sites of the Usatovo group. The eponymous site, which included a settlement, two groups of kurgan barrows and two cemeteries with flat graves, was located on the edge of an elevated plateau facing the Hadjibei liman (estuary), 8 km north-west of Odessa (Patokova 1979). Several kurgans (I-3, I-9, I-11 and I-12) stood out from the rest by their large proportions and the occurrence of cromlechs and anthropomorphic stelae on the top. The cromlech found on the surface of one of the kurgans (I-9) included a bull's head effigy. These kurgans, which are viewed as belonging to local chieftains, contained individual male burials with unusually rich inventories, including Aegean-type arsenic copper daggers, and copper flat axes and chisels (Zbenovich 1976). Rich female graves included pottery and personal adornments. The cemeteries consisted of clusters of flat graves, each cluster apparently belonging to kin relatives, as evidenced by the occurrence of figurines of a similar type. Consequently, Usatovo society may be viewed as a military-oriented chiefdom, with a strong central power consisting of several lineages with conspicuous symbols of group identity.

The further development ended in a total collapse of Late Tripolian agricultural societies. A new cultural unit, known as the Pit-Grave (*Yamnaya kultura*), gradually encompassed the whole area of the steppe. Pit-Grave culture consisted predominantly of groups of pastoral stockbreeders (cattle, sheep/goats and horses being the most common domesticates). None the less, palaeobotanic evidence supports an earlier view that this cultural area also included sedentary agricultural settlements (e.g., Mikhailovka) in areas sufficiently rich in agricultural resources (Pashkevich 1997). The latter settlement in its final stage grew to a size of 1.5 hectares, and was surrounded by fortifications with stone ramparts and ditches. The Pit-Grave Culture reached its peak in the course of the third millennium BC, speading over the whole area of the east European steppe, from the Urals in the east to the low Danube in the west. According to Merpert (1968), the Pit-Grave sites formed a distinct 'cultural-historic entity' based on a common ideology (primarily the kurgan mortuary rite) which resulted from the integration of various local traditions. The most characteristic feature of Pit-Grave culture were male burials found in pits (*yama* in Russian, hence the name *Yamnaya*) of rectangular, rarely of oval, shape, located beneath the burial mounds (kurgans). It should be remembered that the kurgan, which is primarily seen as a symbol of strong personal authority, was not a complete novelty in the steppe area: kurgans were already in existence at the Usatovo sites and still earlier, among Middle Tripolye groups. In several cases, the kurgan burials included wheels or even complete wheeled carts found inside the pits (e.g., Storozhevaya Mogila, near Dnepropetrovsk on the Dniepr). Rich burials usually included imported gold and copper prestige items, as well as maceheads – direct symbols of power (Nikol'ski and Mariupol groups).

The substitution of the Tripolye by the Pit-Grave culture was not always peaceful. There is strong evidence for the existence of trade, social interaction and armed conflicts between the Late Tripolye and Pit-Grave groups (Videiko 1994). There is much evidence for the reciprocal movement of pottery and other items of material culture and Pit-Grave mounds might be erected directly on top of large, fortified settlements of Late Tripolye age (as at Maidanetskoe). It is significant that according to estimates by Ukrainian archaeologists (Videiko 1994), the Late Tripolye population was far higher than that of Pit-Grave groups.

Summing up the evidence of the steppe, one may detect a relationship between the stratification of society, the rise of male-dominated chiefdoms and inter-group conflicts on the one hand, and the deterioration of the social and physical environment and the ensuing shrinking of food resources on the other. It was noted (Hodder 1982; Whittle 1988) that heightened competition for scarce resources may lead to a sharpened sense of group identity and the maintenance of group boundaries – hence the social hierarchy and the emergence of a group-oriented chiefdoms, the increased role of male individuals, and more stringent control over the territory and its resources.

The Neolithic in the boreal zone of Eastern Europe took the form of increased sedentariness and the intensification of hunter-gathering strategies. By contrast to the south, technical novelties (pottery-making, in the first instance) spread in the boreal area at a much slower pace. Recent radiocarbon measurements (Zaitseva & Timofeyev 1997) show that pottery-making started in European Russia much earlier than had been previously thought, in some cases, as early as 5,500–6,000, BC calibrated. The 'forest Neolithic' in all its stages included numerous cultural groupings, primarily identified by pottery styles and other classes of material culture. As in the Mesolithic, these groupings are viewed as the reflection of closed or semi-closed mating networks with few or no symbols either of local power or gender prominence.

Socio-cultural complexity became more apparent during the third millennium BC. As in the south, this was a time of considerable deterioration in the climate, with the massive spread of coniferous forests and repeated flooding episodes, both acting to restrict wild life resources.

In archaeological terms, this period corresponds to the Battle-Axe or Corded Ware 'horizon' which covered the greater part of central and northern Europe. For a long time, the spread of the Corded Ware-related cultures was viewed as a result of a pastoral migration or colonisation (Childe 1958, 159). Contemporary writers (Shennan 1982; Whittle 1981) tend to link the Corded Ware phenomenon with an 'inegalitarian ideology', and particularly, a new form of expression of male status. Several Corded Ware-related cultures were identified in the east European plain: Eastern Baltic Corded Ware, North-Belorussian, Middle-Dneprian and Fatyanovo (Fig. 4). The case of the North-Belorussian was particularly illuminating: corresponding levels dated to 2,500–2,000, BC calibrated, have been identified at a number of pile-dwelling sites in the Upper Western Dvina

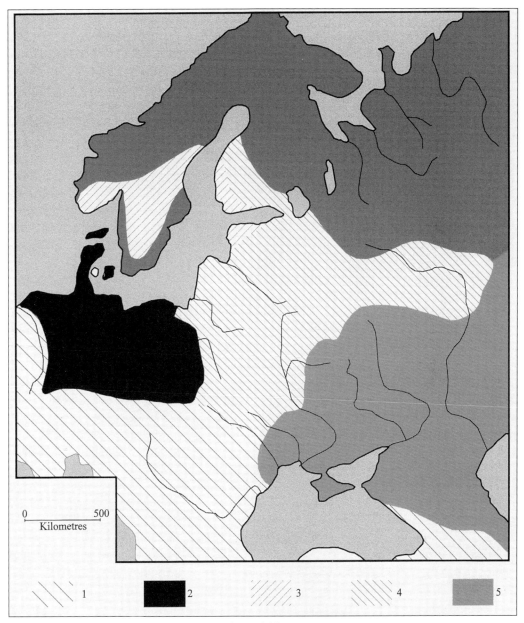

Fig. 4. Corded Ware groups in eastern Europe (after Dolukhanov 1996).

catchment, in north-western Russia and north-eastern Belarus (Usvyaty, Naumovo, Krivina, Osovets and others). Identifiable bone remains include domesticates: sheep, goat, pig and cattle, their total number never exceeding 14 per cent (Dolukhanov & Miklyaev 1988).

Ornamental patterns of the entire pottery corpus of the stratified site of Naumovo were processed by the technique of multivariate analysis (Dolukhanov & Fonyakov 1984). The

85

principal analysis plot for the lower and middle levels of the site produced two clearly distinguishable clusters of signals which merge to form a new entity in the upper level. There is an obvious impression of an intrusion of a new cultural tradition which was gradually absorbed by an old one. A number of 'Late Neolithic' sites in the eastern Baltic area contain elements of the Corded Ware culture. In several cases, these sites (Nainiekste, Kreiči, Leimaniški, Eini, Lagaža) contained typical corded wares, yet they never formed a clear majority in the pottery corpus. Among the domesticates, cattle, sheep/goats and pigs were identified, their overall proportion being less than 10 per cent (Loze 1979).

Hence, the penetration of the Corded Ware into the Neolithic context of the Eastern Peribaltic was essentially peaceful. Archaeological finds fail to produce a single case of destruction or mass killing caused by aggression from outside. Neither can one find sufficiently positive arguments in favour of male dominance. It is true that the bone and wooden figurines found at Usvyaty, Abora, Lagaža and Šventoji are all male. At the same time, amber ornaments widely represented across the area clearly suggest that females were prominent.

Obvious signs of male dominance can be recognised in the Fatyanovo culture area. These sites, almost exclusively cemeteries, were spread over a vast area of northern and north-eastern Russia, forming a compact entity. A particular male status is apparent in the structures of graves and the composition of grave goods. The males were usually found laid on their right side, the head directed to the west, while females lie on their left side, the head to the east. Shaft-hole axes were usually found near the head in male graves; in children's graves, they were placed at the feet. Copper battle-axes, usually in bark cases, were found exclusively in rich graves, apparently belonging to the male élite. Female graves contained numerous ornaments made of animal bones and teeth, and in rare cases, metal and amber ornaments (bracelets, rings, pendants) and pottery. Fatyanovo graves also included animal bones, which belonged largely to domesticates (pig and sheep/goat), bones of wild animals (brown bear, reindeer, elk, wild boar, roe deer, fox, beaver, etc.) being much less numerous. In considering the Fatyanovo phenomenon, one should bear in mind that these sites coexisted, over a significant spread of time and in the same geographical areas, with a distinct cultural unit of a purely hunter-gatherer character: the Volosovo. In contrast to Fatyanovo, this culture included numerous settlements, often large, with both collective and individual burials within the settled areas, either within or in the immediate vicinity of the dwellings. There is evidence for Fatyanovo-Volosovo interaction: Volosovo pottery was often attested in Fatyanovo graves. It may be significant that in at least two sites (Sakhtysh 1 and 2), the Volosovo dead were anthropologically similar to the Fatyanovo individuals.

CONCLUSIONS

At all stages, humankind consisted of social or interest groups of various dimensions, the nuclear (essentially dual) family invariably constituting their basic social foundation. Obvious group symbolism is already recognisable in the late Neanderthal societies (in the form of the 'Mousterian facies'). The internal structure, the degree of cohesion of the age, gender, and interest entities within a group, their social roles and relations of dominance and power were subject to constant changes, primarily dependent on availability of and access to basic resources (both material and spiritual).

Under the conditions of low population density and relative abundance of resources, the social group remains balanced and egalitarian, with less articulated gender dominance. None the less, the symbols of hereditary male power are already recognisable in the Upper Palaeolithic societies of early modern humans. Inter-group relations tended to be peaceful under the conditions of relatively abundant and easily accessible resources. In this case, the proliferation of new cultural and economic packages predominantly took the form of a reticulate process, in which technological innovations and cultural novelties were either accepted or rejected by indigenous individuals.

The inner social hierarchy, with male dominance and inter-group aggressiveness, develops under the conditions of environmental stress and substantial scarcity of resources. Initially developing as an additional survival resource, aggressiveness becomes a superstructural factor, finding its place among culturally patterned beliefs and attitudes. Once emerged, the military élite develops into a self-perpetuating social entity, increasingly involving rank-and-file members. The benefits of being part of an aggressive group were shared by community members, giving them much greater access to material and spiritual resources and mating opportunities. Under similar conditions of acute shortage of resources and the ensuing inter-group hostilities, an 'ethnical myth' can develop, based on the self-identification of an individual with membership of a social group and a mystical perception of common origins expressed by a system of symbols and symbolic behaviour. It may be suggested that this mechanism was largely responsible for a rapid proliferation of Pit-Grave and Corded Ware cultural symbols among initially distinct cultural groups of the east European forests and steppe.

Seven

Neolithic Enclosures in Greek Macedonia: Violent and Non-violent Aspects of Territorial Demarcation

Dimitra Kokkinidou and Marianna Nikolaidou

Introduction

Over the last few decades, the Greek Neolithic has become an active and innovative field of prehistoric inquiry, embracing the study of almost every aspect of past human activity (bibliographic guides are supplied in Rutter 1998). Patterns of cultural change, in particular the emergence of social differentiation and complexity, are increasingly receiving scholarly attention. It has even been argued that the roots of social inequality, which became crystallised in the Bronze Age, can be traced back into the Neolithic (Halstead 1994, 1995). Pertinent to such developments are questions of ownership, incipient accumulation of wealth, antagonism and warfare among early societies.

By the late fifth millennium BC, farming communities in south-eastern Europe had begun to embark upon a course that was to lead, albeit at varying rates, to their hierarchical transformation (e.g., Whittle 1996, 122–43). The Late Neolithic, and especially the Final Neolithic (in Aegean terms) or Chalcolithic (in Balkan terms), were a time of diversification, including the introduction of an integrated and expansive subsistence economy with considerable specialisation (new pottery styles and techniques, craft workmanship, copper and gold metallurgy), increasing cultural interaction and active exchange/trade. Observed innovations in the archaeological record are indications of differential access to material resources and knowledge, which gradually gave rise to social stratification. In this context, substantial perimeter constructions at an appreciable number of settlements can be seen as spatial manifestations – physical and symbolic – of the need for protection of the new goods acquired.

In Greek prehistory, the issue of Neolithic warfare has been a favourite subject of discussion since the publication of Tsountas' classic treatise, *The Prehistoric Citadels of Dimini and Sesklo* (Tsountas 1908). His view about the existence of fortifications in such an early period, dictated by the strong walls of stone that encompass the two Thessalian

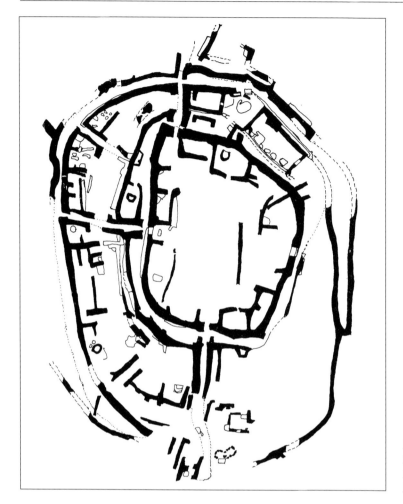

Fig. 1. The enclosures at Dimini (based on Papathanassopoulos 1996, 56 fig. 11).

settlements, is still advocated by archaeologists who rely on recent evidence for comparable discoveries, especially in adjacent Balkan territories (Aslanis 1990a; 1990b; 1993; 1995). At the opposite end, Marxist-orientated scholars have re-analysed the archaeological data on the basis of an alleged economic self-sufficiency of Neolithic social units, which is incompatible with regional or inter-regional hostilities. Hourmouziadis (1979; 1980; 1981), who excavated at Dimini in the 1970s, has postulated that the encircling walls were designed for organising habitational space and for facilitating craft/industrial pursuits and storage (Fig. 1). In a similar vein, there has been a reluctance to acknowledge Neolithic warfare, and enclosures have been collectively correlated with non-defensive purposes such as delimitation of areas of different use (work areas versus living areas), reinforcement of buildings, deterring wild animals or retention of livestock, and, at a symbolic level, demarcation of the community with regard to the outside world (e.g., Elia 1982; Gallis 1996; Grammenos 1996; Halstead 1995; Kotsakis 1996).

It has been common in archaeological and anthropological thinking to treat early agricultural communities cross-culturally as free of the frictions accompanying stratified social formations. These approaches echo a wider intellectual tradition that has sought to reconstruct human history in a continuum of evolutionary and predictable stages from 'primitiveness' and egalitarianism to 'civilisation' and political hierarchy. The evolutionist scheme has favoured the notion of a peaceful distant past, as opposed to a violent present. For a host of reasons pertaining to the disciplinary trends and socio-political debates of the times, there has been a tendency to pacify early social life, even when contextual evidence is in support of the contrary. Warfare has been deemed an integral component of state societies in which inequality is fully institutionalised, but not for non-state populations. Only recently has scholarship refuted the long-held image of harmless farmers, and pointed out that outbreaks of personal and group violence were not uncommon, and 'primitive' war was as effective and deadly as its 'civilised' versions (Keeley 1996; cf. Carman 1997a). This is certainly not to say that violent practices are innate traits of human nature, nor is it claimed that they can exist regardless of any cultural variables. Acts of violence, in any form, are complex phenomena, and as such they cannot have a single cause. In consequence, they have to be construed against the background within which they develop, for they can manifest themselves in a variety of ways, and can take on a multiplicity of meanings that can be understood only by reference to a certain social discourse.

This chapter will assess the defensive and non-defensive aspects of Neolithic ditches and circuit walls in Greek Macedonia (Fig. 2). It proposes that such functions need not have been mutually exclusive, but rather that settlement boundaries may have played alternate roles in times of tension and harmony alike. It then becomes important to examine whether the cultural parameters of artificial boundaries can provide a context for either or

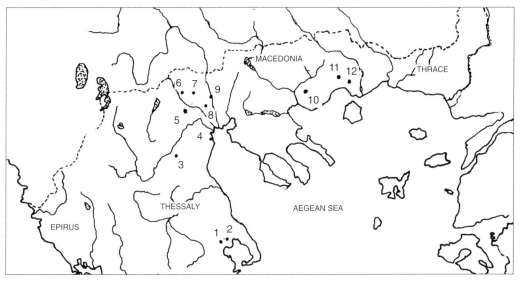

Fig. 2. Map of northern Greece with sites discussed. 1. Sesklo; 2. Dimini; 3. Servia; 4. Makrygialos; 5. Nea Nikomedeia; 6. Mandalo; 7. Aravissos; 8. Giannitsa; 9. Agrosykia; 10. Dimitra; 11. Sitagroi; 12. Dikili Tash.

both modes of behaviour, and under what circumstances. Violence and war are often difficult to deduce archaeologically, since they tend to be reflected only indirectly by material remains. The task becomes more complicated when identification is based on paucity of information, as is the case with the present study. This chapter puts forward some empirical observations and preliminary conclusions which, though qualified by the limitations imposed, seem plausible at the present state of research.

THE ARCHAEOLOGICAL EVIDENCE

Chronology and settlement patterns

The chronological framework for the Neolithic in Macedonia is summarised in Table 1.

Table 1 Chronological divisions for the Neolithic in Macedonia

Early Neolithic	sixth millennium BC
Middle Neolithic	first half of fifth millennium BC
Late Neolithic	second half of fifth millennium BC
Final Neolithic	fourth millennium BC

The Neolithic sequence spans a temporal range of some three millennia, but it is not easy to isolate subdivisions within each chronological division, due to the lack of sufficient excavation data. Specifically, no archaeological horizons have yet been recognised for the initial stages of the period, which elsewhere in Greece are placed in the seventh millennium BC. Likewise, no safe stratigraphies have been established for the Final Neolithic.

Neolithic findings are reported from some 150 sites in Macedonia (Papathanassopoulos 1996, 198–199, fig. 60, 200–1 Nos 18–160; also review article by Andreou et al. 1996, with references). The original number of sites was apparently higher, since several of them must have been destroyed, are invisible as a result of geomorphological changes, or simply remain undetected. Density of habitation increases from the Early Neolithic onwards, to reach its peak in the Late Neolithic, which is also the case for other areas of Greece and the Balkans (e.g., Whittle 1996, 79–85). In the Early and Middle Neolithic, locational preference is concentrated in plains or on gentle slopes and edges of plateaus in proximity to water supplies and arable land, whereas in the later Neolithic phases, a variety of other locations are chosen besides the traditional lowland spots: higher ground, terraces, ridges, naturally defensible positions ('citadels' or 'acropoleis') and inaccessible inland caves.

Settlements vary in duration, size and shape. In terms of morphology, they can be classified into two principal types: mounds or tells of ordered layout, formed by superimposed building horizons, and flat or thin sites with dispersed layout. Both categories, so typical of early sedentary village life across the Balkans, have provided evidence for use over centuries or even millennia (Chapman 1989b). Continuous rebuilding and accumulation of mud-brick or pisé debris has given shape to steep-profiled mounds appearing as outstanding landscape features. Vertical growth can be characteristic of stable residence, but open sites could have been equally long-lived. Perhaps the most important difference between the two groupings is that drifting settlements were not subject to artificial restriction on their expansion: horizontal displacement, possibly related to a greater mobility of population, following relatively short spells of occupation has prevented the formation of tall mounds.

Territorial boundaries

Territorial demarcation in the form of earthworks or stone enclosures is present at the excavated sites identified in Table 2.

Table 2 Neolithic enclosures in Macedonia

Site	Phase		Type
Nea Nikomedeia	Early Neolithic	Late Neolithic	Ditch
Giannitsa		Late Neolithic	Ditch
Mandalo		Late Neolithic	Wall
Makrygialos		Late Neolithic	Ditch
Servia	Middle Neolithic		Ditch

Nea Nikomedeia (Pyke & Yiouni 1996) This mound, 2.5 m in height, lies in the southern part of the alluvial plain of western Macedonia. The exposed portion is 0.2 ha of the total settlement area of 2.5 ha. Three Early Neolithic building phases have been distinguished. Following an abandonment at the end of the sixth millennium BC, the settlement was reinhabited during the Late Neolithic. This layer produced no structures except for a row of ditches enclosing the mound, and no material sequences could be established owing to stratigraphic disturbance. Two narrow, parallel ditches may belong to the Early Neolithic (Fig. 3).

Giannitsa (Hrysostomou 1992; 1994; 1996; Hrysostomou & Hrysostomou 1993; Valamoti 1995) This site is located within the limits of the town of Giannitsa. Excavated levels date to the Early and Late Neolithic. A double ditch is reported for the later settlement, which is estimated to have been 6–8 ha in extent.

Mandalo (Kesisoglou et al. 1996; Kilikoglou et al. 1996; Kotsakis 1987; Kotsakis et al. 1989; Maniatis and Kromer 1990; Papaefthimiou-Papanthimou 1987; Papaefthimiou-Papanthimou & Pilali-Papasteriou 1990a; 1990b; 1991; 1993; Pilali-Papasteriou & Papaefthimiou-Papanthimou 1989; Pilali-Papasteriou et al. 1986; Savvaidis et al. 1988; Tsokas et al. 1986; Valamoti 1989) This small mound is situated on a low ridge near two streams, 8 m above the ground, in the rolling country that separates the Giannitsa plain from the Almopia basin. The excavated area is 0.05 ha of the total settlement area of 0.5 ha. Occupation has been C-14 dated to two major phases, divided by a stratigraphic discontinuity. The Late Neolithic phase corresponds roughly

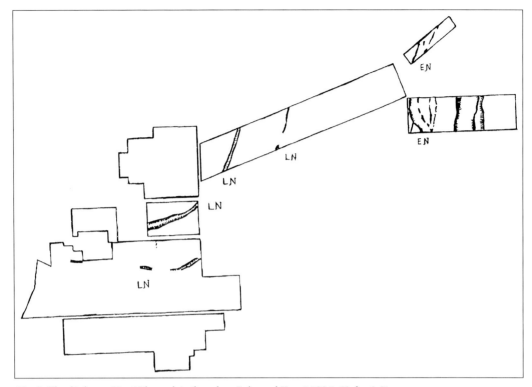

Fig. 3. The ditches at Nea Nikomedeia (based on Pyke and Youni 1996, 53 fig. 3.3).

with the latter half of the fifth millennium BC (4,600–4,000 BC). There follows a hiatus of *c.* 1,000 years until occupation was resumed in the Early Bronze Age, which overlaps with most of the third millennium BC (2,900–2,200 BC). Among the most distinctive architectural features of the Neolithic settlement are two perimetric structures. The inner wall is approximately 18 m long, 2.5 m wide and 1.5 m high. It is made of large fieldstones filled with earth, and stands on the top of the mound, 3 m from another, outer wall (Fig. 4). The upper parts of those walls were associated with Bronze Age finds, which suggests that they continued to be in use during the second phase of occupation.

Makrygialos (Besios & Pappa 1990–5, 1996) This extensive settlement was founded on a low hill slope 2 km west of the coast of the Thermaic Gulf, near ancient Pydna in Pieria. It is estimated to have been at least 50 ha, of which 6 ha was investigated as part of a salvage project – the largest Neolithic excavation ever to be conducted in Greece – before the site disappeared because of construction work on road and rail networks. Occupation falls into two phases, which are datable to the beginning and end of the Late Neolithic respectively. The two phases hardly overlapped in the area they occupied, and there also seems to have been a slight stratigraphic gap. Phase 1 yielded a row of concentric ditches surrounding an area of 28 ha. They were regularly maintained, and

Fig. 4. The circuit walls at Mandalo (based on Papaefthimiou-Papanthimou and Pilali-Papasteriou 1993, 1212 fig. 1).

were reinforced at places by walls of mud-brick or stone. The interior of the system was occupied by Ditch A, up to 4.5 m in width and 3.5 m in depth. It was originally constructed in the form of deep pits which were successively re-dug. A later building episode is represented by a V-shaped trench. The contents of Ditch A included large quantities of cultural residue, such as animal bones, carbonised seeds, shellfish, pottery, figurines, and primary and secondary burials, which suggests that certain parts may have served as refuse dumps after the actual trenches fell out of use. Ditch B was of less substantial construction, and ran parallel to Ditch A. The two structures were probably divided by Ditch C. The enclosure of Phase 1 contained circular timber houses partly sunk into the ground, built reasonably far apart from each other. The space between the ditches and dwellings is likely to have been used for household horticulture or for penning livestock. Parts of the ditches were still in use in Phase 2, as were semi-subterranean houses, set closely together.

Servia (Heurtley 1939; Ridley & Wardle 1979) This low spreading mound lay on a terrace in the riverine zone of the middle Aliakmon Valley. It is no longer visible, having been submerged by the creation of the artificial Lake Polyfyto. The chronological sequence has been established as follows:

Middle Neolithic Phases 1–5
Late Neolithic Phases 6–7
Break in occupation
Late Neolithic Phase 8
Stratigraphic gap
Early Bronze Age Phases 9–10

The early excavator reports a circular fosse of possible Middle Neolithic date, which was dug to a depth of more than 2 m. The ditch was gradually filled up with refuse during the same period of occupation.

TERRITORIAL DEMARCATION IN CONTEXT

A regional perspective

The core argument for considering territoriality and defence as two sides of the same coin is that the former primarily signifies control of access – to land, to people, and to material and non-material goods. Artificial settlement barriers, like the ones in question, can plausibly be interpreted as materialisations of important social objectives: they are costly works of prehistoric architecture, demanding considerable investment of labour, time and symbolic capital, technical expertise, regular upkeep and co-ordination of collective effort (cf. Keeley 1996, 55–8; Sherratt 1982, 25, n. 13).

The practice of spatial delimitation – a reflection of increasing attachment to chosen places – appears to have been an accompanying element of sedentarism from its early stages (McGeehan-Liritzis 1996, 215–16). Neolithic earthworks are present at a number of sites in Thessaly (see Elia 1982; for European parallels, see Bradley 1998; Whittle 1996). Ditches would have been a practical method of digging in open plains with easily workable soils. During the Late and Final Neolithic, a new type of fortification is introduced: a perimeter wall of stone. Examples are known from a wide geographical area, ranging from the Aegean islands (Evans & Renfrew 1968; Hood 1981–2) to Thessaly (Tsountas 1908) to the inner Balkans and the rest of Europe (see Bradley 1998; Whittle 1996). Notable is the concentration of Neolithic enclosures in the western part of our study area, whereas similar discoveries are currently absent in the east. Bearing in mind that the social background was not markedly different inter-regionally, this uneven distribution is intriguing, and in need of further exploration.

Neolithic transactions have been described as reciprocal in character, based on social sharing, to cope with the vulnerabilities of a small-scale economy (see Andreou et al. 1996, 558–9). None the less, intra- and inter-community linkages and networks of obligations would have created not only alliances, but also stress and conflict. The Late Neolithic population expansion would have caused further competition over resources or other valuables, resulting in raiding and other forms of aggression. In this context, an increasing concern for security is explicable by reference to the cultural reality outlined in the Introduction, which virtually verifies Tsountas' early observations regarding the defensive purpose of enclosures referred to earlier in this chapter (Aslanis 1990a; 1990b;

1993; 1995; Renfrew 1972, 392; Theocharis 1973). In addition to artificially fortified settlements, often with metal-working facilities (McGeehan-Liritzis 1996, 217–19), the presence of naturally defensible spots not selected for their agricultural potential is a sign of care for safety. The occurrence of such sites, affording territorial surveillance, has been convincingly linked with dangerous traffic and tactics of warfare (Andreou et al. 1996, 575). Although skeletal evidence of violent injuries and deaths, as well as artefacts identifiable as weapons in post-Neolithic contexts, are absent from the Neolithic record, it could be assumed that any appropriate farming or hunting tool was used in armed conflict, for example axes, mattocks, clubs, mace-heads, projectiles, slingstones, bows, arrowheads or spearheads (cf. Keeley 1996, 49–55; Renfrew 1972, 392).

Social implications

The archaeological findings are suggestive enough as to the types of commodities and their possessors that would have called for protection. A popular material for making ornaments was *Spondylus gaederopus* (the spiny oyster), a prestigious, exchangeable item, obtained from the northern Aegean coast (Shackleton & Renfrew 1970). Makrygialos was a centre for production of adornment accessories cut from this marine mollusc (Fig. 5). Other communities, such as Sitagroi, Dimitra and Dikili Tash in eastern Macedonia (see Nikolaidou 1997) and Dimini in Thessaly (see Halstead 1993), were equally active in procurement, exploitation and circulation of shell objects over the Balkans and up to Central Europe. *Spondylus*, when collected live, must be pulled from the rock by diving 2–4 m, so the spiny valve is hard to handle. Special skills (swimming, diving) and experience were clearly required, and appropriate equipment (knives, nets, baskets or even small boats) would have been used as well. The difficulties involved in acquisition would enhance the value attached to this species which – transported inland from the sea which many might never have seen – would probably have been invested with an 'exotic' aura (Nikolaidou 1997, 180).

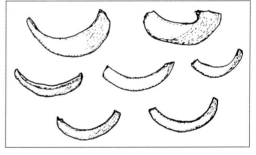

Fig. 5. Spondylus *bracelets or amulets from Makrygialos.*

Possession of metallurgical products and special crafts was apparently an act of status enhancement by emerging social hierarchies. Sixty-five copper objects from Makrygialos (most of them from Phase 2) make up the largest stratified assemblage known from Neolithic contexts in Greece. At Mandalo, the manufacture of textiles and metals seems to have been a flourishing industry. Copper sheets and implements and a clay crucible (Fig. 6) derive from layers C-14-dated to 4,200–4,000 BC. Copper-smelting was also practised at Agrosykia, an 'acropolis' site in the southern part of the Giannitsa plain (*Arhaiologia* 1986, 81; Pariente 1991, 904–5; Touchais 1986, 718). A hoard of gold jewels (though unstratified) from Aravissos, in the vicinity of Mandalo, is reminiscent of the Chalcolithic grave ensemble from Varna in Bulgaria (see Zachos 1996, 167, 339–40, figs 301–3) (Fig. 7). Balkan contacts are further

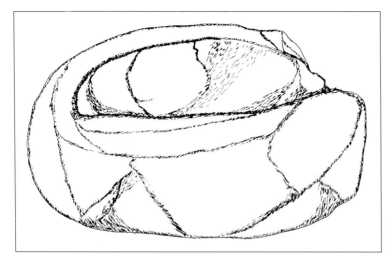

Fig. 6. Clay crucible for copper-smelting from Mandalo (after a photograph in Papaefthimiou-Papanthimou & Pilali-Papasteriou 1993, 1213, fig. 2).

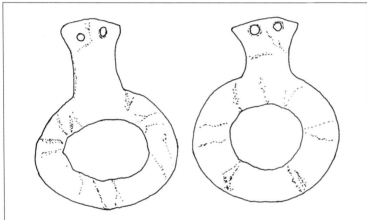

Fig. 7. Gold pendants from Aravissos (based on Papathanassopoulos 1996, 340 fig. 302).

indicated by the use of Carpathian obsidian at Mandalo, attested for the first time in Greece.

Mandalo is currently the only explored site in Macedonia displaying analogies in public architecture with the contemporaneous Dimini in Thessaly: the stone enclosure contrasts sharply with the wattle-and-daub domestic structures which have left but scanty traces in the material remains at the Macedonian settlement. Despite its limited extent, Mandalo seems to have been all but peripheral in the local socio-economic system (Andreou et al. 1996, 572). Its location, affording possibilities for natural guard and overlooking the surrounding plain, hints at a special position in the settlement network, probably an élite residence or a focal point of inter-communal activities, or both (for regional site distribution, see Kokkinidou 1989; 1990; 1995; Kokkinidou & Trantalidou 1991).

To sum up, there is an apparent relationship between settlement barriers and certain artefacts, manufactured locally or imported. The production and exploitation of those precious goods was perhaps manipulated selectively by high-ranking segments of the community – people who controlled the social know-how, and along with their insignia of power, were privately protected.

Settlement organisation is a dynamic process, however, and it is to be expected that its components fulfilled different needs during the lifetime of a site. The ditches at Makrygialos, with their continual rebuilding on the one hand and partial infilling on the other, are an illuminating example of changing uses of space (cf. Andreou et al. 1996, 573). In discussing fourth- and third-millennium BC enclosures in central Europe, Sherratt (1982, 23) has suggested that in times of peace, they are likely to have served as arenas for gathering as part of the concentration or distribution of foodstuffs and livestock, which would have been occasions for general exchange/trade and ritual. His interpretation is quite relevant in envisaging functional alternatives of formalised communal space in our study area beyond the context of hostilities. In other words, boundaries would not only have defined fields of contention, or been defended during actual war, or merely have operated as warning devices and precautions against intruders, but they may well have been associated with peaceful endeavours: loci of major social events, markers of time and continuity, organising metaphors of social cohesion, identity and order, interwoven with local histories and traditions. In any case, the specific nature of such projects remains to be clarified by future research.

CONCLUSION

This case study has attempted to shed light on the role of Neolithic settlement enclosures in one part of Greece by summarising the available evidence and exploring some possible contextual connotations. Fragmentarily as they may have survived in archaeological record, these architectural forms were designed to offer practical solutions as much as symbolic representations.

As implied by the title of this chapter, violent and non-violent aspects of territorial demarcation constitute complementary elements of settlement organisation, though seemingly diverging. Besides, Neolithic life involved a multitude of cultural attitudes that could account for many different expressions of human behaviour, and therefore, different uses of material conditions. It is this web of material, social and symbolic inter-relationships that makes constructional choices meaningful.

EIGHT

THE ORIGINS OF WARFARE IN THE PREHISTORY OF CENTRAL AND EASTERN EUROPE

JOHN CHAPMAN

INTRODUCTION

One of the greatest challenges to the ingenuity and intellectual rigour of prehistorians everywhere is the articulation of views on the incidence of warfare in their periods and regions: ingenuity, because the data informing us about warfare may not necessarily be obvious; rigour, because hypotheses generated about prehistoric warfare can rarely be clear-cut, and indeed, have often been speculative. It must be admitted that until quite recently, this is a challenge which prehistorians have signally failed to address. However, recent work has opened up new arenas for debate and new horizons for research. It is thus timely to address the problems of ancient warfare in central and eastern Europe.

This chapter seeks to contribute to the general debate about the 'pacified past' – the notion that warfare is a recent, state-led phenomenon – and to discuss the evidence for warfare in the Mesolithic, Neolithic and Copper Age of central and eastern Europe. Here, the field of Mars has been dominated by the traditional contrast drawn between (relatively) peaceful Mesolithic and Neolithic pre-Indo-European communities and (relatively) aggressive Copper Age Indo-European invaders – a notion given gendered force by Marija Gimbutas (1978; 1979; 1980). As we shall see, it is not difficult to find evidence for defensive and offensive intentions in the Mesolithic and Neolithic, nor to identify autochthonous strategies for defence and hostility in the Balkan Copper Age.

A PACIFIED PAST?

In his recent synthesis Keeley (1996), outlines the oscillation of intellectual opinions on humans and warfare over the last three centuries between a Hobbesian pole and a Rousseauian pole. For Hobbes, the absence of 'Leviathan' (the centralised, authoritarian state) led inevitably to the outbreak of warfare between communities whose basic biological roots contained the seeds of inter-personal violence. Rousseau opposed this view with the ideal of a 'Noble Savage', whose peaceful nature was only recently betrayed by social complexity into the vigorous promotion of war to achieve political aims.

Keeley indicates how a biased reading of the anthropological record has led most anthropologists to a neo-Rousseauian view of the past, where 'primitive warfare' was rarely deadly, proficient or serious. This view has, in turn, been increasingly supported by those few prehistorians who have commented upon warfare, such that 'prehistorians have increasingly pacified the past' (Keeley 1996, 17). Keeley attempts to demolish this view by creative use of anthropological data, supplemented by a series of snapshots of prehistoric warfare. His Hobbesian conclusion is that 'Primitive warfare is simply total war conducted with very limited means' (Keeley 1996, 175) and 'War has always been a struggle between people, their societies, and their economies, not just warriors, war parties, armies and navies' (Keeley 1996, 176). Keeley maintains that prehistoric warfare was ubiquitous and deadly, with casualty rates just as high as in state warfare, and therefore constituted a major and seriously overlooked factor in socio-cultural change.

However, the evidence cited by Keeley amounts to a dozen sites over a period of 30,000 years in the whole continent. By comparison, Davies's (1994) calculation that one hundred billion people have died on planet earth since the emergence of farming, several million of them at least in the prehistoric period in Europe, indicates that the case from skeletal trauma for ubiquitous prehistoric warfare is slender indeed. In one of the rare studies of long-term regional skeletal data, Bennike (1985) finds remarkably few individuals in the buried population of Denmark, from Mesolithic to Iron Age, who have met violent deaths. Even Keeley admits that 'some prehistoric regions were remarkably peaceful over many generations' (Keeley 1996, 183). In an excellent review of the osteological evidence for Eastern Woodlands prehistoric warfare, Milner (1995, 236) notes that there were more casualties than could be expected from a 'pacified past' hypothesis, but that there was insufficient skeletal trauma to support the Hobbesian scenario of continuous and unregulated warfare. This allows us to conclude that when it happened, prehistoric warfare was bloody and dangerous, and that it happened more frequently than most prehistorians were previously willing to accept. The research questions which arise include the following. How can we identify when and where warfare was a significant factor? Why did warfare begin in small-scale societies, and why was it absent in other regions? Two recent studies enable us to develop a perspective on these issues; the first is Redmond's ethno-archaeological study of tribal and chiefly warfare in South America (Redmond 1994), while the second is Monks's inter-regional archaeological study of prehistoric warfare in the Iberian Peninsula (Monks 1997, 1998).

Redmond is critical of previous attempts to characterise the incidence of warfare in terms of the expectation of particular material traits. Instead, she proposes to extend the interpretative net far wider by studying the whole gamut of social activities related to warfare. The ethnographic detail of tribal and chiefly warfare is used to generate archaeological expectations in a wide range of activities, including preparations for war, organisation of war, pre-war rituals, offensive and defensive strategies and tactics, and post-war rituals, including burials (Redmond 1994, fig. 20). The archaeological difficulty is that there are many possible interpretations of artefacts such as fired clay cylinder seals and effigy vessels which have specific meanings in ethnographic contexts of war-making or remembrance. For example, the seals are used by the Jivaro for the application of the body paints so important to the image of a mighty warrior (1994, fig. 24), while the effigy pots are considered to be images of individual warriors (1994, figs 44–6). However, it is, inadmissible to make similar interpretations of the fired clay cylinder seals (Makkay 1984) or the anthropomorphic vessels (Comşa 1995) of the Balkan Neolithic and Copper Age, at least without complementary supporting evidence. The same is true for the pre-war and postwar feasting and ritual which regularly accompanies raids and battles. But Redmond identifies other warfare-related material traits whose significance has been quite overlooked in prehistoric contexts: an example is the hoarding of weapons in the preparations made for war. Hoards of finely polished stone axes with little use-wear are relatively common finds in the Balkan Neolithic and Copper Age (Chapman forthcoming). While these hoards may well signify communal status, it is valuable to consider the interpretation of cached weapons and the range of possible meanings. Indeed, the principal lesson from Redmond's 'total' approach to warfare is the necessity to look widely for potential evidence, even if the interpretation in favour of warfare may not necessarily be supported in each individual case. Analysis of the widest range of potential data may provide strength in breadth rather than in depth for interpretations of the intentions of prehistoric warfare.

An excellent recent example of this approach to prehistoric warfare is Monks's research on the Iberian Peninsula. Monks demonstrates an intensification of warfare in many regions of Iberia at the end of the Neolithic and into the Early Copper Age, consequent upon increased sedentarism and the caging effects of small, rich lowland valley territories (Monks 1997; 1998, 225–32). She identifies the emergence of new, more permanent war leaders in these periods, who could attract the manpower to build the large new fortifications, of which a total of eighty are known, whose leadership was associated with feasting, ritual, trade and exchange, and whose maintenance led to even longer-term leadership. The most impressive aspect of Monks's hypothesis is that it can explain the absence of fortifications in certain areas, as well as their presence in other zones. For our purposes, however, we recall the important role played in the evolution of Iberian warfare by weaponry, in particular the bow and arrow. Arrowheads were found in skeletons in Copper Age graves, and as grave goods in other tombs (Monks 1998, 210–16); the main representation in later prehistoric scenes of warfare is groups of archers in formation (Monks 1998, 217–22), and many fortifications, such as Zambujal, were designed to deal with the danger posed by archery. An important question is whether or not this weapon played a key role in the intensification of warfare in other parts of Europe, such as the Balkans.

CENTRAL AND EASTERN EUROPE: BEYOND THE LEGACY OF MARIJA GIMBUTAS

An extraordinary omission from Keeley's (1996) account of prehistoric warfare is the work of Marija Gimbutas. She, almost alone of all Balkan prehistorians, has consistently argued for the significance of warfare as the most important single cultural factor affecting social change in the Copper Age of eastern and central Europe. Since the publication of Merpert's (1961) paper on barrow burials, Gimbutas has maintained that a succession of waves of invasion from the north Pontic steppes had dealt the climax Copper Age societies of eastern and central Europe a series of damaging blows from which they never recovered. In her later works, Gimbutas refined the chronology and material consequences of the kurgan waves, which she dated latterly to the Early Copper Age, the Middle Copper Age and the Late Copper Age of the Balkans (Gimbutas 1978; 1979; 1980). But it was only since the mid-1970s that Gimbutas portrayed the communities destroyed by the kurgan warriors as peaceful, matrilocal, matrilinear and creative – an 'Old European' civilisation which represented all that was best about societies ruled by women (Gimbutas 1978, fig. 3; 1989; 1991).

In a biographical sketch of Gimbutas, the author has attempted to demonstrate that the kurgan destruction of Old European civilisation was, in fact, an archaeological replay of Gimbutas's own life, her idyllic Lithuanian childhood shattered by not one but two Soviet invasions (Chapman 1998a). The maps documenting the kurgan invasions show an uncanny resemblance to the invasion routes taken by the Red Army in 1944 (Chapman 1998a, fig. 14.3, A–B). Nevertheless, this biographical interplay between life experiences and academic output should not be used to criticise Gimbutas's hypotheses of warfare and cultural change. This is so mainly because Gimbutas was just one of many central and eastern European prehistorians who have relied upon Indo-European invasions at the end of the Balkan Neolithic and Copper Age to account for markedly less complex material culture and settlements. As a single example, it is worth quoting the late Dragoslav Srejović on the Neolithic of Serbia:

> The Middle Neolithic is a period of peace and good neighbourly relations in the whole of the Balkan Peninsula. The former discrepancies in economic activities which caused friction between the individual culture groups were no longer present. (Srejović 1988, 17)

Srejović goes on to argue that the establishment of cultural boundaries between individual (Early Neolithic) cultures precluded all territorial expansion, and that once in place, the Vinča culture developed independently until the period of great migrations marking the start of the Copper Age in the Central Danubian region (Srejović 1988, 18). The same underlying contrast drawn by Gimbutas is present in Srejović's writings: a peaceful, autochthonous population (related genetically to the inhabitants of modern Serbia) and a warlike invading force from the north Pontic steppe (the homeland of the Red Army). It is important to disentangle modern nationalist assumptions from the archaeological remains which should be studied more carefully to assess the probability of wars, invasions, territorial expansions and changes of population. This task means a careful re-examination of the 'peaceful Middle Neolithic' of the Balkan Peninsula, as well as its dark and dangerous Copper Age, and indeed the 'period of former discrepancies in economic activities' – the Mesolithic–Neolithic transition.

The next section of this chapter will propose a framework for an analysis of the evidence for the offensive and defensive capabilities of communities in the Balkan Mesolithic, Neolithic and Copper Age. This assessment they will be used to give an interpretative account of the development of pre-Bronze Age warfare in central and eastern Europe.

ARCHAEOLOGICAL EVIDENCE: A METHODOLOGY FOR OBJECTS AND DEFENCES

Anyone wishing to assess the incidence of warfare in central and eastern Europe must come to terms with two serious negative aspects of the data. First, there are hardly any examples of skeletons whose cause of death is clearly violent. Second, there are very few examples of representations of individuals or scenes of individuals which include weapons or wounds. While some critics will take this absence of crucial evidence as fatally wounding to the cause of Balkan pre-Bronze Age warfare, the riposte is that the range and depth of evidence pertaining to defences and weaponry is sufficiently strong to make a plausible case.

Let us first examine the skeletal evidence against the background of Balkan Neolithic and Copper Age mortuary practices. It has long been recognised that intramural burial rather than interment in cemeteries characterised much of the period from 8,000–2500 calibrated BC in central and eastern Europe (Chapman 1983; 1994; forthcoming). But taking these cultural practices into account, there is a long list of cemeteries and settlements with intramural burials where no incidences of trauma consistent with a violent death have been found (Table 1).

Table 1 Cemeteries and settlements with intramural burials with no evidence for skeletal trauma

Site	Period	No. of skeletons	Reference
Vlasac I, III	Late Mesolithic	117	Nemeskéri 1978
Lepenski Vir I–II	Late Mesolithic	85	Nemeskéri 1967
Padina A	Mesolithic	25	Živanović 1976
Ajmana	Early Neolithic	14 in mass grave	Radosavljević-Krunić 1986
Velešnica	Early Neolithic	7 in mass grave	Živanović 1986
Anza	Early Neolithic	34	Nemeskéri & Lengyel 1976
Vinča-Belo Brdo	Early Neolithic	12 in mass grave	Schwidetsky 1971/2
Obre I–II	Early-Middle Neolithic	25	Nemeskéri 1974
Zengóvárkony	Lengyel	64	Zoffmann 1972

These data amount to a significant quantity of negative evidence, to be contrasted with the relatively high percentages of skeletons with evidence for trauma recorded in regions with archaeological evidence for warfare (e.g., south-west USA, Eastern Woodlands: Haas 1990; Haas, Chapter 2 this volume; Milner 1995). No Balkan site has yet provided evidence of a massacre such as is found in the partially coeval Linearbandkeramik at Talheim (Wahl & König 1987). The three mass graves comparable in number of dead to Mesolithic Ofnet, with its evidence for decapitation (Frayer 1997), show no signs of violence, and indicate ancestral relations rather than a bloody incident. The claims for cannibalism at sites such as Ovcharovo-Gorata (Nobis 1986) are unverified and the human remains appear to represent the secondary burials of body parts in ancestral rituals. Indeed, human bone deposits of the Ovcharovo type are characteristic of many Balkan Neolithic and Copper Age sites, but there is no evidence here for trauma or cannibalism (for full arguments for kinship rituals, see Chapman, forthcoming). And while there is also much evidence for the deliberate breaking off of the heads of fired clay figurines (Chapman, forthcoming), it is not possible to equate this rite with the decapitation of tribal enemies. So what evidence remains for violent death in the Balkans?

The number of instances is confined to two Late Mesolithic sites downstream of the Iron Gates gorge, and three Copper Age tells in north Bulgaria. In the case of the Mesolithic sites, four burials at Ostrovul Corbului and several burials out of the total of thirty-three burials at Schela Cladovei have been killed by bone points which remained embedded in the skeleton. Radovanović (1996, 338) describes the four Ostrovul Corbului skeletons as: an adult male with wounds to the head; a child with wounds to the chest; an adult female with unspecified wounds, and a second child with unspecified wounds. Nicolăescu-Plopşor (1976) records that bone projectile points were found embedded in the femur of an adult male and in the temporal bone of a second adult male at Schela Cladovei. It is noteworthy that none of the Mesolithic people had been shot with stone projectile points, although this was the fate of several skeletons buried in the Vasilievka 3 cemetery (Telegin 1961; Vencl 1991).

The Copper Age Bulgarian evidence has been synthesised by Comşa (1960) from old anthropological reports by Popov. Popov notes that of the perforations in the five skulls found buried at the tell of Ruse, three were caused by trepanations, and the remainder by blows from a sharp instrument. It is worth testing the notion that the Ruse perforations were caused by a copper battle-axe of the type found on the tell. Popov further claims the same pattern, at the tells of Salmanovo and Kolarovgrad, of human bones broken by heavy blows: long bones at the former, femora and skulls of adults and children at the latter. The heavy blows may well be consistent with attack by an antler battle-axe or any of the heavier bone, antler and stone tools used in the Copper Age. The anthropological evidence is in no way indicative of warfare as opposed to individual punishment or personal revenge, and can thus be considered of limited value.

The negative evidence offered by representations of humans as individuals or in groups is, if anything, more striking because of its numerical strength. The total number of known miniature figures, the vast majority of which represent humans, must total between 50,000 and 100,000 and the figurine corpus currently known from the Cucuteni-Tripolye group alone exceeds 30,000 (Monah 1997). Although there is a steady and increasing percentage of male figures represented in the Balkan Neolithic and Copper Age corpus, this gender is always in a tiny minority, and there are very few examples known to the author which portray either a weapon or a wound. One equivocal group is the Late Neolithic Tisza group of (usually hermaphrodite) figures holding curved objects, from the southern part of the Hungarian plain. While the customary interpretation of this figure is as the 'sickle god' (Csalog 1958; Makkay 1978), the ambiguity of gender and curved object alike render this interpretation problematic – an equally logical name is the 'boomerang goddess'! The object may be a boomerang rather than a sickle, and may be compared to the gold boomerang in the Varna I cemetery (Mazarov 1988, Abb. 36). Trogmayer has pointed out that the most recent addition to this group, a fired clay hermaphrodite from Szegvár-Tüzkoves, is carrying a miniature fired clay hammer-axe rather than a curved object – again a weapon just as much as a tool (Trogmayer 1990, figs. 83–4).

The ambiguity of this group is no great support for the case for representations of warlike activity. We look in vain in the Balkan Neolithic and Copper Age for a group such as the Italian Copper Age stelae depicting adult males carrying daggers (Whitehouse 1993) or the famous Iberian archery battle (Monks 1998, fig. 120). The rarity of warlike items, people and scenes in such a large corpus is a strong argument in favour of a peaceful past in the Balkan Neolithic and Copper Age – a point in favour of Gimbutas's hypothesis of a peaceful Old Europe.

The terrain becomes more fertile when the case for defences is considered. Even here, the evidence is hardly unambiguous. There has been a vigorous debate over the functions of all kinds of enclosed sites in European prehistory, whether Neolithic causewayed enclosures, Bronze Age enclosures or Iron Age hillforts (Thomas 1991; Barrett et al. 1991; Harding 1996; Hill 1995). The main objection to a function of defence has been one of two symbolic principles, the principle of identity and the principle of status: first, enclosure defines the place of the group, rather than defending it, and co-residence in that place in turn defines the group; and second, the defences of some sites are unnecessarily vast for military purposes, so the main function is not defensive but group or individual prestige. But both principles are based upon confusion. An enclosure offers some, even minimal, protection to the residents at the same time as defining a symbolic inclusion of the residents and an exclusion of their neighbours and/or enemies. A massive defensive network may be military overkill, but it still does not remove the defensive function; rather, this function is complemented by the size of the fortifications. Since a fortification protects such a tiny part of the group's home range, it is not surprising that that place is of special importance to the group (for a discussion of place-value, see Chapman 1998a). Even the objection that some ditches were as useful for preventing undesirable stock movement (whether keeping domesticates in or wild animals out) (Tringham 1972) overlooks the point that hindrances to the movements of animals are also likely to deter human mobility sufficiently to improve the chances of rebutting an attack. A general point here is that identification of one function should not necessarily preclude one or more alternative objectives, whether military, economic or symbolic. We should not attempt to exclude interpretational ambiguity, but as we shall see, we should rather seek to revel in it.

The final aspect of the evidence to consider is the most common and also the most complex to interpret – the objects. Childe (1941, 126) made three fundamental points about prehistoric weaponry: weapons can be used for pacific purposes; specifically war weapons are late in the archaeological record; their absence does not exclude warfare. But is the appearance of specifically war weapons really as late as the Early Bronze Age or the Corded Ware period, as Childe and others believed? Any discussion of this question returns us to the very ambiguity noted in the skeletal, representational and site data. This ambiguity turns on the multi-functionality of prehistoric objects. Vencl (1979; 1980) usefully classifies objects in relation to their potential as weapons into specialised, unspecialised and opportunistic. Other archaeologists tend to insist upon one function rather than another in their discussion of objects possibly related to warfare, depending upon their stance in the debate. Keeley (1996, 54) attacks prehistorians for failing to consider the potential importance of arrowheads for warfare, but he errs in the same manner, if in the opposite direction, when claiming of the Danubian shoe-last axe that 'the only *documented* use for them is homicide' (Keeley 1996, 50, original emphasis), or of the

Danubian arrowhead, that 'there is no evidence to suggest that they were anything but war points' (Keeley 1996, 54). Instead of these deliberately rhetorical arguments, it is more helpful to diagnose a specific class of artefacts whose categorisation is based upon the inherent ambiguity of the objects themselves – the tool-weapon. Use-wear analysis of shoe-last axes indicates that some of them were used for heavy woodworking as well as serving as clubs (Lyneis 1988, 315–16). Equally, the few stone points found in the Serbian Neolithic site of Selevac showed no use-wear indications of use as projectiles, even though their morphology favoured such use (Voytek 1990). In other words, the polished stone axe and the flint arrowhead are two good examples of the composite class of tool-weapons.

The tool-weapon can be differentiated from two logical alternatives: those tools which have no potential for warfare, and those weapons which lack any potential for other, more peaceful functions. In the pre-state period, it is not the absence of specialised killing weapons that is important so much as the ratio of tools to tool-weapons to weapons. Hence, the presence of a single tool-weapon (henceforth Tool-Weapon) cannot possibly support the case for warfare, but the deposition of a combination of many Tool-Weapons in different raw materials in a 'defended' site may be a stronger argument. The significance of Tool-Weapons in different raw materials is clear from an example of a site where the high frequency of projectile points may be related to the importance of hunting, but the deposition of many finely polished stone maceheads can hardly be explained in the same manner. Faunal evidence relating to the incidence of hunting will be a necessary part of the argument. There is also a legitimate expectation of the deposition of more Tool-Weapons in a defended than in an undefended settlement, since the commitment to military action is clear in the construction of defences. As Keeley (1996, 55) observes, fortifications were the costliest and largest-scale pieces of pre-industrial technology.

The symbolic richness of the category of Tool-Weapon is an important trait. The person using the Tool-Weapon for peaceful purposes will have been aware of its violent potential, and vice versa. The individual biography of a Tool-Weapon such as an axe (Kopytoff 1986) may have included the killing of several enemies in a raid as well as the construction of a longhouse. The interplay between different functions may have even prevented further specialisation away from Tool-Weapons into weapons and tools. The contextual dimension is also vital in considering the deposition of Tool-Weapons, especially in periods of changing arenas of social power (Chapman 1991).

There is one additional question to consider: the appearance of objects whose primary function is military, but with peaceful secondary functions. This category excludes swords, since it is hard to imagine any but a military function for them, but includes daggers, whose cutting blade may have been applied to materials other than human flesh. It is proposed to term such object categories Weapon-Tools. Weapon-Tools share the same symbolic potential as Tool-Weapons, but there has been a shift in their main aim towards hand-to-hand combat.

A careful assessment of the presence of tools, Tool-Weapons, Weapon-Tools and weapons depends upon an analysis of each raw material before a discussion of changes in Tool-Weapons and weaponry through time. In the absence of the direct association between a Tool-Weapon and a skeleton, or without use-wear analysis, judgements as to function will often have to rely upon the morphology of the objects.

Stone projectile points

In a comprehensive review of the Danish evidence for hunting-arrowheads in the light of experimental studies, Fischer (1989) has defined three technological desiderata, the interplay between which led to design changes over ten millennia: optimal penetrative qualities, the capacity to produce the sharpest possible cut (to induce bleeding), and the greatest possible symmetry along the longitudinal axis to gain maximum directional stability. Fischer presents an idealised typology of arrowhead development from the Late Palaeolithic to the Late Neolithic of southern Scandinavia (1989, fig. 10), on which the author has based morphological comparisons with central and east European materials. While Fischer defines the optimum distance of hunter to prey as *c.* 25 m, it may be that opponents are further apart in open warfare, but rarely so in raids and ambushes. Hence, we shall take it that the same technical qualities in arrowheads apply to warfare as to hunting.

Balkan points fall into two general classes: those objects which can be clearly identified as arrowheads, and those objects whose form matches arrow armatures in the Fischer typology. The bifacial pressure-flaked arrowheads of the Copper Age can be distinguished from spear-points by size. Although the critical variable is weight (<10 g for a well-balanced arrowhead), this information is rarely given. For the less specific stone artefacts, a close match to one of the twenty-five types defined by Fischer has been considered important for the identification of an armature. Fischer also details evidence for arrowhead use as both macro- and micro-scars and wear traces (Fischer 1989). The comparison of the macro-scars with published drawings indicates the same finding as Fischer (1989) – a high proportion of Danish Mesolithic arrowheads had not (yet) been used.

Bone points

The use of bone projectile points is attested throughout the Balkan Neolithic and Copper Age. This object category is one of the few directly associated with skeletons of those who came to a violent end (see above, p. 106), so its status as a Tool-Weapon is not in doubt. A recent comprehensive study of bone projectile points considered the Mesolithic finds from the Volga basin (Zhilin 1998). Zhilin observes that 'compared with flint arrowheads from the same sites, bone ones display a much wider range of specialised types' (Zhilin 1998, 173).

Hafted bone and antler axes

Hafted bone or antler artefacts are also common throughout the Balkan Neolithic and Copper Age. Their varied morphology and size makes them a complex data set to evaluate, since different kinds of weapons require different technical features. For instance, a hafted bone or antler club requires the weight and balance for optimal impact, while a 'battle-axe' requires, in addition, a sharp cutting edge. Hence, two kinds of shaft-hole bone and antler tools have been identified: a generalised axe, which acts as a club, and a more specialised battle-axe with a sharp point. The alternative uses of such heavy-duty objects are related more to cultivation than to hunting, with the use of antler picks and axes for breaking the sod and creating a tilth. The expectation is that the intensification of farming will lead to an increase in the incidence of heavy-duty antler Tool-Weapons.

Fired-clay sling-shots and balls

One of the major differences between the Neolithic of the Near East and Anatolia and that of the Balkans is that the principal weapon in hunting and in war in the former was the sling-shot, while this artefact is rare in the latter (Korfmann 1972). This weapon is also found in the Aegean Neolithic (although rarely: Renfrew 1972, 366) and in the Early Bronze Age at Panormos on Naxos (Renfrew 1972, 392), while stone sling-shots also occur in the Portuguese Copper Age, at the defended site of Castro de Santiago (S. Monks, personal communication). The function of that possibly related development – the fired-clay ball – has been disputed. I have maintained the likelihood that these balls were sling-shots, and that the large numbers found at certain late Vinča settlements indicated stockpiling of weapons for the defence of the village (Chapman 1981, 65–6). More recently, in the Selevac report, Tringham & Stevanović (1990, 336–8) maintain that the balls were most often found near ovens, and that they were temperature-testers for baking rather than weights, toys, pot-boilers or sling-shots. I find it hard to accept that as many as 300 temperature-testers were required at a site such as Jablanica (Vasić 1902), even if round-the-clock baking was the norm! Again, I do not wish to rule out other functions for fired clay balls, but rather see here another example of previously unacknowledged functional complementarity: a Tool-Weapon. The similar size of fired-clay and ground-stone balls is also an indication of at least the potential for violent usage.

Polished stone axes, batons, mace-heads and sceptres

The evidence from Ofnet and Talheim for the use of LBK shoe-last axes to deliver fatal blows to the head (see above, p. 105) is compelling enough to raise the possibility that one of the functions of Balkan Neolithic and Copper Age stone axes was the same. With the exception of miniature trapezoidal axes, almost any medium-sized or large axe, perforated or not, could be a Tool-Weapon. It cannot be excluded that one of the reasons for the high status of axes with little or no apparent use-wear was their function for despatching enemies. But the ubiquity of the stone axe, perforated or not, in Neolithic and Copper Age contexts decreases its value as a discriminating indicator of warfare. The same is hardly true of the baton, the macehead or the sceptre, all of which are confined to specific times and places. However, the possibility that hoards of Neolithic polished stone axes represent not only communal wealth but also caches of weapons in readiness for raiding or warfare opens up new interpretational possibilities (Chapman, forthcoming).

The *locus classicus* of polished stone batons is the Mesolithic of the Iron Gates gorge, where a concentration was deposited at Lepenski Vir I–II. Srejović (1969, 152) identifies the function of a fish-stunner – a function supported by Nandris (1968) with the use of ethnographic evidence – but agrees that the batons would be equally effective as clubs. In the latter case, could the tally marks found on several batons (Srejović & Babović 1984, kat. 99, with 9 marks; kat. 103, with 15 and 18 respectively) relate to the number of human victims, rather than the number of carp stunned?

The polished stone macehead occurs infrequently in the Later Neolithic and Copper Age, generally in contexts of structured deposition. The absence of heavy use-wear and the generally fine finish argue for the attribute of prestige, which may well have been gained through combat use, as the name implies. The well-balanced symmetry and small but dense stone could readily have supplied the *coup de grâce* to an enemy brought down by an arrow. Many of the same traits are found in the so-called zoomorphic sceptres, which are characteristic of the climax and post-climax Copper Age of the east Balkans (Lichardus 1988). The representational aspect – often said to be a horse, but with no good reason – adds the symbolic power of the animal kingdom to a potentially deadly Tool-Weapon. Indeed, it may be queried whether there were ever peaceful uses for these two object categories. If this is not so, we may tentatively identify some of the earliest specialised weapons in Balkan prehistory. But a more cautious step is to identify this category as a Weapon-Tool, to signify the shifting balance of functional probability.

Heavy copper objects

The advent of heavy cast copper objects in the Balkans followed a long sequence of copper usage which lasted over a millennium. Indeed, the presence of shaft-hole copper axes and axe-adzes was a primary reason for Renfrew to propose the autonomy of the Balkan Copper Age (Renfrew 1969). Although he noted morphological parallels between copper and stone shaft-hole axes, Renfrew did not proceed to discuss a military function for the copper objects. Bognár-Kutzian (1972, 139) characterises the Lucska type of shaft-hole copper axe-adze as 'objects of a rather universal use, suitable for being used as weapons, for tree-felling or wood-working'. Patay (1984, 18–20) has usefully summarised the problem of the function of heavy-duty copper axes by proposing three potential uses: as tools, as weapons or as status objects. Patay recognises that particular types (e.g., the Mezőkeresztes axe) were used for mining, whereas others, by dint of the heavy wear on the cutting edges and the frequent breaks across the shaft-hole, were used for felling and heavy woodworking. But he acknowledges that in the Copper Age, weapons were not separated by function from tools, and hence most copper tools, with the possible exception of chisels, could have been used as weapons. This insight clearly encapsulates the notion of the Tool-Weapon, as it applies to many forms of heavy copper axe. Žeravica (1993) suggests that two specific axe types – the Banyabik and the Kožarac types – are particularly suitable as weapons, hence their designation as Weapon-Tools. As with stone axes, heavy copper axes are often found in hoards, many of which are located in remote, upland areas (Chapman, forthcoming). It is difficult to provide an explanation for these upland hoards of one, two or three copper axes – the notion of a cache of weapons is hard to better at present.

Stone and copper daggers

The final object categories to be considered here are the daggers of flaked stone and copper. While there are no flint copies of the Únětice daggers as known in northern Europe, the tendency to produce long flint blades, especially from one of the many varieties of 'pre-Balkan' flint or Volhynian raw material, led to the possibility of offensive use of long, pointed blades. Since a sharp cutting edge is of use in many circumstances, it is likely that the flint knife should be regarded as a Tool-Weapon. However, it is harder to imagine (yet not impossible!) a copper dagger used for cutting leather or reeds, or whittling wood. Thus, it is risky to claim outright weapon status for the copper daggers of the fourth millennium BC (Vajsov 1993), but it is more reasonable to call them Weapon-Tools.

In summary, it is possible to distinguish four general classes of object categories: tools, Tool-Weapons, Weapon-Tools and weapons. While it may be difficult in specific instances to place an object category in one or other of these broad classes, a case can be made for the utility of the general classes in terms of the widespread functional complementarity which went hand in hand with artefact specialisation in later Balkan prehistory. The final section of this chapter will apply this scheme to the artefacts of the Mesolithic, Neolithic and Copper Age of Central and Eastern Europe, attempting to integrate the findings with the evidence for defences and the intensity of social interaction which, as we have seen, is such an important factor in the incidence of warfare. The artefact data will be organised, wherever possible, at the site level, and otherwise on the regional level. In most cases, published site data are insufficient to allow quantification of numbers of artefacts, so a qualitative analysis is used to define variations in the frequency of artefact categories.

WARFARE IN LATER BALKAN PREHISTORY

The Iron Gates Gorge: Mesolithic and Early Neolithic

The only context in the Balkans where it is possible to examine the long-term sequence from Mesolithic to the Early Neolithic is the Iron Gates Gorge. The basis of the analysis is the excellent recent review of the Gorge by Ivana Radovanović (1996), in which she presents her re-analysis of the primary excavation archive of Lepenski Vir, Padina and Vlasac (for revised chronology, see Radovanović 1996, 252). Since there is no evidence for defences on any Mesolithic site, the artefactual evidence is primary. It should be recalled that while economic intensification is attested in the Djerdap Late Mesolithic, a purely foraging subsistence strategy with minimal import of beef, mutton and maybe cereals is maintained until the onset of the Middle Neolithic (Chapman 1989). We can therefore expect a strong emphasis on hunting weapons as well as plant-processing tools, both in the lithic assemblages and the bone and antler inventories.

The evidence from the lithic assemblages of the Djerdap Mesolithic is equivocal. Rather small numbers of armature types are known from sites such as Padina A, where general parallels to Fischer's Types H and T are known (Radovanović 1981, T. VIII/1–5 & 31), and Lepenski Vir, where trapezes show general similarities to Type T (Kozłowski & Kozłowski 1983, Pl. 4/6–7).

The picture is very different in the bone and antler inventories, where considerable diversification is attested (cf. the Volga Mesolithic, Zhilin 1998). Eight assemblages are sufficiently large for statistical analysis (in chronological order): Padina A (Early Mesolithic, 157), Icoana (401), Ostrovul Banului III (140), Vlasac I (281), Vlasac II (754), Vlasac III (648), Schela Cladovei (>107) and Padina B (Early Neolithic, 85). Radovanović (1996) identifies thirty-three types of bone and antler artefact in the Gorge, one of which (bone projectiles/arrowheads) is sub-divided into seven sub-types. Fully 15 out of the total of 39 categories can be identified as Tool-Weapons. This total is remarkably high, even if the majority of them were used in peaceful contexts only (Table 2). The frequencies of the Tool-Weapons by site are presented in Tables 3–5.

Table 2 Types of Tool-Weapon in the Iron Gates Gorge

Artefact Class	No. of types/sub-types	No. and type of Tool-Weapons
Flat bone tools	6	1 (knife)
Pointed bone tools	4/7	2/7 (needle; 7 sub-types of arrow)
Pointed antler tools	3	2 (dagger; projectile point)
Cylindrical pointed tools	4	1 (axe)
Perforated antler tools	2	1 (pick)
Barbed antler tools	5	–
Animal teeth	9	2 (point; projectile)

Source: Radovanović (1996)

Table 3 Frequencies of Tool-Weapons by type at eight Iron Gates sites

	1	2	3a	3b	3c	3d	3e	3f	3g	4	5	6	7	8	9
Padina A		53	4				1	14	2	10		1		2	
Icoana		52	6	3	1	2						3	15	1	2
O. Banului		28			4							2	4	2	
Vlasac I	2	33	14					1		4		5	8		
Vlasac II	15	121	47					7	4	18	10	12			
Vlasac III	11	83	41					3		4	16	2	5		
S. Cladovei		26	2	4	1	3	13					1	1		
Padina B		37	4						1			2			

Key: 1, bone knife; 2, bone needle; 3a–3g, bone arrowhead sub-types; 4, antler dagger; 5, antler arrowhead; 6, antler axe; 7, antler pick; 8, tusk point; 9, tooth arrowhead.

Table 4 Relative and absolute frequencies of Tool-Weapons (TWs) at eight Iron Gates sites

	No. of TW types	% of all types	Total No. of TWs	% of all tools
Padina A	8	32	87	55
Icoana	9	36	85	21
O. Banului	5	28	40	29
Vlasac I	7	30	67	24
Vlasac II	8	31	234	31
Vlasac III	7	27	165	25
S. Cladovei	7	47	48	45
Padina B	5	38	44	52

Table 5 Relative and absolute frequencies of Tool-Weapons by raw material at eight Iron Gates sites

	BONE		ANTLER*		BONE		ANTLER*	
	No. of types	*% of types*	*No. of types*	*% of types*	*No. of items*	*% of assemb.*	*No. of items*	*% of assemb.*
Padina A	5	45	3	21	74	70	13	25
Icoana	5	50	4	27	64	58	21	7
O. Banului	2	40	3	23	32	57	8	10
Vlasac I	4	36	3	25	50	54	17	9
Vlasac II	4	36	4	27	190	67	44	9
Vlasac III	3	30	4	25	138	57	27	7
S. Cladovei	5	63	2	29	46	96	2	3
Padina B	3	50	2	29	42	84	2	6

* Includes tusk and teeth

These data indicate that a high proportion of all bone and antler artefacts can be classed as Tool-Weapons. There may be a trend towards increasing frequencies of Tool-Weapons with time, but this trend may reflect the small sample sizes of the Schela Cladovei and Padina B assemblages. The high frequency of Tool-Weapons is true more of bone than of antler; with the former, over half of all bone artefacts can be classified as Tool-Weapons, although this rarely reaches 10 per cent with the latter. While there can be no doubt that many individual artefacts were used for hunting animals, it is scarcely possible to discount the manufacture of all the projectile points as never having a military goal. This is reinforced by the polished stone batons, found in higher frequencies at Lepenski Vir than at Vlasac III or Hajdučka Vodenica. However, the same is not found in the armature-poor lithic assemblages, in which the Djerdap assemblages are similar to the Mesolithic levels of Montenegran sites such as Medena Stijena and Odmut (Srejović 1989), where projectiles comparable to the range of Fischer's Types E, T are known. The absence of tanged points for ease of hafting distinguishes the Balkan assemblages from those of northern Europe, but does not diminish the significance of lithic projectile points for potential warfare.

These data indicate that Mesolithic communities were potentially well-armed, with Tool-Weapons for attack at a distance (bone-tipped arrows) and for hand-to-hand combat (stone, bone and antler clubs) (Fig. 1). The social context for the military use of the Djerdap Mesolithic and Early Neolithic Tool-Weapons is the intense social interaction between two groups of genetically unrelated communities. Even if the incursions of new farmers were accomplished through small-scale population movements, the potential frontiers for conflict would have been considerable. In previous essays, the author has attempted to diagnose the exchange interactions and ideological power struggles between foragers in the gorge and early farmers at either end of the gorge (Chapman 1989, 1993). There is no doubt that

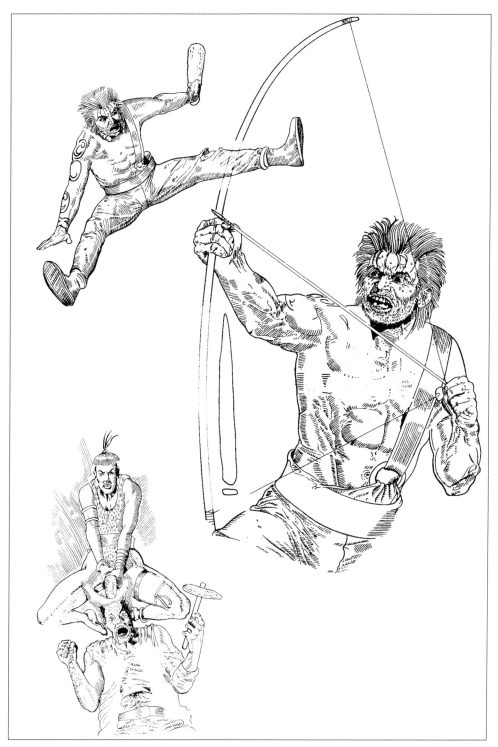

Fig. 1. Mesolithic weaponry in action. Top left: antler pick (Vlasac); right: bone projectile point (Schela Cladovei); bottom left: antler axe (Vlasac).

exchange interactions were intensifying in the latest Mesolithic, and the C-13 isotope evidence from Lepenski Vir could be interpreted as signifying marriage exchange of farmers into foraging sites there (Bonsall et al. 1997). Thus, there may have been only a short period, perhaps of one or two generations, in which there were no genetic links between foragers and farmers, and it was during this period that warlike interactions were initiated. Later, once kinship links and exchange relations were better established, the severity of inter-group warfare may well have diminished, although its frequency may well have increased.

It is very noticeable that in comparison with the Iron Gates Mesolithic, the frequency of Tool-Weapons among the earliest farming villages of the Balkan Peninsula is rather low. There are only seven sites from which qualitative data are available (Table 6).

Table 6 Presence of Tool-Weapon categories and defences from early farming villages

	1	2	3	4	5	6	7	8	9
Rakitovo	*	*	*	—	*	—	—	*	—
Anza	*	*	*	—	*	—	—	—	*
Ceamurlia de Jos	*	*	—	*	*	*	*	—	—
Divostin I	—	*	—	—	*	—	—	—	—
Padina B	*	*	—	—	*	*	*	*	—
Obre I	—	*	—	—	—	—	—	—	—
Gura Baciului	*	*	—	—	*	*	—	—	—

Key: 1, lithic projectile points; 2, polished stone axes; 3, sling-shots; 4, ground stone balls; 5, bone points; 6, antler points; 7, antler axe; 8, boar's tusk point; 9, defences.

Clearly, the range of Tool-Weapons is greatly reduced outside the Gorge compared to within it, and the number of Tool-Weapons on any given site is rather small. A good example is the upland Bosnian settlement of Obre I, where large-scale excavations yielded the polished stone axe as the only Tool-Weapon. The large lithic assemblage boasted not a single projectile point, although the faunal assemblage contained c. 30 per cent (by bone numbers) wild mammals (Bökönyi 1988, table 17.9). Even in Djerdap sites such as Cuina Turcului III, the only possible armature was the trapeze (Paunescu 1987, figs 2/1–3, 6–8, 11–16, 20; 4/1, 12, 20; 5/1, 13). By comparison, bone points were the only projectiles found at the lowland Serbian settlement of Divostin I, where wild mammals accounted for 8 per cent (by bone numbers: 13 per cent by minimum numbers of individuals) of the fauna (Bökönyi 1988, 430). Two hypotheses are suggested: first, that the decline in hunting, which appears to have been both an absolute and a relative process in the First Temperate Neolithic, was responsible for the narrow range of Early Neolithic Tool-Weapons, especially projectile points; and second, that the genetically related early farmers, who maintained social networks over the whole of the Balkans, minimised violent interactions during this period, thus reducing the need for weaponry.

It may appear that the first alternative is favoured by the increasing discovery of defensive ditches in what can be defined as the earliest local farmers in any particular region. Enclosure ditches are now known or claimed from ten of the earliest farming settlements: Schela Cladovei, Anza, Porodin, Asmaška Mogila, Kazanluk, Cărcea-Viaduct, Gornea, Ostrovul Banului and Goljamo Delchevo I (Höckmann 1990; Lazarovici 1990). In addition, a ditch and palisade is claimed from Samovodene in north Bulgaria (Stanev 1982). All the ditches are simple U- or V-shaped affairs, and none of them has been excavated for more than 40 m in length (the longest exposure is at Goljamo Delchevo I: Todorova 1975, Obr. 3). Thus, these 'defences' are the simplest possible barriers, which may or may not have enclosed the whole settlement. None the less, the increased rate of discovery, along with the expansion in aerial photography in central and eastern Europe makes it unwise to dismiss this line of evidence, even in the earliest farming period. There is no question of shortages of land or resources in the First Temperate Neolithic, rather, the possibilities that failures in the relatively non-intensive exchange relations current in the First Temperate Neolithic may have led to small-scale but frequent warfare. Nonetheless, the negative evidence of an absence of skeletal trauma in all the three collective burials so far identified in the First Temperate Neolithic (Vinča, Ajmana and Velesnica) means that the massacres identified at Talheim and Ofnet have not yet been documented in the First Temperate Neolithic.

Mature farmers in the later Neolithic

As mixed farming became more widely established in a landscape of increasingly sedentary village and hamlet communities, socio-cultural differentiation can be seen in the later Neolithic period. This begins with arenas of social power, in which the mortuary domain begins to diversify alongside an already elaborated domestic domain (Chapman 1991; 1995). The range of object categories increases, whether in figurines, ceramic forms and decoration, or tools. There is an increase in the quantity of exotic objects, which are often exchanged over longer distances than before (e.g., the Vinča group: Chapman 1981). The number and size of sites increase in many regions of central and eastern Europe, suggesting local population growth, infilling of the lowland landscapes, and increased colonisation of the uplands. These trends are coeval with the diversification of military structures and Tool-Weapon artefact categories, and conceivably, the beginning of Weapon-Tools.

The incidence of defensive structures on sites increases at the same time as their elaboration. The four classic techniques for defending a settlement in later prehistory are all present: ditches, banks, palisades and stone walls. Simple ditches have been observed at flat sites such as Jakovo-Kormadin, Bicske, Radovanu and Liubcova-Orniţa, across the neck of promontory sites such as Traian, and around the base of tells such as Poljanica, Parţa-Tell I, Vădastra II, Boian-Spanţov and Glina (Höckmann 1990; Lazarovici 1990). The ditch at Traian has been observed over a length of 300 m. The Pre-Cucuteni village at Târpeşti was defended by a double ditch separated by 20 m. A complex defensive system of a ditch and three palisades was in operation at the flat site of Iclod, on the first terrace of the river Someş (Lazarovici 1976; 1990). The ditch and palisade enclosed phase Iclod I, the ditch and second palisade surrounded Iclod I/II and II, and the third palisade defended Iclod II/III or III. In addition, traces of a stone wall dating to Karanovo V have been discovered at the eponymous site (Lazarovici 1990, 113).

The tells of Goljamo Delchevo, Poljanica and Ovcharovo are well-known for the complexities of their defensive systems (Todorova 1982). In the Early–Middle Chalcolithic phases, especially at Ovcharovo, the variation in modes of defence is such that deliberate experimentation is consistent with a response to changed conditions of military practice (Table 7).

Table 7 Variations in mode of defence at two NE Bulgarian tells

Ovcharovo:

Level	Mode of defence
I	triple bank + 2 ditches + palisade
II	double bank + palisade
III	house built over banks & palisade (!)
IV–VI	4 m-wide single ditch
VII	narrow interrupted ditch

Goljamo Delchevo:

Level	Mode of defence
II	2–3 palisades
III	single bank & ditch
IV	single bank & ditch

The Ovcharovo sequence suggests a decrease in defensive capability as time passes – a pattern interpreted by Bailey (1997, 47–8) as supporting the view that flood waters from the adjacent valley were a greater threat in the earliest phases of occupation, a threat which receded as the tell living space rose higher. It is curious that Bailey fails to observe that a similar military pattern may hold – the earliest occupants of a settlement overlooked to the south by high mountains would have been most insecure until their residential choice had been accepted by their neighbours, and as the tell rose, massive defensive structures may have been less vital. The floodwaters in the ditches of Ovcharovo I would have formed a moat – an even better defence than dry ditches. Is this another case of unacknowledged complementarity?

The same problem arises over a whole class of settlements enclosed by a ditch: the 'obrovci' of Serbian Posavina. These settlements have the highest incidence of ditched enclosures known in the Vinča group (Chapman 1981), although the diversity of their material culture is markedly lower, to judge by the excavations so far (Trbuhović & Vasiljević 1973/4). It is therefore difficult to evaluate the claim (echoed by Höckmann 1990) that the obrovci are defended sites. An alternative interpretation is that the obrovcidwellers enclosed their sites against the floods of the Drina, only to realise that their moated sites (cf. Ovcharovo I) provided a valuable defensive potential against local raiding.

In summary, there is some evidence during the mature Neolithic for an intensification of settlement defence, related to the trend towards increased sedentarism found in many regions (Tringham & Krstić 1990). However, as the discussions of Ovcharovo and the Vinča *obrovci* show, the function of banks, ditches, palisades (and even stone walls) at any specific site is no less ambiguous than that of artefacts. The general pattern does, however, support moves towards strengthened defences as compared to the earliest farming settlements. This may indicate an increase in fighting, but the trend may also be explained by a new type of warfare tactics related to a greater degree of sedentarism (S. Monks, personal communication). Does this pattern hold true of the artefacts?

The trend in most regions in the mature farming period is one of marked differentiation in all aspects of material culture. Part of this pattern is the diversification of Tool-Weapons and the appearance of the first Weapon-Tool: the polished stone mace-head. The total number of Tool-Weapons more than doubles in comparison with the early farming period (Table 8).

This series of Tool-Weapons and a single Weapon-Tool incorporates all the nine categories of Tool-Weapon used by the earliest farmers, as well as including five categories similar to those used by the Iron Gates foragers (stone batons, bone arrowheads, bone daggers, antler axes and antler picks). The 'new' Tool-Weapons and Weapon-Tools in this period include the perforated stone axe and hammer-axe, which developed in many areas out of the stone axe. The latter is one of the very rare Tool-Weapons represented in miniature form in the figurine record, at Szegvár-Tüzkoves (see above, p. 106). A related form is the bone axe-adze, which is morphologically related to the polished stone form, at least at sites such as Divostin (Lyneis 1988). Two further innovations were the long spear-point and the bifacial pressure-flaked projectile point, both of which evolved from other forms of projectile point in the East Balkans. Comşa (1987; 1991) identifies the earliest known bifacial arrowheads in the Boian-Gumelniţa transitional period. While this form becomes the standard form of armature in the East Balkan climax Copper Age, it is important to note that there is considerable experimentation with armature design in the mature farming period, with three forms of Vinča arrowhead – tanged, barbed-and-tanged and hollow-based (Chapman 1981) – and as many as nine other types in Romania (Fischer Types H, M, Q, S, T and V, illustrated in Paunescu 1970, figs 23–8).

The significant development of the first Weapon-Tool – the polished stone mace-head – is made in several regions, from north-east Bulgaria to Bosnia. The earliest known mace-head, made of fired clay, was found in the Vinča-A levels at Gornea, and is identical in size to the later Vinča polished stone examples known from Potporanj and the Botoš cemetery (Chapman 1981, 71). The transposition of form in one raw material to design in another, more appropriate to offensive purposes, using polishing techniques perfected on small ornaments, indicates a specialist product whose high status is not just related to its use.

Table 8 The distribution of Tool-Weapons and Weapon-Tools at selected mature farming sites, in relation to defences

Site	1	2	3	4	5	6	7	8	9	10	11	12	13	14	15	16	17	18	19
Divostin	—	—	—	x	x	x	—	—	x	—	—	x	x	x	x	x	—	x	—
Selevac	—	x	—	x	x	x	—	—	x	—	x	—	—	x	x	x	x	—	—
Obre II	x	x	—	x	x	—	—	—	x	—	x	—	—	x	—	—	—	—	—
Danilo	x	x	—	x	x	x	x	x	—	—	—	—	—	—	—	—	—	—	x
Radovanu	x	—	—	x	x	—	—	—	x	—	—	—	x	—	—	—	—	—	x
Târpeşti	—	—	—	x	x	—	x	—	x	—	—	—	—	—	—	—	—	—	—
Kökenydomb	—	—	—	x	x	—	—	—	x	—	—	—	—	—	—	—	—	—	—
Čoka	—	—	—	—	—	—	—	—	—	—	—	—	—	—	—	—	—	—	—
G.Delchevo II–IV	x	x	—	x	x	x	—	—	x	—	—	—	—	x	x	x	—	x	x
Ovcharovo I–IV	x	—	x	x	—	—	—	—	x	x	—	x	—	x	—	x	—	—	x
Ovcharovo V–VII	x	—	x	x	x	—	x	—	x	—	—	x	—	x	—	x	—	—	x

Key:

Tool-Weapons:
1. bifacial stone point
2. other stone projectile point
3. stone spear-point
4. polished stone axe
5. perforated polished stone axe
6. stone balls/pounders
7. polished stone hammer-axe
8. polished stone baton
9. bone point
10. bone arrowhead
11. bone dagger
12. boar's tusk point
13. bone axe-adze
14. antler axe
15. antler point
16. antler hammers/picks
17. fired-clay slingshots.
Weapon-Tools:
18. polished stone mace-head
19. Defences.

There are two sites with detailed information on Tool-Weapons whose occupations span the earliest mature farming period: Divostin and Obre. In each case, there is a major increase in Tool-Weapon categories (Obre I, II from one to eight categories; Divostin I, II from two to ten categories). The level of hunting of wild mammals remains stable in Obre I and II (Bökönyi 1988, 430), while the incidence of hunting almost doubles at Divostin. A second factor is the intensification of cultivation found at both sites, which may well have had an effect on the number of heavy bone and antler Tool-Weapons at Divostin. However, the significant increase in bone points and daggers at Obre II, together with the innovation of the mace-head and the stable hunting strategy, supports an interpretation of increased military potential.

Since there are no sites in the mature farming period with sufficiently detailed accounts to compare actual numbers of Tool-Weapons across the full range of categories, the final analysis will focus on the absolute and relative frequencies of Tool-Weapon categories compared with all categories of bone, antler, lithic and polished stone artefacts. Five units are analysed: three from two defended sites (Ovcharovo and Goljamo Delchevo), and two from undefended sites (Divostin and Selevac) (Table 9).

Table 9 Absolute and relative frequencies of Tool-Weapon categories at selected mature farming sites

Site	Bone		Antler		Lithic		Polished Stone		Total	
	No. of types	% all types	No. of types	% all types	No. of types	% all types	No. of types	% all types	No. of types	% all types
Ovcharovo I–IV	2	50	2	25	2	10	2	25	8	20
Ovcharovo V–VII	—	—	3	38	2	10	3	33	8	20
G. Delchevo II–IV	1	17	3	60	2	18	4	44	10	32
Selevac	2	8	5	42	2	13	3	16	12	17
Divostin II	2	17	3	13	—	—	4	50	9	17

These data show a major increase in the frequency of Tool-Weapons over the earliest farming settlements, while rarely approaching the relative frequency and diversity of the Tool-Weapons in the Djerdap Mesolithic, where Tool-Weapon categories reached 27–47 per cent of all types. However, it should be emphasised that the site with the highest overall frequency of Tool-Weapon categories, Goljamo Delchevo, derives from one of the occupations with the highest incidence of wild mammal hunting, 44 per cent (by both bone numbers and minimum numbers: Ivanov & Vasilev 1975). However, the evidence for mixed farming at Delchevo is also unequivocal in this period (see also Hopf 1975), so the question of the relationship between hunting and warfare may be rephrased: at what point does the significance of status through successful warfare become reinforced by success in the hunt against large and dangerous wild mammals? It should be noted that body parts of species such as the lion, the lynx, the brown bear and the wolf are all represented in the faunal remains at Early Copper Age Delchevo, as well as the more frequent wild boar, red deer and aurochs. At Ovcharovo, the Early Copper Age hunting patterns accounted for

30 per cent (by bone numbers and minimum numbers) of the fauna, with occasional taking of lynx, another big cat, the brown bear, wolf and aurochs (Vasilev 1985, 32). But hunting is far more significant in the Middle Copper Age, where 44 per cent (bone numbers: cf. 39 per cent by minimum numbers) of the fauna derived from the same suite of wild animals (Vasilev 1985, 46). It is interesting that the proportion of Tool-Weapons remains the same in both Early and Middle Chalcolithic levels at Ovcharovo, indicating continuity in hunting as much as in potentially offensive weapons.

Contrary to the notion that hunting pre-adapted humans to warfare, it seems plausible that in certain social contexts, the forms of adult male status achieved in warfare would be reinforced by successes in the hunt which demonstrated key aspects of character, skill, strength, tenacity and bravery.[1] Those contexts may include interactions with an important component of feasting, as well as frontier settlements where a buffer zone between site and environs may be rich in wild mammals. In this sense, an important innovation is the spearpoint, useful only in close combat, in self-defence against a felid's attack, or to finish off a wounded prey or enemy.

In summary, there is a compelling range of evidence for aggressive and defensive potential in the mature farming period. The frequency with which this potential was actualised in warfare remains uncertain, however. Nevertheless, the high levels of categories of Tool-Weapon, the development of the first Weapon-Tools and the increased variety of settlement defences combine to support the proposition that increased sedentism and higher levels of warfare went hand in hand in this period (Figs 2–3). Two other important developments concern exchange and settlement expansion. The evidence for intensification of exchange is constituted by a wider range of objects and raw materials, an increased volume of exchange and the movement of artefacts over longer distances (Chapman, forthcoming; Bíró 1988; Sherratt 1987). Keeley's (1996, 126) proposal that exotic goods may reach a site as a result of warfare as well as through exchange is intriguing, if untestable. The exploitation of a wider range of resources, combined with increased sedentism, leads to the existence of increasing numbers of localised raw material sources which lie within the economic territories of permanent settlements, if not necessarily under their direct and permanent control. A good example is the high-level, possibly seasonal settlement of the Zemplén Mountains in north-east Hungary to monitor and exploit the rich lithic resources of the uplands (Chapman & Laszlovszky 1994). Keeley's (1996: 123) identification of one of the most frequent causes of warfare as the armed struggle for salt and hard rock whose sources are located in a group's exclusive territory is directly relevant to central and eastern Europe, that mosaic of upland and lowland areas, in which the latter are often devoid of such sources, and the former tend to be very rich indeed (Sherratt 1976). The variability in raw material sources is also related to the lowland settlement infilling as much as the expansion of the settlement area into increasingly upland areas, which has the potential for two kinds of violent interaction, warfare against local upland foragers, and struggles between different farming groups, some of whom are primary settlers and others are recent arrivals. While long-distance invasions can never be entirely ruled out in the prehistoric period (Chapman & Hamerow 1996), the strong continuity in forms of defence and Tool-Weapon categories between the earliest and the later farmers would support the notion of

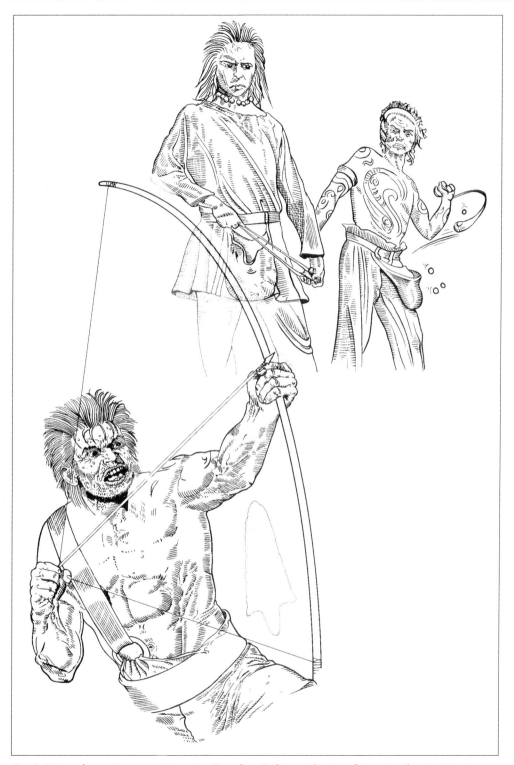

Fig. 2. Mature farmers' weaponry in action. Top: sling (Rakitovo); bottom: flint projectile point (Anza).

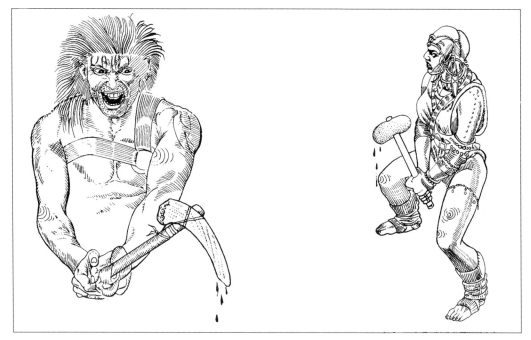

Fig. 3. Mature farmers' weaponry in action. Left: antler hammer (Divostin); right: polished stone mace-head (Goljamo Delchevo).

minimal population displacement. This means that frontier warfare would probably have been limited to upland-lowland border areas, while the main causes of warfare would have been resource competition between neighbouring groups, often with a long tradition of exchange and kin alliances, but where the breakdown of peaceful relations leads directly to warfare.

Climax Copper Age societies

An important part of the differentiation and growth of material culture in the climax societies of the Balkan Copper Age is the continuing upsurge in defensive structures, as well as offensive Tool-Weapons and Weapon-Tools. The issue in question is whether these developments were stimulated by, or a reaction to, Gimbutas's north Pontic invaders, or whether these developments were sufficiently widespread and closely linked to earlier Tool-Weapon traditions to be considered as indigenous to the Balkans. If the latter, it is a serious blow to Gimbutas's hypothesis of a peaceful, woman-creatress-dominated Old Europe rigidly opposed to the warlike Indo-European male invaders.

The only north Pontic candidate coeval with the Balkan Copper Age climax societies is the Sredni Stog group of the Dniepr, Donets and Oskol valleys (Telegin 1973). This group is characterised by small communities living for the most part in villages and practising intramural burial in oval pit-graves not under barrows. The early phase of the Sredni Stog group is dated by radiocarbon to 4,400 – 3,700 calibrated – BC, with later sites dated as late as 3,300 calibrated BC (Mallory 1977, 348–57). There is strong evidence for the exchange of pottery between Cucuteni-Tripolye and Sredni Stog communities (Mallory 1989; Ellis 1984; Anthony 1986). All other north Pontic groups practising barrow burial are dated post-3,000 calibrated BC.

In addition to the intensification of previous trends, four new military developments characterise Copper Age climax societies: the production of the first metal Tool-Weapons, Weapon-Tools and weapons; the widespread diffusion of two Weapon-Tools identifiable as the earliest standardised Weapon-Tools; the imitation of Tool-Weapons and Weapon-Tools made of higher-status materials in lower-status materials, and the inclusion of Tool-Weapons and Weapon-Tools in the mortuary domain. While not in themselves certain indications of heavily militarised societies, these developments, in combination with other trends, suggest that climax societies had reached a military as well as a ritual climax.

The emergence of copper metallurgy can be dated to the earliest farming period, but the earliest objects capable of use as Tool-Weapons or Weapon-Tools date to the climax Copper Age, when heavy cast copper axes, hammer-axes and axe-adzes were manufactured. Given the strong probability that stone, bone and antler shaft-hole Tool-Weapons were used in battle, it is inconceivable that objects of similar form made in a heavier, more deadly material would not have been used in warfare. The *Prähistorische Bronzefunde* volumes on copper axes (Patay 1984; Todorova 1981; Žeravica 1993; Vulpe 1975) indicate that most groups from the late fifth Millennium calibrated BC onwards had access to plentiful copper sources, and used them to manufacture heavy Tool-Weapons and Weapon-Tools. This new material must have made a significant difference in arming warriors for hand-to-hand combat. The same is true for copper daggers, found first in Cucuteni AB – Ariuşd settlements such as Mastacari and Ariuşd, dated 4,200 – 3,800 calibrated – BC, and the Tiszapolgár cemetery of Vel'ké Raskovce, dated *c.* 4,000 calibrated BC, as well as in the later Tripolye C1 settlements and cemeteries (Vajsov 1993). It is important to note that no copper daggers are yet known from the Sredni Stog group, whose only known use of copper is for ornaments.

Appearing in the Boian-Gumelniţa transitional phase, the pressure-flaked bifacial arrowhead rapidly became the preferred armature in the East Balkans and in parts of the West Balkans. Its three main qualities – the symmetrical form for precise direction, the thin cross-section for maximum penetration, and the size, heavy enough to penetrate deeply into the flesh, but harder to propel in flight – combined to produce a successful Weapon-Tool widely found in the Cucuteni-Tripolje-Ariuşd group and the Karanovo VI group, as well as in the Salcuţa, Tiszapolgár and Lengyel groups. The bifacial point is also widespread in the Sredni Stog group. The related but larger form – the pressure-flaked bifacial spear point – represents the extension of the principles of the armature into face-to-face fighting. The relatively rapid diffusion of pressure-flaked arrowheads over most of the East Balkans is comparable to the rapid spread of similar arrowheads in the Iberian Copper Age (Monks 1997). The increasing use of in-depth defences with two or more concentric lines of fortification (see below, pp. 133–4) may well be linked to the efficacy of this new Weapon-Tool.

The imitation of copper Weapon-Tools and Tool-Weapons in bone, antler and stone is an indication of the process of skeuomorphism characteristic of societies with incipient status differentiation, where higher-status warriors have the use of copper forms, while lower-status warriors produce imitations in more available materials. Examples are the imitations in bone, the polished stone mace-head, and the flint or copper spearpoint. The appearance in climax societies of particular forms of stone, bone and antler battle-axes may be interpreted as a process of differentiation from a previously existing series of Tool-Weapons, but the influence of new copper forms may well have been decisive. This development may indicate that weaponry had assumed a stronger symbolic significance.

The final innovation is the deposition of weapons, Weapon-Tools and Tool-Weapons in the emergent mortuary domain. While relatively few cemeteries have been identified in mature farming contexts, their frequency rises in most climax societies, (Chapman 1983). One of the key new patterns of structured deposition was the inclusion of gold and copper objects in selected graves, whether inhumations or cenotaphs (graves without a skeleton). The salient Copper Age example is the Varna I cemetery, where a small percentage of graves contained large numbers and a great diversity of gold and copper objects (Ivanov 1991). Few commentators have emphasised the potential significance of the inclusion of Tool-Weapons and Weapon-Tools in this new arena of social power. If warrior prowess is associated with high male status, its expanded representation in the mortuary domain marks a statement by adult males about the basis of their social power and the importance of male social power in the whole community.

Lichardus (1988) has claimed that the combination of four different kinds of copper tool – chisel, axe, adze and wedge – in Grave 36 at Varna I – indicates the grave of a high-status carpenter. An alternative may be proposed that these copper objects formed part of the weaponry of a mighty warrior. The same pattern can be identified in the rich Reka Devnja grave, where the majority of grave goods comprised Weapon-Tools, such as a set of 5 bifacial stone projectile points, 27 pointed knives, a flat copper axe and a long copper point (Mirchev 1961). Taking this insight further, however, depends upon a more systematic analysis of the mortuary domain.

An analysis of the Varna I weapons, Weapon-Tools and Tool-Weapons based upon Ivanov's (1991) publication of the core grave and selected rich outer graves indicates a wide range of combinations of potential weapons, ranging from zero in some cenotaphs to eight categories in Inhumation Grave 43 (Table 10).

The large numbers of potentially offensive weapons found in some major cenotaph graves are surprising. A moderate proportion of the objects represent Weapon-Tools, such as the copper spear points of Graves 97 and 43, which have no other function except killing humans and hunted animals. Other objects have resonances with distant Weapon-Tools, such as the perforated stone axe with gold mounts, paralleled in the Szegvar-Tüzkoves figurine with the fired clay axe. The widespread inclusion of superblades whose length is closely correlated with total grave wealth (Manolakkakis 1996) is a symbolic representation of the blades whose military use could have included scalping or stabbing – symbolic, since many are so long and curved that they had no practical use. But the sheer number of object categories with offensive potential is a clear

Table 10 Weapon, Weapon-Tool and Tool-Weapon combinations in Varna I graves

Cenotaphs	Inhumations	Object Combination
18, 06, 07, 08, 11	8, 16, 17, 20, 25, 34, 42, 48, 134, 04	No weaponry
2, 3, 15	19, 45	Flint blade
	23	Polished stone axe
	32	Copper hammer-axe
03		Flint blade + stone axe
	7	Flint blade + perforated stone axe
	13, 14	Flint blade + antler pick
5, 36	6	Flint blade + copper hammer-axe
53		Flint blade + copper axe-adze
41		Flint blade + obsidian point + bone point
40		Flint blade + curved copper axe + rectangular cross-section copper axe
1		Flint blade + copper hammer-axe + flat copper axe + round copper axe
97		Flint blade + stone axe + boars' tusk point + copper axe-adze + copper spear point
4		Flint blade + stone axe + perforated stone axe (with gold mounts) + antler pick + flat copper axe + copper hammer-axe + copper axe-adze
43		Flint blade + flint projectile point + stone axe + bone point + copper point + flat copper axe + copper axe adze + copper spear point

signal of the increased reliance on warfare for the creation of adult status – and adult male status at that. Four grades of status are apparent at Varna: those graves with no weapons; graves with a blade or an axe; graves with a blade and an axe, graves with a blade, an axe and other weapons.

The high status of 'weapon'-rich graves is corroborated by an analysis of the rank order of graves by number of 'weapons' compared to numbers of gold objects, indicating a close correlation. Spearman's rank correlation test on the fourteen grave assemblages containing both gold objects and Tool-Weapons/Weapon-Tools gave a score of 0.822, which, on a Student's t-test with twelve degrees of freedom, indicated a highly significant degree of agreement (at 0.1 per cent) between the two rankings. The Varna I graves indicate that prowess in warfare, as signified by 'weaponry', is but one way for the living to signal the male status of the newly dead in the climax Copper Age, but that it is closely related to other statements about status, including the ability to accumulate exotic prestige goods.

There is little relationship between the ages of the inhumations and their varying object combinations: youths, young adults and mature men have differing combinations, or no 'weapons' at all. But the gendered message of this sample of Varna I graves is explicit: apart from the ungenderable cenotaphs, all the core inhumations and the rich outer inhumations are identified as males, and there is not a single female in the Varna I cemetery core.

The links between 'weaponry' and males in the mortuary domain is also encountered in the Hungarian Copper Age. In a general analysis, Nevizansky (1985) identifies a major increase in the frequency and diversity of weapons in Bodrogkeresztúr graves compared to Tiszapolgár graves. J. Sofaer Derevenski (1997) shows that the weapons in the Basatanya cemetery are restricted to male graves in both periods (Period I, long blades, boars' tusk points; Period II, blades, projectile points and stone hammer-axes). It is also significant that one of the first true weapons – the copper dagger – appears first in the mortuary domain in the Middle Danube area, in the Tiszapolgár cemetery at Vel'ké Raskovce and in several Bodrogkeresztúr cemeteries (Vajsov 1993).

While it is not being suggested here that there is an absolute correlation between male gender and the presence of 'weaponry' as grave goods, there is clearly a strong tendency for the association between male burials and potential weaponry. This finding may have wider implications, since Marsh (1978, 62) has argued that once sex becomes associated with aggression and dominance, a gendered social divide is inevitable, with females as the prizes. But this contrast may not be so sharp in the Balkan Copper Age. It is important to note that in those rare cases where artefact assemblages from both the mortuary and the domestic domains are available, there is a strong distinction between 'weaponry' found in the graves and that found in the settlement. The two north-east Bulgarian instances are Goljamo Delchevo and Vinica, where small cemeteries are associated with Late Copper Age tells (Todorova et al. 1975; Raduntcheva 1976). In both cases, 'weaponry' on the tells is limited to stone, bone and antler forms, while at Vinica and Delchevo, copper Weapon-Tools occur predominantly in the graves of adult males (there are two exceptions in Vinica Graves 41 and 42, where adult females are buried with a flat copper axe: Raduntcheva 1976, 89–90 & obr. 92/2, 93/2; Chapman 1996). Rather than a notion of domains strongly differentiated along gender lines, there is a conversation expressed by both male and female statements in both domestic and mortuary arenas, with males often having more success at putting across their message of status achievement through metal 'weaponry' in the latter, and stone, bone and antler 'weaponry' in the former.

In summary, the innovations in climax Copper Age communities make the waging of war more deadly through the introduction of an improved design for armatures for long-distance attacks, and a series of metal weapons (battle-axes, daggers) and the spear point for hand-to-hand combat. These new weapons were imitated in lower-status materials such as bone, antler and stone to produce effective Tool-Weapons and Weapon-Tools. The development of the mortuary domain increased the opportunities for adult males to make statements relating male status to warfare through the use of mortuary symbolism and grave good deposition. How do these developments relate to the differentiation of the previous tradition of defensive structures and offensive weapons?

The 'weaponry' found in Copper Age settlements and cemeteries may be divided into Tool-Weapons (Table 11) and Weapon-Tools (Table 12).

Table 11 Tool-Weapons found in climax Copper Age contexts

Site	1	2	3	4	5	6	7	8	9	10	11	12	13	14	15	16	17	18	19
Ovcharovo VIII–XIII	x	x	—	—	—	—	x	—	x	—	x	—	x	x	x	—	—	—	—
G. Delchevo V–XIII	x	—	—	—	x	x	x	x	—	—	x	x	x	x	—	—	x	—	—
Vinica	x	—	—	—	—	—	x	x	—	—	—	—	—	x	x	—	x	x	—
Varna I	x	—	—	—	—	—	—	x	x	—	x	—	x	x	—	x	x	x	x
Reka Devnja	—	—	—	—	—	—	—	—	—	—	x	—	—	—	—	x	x	—	—
Brailiţa	x	—	—	—	—	—	x	—	—	—	—	—	x	x	—	—	—	—	—
Draguşeni	x	—	—	—	—	—	—	—	—	x	—	x	x	x	x	—	—	x	—
Hârşova	x	—	—	—	—	—	x	—	—	—	—	—	—	x	x	—	—	—	—
Luka Vrublevetskaya	—	—	—	—	—	—	—	—	—	—	—	—	—	—	—	—	—	—	—
Târpeşti	—	—	—	—	—	—	—	—	—	—	—	—	—	—	—	—	—	—	—
Tiszapolgár-Basatanya	—	—	—	—	—	—	x	—	x	—	x	—	x	—	—	—	—	—	—
Zengóvárkony	x	—	—	—	—	—	—	—	x	—	—	—	x	x	—	—	—	—	—

Key:

1. bone arrowhead
2. bone spear point
3. bone dagger
4. bone hammer-axe
5. bone boomerang
6. antler projectile point
7. antler hammer-axe
8. antler pick
9. boar's tusk point
10. flint projectile point
11. long blade
12. flint core-axe
13. polished stone axe
14. perforated polished stone axe
15. ground stone ball
16. copper point
17. flat copper axe
18. copper hammer-axe
19. copper axe-adze.

Table 12 Weapon-Tools found in climax Copper Age sites

Site	Bone mace-head	Antler battle-axe	Flint arrow head	Bifacial spear-point	Stone battle-axe	Stone mace-head	Copper spear	Copper dagger
Ovcharovo	—	x	x	x	x	—	—	—
G. Delchevo	x	x	x	x	—	x	—	—
Vinica		—	—	—	x	x	—	—
Varna I	—	—	x	—	x	—	x	—
Reka Devnja	—	—	x	—	—	—	—	—
Brailiţa	—	—	x	—	x	x	—	—
Draguşeni	—	—	x	x	—	—	—	—
Hârşova	—	—	x	x	—	—	—	—
Tiszapolgár	x	—	x	—	x	—	—	x

In comparison with the 'weaponry' of the mature farming groups, with its ratio of 1:17 Weapon-Tools:Tool-Weapons, the climax Copper Age communities used a higher ratio (1:2.4) of Weapon-Tools (Fig. 4). The combined increase in object categories of 50 per cent included new Weapon-Tools, such as the bone mace-head, the antler battle-axe, the flint spear point and the copper spear point and copper dagger, as well as Weapon-Tools differentiated from earlier forms (e.g., the polished stone battle-axe and the bifacial projectile point), and the continuing use of the stone mace-head. Several Tool-Weapons continued on in use (bone daggers, antler picks, boar's tusk points, flint projectile points, stone balls and stone axes), but there was differentiation of some bone and antler forms (the bone arrowhead, spear point and hammer-axe, the antler projectile point and hammer-axe) and the 'improvement' of the flint blade into a longer and sharper design. The only new Tool-Weapons recorded are the bone boomerang and the flint core-axe.

These observations show that there is strong evidence for continuity in the manufacture of 'weaponry', combined with the local innovations that characterise climax Copper Age communities. Although the new copper dagger has a predominantly eastern distribution, the case for linking its diffusion to north Pontic migrants is severely weakened by its early appearance in Transylvania, Moldavia and eastern Slovakia (Vajsov 1993). The main Sredni Stog Tool-Weapons include bone and antler adzes, antler battle-axes, long flint knives and bifacial arrowheads and spear points. This range of 'weaponry' falls well within the range of climax Copper Age Tool-Weapons and Weapon-Tools, if on the less diverse end of the spectrum. There is no evidence that Sredni Stog communities were military innovators, rather that groups shared part of the typical 'weaponry' of the day, but at a severe disadvantage against Cucuteni-Tripolye groups with heavy metal Weapon-Tools, stone mace-heads and daggers.

The development of Weapon-Tool and Tool-Weapon categories can be quantified at two north-east Bulgarian tells, using the Late Chalcolithic data from Ovcharovo (levels VIII–XIII) (Todorova 1983) and Goljamo Delchevo (levels V–XVII) (Todorova 1975) (Table 13).

Fig. 4. Climax Copper Age weaponry in action. Top pair: right, shaft-hole copper hammer-axe (Vinica), left, copper dagger (Tiszapolgár-Basatanya); middle left: bifacial flint spear point (Ovcharovo); bottom right: bifacial flint projectile point (Brailiţa).

Table 13 Absolute and relative frequencies of Tool-Weapon categories at selected mature farming sites

Site	Bone		Antler		Lithic		Polished Stone		Total	
	No. of Types	% all Types	No. of Types	% all Types	No. of Types	% all Types	No. of Types	% all Types	No. of Types	% all Types
Ovcharovo VIII–XIII	2	50	3	38	3	14	4	40	12	28
G. Delchevo V–VII	2	40	4	44	1	13	3	43	10	34
G. Delchevo VIII–X	1	20	3	50	2	22	4	67	10	38
G. Delchevo XI–XIII	3	38	3	38	2	22	3	43	11	34
G. Delchevo XIV–XVII	3	30	5	45	4	31	3	43	15	37
G. Delchevo All LCA	2	18	5	45	4	31	4	44	15	35

These data indicate a relatively high proportion of Tool-Weapons and Weapon-Tools throughout the Late Copper Age, with increases over the Middle Copper Age totals in each case (Ovcharovo, 20 per cent of all types, rising to 28 per cent; G. Delchevo, 32 per cent of all types, rising to 35 per cent). Over this period, the incidence of hunting declines at Ovcharovo from 47 per cent (bone numbers: cf. 39 per cent minimum numbers) to 32 per cent (bone numbers: cf. 31 per cent minimum numbers), while remaining the same at G. Delchevo. Thus, it is difficult to argue that the increasing diversity and frequency of 'weaponry' is a reflection of a greater reliance on the hunting of wild mammals. As in the mature farming period, a range of dangerous species was successfully hunted at both sites – wolves, bears, big cat, lynx, aurochs and boar – supporting the notion of continuity in status hunting in the Late Copper Age. No conclusion from these north-east Bulgarian tells weakens the idea of increasing militarisation of climax Copper Age communities, not least those tells surrounded by defences.

The pattern of diversification and increasing frequencies in 'weaponry' is also matched in settlement defences. While all the basic forms of defence – ditch, earthen bank, palisade and stone wall – had already been developed in the mature farming phase, the variety of defensive combinations in the later Copper Age is remarkable, not least in the Cucuteni-Tripolye group.

The locations of many Cucuteni settlements have long hinted at a widespread defensive strategy, not least the type-site of Cucuteni-Cetăţuia (Schmidt 1932). A statistical analysis of the locations depends upon a clear distinction between the often overlapping topographical variables. Especially important is Monah & Cucos's (1985) observation that even sites low in a valley can have a height advantage of 8–10 m relative to the surrounding terrain. This point may explain the virtually identical frequencies of high-terrace, medium-altitude and low-terrace sites throughout the Cucuteni sequence (Table 14).

Table 14 Summary of the distribution of Cucuteni locations by period

Period	High terrace	Medium	Low terrace
Cucuteni A (n = 349)	269 (77%)	3 (1%)	77 (22%)
Cucuteni AB (n = 87)	63 (73%)	2 (2%)	22 (25%)
Cucuteni B (n = 234)	165 (70%)	2 (1%)	76 (29%)

Source: Monah & Cucos (1985, 42–3)

There is therefore no evidence to support the specific selection of high-terrace locations with increasing time, perhaps also reflecting the advantages of proximity to fertile arable soils for low-terrace settlements. Monah & Cucos take this stable pattern to reject the possibility of inter-tribal conflict (Monah & Cucos 1985, 47). However, the strength in depth of some of the defences suggests that warfare is indeed highly probable in the Cucuteni region. The following data summarises Häusler's (1990) observations on Cucuteni-Tripolye defences (Table 15).

Table 15 Types of Cucuteni-Tripolye defences by period

Type of defence	Cucuteni A/Tripolye B1	Cucuteni AB–B/Tripolye BII–C1
Ditch	Târpeşti IV	Cucuteni-Dâmbul Morii
Double ditches	Polivanov Jar Hăbăşeşti	
Bank & ditch	Truşeşti	Traian-Dealul Fântinilor III
Double bank & ditch	Starije Kukonesty	
Triple bank & ditch		Costeşti IV
Stone-lined bank		Zvanec-Scorb
Double palisade	Ariuşd	
Bank, ditch & ?stone counterscarp bank	Mâlnas Băi	Cucuteni-Cetăţuia

Sources: Häusler (1990); László (1993).

There is no clear evidence for an intensification of defensive structures with time in the Cucuteni-Tripolye sequence, suggesting that the military impact of any hypothetical Sredni Stog incursion was in reality, if not minimal, then no greater than that suffered from generations of local intra-tribal warfare. The case for the military impact of Sredni Stog attacks on Tripolye settlements has been advanced by Gimbutas (1979) in respect of the massive nucleated settlements of the Majdanetske type. However, there is no evidence from Sredni Stog sites to suggest the existence of the social structure necessary to organise attacks on the largest nucleated settlements in fourth millennium BC Europe. The widespread nature of similar small-scale defensive structures across the climax Copper Age communities of both the east and west Balkans suggests similar intensities of hostilities. Ditches are known from the Bubanj-Hum tell as well as the hillfort of Gadimlje. Ditches and palisades are well known from a series of Lengyel enclosures, such as Sé, Svodin, Aszód and Zengóvárkony (Zalai-Gáll 1990). Stone walls are known at the Bubanj-Hum settlement of Krivelj, as well as at Gradac-Zlokučani, where traces of a ditch and palisade were also found (Vasić 1911). It is important to note that no evidence for fortifications has yet been found on Sredni Stog villages (Telegin 1973).

The changing fortunes of inter-communal relations are also clearly shown at the two north-east Bulgarian tells of Ovcharovo and Goljamo Delchevo, whose Late Copper Age occupations are defended by a variety of means (Table 16).

Table 16 Variations in mode of defence at two north-east Bulgarian tells (Late Copper Age)

Ovcharovo:

Level	Mode of defence
VIII–IX	broad bank + palisade
X	narrow bank + palisade
XI	broad rectangular bank + palisade
XII	interrupted bank + palisade

Goljamo Delchevo:

Level	Mode of defence
V–XIII	broad bank + ditch + some palisade elements
XV	large ditch
XVI–XVII	? no fortifications

The general conclusion is that during most of the Late Copper Age, these tells were defended with moderate strength, but that near the end of the period, the defences were not as strong. It is possible that poor preservation of the uppermost levels has destroyed some traces of the latest defences, but there is no sense that the defences were extended or improved in this phase. This pattern is hardly consistent with an additional threat from the north Pontic region less than 250 km to the north-east. Rather, the threat posed to these tells throughout the Late Copper Age was no less serious than immediately prior to the Transitional Period.

A potential military innovation in the climax Copper Age is the earliest domestication of the horse. However, there is little evidence of the military use of those horses which appear to represent the earliest stages of domestic use.

If the intensification of fortifications and the increase in numbers and diversity of 'weaponry' are to have any meaning, it is hard to resist the conclusion that the climax of military action took place in the climax Copper Age (Anthony 1995). It is clear that it is patently absurd to describe the climax Copper Age in Gimbutas's terms as a peaceful era. We should, rather, accept the strong probability that a significant number of innovations in this period are primarily, if not wholly, military in nature, and that they are supported by a range of similar or differentiated Tool-Weapons which link this period to the earlier mature farming period. A similar range of defensive techniques is combined in new and extended ways to provide ever-increasing numbers of settlements with fortifications against local rather than inter-tribal raids. Far from posing a danger to the much larger Cucuteni-Tripolye communities, the Sredni Stog group played a minor role in military innovations in this period.

Settlement and exchange data combine to indicate two processes of change in the social networks of the climax Copper Age: network densification and network linkage. In terms of social relations, denser networks bring related people closer together, while wider networks bring unrelated people into more regular contact (Chapman forthcoming). Both processes lead to increased intensity of social interaction, which would have stimulated both violent and peaceful results. The densification process would have led to especially violent interchanges if unrelated groups from a distance settled in the vicinity of well-established core settlement. An example is the Tiszapolgár occupations in central Transylvania, over 100 km from the core Tiszapolgár settlement zone, and close to settlements where Petreşti and post-Petreşti material culture is in use (Bognár-Kutzian 1972). Another example is the Bodrogkeresztúr settlement cluster around Višesava in north-west Serbia, over 200 km distant from the nearest Bodrogkeresztúr site, and close to communities using very different material culture (Zotović 1972; Chapman 1981). The fact that both remote clusters are close to rich sources of polymetallic ores leads to the third factor stimulating warfare: the localisation of valuable resources. Although there are large numbers of copper, gold, silver, lead and antimony sources in central and eastern Europe, these sources are often localised within the territories of particular groups (e.g., the Ai Bunar sources: Chernykh 1978). Groups with no access to local metals may raid as well as trade for these valuable objects. The rapid increase in the variety of raw materials used for tools, weapons and ornaments in this period implies a growth in demand for prestige and other materials – in turn a potent source of competition which could escalate into warfare.

The post-climax period

In many regions of south-east Europe, the period following the demise of climax Copper Age societies is characterised by settlement dispersion, minimal deposition of material culture outside graves and hoards, and an overall reduction in the complexity of material culture. There is little doubt that this demise constitutes a major social and economic transformation, whose causes are still hotly debated (Gimbutas 1980; Tringham & Krstić 1990; Anthony 1986; Greenfield 1986; Sherratt 1996). The strong differences in depositional practices mean that it is particularly difficult to compare this period with the preceding climax.

The basis of Gimbutas's explanation for what she termed 'the collapse of Old Europe' is a series of waves of invasion by horse-riding north Pontic warriors (the kurgan groups, after the Russian term for 'barrow': Gimbutas 1978, 1979, 1980). The absolute dates for the earliest north Pontic group to bury their dead under barrows – the Yamnaya (Pit-Grave) group – range from 4,400 calibrated BC to 2,000 calibrated BC, but Telegin (1977) rejects both the earliest dates (Zaporozh'e 1/14, Utkonosovka 1/13) and the latest (Pervokonstantinovka 12/6), leaving a date span of 3,200–2,300 calibrated BC (Mallory 1977, 348–57). The very few radiocarbon dates from barrow burials in the Balkans indicate contemporaneity with the later (Yamna) phase, after c. 2,600 calibrated BC. Thus, the Balkan evidence for Yamna-type barrows is later than the demise of the climax societies by over 500 years. But, even more interestingly, the 'weaponry' deposited in Yamnaya graves is limited to a small number of Weapon-Tools, polished stone zoomorphic sceptres, copper daggers and long flint blades. The same pattern is found in the Hungarian barrows, where the only 'weapon' is the long obsidian blade from the Csóngrad burial (Ecsedy 1979, fig. 2).

The limited range of this 'weaponry' makes it hard to argue for the strong influence of the north Pontic Yamna group on the military practice of post-climax Balkan communities. But this view ignores two aspects of mobility which leave the status of Yamna warfare ambiguous. First, equid-based mobility means that nomadic warriors use a very limited range of weaponry, little of which is deposited in the mortuary domain. Secondly, equid-based mobility is based upon the tactics of the surprise raid or ambush, followed by an equally rapid retreat. These tactics may have proven difficult for place-based post-climax communities to counter, given that at least some of their 'weaponry' was more adjusted to hand-to-hand combat. A possible analogy is the alleged defeat of the Aegean kingdoms by 'barbarian' forces using guerrilla tactics and new weapons (Drews 1993). To investigate the first question, we need to consider the emergence and spread of horse domestication and the likelihood of armed cavalry in the post-climax period. For the second question, we need to examine the evidence for post-climax weaponry.

The data on horse domestication is as equivocal as in the climax Copper Age period. Domestic horses are claimed for the Yamna group (Anthony 1995), but the methodology in support of the claim is not clear. The increase in the frequency of horse bones at the Gorodsk-Horodiştea site of Folteşti is scarcely replicated on Hungarian Baden sites (Bökönyi 1978, 30–4, 51). It seems unlikely that Yamna warfare was based upon equine hit-and-run tactics; however, the failure to deposit horse remains in mortuary contexts and the rarity of deposition of animal bones in the few known settlements make this conclusion equivocal.

The range of Tool-Weapons and Weapon-Tools associated with post-climax groups is considerably attenuated in comparison with climax Copper Age societies. Whether this is a function more of the paucity of depositional contexts of preservation or more a genuine paucity of weapons, perhaps related to new military strategies, is hard to assess. In most cases, the number of categories of 'weaponry' found on individual sites is so small that the cultural group is used as the unit of analysis (Table 17).

Table 17 Presence of Tool-Weapons and Weapon-Tools in post-climax groups

Site/Group	1	2	3	4	5	6	7	8	9	10	11
Hotnica-Vodopad	x	—	—	—	—	—	x	—	x	—	
Hârşova (Cernavoda I)	x	—	x	—	x	x	—	—	—	—	—
Vučedol	—	—	x	x	—	—	—	—	x	x	x
Coţofeni group	—	—	—	—	—	—	x	—	—	x	x
Lasinja group	—	—	x	x	—	—	—	—	—	—	—
Baden group	—	x	—	x	—	—	x	—	—	—	x
Laznany/Hunyadi h.	—	x	—	—	—	—	—	—	—	x	—

Key: Tool-Weapons: 1, bone point; 2, long flint blade; 3, polished stone axe; 4, perforated polished stone axe; 5, ground stone ball; 6, copper axe-adze; Weapon-Tools: 7, antler battle-axe; 8, flint bifacial arrowhead; 9, polished stone battle-axe; 10, copper dagger; 11, copper battle-axe.

This assemblage of 'weaponry' is greatly reduced from the climax set in the numbers of Tool-Weapon categories (from 19 to 6), in the number of Weapon-Tool categories (from 8 to 5) and in raw materials (in bone, from 6 to 1; antler, 5 to 1; chipped stone, 5 to 2; polished stone, 5 to 4; copper, 6 to 3). But this reduction in 'weaponry' categories conceals a strong element of continuity, since 10 out of the 11 categories were present in the climax societies' repertoire. Only the copper battle-axe (of Banyabik or Kožarac type) represents a development out of a previous Tool-Weapon, the copper hammer-axe for the latter. What is different about the post-climax 'weaponry' is the ratio of Weapon-Tools to Tool-Weapons: 1:1.2 compared to 1:2.4 in the climax repertoire. This indicates a selection of artefacts more specifically prepared for combat than for multi-purpose uses – the only artefactual sign in this period of increased militarisation. The majority of these Weapon-Tools are designed for hand-to-hand-combat rather than mounted attacks (Figs 5–6).

A similar change in military strategy is found when the evidence for post-climax fortifications is reviewed. The main strategy for defence in this period is undoubtedly the maximum dispersion of settlements. The comparatively rare examples of nucleated settlements are often on naturally defended hills, but without fortifications (e.g., the Bubanj-Hum hilltop site of Humska Čuka and many Coţofeni hilltop sites (Roman 1977). Perhaps the strongest fortifications are found in the Vučedol group, with ditches at each of the Vučedol settlements and palisades around several Vučedol-group tells (e.g., Vinkovci) (Dimitrijević 1979). Other ditched or palisaded sites are rare, and include the Hunyadi halom enclosed site of Tiszaluc (Patay 1990) and the ditched tell occupations at Gomolava (Tasić 1979). This makes Dimitrijević's (1979, 330) claim that the Vučedol culture is transitional to a warlike economy rather dubious. The rarity and lack of complexity of post-climax defensive structures is consistent with a more dispersed, mobile approach to defence and settlement.

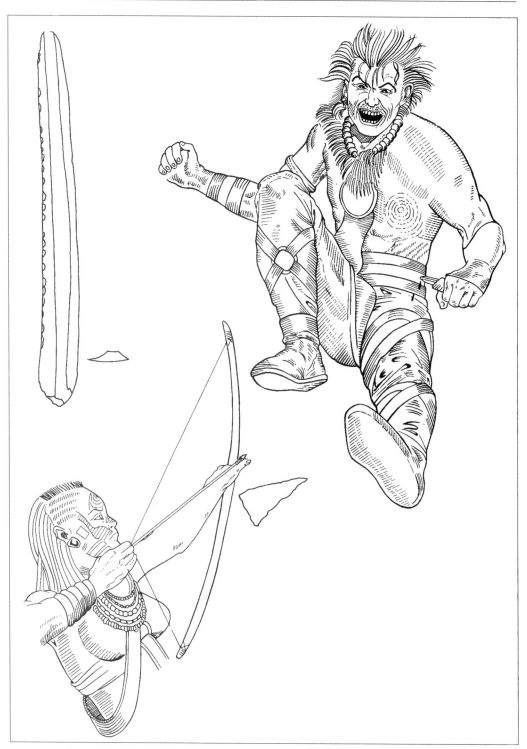

Fig. 5. *Post-climax weaponry in action. Top: long obsidian blade (Csóngrad); bottom: bifacial projectile point (Hotnica-Vodopad).*

Fig. 6. Post-climax weaponry in action. Left: zoomorphic sceptre (Drama); right: copper battle-axe (Vučedol).

In summary, the post-climax communities of south-east Europe were less heavily armed, less sedentary and less dependent upon fixed-place fortifications than the preceding climax Copper Age communities. Ignoring the dating problems for this explanation for the end of Old Europe, Gimbutas's scenario of horse-riding nomadic pastoralist warriors sweeping in from the north Pontic steppes is based upon remarkably little evidence for warfare, whether in terms of 'weaponry' or domesticated horses. Without domestic horses for hit-and-run raids and rapid retreats, the probability of

Yamna groups overcoming the post-climax communities seems remote. If these groups made any contribution to south-east European warfare, it may have been the emphasis on military expansion in small, self-contained, mobile groups which settled down far from their homeland. Lacking any genetic relations with the more settled local populations, such groups would have been ideal targets for an ideology of in-group/out-group identity. But an alternative hypothesis proposes that the people who buried their dead in barrows were equally local groups who transformed the symbol of the domestic domain – the settlement tell – into a mortuary monument (Chapman 1994, 1995). This alternative rests on the strong continuity in material culture between barrow-burying groups and earlier Copper Age mortuary practices in Hungary, and may end the quest for north Pontic invaders once and for all.

CONCLUSIONS

There are three principal contexts for the increasing probability of severe warfare: (1) frontier contexts, involving either new populations settling adjacent to established groups, or new populations infilling niches within a settled landscape; (2) the differential distribution of resources, whether arable resources which are richer in the floodplains than in the interfluves, or specific rock, salt or metal ore sources with limited distributions, which could provoke long-distance raids designed to accumulate prestige goods or resources from non-kin-related communities; and (3) the cultural factor of the emergence of warrior lifestyles.

Methodological approaches to the Balkan data lead to the identification of two strong fields of negative evidence concerning the incidence of warfare: the palaeopathological data and representational data. The extremely low incidence of skeletons whose deaths were caused by violent trauma is matched by the absence, so far, of any evidence for the massacres found in the Bavarian Mesolithic, the French Neolithic and the Linearbandkeramik. Similarly, the representation of weaponry on the many thousands of Balkan Neolithic and Copper Age figurines is limited to a very small number of cases. This leaves two classes of evidence for warfare: fortifications and objects of 'weaponry'. The four means by which settlements are defended – banks, ditches, palisades and stone walls – have been discussed, and the false dichotomy between symbolic defences and militarily functioning defensive structures has been criticised. In the case of 'weapons', a solution has been proposed to the problem of overlapping function of objects equally useful for warlike or peaceful aims: a continuum with four classes of artefact category: tools, Tool-Weapons, Weapon-Tools, weapons. The inherent categorisational ambiguities of objects have been accepted as the basis for analysis, rather than being seen as a hindrance to further study. In this sense, 'weapons' are no less ambiguous than many other classes of object or monument. This methodological scheme allows a diachronic analysis of Balkan Mesolithic, Neolithic and Copper Age objects and settlements within the same framework. This analysis attempts to define the probability of warfare in any of the four specific periods defined: the Late Mesolithic, earliest farming transition, the mature farming period, the climax Copper Age, and the post-climax period.

The Iron Gates gorge was selected for an analysis of the forager–farmer transition. Although many Late Mesolithic Tool-Weapons must have been used for hunting and gathering, the high percentages of all bone and antler categories which can be identified as Tool-Weapons suggests the likelihood of warfare using attacks at a distance with bows and arrows (using bone points more often than flint armatures) as well as hand-to-hand combat using bone, antler and stone clubs. The steep decline in the number and variety of Tool-Weapons among the earliest farming communities is related to the decline in hunting practices as well as the extended kin-based networks linking the regional groups of the First Temperate Neolithic. It seems probable that despite the occurrence of the first settlement defensive ditches and palisades, there were many areas where warfare was relatively rare, and certain regions, such as the Iron Gates gorge, where more intensive exchange and warfare may be identified.

There is a clear diachronic trend, from the earliest farming settlements through to the climax Copper Age sites, of increasing frequencies and diversities of both 'weaponry' and defences. Later in the sequence, it is possible to identify the emergence and differentiation of Weapon-Tools, together with a long-term tendency for an increase in the ratio of Weapon-Tools to Tool-Weapons. The cumulative nature of the increases in weaponry and defences betoken strong continuity in this process of differentiation. Long-distance attacks are based upon bows and arrows, using flint armatures, and in the climax Copper Age particularly, bifacial pressure-flaked points, and slingstones (fired clay less often than ground stone). Hand-to-hand combat became increasingly lethal, Tool-Weapons gradually being superseded by a range of Weapon-Tools, such as stone and bone mace-heads, flint and copper spears, copper, stone and antler battle-axes as well as copper and bone daggers. Settlements tended to be surrounded by increasingly elaborate combinations of the four basic means of defence known from the sixth millennium calibrated BC. One of the results of the emergence of a distinctive mortuary domain was the increasingly close association between Weapon-Tools, heavy copper objects, and burials of adult males – a trend found in particular at the Varna I cemetery. The acquisition of high male status through warfare and the hunting of fierce wild animals (lions, lynxes and big cats) was institutionalised in the mortuary domain. The climax Copper Age defences and weaponry were more complex and elaborate by several orders of magnitude than those of the coeval Sredni Stog group in the north Pontic region, a conclusion that renders the early phase of the Gimbutas kurgan invader hypothesis extremely improbable.

The post-climax reduction in object and settlement complexity affected weaponry and defences as well as every other domain of activity. But, interestingly, the much-reduced repertoire of Weapon-Tools and Tool-Weapons in the local groups is still more complex and differentiated than the weapons found associated with barrow burials, whether in the north Pontic zone of the Yamnaya burials or in the Hungarian barrows. Hence, the later part of the Gimbutas hypothesis can also be rejected. On a broader front, the Gimbutas notion of a peaceful Neolithic and Copper Age matriarchal Old Europe which was destroyed by male Indo-European invaders can be seen as a gross distortion of the evidence, which points to a far higher probability of warfare in Old Europe than in the post-climax period.

ACKNOWLEDGEMENTS

I am grateful to Linda Ellis and Peter Biehl for comments on figurines, David Anthony for comments on horse-riding, Sarah Monks for comments on the overall text, Graham Philip for help with references, Sandra Rowntree for illustrations, and the editors for their patience and comments.

NOTE

1. This idealised characterisation of adult male qualities is not meant to deny that similar qualities may be displayed by women and children in other contexts.

NINE

THE ORIGINS OF WARFARE IN THE BRITISH ISLES

R.J. MERCER

A fishbone pattern of flint arrows flattened
A fossil vision of the Age of Stone –
And sages in war-weary empires quarrel
With those quaint quarrels and forget their own.
What riddle is of the elf-darts or the elves
But the strange story riddle of ourselves.
(G.K. Chesterton, 'Outline of History', in *New Poems*, 1932)

INTRODUCTION

The role of warfare in European prehistory has not received the consideration that perhaps it should have over the last half century. In the author's view, two all-pervasive influences have created this vacuum: first, the dominance of Marxist and post-Marxist models of earlier prehistoric social development saw conflict as indissolubly associated with the alienation of the fruits of production from the individual worker – a situation certainly not seen as existing within an early farming context in Europe; second, European scholars, looking around themselves in the late decades of the twentieth century, can perhaps be readily forgiven, in the open vistas archaeology provides, for avoiding consideration of an aspect of human conduct that has brought so much protracted and intense pain to the entire continent for nearly a century of European civil war.

We know that warfare has been a consistent feature of human conduct for at least 3,000 years in Europe, but our sources of information tend to be documentary and pictographic, and archaeology tends to be somewhat opaque as a source. The old soldier's dictum, 'warfare comprises extended periods of boredom spent in preparation for short periods of frenzied activity, themselves in preparation for further periods of boredom', emphasises the ephemerality and 'event-centredness' of warfare. Certainly, in terms of archaeological evidence, the clearest indicators of violent intention are the existence of tools which we (sometimes rather subjectively) term 'weapons', and of structures that we term 'defences'. Both may hint, at second hand, at the existence of warfare, but first hand evidence of the events of warfare is – as any battlefield archaeologist will confirm – notoriously difficult to come by.

Further difficulty arises with any definition of the nature of warfare. Warfare is not synonymous with conflict or violence. Inter-personal violence is likely to have a very long pedigree reaching back beyond the tenure of *Homo sapiens* in the world. Conflict, which this chapter will consider a collective activity, may include a wide range of activities, including raiding, revenge, display, feuding, 'sport' and initiatory activities, none of which sit comfortably with the word 'warfare'. Indeed, violence, and even conflict, is not restricted to humans, and many mammals employ fighting (often deploying display as much as actual violence) to assert 'rights' of reproduction and territory. We have, perhaps, to turn again to the famous dictum of Carl von Clausewitz (1976 [1832], 87): 'War is merely the continuation of policy by other means.'[1] It is in the context of social policy that the word 'warfare' has to be considered and defined.

The existence of social policy implies, in turn, the existence of a social network which has within it conflicting interests from which an agreed policy is able to emerge via a sufficiently sophisticated system of communication. The emergence of 'policy' – an imposed or accepted communal will – may take on great strength by virtue of the rigour of the fire in which it is forged. There may – though there need not – be a difference of policy with another group large and complex enough in its organisation to have evolved similar networks.

Traditionally, the causes of warfare have been summarised under three headings: *commercium*, *conubium* and *territorium*. Thus, differences of policy arise over issues relating to trade and its successful prosecution, dynastic ambition and intermarriage as a means to advancement, and the acquisition of land to enhance economic productivity or to gain access to the means of such enhancement. Very often, policy is developed with two or three of these fundamental causes of war brought into alignment. Sometimes, one cause is selected as 'cover' for another which could not be communally agreed as policy. In those first wars to receive any detailed written explanation of their cause and course by Homer, the problems of *conubium* that launched a thousand ships had achieved a policy (political) symbolism well understood by every fighting man on both sides – a symbolism which, among nascent city states seeking at that early time to establish *commercium* in the Euxine area, may have spoken of a rather different agenda.

A key issue for an examination of the origin of warfare in Britain is a consideration of the above media and causality within which warfare may emerge. When did these conditions first become current in Britain, as demonstrated by archaeology? The existence of networks of communication between communities politically united enough to undertake large-scale engineering tasks is demonstrated by the monuments of the British Early Neolithic – long barrows, causewayed enclosures and quarries for implement materials – some of which are calculated to have taken over one million man hours to construct or work. Intercommunication is also clearly demonstrated archaeologically by the movement of raw materials and the finished products of a wide range of varieties and sources. Stone is but one of these materials, which is transmitted both in a down-the-line and direct fashion between sites which, as we shall see, occasionally appear to have been fortified. The evidence of selective and minority burial in tomb structures of considerable elaboration may hint at dynastic concerns, as may the evidence (admittedly rare) for genetic linkage between individuals, such as may have occurred at Lanhill Barrow near Chippenham in Wiltshire (Piggott 1954, 141).

THE NATURE OF ARCHERY AS A WEAPON

The last battle involving the use of the bow on British soil reputedly took place at Tippermuir, 8 km west of Perth, on Sunday 1 September 1644, between the Duke of Montrose and the Covenanter Army commanded by Lord Elcho. Montrose had no supplies, and was desperately short of ammunition – his musketeers apparently possessed only one round each. The stones liberally available on Tippermuir Hill were much used on that day, but so was a contingent of 500 bowmen raised rapidly among the local peasantry by Lord Valpont (Buchan 1928, 191).

This anecdote illustrates precisely the great virtue of the bow as a battle weapon. It uses a technology which can easily be supported within a simple economy, the most advanced technological aspect probably being the ability to manufacture and maintain cord of sufficient quality. Throughout the Middle Ages, the bow, while ideally made from (Spanish) yew, was frequently produced from wych-elm or ash. This ease of production and maintenance promoted the bow's wide use within a peasant community (and this was encouraged in Medieval England, Wales and Scotland by both legislative and social means). The skills of archery are of some relevance within the subsistence patterns of a peasant farming economy at whatever stage of development. Although the evidence for hunting seems to be minimal in the British Early/Middle Neolithic, there is nevertheless sufficient evidence for the use of pelts of beaver and other animals (Mercer & Healy forthcoming) and for the taking of red and roe deer, if only in small numbers, to support the development of archery skills.

THE ANATOMY OF NEOLITHIC ARCHERY IN BRITAIN

The bow in Britain – both in the Neolithic (Clark 1963) and in the single instance of a Mesolithic example – was made of yew (*Taxus baccata*), which is well known as a slow-growing tree that provides staves characterised by the narrowness of their growth rings, resulting in excellent tension under torsion. Yew is certainly present in the charcoal assemblage at Hambledon Hill and at a number of other causewayed enclosure sites, and would have flourished widely in localised concentrations – notably on the edge of wetland areas, beside the flood-plains of rivers. Extreme cold temperatures of winter will damage the tree, but otherwise the temperate English climate suits it well (Godwin 1975, 115). However, even in the Somerset Levels, at the limits at which yew could have flourished, only six artefacts over the whole length of the Sweet Track were formed on yew (Coles et al. 1984, 43), comprising pins of unknown function (possibly dress fasteners), and possible bow fragments. In sum, yew is a specialist wood, of great longevity and very hard – so hard that it will simply turn the axeman's blow. Its limited occurrence on sites is thus easily explained, and its consistent use for bow manufacture is attested by Clark (1963, 89–95) for all of Europe, other than those areas of Scandinavia where yew could be expected to be rare or absent.

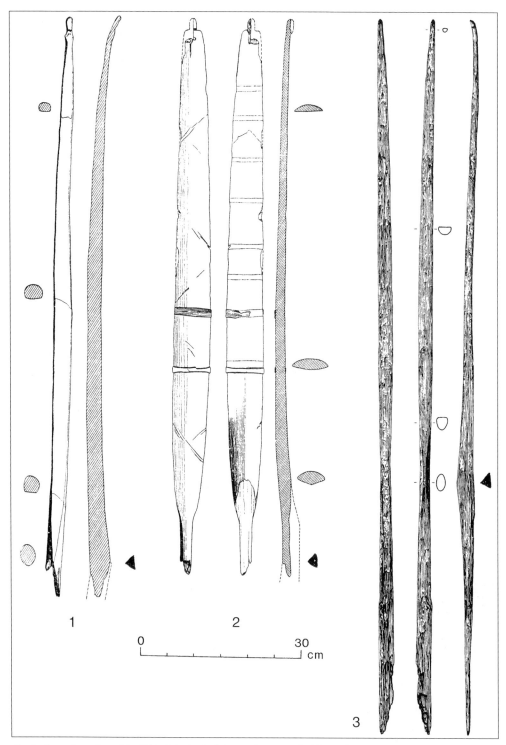

Fig. 1. Long bows from Neolithic Britain. 1. Ashcott, Somerset; 2. Meare, Somerset; 3. Rotten Bottom. Sources: 1–2, Clark 1963; 3, drawing by permission of the National Museums of Scotland.

The weapons of Neolithic date discussed by Clark, from Ashcott and Meare in the Somerset Levels (Fig. 1, 1–2), gave C 14 dates of 2,665 ± 120 uncalibrated BC (Q-598) and 2,690 ± 120 uncalibrated BC (Q-646) (calibrated range 3,530–3,300 BC). The bows are 1.72–1.9 m long, with nocks for string attachment, which may be compared with 1.87–2.11 m for longbows from the *Mary Rose*, which sank in AD 1545. A replica of the stouter of these two Neolithic bows, when tested in the hands of skilled archers, was able to project an arrow 60 m and penetrate a target (Clark 1963, 59).

The Rotten Bottom longbow, found in the Tweedsmuir hills, Peeblesshire (Sheridan 1992), was radiocarbon dated at 4,040–3,640 calibrated BC (OxA-3540), which might suggest either a Mesolithic or an Early Neolithic date. The bow was D-sectioned, like its southern English counterparts, with an estimated original length of 1.74 m and no nocks visible for string attachment. Whatever its cultural status, this bow is a lighter implement – amply demonstrated when a replica was tested, suggesting that it had roughly half the drawing weight of the Ashcott bow.

Neolithic arrowshafts are less commonly found, but some evidence exists to suggest that Guelder rose (*Viburnum opulus*) may have been one favoured wood used in their manufacture – the mounted arrowhead of lozenge form from Blackhillock Bog near Fyvie, Aberdeenshire, was certainly manufactured on this wood (Fig. 2). In this instance, the shaft, when found, was only 'about 9 inches [23 cm] long', according to the workmen who found it, and this account, if the object represented was complete, may introduce the possibility of a two-component shaft – a fore-shaft that remained in the wound, while the back-shaft easily broke away, making the projectile point more difficult to extract, and perhaps allowing recovery of the shaft. Arrowshafts from Ireland are formed on ash, alder and hazel wands, and it is likely that the

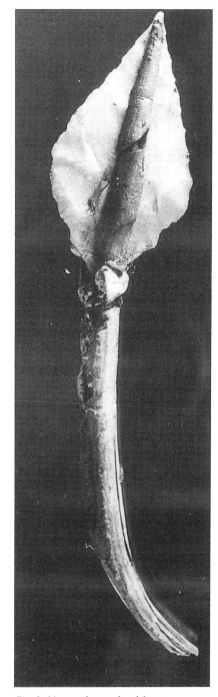

Fig. 2. Mounted arrowhead from Blackhillock Bog, Fyvie, Aberdeenshire. Photo: copyright National Museums of Scotland.

specification for the shafts was less exacting than that for the bow. Few complete shafts have been found, but Mesolithic evidence and modern studies are used by Clark (1963, 74) to suggest that around 1 m would be a suitable length for weapons such as the Meare and Ashcott bows.

If the arrows were fletched – and fletching *is* visible in Upper Palaeolithic representations of archery – then further work was necessary at the butt end of the shaft, binding (and glueing) the feathers into place in the grooves prepared there. Traditionally, goose or swan feathers have been used for this purpose.

Throughout northern and western Europe, during the Mesolithic there had been a common tradition of arrowhead production where the functional emphasis was as much on the projectile's ability to lacerate and remain in the wound as in the depth and impact of the wound puncture. With the first Neolithic, that tradition changes in apparent functionality – although, interestingly, in diverse ways. The universal development is away from the multiple-armature arrowhead to the single, heavy armature, often precisely worked to achieve symmetrical form. This transition occurs whether in the northern tradition of the Polish/north German/Danish Middle Neolithic or in the western tradition of France or Spain – leaf, triangular, hollow-based, triangular-section arrowheads completely replace earlier microlithic traditions. Indeed, this process had started within the central European Linearbandkeramik tradition.

While the picture is far from even, the bulk of the available evidence indicates a strong tendency for hunted animals to be poorly represented on settlement sites of this period. The general picture is of fine, heavy arrowheads forming one of the diagnostic lithic types that distinguish Early and Middle Neolithic cultural diversity in north-west Europe, but generally speaking, there is little evidence of hunting associated with them. As Case remarked of the British Neolithic: 'Large numbers of arrowheads combined with small evidence for hunting suggests that warfare may have been a seasonal occupation of stably adjusted Neolithic communities in our islands' (Case 1969, 171).

In this respect, therefore, as in so many other aspects of Middle Neolithic culture, Britain would appear to be operating in parallel with the broad trend of north-west European development, but at arm's length. Whittle (1977, 103) notes that while all the techniques for the production of bifacially worked arrowheads are present in the Mesolithic of Britain, no such production appears to have taken place, and while bifacial arrowhead production is widespread in Europe, there are very few specifically and clearly visible progenitors for the British leaf arrowhead on the continent. It would be interesting if the advent of a new type of (more powerful) bow, perhaps hinted at by the Rotten Bottom evidence (see above), were to be linked with the new single-armature arrow.

Another reflection of Neolithic reality in Britain is the fact that in stark contrast to the difficulty experienced in observing precise parallels for the bifacially worked arrowhead across the narrow seas that separate north-west Europe and Britain, within the British Isles the leaf arrowhead is a standard cultural type that is part of a continuum that persists for 700 miles into the farthest recesses of the archipelago, and lasts over a period of at least a millennium. Green (1980, 184–5) concludes that other than some broadly sketched trends – for small-scale arrowheads to occur in the Highland Zone (away from sources of large-scale raw material), for ogival arrowheads to occur in the south-west and along the Irish Sea corridor (but not exclusively so), and for slender types to concentrate in the south and east – little regional variation exists. Apart from these broad and far from exclusive trends, the form of the leaf arrowhead is remarkably homogenous throughout Britain and Ireland. Such homogeneity might suggest specialised production of a relatively high-status product.

Such high-status allocation might account for the relatively high frequency of occurrence of leaf arrowheads in graves. Thus, the indisputable involvement of the leaf arrowhead in human fatality in the British Neolithic is much in evidence. Besides the two examples at Hambledon, where leaf arrowheads have been located within the ribcages of intact male skeletons lying within the ditch of the fortified complex (see below), the best-documented example is the burial at the Cat's Water site at Fengate, Peterborough (Pryor 1976, 1984). Here, in a randomly disposed and apparently unmarked grave, a male aged between twenty-five and thirty is accompanied by at least three other individuals: one an infant, one a female of similar age, and one a child of eight to twelve years old. The male had a leaf arrowhead lodged between the eighth and ninth ribs. The arrowhead – of Green's (1980) type 4C – is a slender leaf with the tip apparently broken off, probably as a result of the wound impact. The circumstantial evidence suggested by this interment does not allow the inference of warfare, but it does indicate the use of the bow as a human-killer.

The same is suggested by the evidence from a number of burial deposits in more formal circumstances. At Ascot-under-Wychwood, Oxfordshire, the southernmost cist (No. 2) contained at least four individuals: three adults and one juvenile (Selkirk 1971). One of the adults, 'a male of robust construction', appears to have constituted the primary deposit, his upper body being disturbed by the insertion of the other burials, but his lower body remaining intact. In his third lumbar vertebra was embedded a leaf arrowhead 'which had pierced beneath his ribs and then broken off'. The southern inner cist (No. 3) also produced a leaf arrowhead 'beneath a rib' of an adult secondarily interred there. Both arrowheads at Ascot were of Green's type 3C.

Piggott (1962, 24–5) recovered similar evidence at the West Kennet Long Barrow, where, in the north-east chamber, in the north-west angle, lay the burial of an 'elderly' male, tightly flexed on his right side, with a leaf arrowhead 'in the region of the throat . . . conceivably the cause of death'. In similar vein, Corcoran (1967, 44) discovered in the innermost element of the tripartite chamber at Tulloch of Assery B a broken leaf arrowhead embedded in a lower thoracic vertebra of a fully grown adult, who formed part of the primary burial deposit.

If the above instances refer to associations of a very positive nature between leaf arrowheads and human remains, they should perhaps be set alongside the extraordinary wealth of more generalised associations in British Neolithic funerary contexts. Green (1980, tables IV, 14–29) tabulates 136 examples of Early/Middle Neolithic funerary contexts in which leaf arrowheads have been recorded as 'deposits' associated with burials. If we pause to consider the circumstances of the burials in question, frequently disarticulated, often re-ordered, and very often disturbed by animals and later human activity, it seems perverse (and curiously archaeocentric) to regard the very occasional, and often single, arrow as a 'votive deposit', as opposed to its arrival in the grave within the corpse, either as a cause of death or as a long-term legacy of some earlier conflict.

If the evidence for the use of the bow – and a bow fully adequate to the task of human-killing – in the British Isles during the Neolithic is clear, and if the evidence for the frequent occurrence of leaf-shaped arrowheads in association with the interment of human remains indicates the use of arrows for killing, then we are still left with the task of demonstrating that human killing by arrow-shot was a process not only of assassination and execution (ceremonial or not), but also essentially a component of organised warfare.

As we have already hinted, evidence for organised warfare retrieved by purely archaeological means is notoriously hard to come by. Defensive function in site design is largely a matter of interpretation based upon current conceptions of defensibility, which may be inappropriate to the period under consideration. However, evidence of killing is not evidence of warfare, and the existence of artefacts readily interpretable as weaponry is again an interpretative leap, founded in modern and possibly quite inappropriate perceptions. In the absence of pictographic or written material, an intersection of evidence is required to demonstrate the occurrence of warfare. The presence of human remains that are clearly the subject of violence, in close proximity to apparent defences that themselves reveal evidence of destruction, would, if repeatedly registered, appear to indicate the systematic execution of 'policy' that we have argued lies at the core of warfare as opposed to other forms of conflict and violence.

Such indications exist in sufficient quantity within the British Neolithic to allow the suggestion that regular episodes of warfare were a feature of at least the southern British Neolithic. Indeed, the archaeological evidence for warfare is arguably clearer during the Neolithic than at any time in Britain prior to the Roman period.

THE SITE EVIDENCE FOR WARFARE

In the early 1930s, Dorothy Liddell commenced the excavation of the Iron Age promontory hillfort at Hembury, north-east of Exeter (Liddell 1930, 1931, 1932, 1935). Although it was largely masked by the later defences, she recognised a causewayed ditch which was clearly of Neolithic date, matching the enclosure and finds of the same date being recovered by Alexander Keiller at Windmill Hill, Wiltshire. The Neolithic ditch seems to disappear on to the steep slopes of the promontory (although the possibility of a complete circuit remains), so at present the Neolithic site is assumed to have been a promontory enclosure about 150 m in length and 100 m wide at its broadest point (i.e., about 1 hectare in size); 150 m to the north, a further stretch of Neolithic ditch (uncausewayed over its 20 m of excavated length) would, if it swings away to the west, cut off the spur, enclosing a further 2.5 hectares.

Throughout the 'inner' causewayed enclosure ditch, Liddell located slow silting that had been allowed to accumulate there prior to the almost ubiquitous presence of a mass of burnt material which it was apparent had burnt in situ, the heat turning the exposed natural greensand of the ditch sides to a 'deep wine colour'. It had also discoloured bank material which had apparently been deposited directly on top of it. Liddell noted that the charcoals that made up this mass of burnt debris, which was never less than 15 cm and could be up to 60 cm thick, comprised the remains of oak, hazel and ash, which could be associated with hurdling strapped to a timber framework that had reinforced the forward face of the inner bank or rampart accompanying the ditch (cf. Hambledon Hill, p. 154). Whole blocks of oak charcoal as well as burnt stone were noted in this mass. During the excavation, Liddell sampled something like 50 per cent of the causewayed ditch at Hembury, and also excavated a considerable area (about 600 m²) around the area of a likely timber-built gateway. At least 120 arrowheads – the majority calcined by fire, and a high proportion broken – were located in the area excavated, with, apparently, a major concentration in the region of a likely timber-lined gateway (also burnt) situated at the western side of the promontory enclosure. Sadly, the area of the Neolithic bank and its immediate surroundings had been heavily denuded in the garnering of material for the later Iron Age rampart. However, burning was ubiquitous in the area excavated, and in the very small area at the interior of the promontory enclosure excavated, was represented by an 18 cm-deep layer of charcoal.

The site appears to have been a focal point of both local and wider exchange networks, evidenced by stone axes (of petrologically identified Groups IIa IVa and XVII) and pottery from Cornwall (more than 150 km away), chert and jet from south Dorset (more than 50 km distant) and flint, possibly from further afield. Bone hardly survived at Hembury, so relatively little can be said of the economy of the site (or indeed of its population), but carbonised seed evidence hints at a range of crops – emmer and einkorn, naked and hulled barley, flax and spelt.

Curiously, neither Liddell nor other scholars explored the implications of the violence that had so clearly destroyed the Neolithic site of Hembury, and further advancement of the argument concerning the nature of warfare in Neolithic Britain did not take place until the early 1970s, when excavation taking place at two sites brought the issue back to general attention.

At Crickley Hill, on the Cotswold scarp 6 km south of Cheltenham, Philip Dixon, like Liddell, located the traces of a hitherto unknown causewayed enclosure (or series of enclosures) while undertaking the excavation of a later prehistoric promontory fort (Dixon 1989). After a preliminary stage of unenclosed activity, a complete enclosure was built on the promontory (Dixon's Phase Ibi), comprising a single ditch circuit which was to become the outer ditch of the site as it developed. The ditch of this initial 1 ha enclosure was broad, shallow and flat-bottomed, with at least three, but probably five, entrances aligned radially on the centre of the site. The material quarried from the ditch had been used to construct a broad and very low bank on its inner side, at the rear of which was erected a palisade of no great height. It seems likely from the distribution of leaf arrowheads on the site (Fig. 3) that this enclosure was attacked by arrow-shot, so even at this inceptive stage, Crickley may have had some defensive connotation. It is possible that structures stood within this enclosure, but it proved impossible for the excavator to distinguish any of this phase from those of successive phases.

Probably after the attack by arrow-shot, associated with the outer enclosure, this system appears to have been deliberately levelled, burning brushwood being thrown into the ditch and promptly buried. Five phases of re-cutting (Dixon's phases Ici-iii) in the upper part of this backfilling occurred over a prolonged period. After this interval of unknown length, there was second phase of apparently defensive construction on the site (Dixon's phase Id), with a single massive ditch and only two gateways, both timber-lined, leading to the

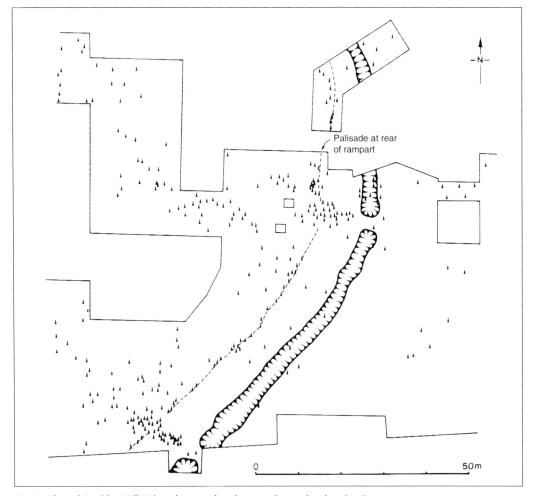

Fig. 3. Plan of Crickley Hill, Glos, showing distribution of arrowheads (after Dixon).

interior. The body of material quarried from this massive ditch was used again to construct a low (0.5 m high) bank some 10 m in breadth with, again, a palisade on its inner edge. The two gateways led from their timber-lined gate-passage on to discernible fenced and cobbled road surfaces within the enclosure. Beside these roads, rectangular house foundations were located in what would appear to be a densely packed settlement, although in the western sector of the enclosure, other activities of a ceremonial nature probably took place in a separately enclosed and gated space.

This Phase Id enclosure also seems to have met a violent end. A massive concentration of leaf arrowheads lies along the line of the palisade, with a dense clustering of over 400 arrowheads in the two entrances. This enclosure seems to have been the target of intensive and probably tactically marshalled archery. It is perhaps significant that no further occupation appears to follow this devastating assault. Dixon states:

The enclosure had quite obviously been defended against archery attack and it is highly likely that it was built with this intention, for the low palisade formed no more than a breastwork. The ditches were presumably designed to break up and slow down an assault, and the low bank, or rather platform, would then serve as a killing-ground, at point blank range, against aggressors clambering out of the ditch. It is worth noting that despite ditches slighter than those of phase Id, the bivallate interrupted ditch enclosure would, on this interpretation, be a defence in depth more effective than the final rampart of phase Id even though their (the latter) larger size gives them a greater appearance of strength'. (Dixon 1989, 82)

One might also add that the causeways, by inviting almost inevitable 'bunching' at a known distance, might well have been a designed aspect of this strategy. Like Hembury, Crickley finds itself at the focus of lines of distribution of both raw materials and finished artefacts over substantial distances.

In 1970, the author commenced excavation of the hilltop enclosure at Carn Brea, near Redruth, which revealed a walled area of about 1 hectare – the wall being built of massive granite blocks, many of them 2–5 tonnes in weight (Mercer 1981). This vastly impressive wall, even in its current collapsed state, joins impregnable outcrops of bedrock granite to form an enclosure within which are a dozen or so terraces, many of them artificially created or enhanced by stone clearance, upon which timber structures containing pits and hearths had been built. All the structures recovered had been burnt. Some 800 arrowheads, many calcined by intense heat, were located all over the site (and hundreds of others had been found in earlier excavations and as casual finds) – this in the approximately 10 per cent of the site excavated. The only feasible place for a gateway to the site had, sadly, been dynamited in the nineteenth century to create the existing access road, but a major concentration of arrowheads (over double the norm) occurred in this immediate area. The degree of dilapidation of the enclosure wall might even be taken to suggest deliberate slighting – paralleling, perhaps, the deliberate infilling of ditches at Hembury and Crickley. The conclusion that the site's occupation had been terminated by an assault involving massed archers followed by frenzied destruction was difficult to resist.

Carn Brea, like Crickley and Hembury, lay at the focus of extended and complex lines of the distribution of raw materials and finished artefacts. The site imported all its pottery from the gabbroic grit source-area at least 25 km away in the Lizard Peninsula (at least 550 vessels were represented on the 10 per cent of the site excavated). Flint axes from Wessex were located, as well as axes and axe-polishers relating to local stone sources (Groups I, XVI, XVII). Chert from Somerset formed 8 per cent of the arrowheads. The community must have been an influential and prosperous one, whose very wealth may have provoked its downfall. Of its economy, little can be said, as the searingly hostile soil conditions on the site allowed little that was organic to survive intact. Certainly, no bone – human or animal – survived, charcoal was reduced to dust, and even pollens were abraded to an unrecognisable state. Nevertheless, outside the 1 ha Eastern Summit enclosure, the remains of cultivated fields were to be seen, with only Neolithic material occurring within their cultivated surface. Furthermore, a 10 ha enclosure had been constructed around the 1 ha Eastern Summit enclosure, furnished with complex gateways that were defended in depth, and which excavation clearly demonstrated were also of Neolithic date. This outer rampart comprised a flat-bottomed ditch 1.5 m deep, cut down to, but not into, bedrock, with a stone-revetted, potentially reinforced rampart. The sockets of the orthostats that lined the gateway, the primary silts of the ditch and the sockets of the orthostatic settings that reinforced the rampart all contained unabraded Neolithic material – pottery, a greenstone axe, and diagnostic flintwork. However, there was no trace of an assault upon this outer feature, which it is difficult to interpret other than as defensively inspired.

With the completion of the excavation at Carn Brea in 1973, there was naturally a push to recognise other sites of similar type. Carn Galver, 8 km west of St Ives, is a very likely parallel, as is the site at De Lank on the south-west fringe of Bodmin Moor (discovered by Peter Herring and Jacqueline Nowakowski). Others doubtless exist and await a systematic survey approach, but the most likely parallel from the outset was the site at Helman Tor, near Lostwithiel. At this site, briefly explored by the author in 1986 (Mercer, forthcoming), a situation precisely parallel with that at Carn Brea was discovered – a granite hilltop with its outcrops linked by a massive defensive stone wall with a series of at least nineteen terraces set on its 1 ha interior. Once again, there was ample evidence of long-distance distributive communication, and flint arrowheads were also present in quantity from this small-scale excavation. They were not as ubiquitous or numerous as the average at Carn Brea, but their number compared with the least productive area at that site. Any question of an attack and destruction could not be addressed by the scale of the 1986 investigation. What is clear is that Carn Brea is not a unique site, and whether its fate was shared by others or not, the evidence suggests a network of interacting sites, linked by shared sources of raw materials and artefacts, demonstrating an interaction within which the seeds of warfare may easily have been sown.

In 1974 the author began the major series of excavations at Hambledon Hill in Dorset (Mercer 1980; 1988; forthcoming). The excavations were initially designed to explore the 9 hectare enclosure on the central summit of the trilobate hill at Hambledon. However, the excavation was accompanied by a field survey exercise that had soon located what appeared to be a range of associated earthworks on the east, south and west slopes of the hill. Excavation of these between 1979 and 1982 produced evidence of a cumulative trivallate defensive system on the southern spur of the hill, comprising causewayed ditches and banks, with the innermost ditch backed by a box-framed rampart, possibly rebuilt at one stage, with two timber-lined entrances (Fig. 4). There is no doubt that at the end of one stage of the site's occupation, this rampart was on fire for over 120 m of its length, and within the ditch segments that fronted it, two absolutely intact, robust male skeletons were buried in the rubble of the rampart collapse (Fig. 5). Both individuals had leaf arrowheads located in the thoracic cavity and near the throat.

CONCLUSION

The intersection of evidence to prove the existence of warfare by purely archaeological means can never be complete. None the less, the evidence for organised warfare in the Early Neolithic in Britain is now compelling. Indeed, the author would go so far as to say that the archaeological evidence for warfare (as opposed to weaponry or defences) is more

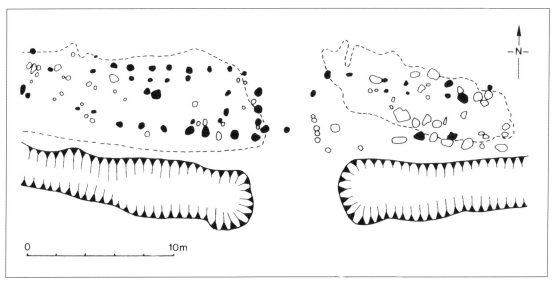

Fig. 4. Plan of the box rampart at Hambledon Hill, Dorset.

Fig. 5. Male skeleton in the rubble-filled ditch at Hambledon Hill.

Fig. 6. Flint arrowhead embedded in the chest of the male skeleton shown in Fig. 5.

convincing for the Early Neolithic than for any other period of British prehistory. It is not an adequate objection that the warfare was in some way 'ceremonial' or 'ritualised' – *all* warfare is ceremonialised and ritualised, but the footballers at Ypres on Christmas Day 1914 (ritual, if you like!) were there in deadly earnest, as were at least two of the men at Hambledon Hill on that day some time around 3,400 calibrated BC, when the site came to its end.

During the Early Neolithic in north-west Europe, the bow and arrow became an efficient human-killing weapon. Arrowheads are frequently found in conjunction with human remains, and human remains with arrowheads as their certain cause of death are found in direct association with constructed defensive systems. It can be argued that those defensive systems, which are often associated with settlements, would appear – as at Crickley and Hambledon – to be specifically laid out to favour the archer, and there is good evidence on at least four sites that the defensive works were massively slighted at the end of the episode involving archery assault (and defence).

The author does not argue that all Neolithic enclosures were defensive – many were clearly not, and indeed components of the site at Hambledon Hill were not. However, the fact that some sites were defensive, and were attacked in an organised and utterly destructive way during the early period of British farming prehistory, is now beyond doubt.

NOTE

1. However, Keegan (1993, 3) points out that von Clausewitz's words actually mean: 'the continuation of political intercourse with the intermixing of other means' (eds).

TEN

WARFARE: A DEFINING CHARACTERISTIC OF BRONZE AGE EUROPE?

ANTHONY HARDING

INTRODUCTION

In November 1985, a farmer on Fröslunda Manor in the Kålland Peninsula on the southern side of Lake Vänern in central Sweden was ploughing a fen area deeper than usual when a large, green disc appeared in his furrow (Hagberg 1988). He initially thought this was a modern lid of some sort, but later realised it was something much more special. It turned out that the object was a bronze shield. In excavation the following year, a further thirteen shields, whole or fragmentary, were recovered (Fig. 1). They had been deposited in wet ground, or shallow water, in what was at the time a bay on the edge of the lake, and their number, variety, disposition and condition (at least some were apparently perfect when deposited) indicate that they were all deposited at one time, and intentionally.

The shields are of the so-called Herzsprung type, named after a site in eastern Germany, and date typologically to the Late Bronze Age. The Fröslunda finds are not unusual, except in so far as their number is concerned; shields have been studied by a series of scholars (Sprockhoff 1930; Hencken 1950; Coles 1962; Gräslund 1967; Thrane 1975; Needham 1979). The Herzsprung and other shield types are distributed across much of Europe: where actual finds do not occur, depictions may do (as, for instance, with stelae in Iberia). Many *in corpore* finds come from wet places, particularly in Ireland and Britain. In the former, the shields may be of leather or wood as well as bronze, and famous examples come from Clonbrin, Co. Longford, Cloonlara, Co. Mayo, and Lough Gur, Co. Limerick. On the European continent, well-known pieces come from Plzeň, from Nackhälle in Halland (Sweden – geographically the closest to Fröslunda), from Ognica (formerly Nipperwiese) near Szczecin, and from the Rhine. There has not been a complete corpus of these shields for some years, but there are at least eighty metal examples in central and northern Europe, with more turning up unexpectedly at intervals (e.g., a new find from South Cadbury, Somerset, discovered in excavation in 1997: Coles et al. 1999).

All this indicates that the deposition of Bronze Age bronze shields was far from rare – and it was not only shields that were deposited: other types of weaponry, particularly swords, also found their way into the ground in large numbers. It was by no means only

Fig. 1. The shields from Fröslunda, Sweden, under excavation. Photo: Lars Hasselberg, by kind permission of Västergötlands Museum.

weapons and armour of which this is true (ornaments of various kinds, for instance, were also deposited very frequently), but they do constitute one of the principal categories of material thus situated. Why? What was the special importance of war-related artefacts in the Bronze Age world?

A second remarkable set of finds was made between 1984 and 1995 on the Middle Bronze Age site of Velim, district of Kolín, in the Czech Republic. A series of large pits, conjoining to form discontinuous ditches, were found to contain numerous human bone deposits (Hrala et al. 1992). Some of the bones were complete and articulated, some scattered or incomplete; groups of skulls were found in certain pits; infants and children were represented, as well as adults, of both sexes, mostly lying in disorder in the pits (Fig. 2). As if this were not strange enough, some of the bones bore cutmarks, usually taken as evidence of butchery, and possibly cannibalism. Velim is not a cemetery, at least not in the normal sense (it belongs mostly to the Tumulus Bronze Age, the burial rites of which are well known). As yet, there is no indication of the total extent of the site and thus of the dead occupants of the ditches, but it must run into hundreds. It seems certain that most if not all of the persons deposited here were killed, and warfare is one of the likelier explanations for this extraordinary congeries of death and destruction.

Fig. 2. Human bone deposits from the ditches at Velim, Czech Republic. Some of the bones bear cutmarks, and were probably the subject of violent deaths. Unusually, the individual in the foreground had a pot placed alongside. Photo: M. Vávra.

This chapter will examine various aspects of the occurrence of warlike material in Bronze Age Europe, and ask the question: did war and warlike behaviour play a particular role in the Bronze Age? If so, what was it? Can one even characterise the Bronze Age by reference to its war-related attributes?

WEAPONS AND WARFARE, 2,500–1,200 BC

No one looking at the artefactual record of the European Copper and Bronze Age can fail to be in any doubt that objects of warlike appearance played a major role in the period. That role is a matter for discussion, but the sheer numbers of artefacts, and their ubiquity, speak eloquently of large-scale production and large-scale deposition.

In the Copper Age, depictions on grave stelae and finds of arrowheads (as well as the remains of an actual bow and a quiverful of arrows with Ötzi, the Ice Man) indicate that the bow and arrow was the main long-distance weapon. Mercer (see chapter 9) has considered the importance of warfare by archers in the British Neolithic, and there is every reason to believe that such war technology was widespread throughout western and central Europe, providing an ancestry for the Copper Age manifestations in the west, most tellingly exemplified by the statue-menhirs or stelae that extend from Italy to Iberia and western France (Arnal 1976).

Fig. 3. Anthropomorphic stela (statue-menhir) from Petit Chasseur, Sion, Switzerland, showing bow slung across the chest and lozenge and triangle designs probably representing patterned textiles. Musée cantonal d'archéologie, Sion. Photo: H. Preisig, courtesy of Musées Cantonaux du Valais.

The depictions on the stelae from Petit Chasseur give a lively impression of the Copper Age warrior in central Europe (Fig. 3).[1] Some of these are abstract in nature, but taken as a whole, the anthropomorphic nature of the figures is not in doubt (Sauter 1976, 76ff. fig., 22; Bocksberger 1978, pl. 18–20). The bow is slung across the chest, and in some cases arrows are also visible, or a dagger is present on the lower trunk. The daggers are markedly triangular with a rounded pommel, and have been considered to be most akin to those found in the Remedello culture of northern Italy, dating to the Copper–Bronze Age transition. In north Italy, for instance in the Lunigiana behind La Spezia or the Alto Adige between Bolzano and Merano, the stelae have daggers at the waist and L-shaped implements (thought to be hafted battle-axes) on the chest, though not bows (Barfield 1971, 65ff.; Ambrosi 1988).

It seems, therefore, that two different forms of fighting are visible. In the Rhône Valley in Switzerland, the warriors were either using bows for long-distance offence directed towards humans or animals, or daggers for fighting at close quarters; on the other side of the Alps, they were equipped with daggers and battle-axes. A third variant may be present in southern France: the L-shaped implements (battle-axes) are present, as are a group of mysterious 'objects' slung on a strap across the chest, having a triangular shape with a circle at the wide end (Arnal 1976; D'Anna 1977).

But was this really such a contrast? Can we assume that the appearance of these statues really reflects the way dominant or bellicose males (all those with weapons seem to be male – at least they do not have the obviously female characteristics seen on some stelae) dressed and the arms they carried? Not necessarily. The statue-stelae are unusual enough for it to be quite likely that what are represented are exceptional depictions – exceptional people or exceptional events. We cannot even tell whether these are meant to be specific individuals (e.g., in commemoration of the deceased who lay nearby in an associated tomb) or genre scenes. What is certain, however, is that bow and arrow and dagger were carried by particular individuals in the Copper Age of these circum-Alpine regions, and it is likely that the bow and arrow at least was in widespread use for hunting, probably also for human combat. The dagger, by contrast, is likely to have been mainly intended for human fighting rather than hunting, though it is possible that it was used to deliver the *coup de grâce* to wounded animals, and in the absence of other implements identifiable as knives, it could have been used to butcher them.

Daggers continued as one of the most popular weapons of the Bronze Age, and were still in common use in the Early Iron Age. Daggers are found throughout the Aegean Bronze Age, often elaborately decorated, and certainly not intended for use in fighting. We know little about the Aegean warrior until the Late Bronze Age, however, when a suite of other weapons is also found (see below).

The same is probably true for the bow and arrow (Rausing 1967), though usually it is only the arrowhead which survives. While arrowheads are not generally distinctive in type or origin (Mercer 1970), there are exceptions – most notably in the latter stages of the European Bronze Age, when a particular form is present on fortified sites in central Europe (presumably the aftermath of attacks), thought by some scholars to attest the presence of invaders from the steppe zone, 'Thraco-Cimmerians' or Scythians. A one-to-one correspondence is perhaps unlikely, but it is certainly true that there are many indications of conflict in the earlier first millennium BC in this part of the world. In Greece, the bow and arrow (as attested both by depictions and by finds of arrowheads) had existed probably for thousands of years (Buchholz 1962; Avila 1983). Arrowheads are well known from the Shaft Graves of Mycenae and the chamber tombs of Prosymna and elsewhere, in flint and other stones, and are usually hollow-based in form; bronze arrowheads occurred in great numbers in the workshops and storerooms at the Palace of Pylos and elsewhere (Buchholz 1962; Avila 1983, 86ff. Taf. 23ff.; Blegen 1966, 321ff. fig. 316, 1, Room 99, 325f., fig. 317, Room 100: 'more than 501 small barbed arrowheads'). They were also found by Evans in quantity in the Knossos 'armoury' (Evans 1935, 617, 836ff. figs 816, 818; Avila 1983, Nos 597, 7242[2]). There is also the evidence of the Linear B tablets: those listing items in the 'armoury' at Knossos indicate many arrows or javelins held in store (Chadwick 1973, 361), and also swords or daggers (the Ra series of tablets). A tablet at Pylos (Jn09) listing bronze allocations specifically states that bronze was collected in order to make points for arrows and spears (Chadwick 1973, 357).

161

The really significant developments in warfare technique, however, came with the creation of quite new weapons during the course of the Bronze Age. The halberd, if it really was utilised in battle, was clearly cumbersome to handle, and because of the angle at which force would be directed to the fastening rivets, weak in attachment, and likely to come adrift. Any Early Bronze Age warrior who relied on it in battle against an enemy with more solidly conceived and executed weaponry would have an untimely end, but it is possible that the 'fighting' involved was purely of a ceremonial or ritual nature, as we will see in other contexts shortly.

Much more significant were two types of weapon that emerged quite early on in the Bronze Age: the spear and the sword. The spear developed out of a dagger-like blade with a long tang that may have been mounted on a long shaft rather than held close to the body. By the developed Early Bronze Age in central Europe (*c.* 1,800 BC), the socketed form was in production, and with only small differences this was the form that existed throughout the rest of the period (Jacob-Friesen 1967). In the Aegean, the spear started its life around 2,000 BC, but the fully functional socketed form only arrived with the Late Bronze Age (Höckmann 1980a, 1980b; Avila 1983).

From their abundance, spears were obviously important, but in central Europe they were not usually decorated or given the appearance of prestige weapons – unlike the other new invention, the sword. There are many fewer surviving swords than spearheads, but this is probably a good reason for considering them to have been of greater importance. The developmental history of the sword is well known (Cowen 1955; 1966). Early versions of swords were already present in east central Europe in the Early Bronze Age, and during the Middle Bronze Age Tumulus period, the standard 'cut-and-thrust' sword developed. In Greece, the sword was a new arrival at the end of the Middle Bronze Age, probably building on a Near Eastern ancestry (Sandars 1961), whereas the dagger had existed since the Early Bronze Age. At first, long, narrow rapiers were produced, with a small tang for fastening to the hilt; later, flanged hilts were used, though the blade was still tapering and officially a 'rapier'. Finally, in the later centuries of the Greek Bronze Age, the fully functional cut-and-thrust sword appeared in Greece, and the significance of this is examined below.

How were the weapons used?

In Greece, depictions and *in corpore* finds make it clear that by the middle of the second millennium BC, the weaponry available consisted of the rapier, spear, dagger, and bow and arrow. Warriors also had access to defensive weaponry, notably helmets and shields, and to chariots (Crouwel 1981). A series of Linear B tablets from the 'armoury' at Knossos refers to chariots (without wheels), and others to the wheels themselves (So series); similarly, at Pylos, the Sa tablets list wheels (Chadwick 1973, 361ff.). A related matter, not the subject of discussion here, is the occurrence of fortifications, which are prevalent in certain areas and periods – though not on Crete, at least not in the Palace periods.

Kilian-Dirlmeier's (1993) full consideration of the use of swords has placed the study of Bronze Age warfare in the Aegean on a new and sounder footing. She has tabulated the occurrence of swords in combination with other weapons throughout the Late Bronze Age. In the earliest Mycenaean period, swords were usually accompanied by daggers or

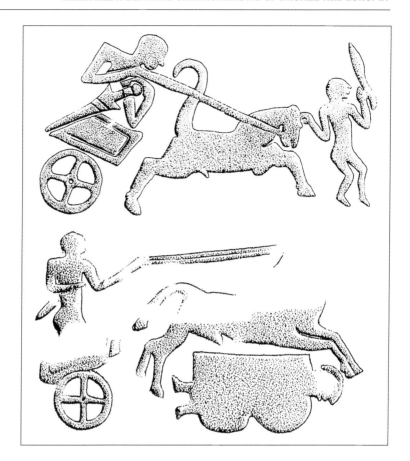

Fig. 4. Grave stelae from Mycenae, found above Shaft Grave V, showing chariots, a swordsman (upper) and a fallen warrior with figure-of-eight shield (lower). Source: Crouwel 1981.

knives, sometimes by spears. By contrast, in the middle to late period, the spear was a much commoner accompaniment. Interestingly, in the early to middle Late Bronze Age on Crete, the sword and spear duo was also common; some of the so-called Warrior Graves at Knossos have a spear but no sword. These occurrences allow the reconstruction of several weapon combinations, which could have reflected either ownership and deposition practice, or warfare technique. If the latter is true, not everyone fought with a sword – a few relied on spear or dagger. However, swords were much the commonest weapon provided and (presumably) used.

Depictions of the Shaft Grave period show warriors in hand-to-hand combat wearing boar's tusk helmets and using swords, spears and shields (full discussion in Kilian-Dirlmeier 1993, 130ff.; Foltiny 1980; Höckmann 1980a). A larger scene on a silver vase from Shaft Grave IV shows a number of fighters, some armed with bows. The grave stelae and daggers of the Shaft Graves depict hunters wielding bows in pursuit of lions and leopards but also engaged in fighting other warriors, both on foot and mounted in chariots (Fig. 4). Shield and spear are shown on other depictions of this period (Höckmann 1980a, 277). A warrior with boar's tusk helmet and spear occurs on a fresco from Pylos, and other depictions from Tiryns and elsewhere confirm the picture, suggesting that the same method of fighting (and/or hunting) was present in the later (but not the latest) part of the Mycenaean period as in the earlier.

To what extent Homer may be used as a model for understanding Mycenaean warfare is a much-discussed question (Lorimer 1950, ch. 5; most recently, van Wees 1994). Clearly, there are elements of Homeric warfare that correspond well with what we can reconstruct of Late Bronze Age warfare, but the whole question of which parts of Homer were late insertions and which relate to a genuine tradition handed down in bardic memory from ancient times is highly controversial. Most commentators assume that chariots were used to transport the warrior to the scene of battle, where he dismounted and proceeded to engage with one or more opponents (e.g., Crouwel 1981). In spite of some passages implying the massed warfare that resembles what happened in the hoplite age, most encounters described by Homer are man-to-man, which tallies with most of the pictorial evidence. It is certainly hard to imagine that on Greek terrain, the moving chariot could have served as an effective platform for accurate archery, and in spite of assertions to the contrary by Drews (1993), there is no evidence that massed chariot charges took place in Greece at this period.[3]

In considering the nature of Mycenaean warfare, it is important also to bear in mind the evidence of protective armour. The shield was the most frequently used item of armour, but it was not the only one: helmet, cuirass or corslet, and greaves were used to protect the head, torso and shins respectively. Most of what we know about these objects comes from those examples that were fashioned in sheet bronze and have therefore survived, but it is highly likely that the majority of such items were made in leather. Shields certainly were, and there are even wooden examples known. It is highly significant that experimental reconstructions of metal and leather shields have shown that the latter are very much more effective in real combat than the former (Coles 1962), and as a consequence, that sheet metal armour was much more likely to be intended to be seen than to be used in real combat.

Most of the earliest examples of body armour in Europe appear at the start of the Urnfield period (Br D, thirteenth century BC), though in Greece armour was in use in the LH IIIA period (the Dendra corslet), the fourteenth century (Snodgrass 1971), and a radiocarbon date on a wooden shield form now indicates that shields were produced in Ireland as early as the Early Bronze Age (Hedges et al. 1991, 128f.). Unlike the thin sheet armour that occurs in continental Europe, the Dendra panoply is made of quite thick metal, and would have been relatively effective at keeping blows from sword and spear off the body. But it would have been extremely heavy and hot to wear, and if its bearer tripped or fell, he would have needed help to get up again. The Linear B tablets show that cuirasses like this were a standard part of the armoury, and in spite of some objections, it seems inescapable that this was how Mycenaean warriors operated, in the middle period at least. This contrasts with the commonly presented view of the 'Urnfield warrior', with light bronze shield, helmet, corslet and greaves (Fig. 5). In truth, this bronze-clad warrior was only ever around in the late part of the Bronze Age, and then only for display. Earlier, he was protected by leather, and one must hope that one day such a panoply will turn up, perhaps preserved in a peat bog.

This brings us to the question of how weapons were used. In the case of spears, debate centres on whether they were held or thrown – a question that has vexed scholars for decades. In the Aegean, there is some pictorial evidence to show that both modes were used, and if Homer is relevant to the debate, the throwing of spears was the standard mode

Fig. 5. The 'Urnfield warrior', an idealised reconstruction by J.M. Coles showing bronze helmet, corslet, shield, sword and greaves.

of engagement in the *Iliad*. In European contexts, two quite distinct sizes of spearhead became known – one large and the other small – though there are also most intermediate sizes in between. Although either could have been used in either way, it is most likely that small spearheads were intended for light javelins that could be thrown over a distance of several tens of metres, and large ones for heavy spears that were held firm by a warrior or group of warriors under close-quarters attack, or thrust at the opponent. Indeed, Klavs Randsborg (1995, and Chapter 12 this volume) maintains that hoards or collective finds of spears in the Nordic Early Bronze Age are to be interpreted as the weaponry of warrior collectives. Perhaps such spear-owners acted and fought in collaboration – if not as a hoplite (very unlikely), at least as a co-ordinated group, with some throwing their spears and then taking cover behind the others, who advanced holding theirs. At the moment of encounter, the lancers (as we may call them) could then have emerged to use cutting or thrusting weapons (daggers, rapiers, swords) in hand-to-hand combat.

Daggers and rapiers can only have been used for thrusting, to penetrate deep into the body of an opponent – though only creating a narrow wound. It is quite possible that a rapier thrust could penetrate the body and yet cause no fatal or even debilitating wound (in the short term). A rapier wound would need to be deep and on target, which is to say accurate (or lucky) enough to penetrate a vital organ or artery. Swords, with their broader and heavier blades – especially those with leaf-shaped (splaying) blades – could be used to deliver cutting or slashing as well as thrusting blows. In this way, a swordsman could use a much greater variety of skills in combat, and in the event of landing a blow, could cause significant injury even through glancing blows, which would cause lacerations and bleeding, and potential damage to muscle and tendons. Danger spots might include the neck, the back of the knee, the groin, or the inner thigh, all of them dangerous because of the tendon damage, pain and bleeding that might ensue. On the other hand, the long blade and sharp point of the rapier would mean that a moment of inattention could allow an opponent to land a dangerous thrust on the face or other vulnerable body part.

In view of the above, it is confusing to find that depictions from the Aegean, which can only be referring to weapons with a narrow, tapering blade (i.e., rapiers), frequently show warriors with their sword arm raised above the head, delivering blows that certainly appear to be bringing the sword down on their opponent's head or trunk (Fig. 6). I believe that in spite of what we would regard as the 'logical' way of using swords (as presented by experts in the art: Gordon 1953), Mycenaean fighters used their weapons in a variety of ways. Many of their finest swords and daggers can hardly have been intended for use at all, so elaborately are they decorated. There is undoubtedly a display element to what comes from the rich graves of Mycenae or Dendra or the tholoi of the Pylos area. I also believe that the effectiveness of Bronze Age cut-and-thrust swords has been exaggerated. I have not experimented with striking an object, let alone a living body, with such a sword, but I have waved a few around, and find it hard to believe that a slashing blow landing on a clothed body would have done more than produce bruising. Even freshly sharpened, it is hard to see how they could have produced more than superficial cuts where the skin was protected. Thrusting blows, delivered in a moment of inattention during a fencing duel, are much more likely to have been effective.

In Europe, much speculation has centred on the degree of wear swords have, and the indications this provides of how much and how often they were used in battle. It is certainly striking that many sword blades are nicked or battered (Bridgford 1997), and Kristiansen (1984) maintains that the degree of resharpening or edge-grinding (as shown by the steepness of the edges) indicates the degree of wear and usage. This hypothesis assumes that swordfights were conducted in the manner beloved of Shakespearean actors – essentially for fencing, with the sword used as much to parry blows as to land them on the opponent. There is a big difference between fencing weapons and Bronze Age swords, however, the most significant being the difference in length. Unlike fencing foils, European Bronze Age swords are typically 50–80 cm long, which means that the warriors were very close to each other (Minoan and Mycenaean rapiers were typically 1 m or more long). Their balance is also frequently less than ideal – a factor compounded by their rather short grips. The degree of wear (use) is also related to the type of sword. Most notably, solid-hilted swords (*Vollgriffschwerter*) are more

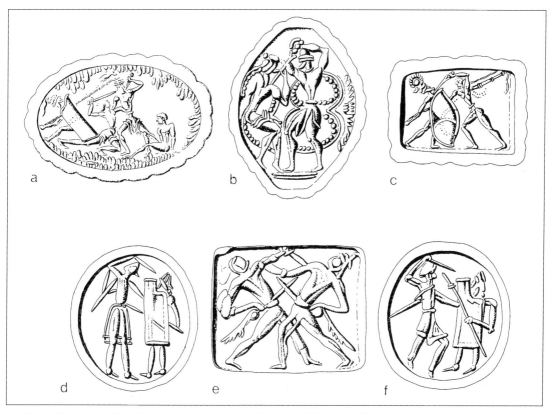

Fig. 6. Depictions of combat involving swords and shields from Minoan and Mycenaean rings, gems and seals. a: Mycenae, Shaft Grave IV; b–c: Mycenae, Shaft Grave III; d, f: Unprovenanced, Crete; e: Pylos, Gouvalari tholos grave 1. Source: Kilian-Dirlmeier 1993 (after Corpus der minoischen und mykenischen Siegel).

commonly in pristine condition than other types, suggesting that their function was not necessarily for real fighting, but rather for ceremonial fights or display (Figs 7–8).

The Bronze Age sword provides an ideal subject for study, since detailed catalogues have been published covering large parts of Europe. In eight geographical zones, covering all or part of ten countries, 3,390 organic-hilted and 1,547 metal-hilted swords have been recovered – a total of 4,937.[4] In some areas, the density of finds was extremely high: in Ireland, for instance, there are 624 swords in the published catalogue (Eogan 1965), amounting to 7.61 swords per 1,000 square kilometres. Though that may not at first sight seem a particularly high density, over 600 swords in a country the size of Ireland, all emanating from the 500–600 years of the Late Bronze Age, is truly remarkable. Ireland is also the place where shields are most abundantly known. What exactly was going on there, and was it different from anywhere else?

This question cannot realistically be separated from the wider one of bronze deposition in general. Much ink has been spilt in recent years to try to determine the reasons why people in the Bronze Age left so much bronze in the ground. This is not the place to review these interpretations in detail; suffice it to say that there has been a marked shift from a tendency to consider bronze hoards as industrial or commercial in nature, to considering

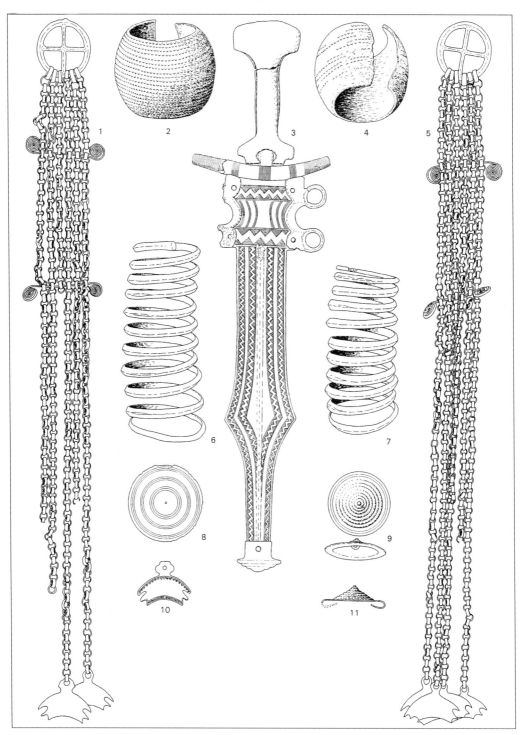

Fig. 7. Parade weaponry from the Late Bronze Age Balkans: the solid-hilted sword with scabbard (3), arm-guards (6–7), bracelets (wrist-guards?) (2, 4) and elaborate chain pendants (1, 5) from Veliki Mošunj, Vitez, Bosnia. Not shown is a large decorated bronze disc that might have formed the centre of a shield. Source: Harding 1995 (after Truhelka).

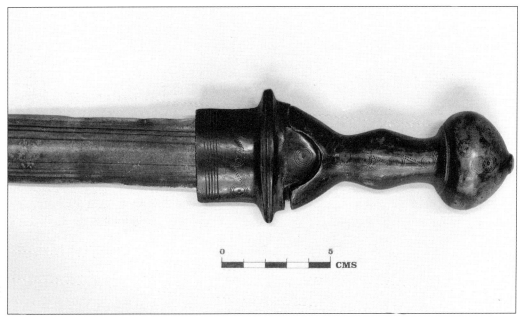

Fig. 8. Solid-hilted sword from Kulen Vakuf, Bosnia, showing integral hilt and pommel and the bronze scabbard mouth (the rest of the scabbard would have been of leather or wood). Naturhistorisches Museum, Vienna. Photo: author.

them votive – intentionally placed in the ground, and abandoned for ever. Weapons are far from being the most common artefact group to be treated like this, but there are plenty of cases where they were lost to living Bronze Age people, either by being hoarded in the ground or by being thrown into rivers. A well-known example is the group of swords (and other objects) from the Porta Bohemica at Velké Žernoseky in northern Bohemia (Plesl 1961, 155, pl. 54); there are also examples from the Danube in Hungary and elsewhere (Mozsolics 1975). In Britain, many finds come from the Thames and the wet ground of the Fenlands (Burgess & Colquhoun 1988). In other words, there are plenty of finds to show that weapons were treated in comparable ways to other artefact classes. In addition, there are relatively few cases where swords were placed in graves. An exception is the Seddin area of eastern Germany, where a hierarchy of graves has been suggested (Wüstemann 1974, 1978). Here, a topmost layer of graves (and therefore, presumably, people in society) were equipped with swords, spears and other rich goods, the 'King's Grave' at Seddin itself being the prime example, but with other rich groups placed in a territorial pattern across the landscape. As well as these 'sword graves', there were spear graves, harness graves and so on, and at the bottom of the pile, the great mass of poorly differentiated and poorly provided for graves that constituted the norm in Urnfield cemeteries. In the west, weapons in graves were exceptional, and there is certainly no comparison with the situation in the central European Urnfield world.

How does this relate to the bearing of arms in combat? If much, or some, of this deposition was concerned with votive and not utilitarian acts, does the number of weapons have anything to do with the bearing of arms in battle? Yes and no. On the one hand, there is little to suggest that the depositions themselves were directly connected with warlike acts. While the few graves with swords are plausibly those of the warriors who bore them, and a few instances might be interpreted as losses, in general, deposition in wet places, or in hoards, or involving intentionally bent weapons, cannot have anything directly to do with a context of fighting. On the other hand, the clear indication that swords were used, were constantly changing, and achieved celebrity status by the end of the Bronze Age, with extra length and decoration becoming the order of the day, shows that swords were no mere cipher to be deposited in the ground, but a vital and regular part of the Bronze Age arsenal. It is not clear that many people actually owned a sword, but sheer numbers suggest that plenty of people used them over the years. In any case, there may have been a number of prohibitions on burying swords with dead warriors, ranging from sheer pragmatism (the desire to retain them for further use) to beliefs involving magical powers (Notung, Excalibur), in which burial of a sword with a warrior would be profane or otherwise undesirable.

WARFARE AFTER 1,200 BC

Around 1,200 BC a new set of arms and armour came into use in the Aegean area (Milojčić 1955; Harding 1984, ch. 6; Sandars 1985, 91ff.). Most visible was the arrival in Greece of the flange-hilted sword of European type ('Naue II' sword), with a broad, sometimes leaf-shaped blade that was suited to both cutting and thrusting blows in combat. Flange-hilted daggers ('Peschiera daggers'), flame-shaped spearheads and certain items of defensive armour also came into use. These changes have often been considered part of a general shift, not only in warfare practices, but also, potentially, in populations, with northern influences, or at any rate forms that started life in central Europe, becoming widespread in the south. According to Drews:

> the catastrophe [the decline of the major East Mediterranean cities around 1,200 BC] can most easily be explained . . . as a result of a radical innovation in warfare, which suddenly gave to 'barbarians' the military advantage over the long established and civilized kingdoms of the eastern Mediterranean. (Drews 1993, 97)

Specifically, the innovation was the invention of a new form of infantry warfare which was capable of resisting chariot attacks, and the means the infantry adopted was the javelin and the long sword:

> Until shortly before 1200 BC . . . it had never occurred to anyone that infantrymen with such weapons could outmatch chariots. Once that lesson had been learned, power suddenly shifted from the Great Kingdoms to motley collections of infantry warriors. These warriors hailed from barbarous, mountainous, or otherwise less desirable lands, some next door to the kingdoms and some far away. (Drews 1993, 97)

In other words, these newly rising warriors were those of the continental European Bronze Age, perhaps the Balkans.

The changes in the armoury of warriors in the Late Bronze Age, long known and long debated, are undoubtedly of significance, but can they really be assigned the role of destroyer of great civilisations? Two questions are crucial in determining the likelihood of the Drews scenario: was it indeed the case that warfare in Greece prior to the twelfth century was conducted solely (or mainly) by archers riding in chariots, and do the changes in weaponry really indicate to us a major shift in that practice, with spear and sword-wielding infantry replacing chariot-riding archers?

The first question has already been answered in the negative. Chariots were important, but not supreme; there is, for instance, abundant pictorial evidence for foot soldiers, using the two shield forms that are also depicted, the boars' tusk helmet, and the many swords and spears that belong to the period before 1,200 BC. There is also plenty of evidence that chariots were used for other purposes than fighting (Crouwel 1981).

The answer to the second question is more difficult to elucidate. The Naue II sword was certainly better balanced and more versatile than the Mycenaean rapier. It is very striking, however, that only two main forms of the several dozen that were developed within Europe ever penetrated to Greece: the common form (Nenzingen/Reutlingen), and that with a pommel tang (Stätzling, Allerona in Italy) (Schauer 1971; Bianco Peroni 1970). We see none of the variety found in the Balkans and Central Europe, and none (or no convincing cases) of the highly important *Vollgriffschwerter* that characterized many of the European industries. In Cyprus and the Levant, local variations on the theme were created – a good indication that the weapons were produced locally. Elsewhere, Greek smiths produced only this limited repertoire of Naue II forms (though admittedly, they quickly moved on to producing them in iron, where a further rapid development of the type is seen: Kilian-Dirlmeier 1993).

This must mean that if 'European' warfare techniques were introduced to Greece, it was only some of them, or some aspects of them, that were introduced. Why, if Drews is correct that the effects were so far-reaching, was this the case? It is clear both from experimentation and from pure practicality that much of what we see in the archaeological record is remote from the utility of the objects concerned. Deposition in graves, and deposition in wet places, took the form of a structured selection of the repertoire of bronzes available at a given moment in time. The provision of swords, in combination with other objects, relates to the marking of the burial or deposition as a significant moment in the social life of the community. Rock art panels in Scandinavia show many instances of figures, very obviously male, wearing or wielding swords, and taking part in what appear to be dances or ceremonial fights. Swords represented the tangible evidence of prowess in combat, regardless of whether any particular sword belonged to any particular buried individual. Artefacts had a 'social life', they reflected the social conditions from which they emanated. In this sense they indicate that warfare can be considered defining for the Bronze Age.

All we know of early Mycenaean Greece would suggest that this was true there as well as in Central Europe. The many depictions of combat and hunting show that these were important events in the life of individuals, and in view of the special way certain people were buried, of communities too. What changed in the decades around 1,200 BC was, on the face of it, a purely technical thing, in that sword blades became stronger and their attachment to the hilt more secure, and spears were thrown more than previously. On the other hand, the change was reflected also in the way metalwork was treated. In

Continental Europe, very large quantities of metal were consigned to the ground in circumstances which must frequently have prevented its recovery – in other words, it was intentionally thrown away. That practice was rare in Greece, though some have argued for its existence (Matthäus & Schumacher-Matthäus 1986). Metal forms that originated in Europe were therefore treated in 'Greek' ways, and in the process underwent a subtle change of meaning. It is not necessary to suppose that Naue II swords indicate northern mercenaries or northern smiths, though admittedly, the form did not arise by chance in Greece: it was 'brought' there by human action. Swords in Greece remained what they had been before – the physical means of warrior supremacy – even if they were used in combat somewhat differently. Swords in Europe possessed and continued to acquire a symbolic aspect that is absent in Greece.

In just the same way, the shields from Fröslunda, and the slaughtered bodies from Velim, with which we started, reflect a set of processes and conditions that led to their deposition. To the extent that the shields are material objects, created with a particular technology that was characteristic of the period from which they emanate, they are mere arrangements of atoms of time past; but through the way in which their material being was structured and organised, from the moment of their creation to that of their deposition, they are much more. They reflect the society that placed them in the ground, their form and function referring to a set of social conflicts that had to be resolved, their placement referring to one of the ways in which that resolution was to be achieved: not necessarily by use in battle, but by symbolic deposition in wet ground. Warfare – or to be more accurate, warlike objects – was just one of a number of defining characteristics of the Bronze Age, and to assume that weapons equate with warfare in a modern sense is misleading. Weapons and the real or imagined combat they reflect were just one of the ways in which life was structured, society was reproduced, and individuals learnt and expressed their place within that life and that society. For the unfortunates of Velim, the lesson may have been a hard one, and their ability to express themselves on those fateful days limited, but both they and the weapons (? weapon-tools, ? tool-weapons) that killed them were part of what it was to be a Bronze Age person on the Elbe in the middle of the second millennium BC. Whether or not their fate is a defining characteristic of the Bronze Age, for them personally, the lethal blows that killed them were definitive enough. Small sign of warriors here. Clearly, there were many aspects to the making, bearing and using of weapons in Bronze Age Europe, and warrior societies, while important at particular areas and times, were not ubiquitous. Fröslunda and Velim are perhaps two sides of the same coin: the (? symbolic) remains of the warrior elite in fighting mode, and the squalid deaths of those who were unlucky enough to have to face unarmed the weaponry that the Fröslunda shields notionally guarded against. For both, warlike behaviour and its consequences were definitive.

ACKNOWLEDGEMENT

I thank Colin Burgess for comments on an earlier version of this paper.

NOTES

1. Comparable finds came from Saint Martin de Corléans (Aosta): A. Cardarelli in Guidi & Piperno (1992); Mezzena (1988).

2. The many other arrowheads found in this spot are curiously not listed in that work.

3. Drews opposes the views of, among others, Terence Powell and Trevor Watkins, who saw the role of chariots in Mediterranean warfare as more or less incidental to the main business, which was conducted by infantry. He describes how opposing lines of advancing chariots would have had to have 'slowed as they closed and then somehow slipped around or through each other . . . After the surviving teams had made their way past each other, the archers may have faced the rear of their vehicles and fired once or twice at their opponents as they receded. Then the two forces, if they were still cohesive, must have wheeled around and begun their second charge, this time from the opposite direction' (Drews 1993, 128). As fuel to this fire, Drews believes that the Dendra cuirass could not have been worn by an infantryman, in view of its weight, but by someone who would be mostly stationary – a chariot warrior (Drews 1993, 175). So, according to this view, for most of the second millennium BC, chariots bearing archers were the main means of carrying out attacks in battle.

4. The actual number must be considerably higher than that: some of these catalogues go back many years, and no attempt has been made here to add in recent finds. It is believed that these figures are adequate to give an order of magnitude idea of the situation.

ELEVEN

THE EMERGENCE OF WARRIOR ARISTOCRACIES IN LATER EUROPEAN PREHISTORY AND THEIR LONG-TERM HISTORY

KRISTIAN KRISTIANSEN

INTRODUCTION: THE PACIFIED PAST[1]

The archaeological record in Europe is full of evidence of warfare: thousands of weapons from burials, hoards and even settlements have been classified and published. Paradoxically, this rich evidence has never been employed in a systematic study of the role of warfare in later prehistory.[2] In this way, archaeology has set itself apart from some of the central debates over the nature and role of violence and warfare that have taken place especially in social anthropology during the last generation or so (Bohannan 1967; Ferguson 1984; Haas 1990). This is regrettable, since the archaeological record holds the potential to answer some of the most basic questions as to the role of warfare in the evolution of human societies, especially pre-state societies.

It has been suggested that the post-Second World War resistance to coming to terms with the more brutal aspects of prehistoric European societies, including warfare and migrations, is rooted in archaeology's ideological role of legitimising a peaceful perception of human society in accordance with the welfare society (Kristiansen 1989; Keeley 1996, ch. 1; Carman 1997b). Consequently, modern post war archaeology saw ritual and monument-construction as a collective mobilisation for peaceful ends, fortifications as mainly ideological or religious, and the victims of warfare as ritual sacrifice (e.g., Renfrew 1973; Neustupný 1995, 199f.).[3] Although such aspects should not be denied, it is indeed remarkable to what extent the past became pacified after the Second World War. Accordingly, it should come as no surprise that the changing political configuration in Europe during the last decade has reintroduced identity, migrations and warfare to the archaeological agenda, reflected in a series of books and conferences on warfare (Randsborg 1995; Keeley 1996; Carman 1997a).

This chapter will develop a long-term perspective on the concept of 'warrior chiefs' or 'warrior aristocracies' in later European prehistory and their implications for understanding decentralised political leadership (Kristiansen 1991, fig. 2.1). It will demonstrate that the basic elements of aristocratic warfare and retinues were a more or less continuous feature of European history from the beginning of the second millennium BC until the rise of medieval states in temperate Europe. But before presenting this argument, it is necessary to place the study in theoretical context.

SOME THEORETICAL PRECONDITIONS

Theoretical concepts need to be in accordance with the historical context being studied if they are to serve their role effectively as interpretative tools. Turning to Europe in the first and second millennium BC, we observe that: rank was mostly ritualised, as reflected in monumental burials and ritual centres; prestige goods of bronze and gold were employed in social strategies, including their ritual destruction and deposition; and such depositions were subject to cyclical fluctuations and contextual changes in time and space.

Ritual is a powerful way of legitimising and institutionalising new positions of rank, but having done so, it also constrains further developments towards power and hierarchy (Bloch 1977). This dialectic is probably decisive for understanding the permanence of 'warrior chiefs' in later European prehistory, and it should lead us to focus attention on those periods and regions where there were attempts to disconnect rank and ritual. It can be suggested that during the millennia under study, we see repeated moves back and forth between the formation of ritually sanctioned rank, and attempts to separate rank and ritual.

However, the ritualized formation of rank cannot be separated from the potential and factual use of force (coercion), as reflected in the dominance of weapons in burials and hoards in certain periods and regions. As has been demonstrated, weapons were not only for display, but show clear signs of use in combat (Kristiansen 1984a; forthcoming).

Ritual, rank and coercion are thus intrinsically interlinked in pre-state societies (Fig. 1), and should never be studied in isolation. The balance between them should instead be the object of study, defining different strategies and historical phases in the formation of power and in the playing out of conflicts, which may correspond to different organisatonal structures. War is thus embedded in society and ritual, which means that we have to treat these interpretative categories as theoretically interlinked (Fig. 1).

The archaeological evidence of warrior aristocracies

In temperate Europe, the archaeological evidence of warrior aristocracies is consistent over 3,000 years, from 2,000 BC to AD 1,000. Shortly after 2,000 BC there appear in the Wessex Culture in southern England and in the Únětice Culture in central Germany rich,

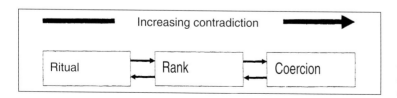

Fig. 1. Concepts and strategies for establishing and maintaining power.

chiefly burials under barrows furnished with new personal status items, such as dagger/short sword and axe, along with complex, gold-decorated ornaments, buttons and other insignia of ruling elites, such as sceptres and golden drinking cups (Clarke et al. 1985). This reflects the first merging of Near Eastern and traditional European ruling symbols. From the eighteenth to the seventeenth century BC, two interlinked phenomena spread across Europe: a new weapon complex that employed long sword, lance and chariot. It represented new military tactics, originating in the empires and palace cultures of the Near East and Eastern Mediterannean, based upon the employment of chariots to supplement infantry. The new weapons meant heavier man-to-man fighting, and demanded new military skills and the employment of protective armour. It thus put new demands on the training of warriors, and subsequently on their social and economic support. The professional warrior, well trained and organised, was introduced.

In temperate Europe, the new weapons were linked to the rise and expansion of a new, aristocratic warrior elite, above the traditional tribal warrior, which had employed bow and arrow and dagger/battle axe since the third millennium BC or even earlier (Kristiansen 1987a). In the archaeological record, the new warrior aristocracies set themselves apart by being buried in richly furnished graves, often in a barrow with sets of weapons, which could also be deposited in hoards. From the sixteenth to the fifteenth century BC, the new warrior chiefs became a common phenomenon at both local and regional levels in temperate Europe; social and military differentiation was recognisable in different combinations of weapons in grave goods, and in different uses of weapons (Coombs 1975; Kristiansen 1984, 1987; Schauer 1984, 1990). A study of the use and resharpening of Danish and Hungarian sword blades, for example (Kristiansen 1984a; forthcoming), demonstrated the following:

• Sword blades showed clear and recurring traces of resharpening and repair as a result of actual use. The pattern of resharpening could be linked to both attack and defence (Fig. 2), and edge damage in the form of notching was often visible. Similar evidence is testified on Irish Late Bronze Age swords (Bridgford 1997, 103ff.)

• There occurred a distinctive difference in the degree of use between full-hilted, richly ornamented swords and flange-hilted, highly functional swords. The latter always showed heavy traces of use in combat, the former only minor traces of use. This reflected a difference between chiefs and warriors that could also be sustained in grave goods. However, warriors belonged to the chiefly line, as they received the same kind of chiefly burial in mounds (Fig. 3). Therefore, it might also reflect a dual leadership between ritual/political leaders and war-leaders.

• A similar study of spears or lances by Schauer (1979) demonstrated the use of lances in combat. In burials, they were often found in pairs, and belonged to a consistent complement of warrior equipment. However, lances were more often found in hoards, and seem to have been the basic weapon of the infantry from Greece to northern Europe. This is demonstrated both in pictorial scenes of warriors (Fig. 4) and in the deposition of lances in single graves and in hoards. The evidence suggests that the numerical relationship between spearmen/infantry and chiefly warriors/swordsmen was about 10:1.

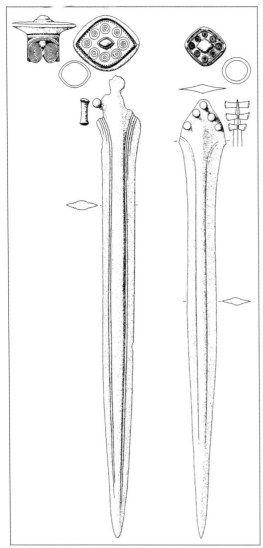

Fig. 2. Patterns of resharpening and blade transformation on Nordic Bronze Age sword blades. Distinctive resharpening occurs under the hilt (defence) and around the point of the blade (attack). Sometimes unrepaired edge cuts from warding off a slash from an enemy occur under the hilt, or at one side towards the middle part of the blade and the tip, deriving from from attacking/slashing towards an enemy sword.

• Defensive armour was already in use from the early second millennium BC, but was normally made of organic material – leather, wood and bone – as reflected in a few burials with good preservation (Makkay 1982; Schauer 1990). From the thirteenth century BC onwards, protective armour of hammered bronze came into use, mostly for military display and status emblems for chiefly war-leaders. Leather shields remained the norm (Osgood 1999, ch. III).

• Chariots are regularly displayed on rock art in Scandinavia, sometimes with detailed constructional indications (Fig. 5); similarly, bronze wheels for model vehicles are known, also displaying great attention to detail (Kristiansen 1987, n. 6; Rausing 1991), all of which points to the existence of real prototypes,[4] as in the Pontic steppe region (Piggott 1983, 91ff.) and at the chiefly courts in the Carpathians, where elegant, full-size spoked wheels with bronze frames demonstrate the use of chariots of Minoan/Mycenaean origin or inspiration.[5]

This pattern of chiefly war-leaders with a retinue of lance warriors and a smaller group of chiefly warriors is seen to be consistent over wide regions from the sixteenth century BC onwards. Functional changes in the nature of combat and the preference of weapons occur through time, and were quickly adopted from the Mediterranean to northern Europe, such as the introduction of the efficient, flange-hilted warrior sword from around 1,500 BC. During the early second millennium BC, the lance and the short sword/dagger combination was dominant, to be replaced by the long sword from the seventeenth century BC. A shift from rapier/axe combinations to slashing swords/knife took place from the late fourteenth century BC, while after 1,000 BC lances again win dominance as the standard weapon of the hoplite, also in central and northern Europe. Numbers in battle are difficult to estimate, but they

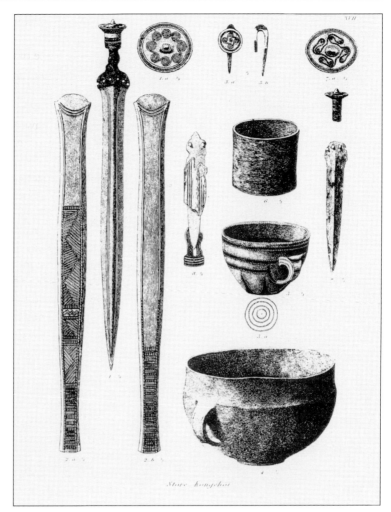

Fig. 3. Personal grave-goods from Nordic Bronze Age barrows: the chiefly sword and dagger from 'Store Kongehøj' in Jutland representing political/ritual leadership. Note the wooden drinking cups, imitating metal forms. Here they are decorated with tin nails to indicate status and the participation in international trade networks. Source: Boye 1896.

probably varied from small raiding parties, reflected in small weapon hoards, to armies numbering in the hundreds attacking fortified settlements, as suggested by studies by both Randsborg (1995, 44ff.) and the author (Kristiansen 1998).[6] In his study, Randsborg suggested that Bronze Age hoards with weapons might represent ritual depositions from battle. This hypothesis can be further substantiated by the observation that the swords in weapon hoards show traces of battle (unrepaired scars on the edge) and thus had not been resharpened, as is often the case in burials (Kristiansen 1984). A similar observation has been made in my later study of central European Bronze Age swords (forthcoming). Randsborg's method of using a few distinctive weapon hoards to reconstruct war parties thus seems partly justified (selection also occurred, so hoards are not representative, in a strict sense, of what constitutes war equipment), and suggests variations in the scale of Bronze Age warfare from small chiefly combats to a larger military phalanx of 50 (10 commanders and 40 commoners). To this, we should probably add a larger group of

Fig. 4. Bronze Age infantry with shield and lances, the military backbone of chiefly retinues during the second and first millennia BC. (A) Nordic warrior from the Wismar bronze horn (Middle to Late Bronze Age, Period II/III); (B) Mycenaean warrior from an amphora; (C) Greek warrior from a Geometric krater.

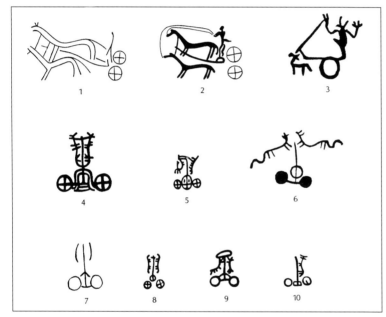

Fig. 5. Chariots displayed on rock art in Scandinavia during the sixteenth–fourteenth centuries BC. Note the very accurate representation of the basic construction of the chariot as seen from above on no. 4.

warriors armed with slings and bows and arrows, the evidence of which only rarely can be documented archaeologically (but see Cunliffe 1986, 80; Keeley 1996, fig. 1.1).

Thus, the archaeological evidence speaks conclusively about the impact of warfare in Bronze and early Iron Age Europe. This development was linked to the rise of so-called warrior aristocracies – a chiefly organisation of warfare whose social and cultural context we shall consider next.

THE SOCIAL AND CULTURAL CONTEXT OF WARRIOR ARISTOCRACIES

The appearance of warrior aristocracies represents the formation of a new chiefly elite culture in Europe (Kristiansen 1987a; Treherne 1995). It was embedded in new rituals, in new ideas of social behaviour and lifestyle (body care, clothing, etc), and in a new architecture of housing and landscape (Kristiansen 1998b). It centred around values and rituals of heroic warfare, power and honour, and it was surrounded by a set of new ceremonies and practices. They included ritualised drinking,[7] the employment of trumpets or *lurs* in warfare and ritual, special dress, special stools, and sometimes chariots. It meant that chiefs were both ritual leaders and leaders of war.

Thus, the new chiefly elite culture spread as a cultural package – a new social value system – rather than as separate elements. We may characterise it as a new social institution of chiefly leadership. It therefore became a penetrating phenomenon, crossing cultural boundaries throughout Europe. Although it was adapted to local or regional cultural traditions, its main components are easily recognisable from the Mediterranean to northern Europe. And since appearance was an important factor, it left rather good archaeological traces, as demonstrated above. We shall now proceed one step further, and try to characterize the social and cultural institution of warrior aristocracies. It comprises the following interlinked elements:

• New body culture and dress codes – appearance and body care gains new significance, reflected in the universal employment of razor and tweezer, and in needles for tattooing (Treherne 1995; Willroth 1997, Abb. 6). Men wore elaborate hats and capes, women had complex hair styles and elaborate ornaments, sometimes constricting their physical movements (Stig Sørensen 1997). Chiefs sat on stools and drank mead from valuable metal vessels and amphorae – or, more often, from imitations made of wood, but sometimes decorated with tin nails to signal status.

• A new architecture – large chiefly halls/farms that could hold the chiefly lineage and its attendants, and sometimes also the cattle. In western and northern Europe, the landscape is reorganised, with chiefly barrows placed on hilltops, surrounded by grazing cattle/sheep (Kristiansen 1998b). In central Europe, fortified chiefly residences and villages, sometimes with an acropolis, emerge (Jockenhövel 1990). Specialist metalworkers were attached to the new residences.

• A new warrior lifestyle – the new forms of combat demanded regular training, as well as specialists to produce weapons and wagons. Thus, a new warrior lifestyle became an integrated part of traditional life at every local chiefly farm. In opposition to a state society with a professional army separated from daily life, daily life was dominated by warrior values in addition to harvesting the fields and raising the cattle. Warrior ideology and lifestyle was an ingredient in everyday life, and was the meaning of life to most chiefs' young sons. Since every parish had its local chief, sometimes several, the influence of the chiefly warrior culture penetrated social life.

• New social organisation of warfare. This was reflected in the new system of clients/retinues, which was the basis for mobilizing war-parties for raids, trading expeditions etc. But it was also the economic basis for the chiefs, since clientship allowed the collecting of surplus to finance feasts, boats for trading expeditions, rituals, and warfare. While the chiefly barrows and feasts reinforced chiefly power and generosity, the professionally trained warriors were the means to extract tribute from unwilling clients and to enlarge tribute through raids when needed.

Thus, in the Bronze and early Iron Age of central and northern Europe, warfare was an integrated aspect of daily life. Every local community would regularly bury its dead warriors. Farming and warfare were the two axes of male activity, war training being a main concern of the young, local, chiefly males. During seasons of war, local retinues were mobilised along lines of rank. Changes occurred in sword combat – during the earlier second millennium BC, the long and narrow rapier was dominant (thrusting), while from the thirteenth century BC, the wide-bladed and heavier slashing sword took over. The size of armies may have developed over time, and thereby increased the scale of combat and political control, but this is mainly based upon the size of fortifications (Kristiansen 1998, fig. 200), whereas the overall social organisation of warfare based on the chiefly retinue remained largely unchanged. The impact of warfare on Bronze Age populations has never been studied systematically, but can sometimes be demonstrated in the age statistics of cemeteries. Here we find a recurring gender variation: young women show higher mortality than men due to the risks of giving birth, while adult men demonstrate highly increased mortality compared to women, most likely due to warfare (Kristiansen 1998, fig. 198; O'Shea 1996, fig. 6.1). In some cases, we also find the victims of warfare quickly buried or sometimes even thrown into mass graves, examples numbering from a handful to several dozen (Louwe Kooijmans 1998, Abb. 12; Chochorowski 1993, figs 47–8).

In all this, the Bronze Age and early Iron Age societies of the second and first millennia BC resemble historically known chiefdoms, which were characterized by systematic warfare, including a rather high proportion of the male population, and many casualties (Keeley 1997, figs 4.1, 6.1, and tables 2.1, 2.6, 3.2 and 6.2). A few ethnographic accounts may exemplify the nature of warfare as it might also have taken place in Bronze Age Europe, since there are many parallels between the organisation of warfare in historically known chiefdoms, and the picture painted above of the organisation of Bronze Age and early Iron Age warfare.

Carneiro (1990, 195ff.) writes about Fijian chiefdoms: 'Hostilities are now often attended by a certain amount of protocol and ceremony . . . The paramount chief typically leads his warriors in battle . . . Warfare is much more likely to be fought hand to hand' (cf. sword-fighters of the Bronze and Iron Age). In battle, there was 'trumpet blowing and drums were beaten' (cf. the *lurs* of the Bronze Age). In most battles on Fiji, the number of persons killed range from 20 to 200 (1,500–2,000 a year in the nineteenth century). Skulls were taken as trophies (cf. the Celts). The motives included the desire to increase the amount of tribute and slaves. It meant that success in warfare was crucial for maintaining chiefly power.

Carneiro observes cycles of expansion and regression of territorial power by a single chiefdom. It means that periods of warfare alternated with periods of peace. Barbara Price notes in ranked societies a 'regular pulsation of scale among large complex ranked groups: relatively brief periods of unity over wide areas alternate with longer periods of fragmentation' (Price 1984, 230).

Thus, while chiefly power over larger areas is short-lived, the chiefly structure itself is long-lived. This picture of a chiefly warrior culture linked to honour and power is also what we find in the later European sagas and myths, some of them – like the Celtic ones – with probable Bronze Age roots (Enright 1996).[8] It suggests a world-wide regularity in the history of warrior aristocracies, whose historical foundations in Europe we shall now explore further.

ECOLOGICAL AND ECONOMIC FOUNDATIONS OF WARFARE: POPULATION INCREASE AND THE FORMATION OF OPEN LAND

One of the classical debates about the causes of warfare concerns the role of population pressure and/or ecological stress and degradation. Carneiro (1970) saw warfare and territorial conquest as an inevitable outcome of population increase, and increasingly scarce resources under conditions of circumscription, such as island environments or valleys. Some confirmation of this has been found in Polynesia (Kirch 1984, ch. 8), where ecological degradation would sometimes result in endemic warfare and internal competition between priests, warriors and chiefs (Kirch 1991). This may not be the only or most common scenario, however. In an evolutionary process from extensive to intensive farming practice, warfare becomes a profitable investment as a means of getting access to new producers and clients, as pointed out by Earle (1978, 183).

In prehistoric Europe, the second millennium BC saw the formation of open land, and development from extensive to more intensive farming practice, but with great regional variation. From evolving pastoral economies of the steppe environment in eastern Europe to intensive downland agriculture and upland transhumance in central Europe, Bronze Age societies were able to organise the landscape on a grand scale. Everywhere, settlement and population expanded rapidly, as did agricultural practices (Kristiansen 1998, ch. 4). Ecological and demographic boundaries were already reached and even crossed during the Bronze Age in several regions, leading to local and regional regressions in economy and settlement. Capital investments were made in some regions in the form of field systems, while in others they were linked to mining.

In terms of settlement and farming economy, we can make the following observations. Fortified settlements and settlement hierachies are found only in some periods and regions. They alternate with regions and periods where no or few fortified settlements are found; instead, the landscape is dominated by individul farms or hamlets. This variation in settlement is linked to variations in economy, fluctuating between predominantly agrarian (intensive) and pastoral (extensive) strategies.

Thus, ecological and economic conditions which were to characterise Europe into the Iron Age and the Medieval period emerged during the second millennium BC, and in some regions even earlier. In this unstable environment, agricultural technology and the low-level industrial capacity of copper and iron mining defined some absolute barriers to economic and political development. It meant that one of the ways to increase political power was not via production, but via warfare – either to raid for booty or to control the production or trade of neighbours. It also meant that temperate Europe during the first and second millennia BC and the first millennium AD exhibited many of the demographic and ecological characteristics which defined historically known chiefdoms/kingdoms in Polynesia, America or Africa, such as high population figures in relation to highly exploited and unstable environments, and which all exhibited developed warrior cultures and warrior aristocracies. However, it is the organisation of people and resources, the size and nature of political control, that allows us to define the political organisation of society – a task to which we shall now turn.

POWER AND POLITIES: THE FORMATION OF POLITICAL TERRITORIES
AND THE ROLE OF LONG DISTANCE EXCHANGE

In order to understand both the nature and the scale of Bronze Age warfare, we need to consider the size of polities – areas characterised by social and political integration. This can be determined through a mapping of diagnostic cultural features (Kristiansen 1998, ch. 4.1; Harding 1997). A comparative analysis in central Europe reveals that territories were quite marked and well defined, with culturally distinct borders and empty zones between them. A recurring pattern emerges: local polities corresponding to a community level of integration 20–40 km wide, in some periods with one or a few fortified settlements. The next level is 100–200 km, reflecting networks of alliances between local polities. This corresponds quite well to the general characteristic of chiefdoms, being described as regional polities (Johnson & Earle 1987, 207ff.), and represent what is typically described as a local group or culture in Bronze Age literature.

These territories were linked together in networks of prestige goods exchange and metal trade, some of which was meant for local consumption (prestige goods and metal in areas without copper and tin), and some of which was meant for further exchange to more distant centres (such as amber from the Baltic area, also in high demand in the east Mediterranean). Recent research has made it possible to describe in some detail not only the size of political units, but also the nature of intermarriage and exchange (Jockenhövel 1991; Kristiansen 1998, figs 206–7). Intermarriage was frequent between community groups (the local chiefdom) inside the regional polity, which was characterised by small local variations in metalwork. Between regional polities 'dynastic marriages' took place to secure alliances and trade networks. These were less frequent, and are recognised by the occurrence of a 'foreign' set of female ornaments in burials or hoards. Typical distances are 100–200 km. While women maintained their local material culture, male chiefs were more inclined to signal participation in international networks by adopting foreign weapon types and bronze vessels, including the social institutions linked to warrior aristocracies (described above).

Thus, competition for access to exchange networks also implied access to prestige, metal and social and religious information that could be transformed into social and religious institutions, all of which was crucial for social and political reproduction. Participation in alliances meant participation in an international chiefly culture that was translated into local dialects of material culture, but which maintained a degree of international hegemony in terms of the social and religous institutions that accompanied it. Among other things, this was due to the international demand for the valuables circulating in the system, connecting regional polities of the east Mediterranean, central Europe and northern Europe. The system was highly competitive, as reflected in frequent changes in the dominant exchange networks. At the local level, participation in this Europe-wide chiefly network implied that chiefs had to organise trading expeditions and visits to political allies, and secure their protection by warrior retinues, over distances of 10–20 km to sometimes more than 100 km. A chief also had to mobilize the necessary economic means to participate in trading networks, by exploiting and, if possible, expanding his economic base to gain control over new producers/clients, and if that did not suffice, by raiding, to increase his productive basis by capturing labour (slaves, women) and cattle. All of this tended to boost both production and warfare, which in the long run might lead to overexploitation, endemic warfare and political fragmentation. This is the probable scenario behind the observed regional changes in trade networks.[9]

Some of this mobilisation was secured by the traditional political and religious power of old chiefly families, reflected in their large family barrows, and reproduced through complex rituals, as evidenced in religious centres of rock carvings (Kristiansen 1987b). But it was inevitable that these strategies had to be supplemented by warfare and raids, considering the competitive nature of society, the penetrating role of warrior culture, and the need to maintain and demonstrate chiefly power. Thus, we have to envisage a society where local and even regional warfare was an integral part of daily life.

The next section will combine the theoretical and empirical building blocks of the previous sections into a structural and historical model that accounts for the observed variations from a long-term perspective.

LONG-TERM TRENDS: SOCIAL AND HISTORICAL DYNAMICS

While the warrior elites are a general phenomenon throughout Europe, they may be embedded in different social and economic systems. Thus, a marked difference can be observed in the archaeological record between a political and economic system based upon stable finance, which controls land and producers in a vertical and hierarchial territorial settlement system of central places and villages, and a political economy based upon wealth finance, which is expansive, and which controls producers in a horizontal settlement system of individual farms with a less marked hierarchy (Kristiansen 1998, figs 224–5).

In the wealth finance system, the warrior aristocracies are ritually visible by employing barrows for chiefly burials and by abandoning commoners in rituals and burials, who consequently remain ritually invisible. The economy is dominated by moveable wealth (e.g., cattle) and the exchange of prestige goods. In the stable finance system, farmers/peasants are organised in small hamlets or villages with communal cemeteries linked to them, making them ritually visible. They form a social group or class distinct from the chiefly families, who live in fortified chiefly compounds placed at nodal points and controlling trade, producers and specialist production. The economy is dominated by non-moveable wealth (e.g., land). Hoarding is often the most common form of wealth-consumption. The social dynamics of these two political economies in Bronze Age Europe are summarised in Table 1 (based upon Goody & Tambiah 1973).

Table 1 Comparison of stable-finance and wealth-finance societies

Settled agrarian societies	*Warrior societies, expansionists*
Stable wealth	Mobile wealth
In-marriage, dowry	Out-marriage, bridewealth
Rich female burials, hoarding (fertility/payment)	Rich male burials, prestige goods in burials, no hoarding

These two social and economic strategies are interlinked, and compete for dominance according to a set of rules. Thus, the European societies of the first and second millennia BC contained the building blocks of two social and economic strategies that were never totally separated. In their basic or dominant forms, they represented two different types of investment, in labour, land and in ritual – those aspects of material culture most visible to archaeologists. During periods of settlement, expansion and agrarian intensification, labour investments were directed towards land improvement, while ritual investments took the form of votive offerings and fertility cults. Whenever new warrior elites expanded and took over, investments were directed towards moveable wealth and ritual investments in burial monuments, and only rarely in hoards. The two strategies also employed different rules of marriage and inheritance, although they were probably both based upon the highly flexible Indo-European 'Crow-Omaha' kinship system. As demonstrated by Rowlands (1980), it entails all the basic elements of competitive, expansionist social strategies described above, with the potential of forming gradually more endogamous chiefly elites.[10]

The two systems were inter-related historically, as warrior societies tended to develop on the periphery of the politically more developed and hierarchical sedentary societies of stable finance. The balance between them depended on a complex interplay between local conditions of economic expansion or regression and international conditions of exchange. In periods of economic regression in the agrarian economies, the warrior societies would sometimes run down the old centres. In due course, they would expand again and raise to dominance, creating a cyclical pattern of dominance by one or the other political and economic strategy (Fig. 6). These temporal and regional dynamics created a cyclical pattern of evolutionary and devolutionary processes that tended to halt a process towards true state-formation. It favoured a political culture of warrior aristocracies and relatively autonomous villages/farms which checked each other in repetitive cycles of expansion and recession. However, these conditions were rooted in basic economic and demographic constraints.

Thus the long-term dominance of warrior aristocracies in Europe from the second millennium BC onwards was due to the evolutionary constraints of the continent, reflected in its role for several millennia as a periphery to the more productive centres of urban culture and states in the Near East and the Mediterranean. This macrohistorical perspective may offer a possible explanation for the persistence of chiefdoms and warrior aristocracies in other parts of the world, being a structural outcome of centre–periphery relations between states, their peripheries and margins in less productive and unstable environments.

CONCLUSIONS

The introduction of the sword/lance/chariot and aristocratic warfare throughout Europe from the early second millennium BC and onwards coincides with the rise of a new type of chiefdom structure based upon the institution of warrior aristocracies and retinues.

It evolved along two lines of social organisation: vertical, agrarian-based systems of stable finance with settlement hierarchies (complex chiefdoms/archaic states), and expansionist horizontal warrior societies based on wealth finance, with no marked settlement hierarchy beyond local differences in the size of households and farms.

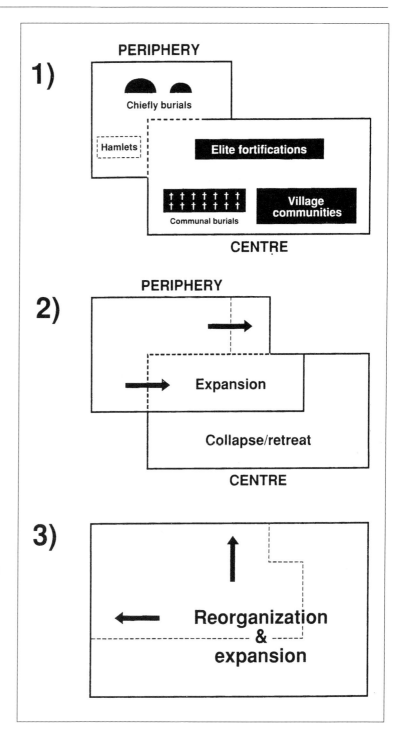

Fig. 6. Geographical model of the changing relationships between centres of metal production/agrarian production and warrior peripheries supplying special products and services, suggesting regular shifts in dominance through time.

Territorial control of tribute was usually limited to 20–40 km, but could be extended through confederations or alliances into a larger regional polity up to 100 km or more across. Warfare was linked to control over production (tribute, cattle and slaves), trade in metal, honour and prestige.

Although this social system entailed many of the building blocks necessary for state-formation, such as chiefly retinues and the extraction of tribute, the process was constantly being held back by internal dynamics and the constraints described above. Social dynamics were mainly linked to the ritualisation of power in combination with the competitive nature of exchange, whereas constraints were ecological and demographic.

Chiefly warrior aristocracies and warrior culture consequently remained an inherent feature of the social and ideological organisation of the European Bronze Age and early Iron Age societies for 2,000 or probably 3,000 years. We thus have to project back in time the old notion of a *Militärische Demokratie*, as coined by Morgan and later absorbed by Engels, another 2,000 years.[11] This raises a series of questions about the historical role of warrior aristocracies in the evolution of early states, characterised by a decentralised political economy. This chapter suggests that this social form was long-lived, lasting for several thousand years, not as a cause but as an effect of its structural position in a larger world system in combination with environmental constraints.

NOTES

1. This title is borrowed from the first chapter in Lawrence Keeley's inspirational book, *War Before Civilization* (Keeley 1996).
2. A few notable exceptions should be mentioned: in the United States, the work of Jonathan Haas (Haas 1990a; Haas & Creamer 1993), and in Europe, that of Vencl (1984), Kristiansen (1984; 1987), Randsborg (1995) and Osgood (1998).
3. In a recent book, Evžen Neustupný, in a section on prehistoric wars, restates the position that warfare played no significant role in European prehistory, and that Bronze Age weapons were not suitable for practical use (Neustupný 1998, 27ff.). He considers most prehistoric warfare to be ritualised, symbolic and peaceful. The present author does not deny the role of rituals and symbols in warfare, which is evident even in modern military organisation. However, there can be no rituals or symbols without the reality of what they signify. This chapter seeks to demonstrate that Neustupný's opinion is a myth based upon neglect of relevant evidence (see note 2 above), and based upon a lack of insight into the nature and role of warfare in social evolution, and more specifically in pre-state societies (Turney-High 1949; Keeley 1996). It should be stressed that this critique does not affect the book as a whole, which contains important new information on settlement systems in later prehistory.
4. In an interesting article, Willroth has surveyed rich Nordic, chiefly, male burials from the transition period I/II (*c.* 1500 BC) containing a bronze handle with a spike at the end (Willroth 1997, Abb. 7). With reference to the early Iron Age so-called 'Treibstacheln' (= 'driving stick'), he interprets them as hafted on a long, wooden shaft (wood is preserved in the bronze handle) to control chariot horses and/or cattle (a symbolic herding staff). This is an original and important observation to explain a hitherto unexplained tool. However, they could also have served as handle for a whip, the leather being hafted to the spike, and the remaining leather cord being wound around the midribs of the bronze handle to secure the hafting. This would explain the function of the otherwise strange midrib or midribs of the bronze handle (which swells slightly and has a supplementary wooden handle). Whichever interpretation is correct, the function remains basically the same, and supports the proposition that chariotry was practised in central and northern Europe from the earlier to mid-second millennium BC.
5. In a recent article, Stefan Winghart (1993) has convincingly demonstrated how specific constructional details – thickened spoke ends and 'double felloe' (the bronze rim frame and the added wooden felloe look like a double rim, basically the same principle as on a modern wheel) – link the Carpathian wheels from Arcalie, Transylvania, and Obišovce, Slovakia to Minoan and east Mediterannean types, as depicted, for example, on

the chariots of the Aghia Triada sarcophagus. They are thus safely anchored in a (later) Middle Bronze Age context (certainly pre-Urnfield), and represent Minoan/Mycenean influence (see also Pare 1992, figs 23–4). As they were deposited in pairs, they quite certainly represent a chariot, but find circumstances are otherwise missing. The big model bronze wheel from a chieftain's burial in Tobøl, Jutland, from early Period II, fifteenth century BC, shows decorative details that could represent the double metal/wooden felloe construction, and the joining of spoke ends and felloe is also shown (Thrane 1990, fig. 3a–b).

6. In a recent book, Robert Drews has suggested that the military organisation of the central European Late Bronze Age infantry was superior to east Mediterranean armies employing chariots and small groups of foot soldiers. The 'barbarian' armies were therefore able to overrun the more traditional organisation of the east Mediterranean armies during the turbulent thirteenth–twelfth centuries BC, which changed both the balance of power and the military organisation (Drews 1993).

7. In a most interesting book, Michael Enright (1996) has demonstrated continuity in the drinking rituals and social reproduction of chiefly retinues from La Tène to the Viking Age, based upon literary evidence, but also supported by archaeology. However, his findings, are echoed in the material culture of the preceding millennium. From the Early Bronze Age of Scandinavia, we find cups with relics of mead in both male and female burials (among them the famous Egtved woman, wearing a corded skirt employed in rituals, as demonstrated in female figurines, since one of them holds a cup). Drinking sets for several persons in bronze and gold are likewise associated with both male and female depositions during the Late Bronze Age (Kristiansen 1984b, figs 10 and 11).

8. This theme and the relationship between Bronze Age and later Iron Age retinues, in archaeology and in texts, has been systematically analysed in a recent doctoral thesis by Paul Treherne.

9. It might also lead to periodical conquests of larger areas, something which is hard to trace archaeologically, but is likely by reference to ethnohistorical cases, such as the Iroqouis or the Zulu (Otterbein 1967a, 1967b). However, by analogy with the material culture of the Celtic conquest migrations of the later first millennium BC, future research may also prove it possible to infer similar phenomena during the second millennium BC (Kristiansen 1998, ch. 8).

10. Rowlands's study of kinship and alliance still stands as an isolated classic that has not been followed up in Bronze Age research. More detailed studies, like those of Wels-Weyrauch (1989), would allow the application and testing of models of kinship and marriage strategies.

11. The vast literature on '*Militärische Demokratie*' or the Germanic Mode of Production (Herrmann 1982; Gilman 1995), is not discussed here since we need more up-to-date case studies to establish a better empirical and historical platform for discussion.

TWELVE

INTO THE IRON AGE: A DISCOURSE ON WAR AND SOCIETY

KLAVS RANDSBORG

INTRODUCTION

This chapter has three theses: that a number of human issues and phenomena transcend the recognised patterns of culture; that Europe, towards the close of the second millennium BC (at some time after 1200 BC), experienced a highly important challenge to the common aristocratic norms of society that had built up since the Stone Age, and that the social discourse of the idea of equality found new force, both north and south of the Alps, after about 700 BC and in the middle centuries of the first millennium BC (Table 1).

Table 1 Chronological/cultural framework for Bronze/Iron Age Europe

BC	Greece	Central Europe	Denmark
2000	Palaces (Crete)	Early Bronze Age	Late Neolithic
1500	Palaces (mainland)	Middle Bronze Age	Early Bronze Age
1200	Collapse	(Cremation, grave-goods disappearing)	
1000	Centres	Late Bronze Age	Late Bronze Age
800	Aristocratic 'backlash'*		
500	City States	Early Iron Age (the west elitist)	Late Bronze Age

* Mostly petty aristocracies, partly egalitarian ideology, stress on sanctuaries

---

The puzzled reader may ask what this has to do with warfare. The quick answer is that the spearmen and shieldsmen in question, similarly equipped and fighting shoulder-to-shoulder in small and large 'regiments', were mostly full members of society – indeed, its citizens – not the mercenaries or conscripts of later regimental armies. The classic example is the Greek hoplite, in full panoply from 700 or 650 BC onward (Hanson 1991). Less well known is a related military development in other parts of Europe.

Although replete with guesswork, these theses seem to work both as a general model of the social discourse from the Bronze to the Iron Age and of the military development of the period. Let us first go north, and into detail.

HJORTSPRING

The find, the boat and its crew

One of the truly famous archaeological finds from the Iron Age in Europe is the huge military sacrifice from a tiny bog at Hjortspring, on the island of Als (off south-eastern Jutland) in Denmark (Randsborg 1995). It contains a magnificent boat or huge canoe with room for some twenty-two paddlers-cum-warriors, plus the weaponry and other equipment for a small fighting force substantially larger than the crew of the boat. The

Fig. 1. The Hjortspring find under excavation in 1921–2. Photo: National Museum, Copenhagen.

date of the sacrifice is *c.* 350 BC, or Late Classical Greece, the time of Philip II of Macedonia.

The Hjortspring find was expertly excavated in the early 1920s (minor digging for peat before the excavation implies that the find is not complete), and the work on preserving the delicate wood was outstanding for its period (Rosenberg 1937). The finds have recently been conserved anew, and are beautifully exhibited in the Danish National Museum. But perhaps its deeper secrets are only beginning to be revealed.

The boat is of knot-free lime from very tall trees, and weighs only about 500 kg. It is 19 m long in total, the interior measuring a little more than 13 by 2 by 0.75 m. It is made of five thin boards, and has identical, prominent double-prows at both ends, the lower 'beak' being by far the most powerful, although it does not show. At one end is a small quarter-deck with three ornamented seats: one for the steersman, the other two facing the crew. A rudder was also found at the other end, where a fourth 'commander' or 'veteran' warrior is implied, his function being to indicate the timing of the stroke to the two ranks of nine paddlers who faced away from the quarter-deck. Up to eighteen long, narrow paddle-oars (common warriors) and two punting-poles (commanders) were found, corresponding to the suggested crew, omitting the steersmen for obvious reasons.

At sea, it would have been possible to ram enemy vessels of similar construction amidships with the strong lower beak of the prows, perhaps using the quarter-deck as a fighting-platform.

The warriors would no doubt have exercised together frequently, and the disciplined life on the boat would have created further bonds, for instance between paddlers on the same bench. Thus, fighting on land, and following the order of seating in the boat, a small phalanx might have formed of two ranks of nine warriors, with the veterans on the wings. However, the weaponry implies that the seniors would more likely have made up a third rank of four. The weapons found are sufficient to equip at least four boats at the size of the preserved vessel, and thus more than four phalanxes with a total front at least 100 m wide.

Weaponry and fighting force

The offensive weaponry found at Hjortspring includes 11 short one-edged iron swords, 8 lances with bayonet-shaped heads, 65 common spears with heads, 65 spears or javelins with heads (31 broad, 34 narrow), and 31 javelins with small antler/bone heads (Fig. 2). The defensive weaponry comprises some ten coats of chain-mail – in fact, the earliest in Europe – 52/53+? broad wooden shields, and 11/12+ narrow ones (Table 2). There are 67/68 shield-handles, plus ten unfinished spares. It is striking that the bow and arrow is missing. Obviously, this common and highly useful weapon was not up to contemporary military standards, perhaps because of its allusion to hunting rather than fighting between honourable men, perhaps because it prolonged the period of fighting and increased the number of casualties.

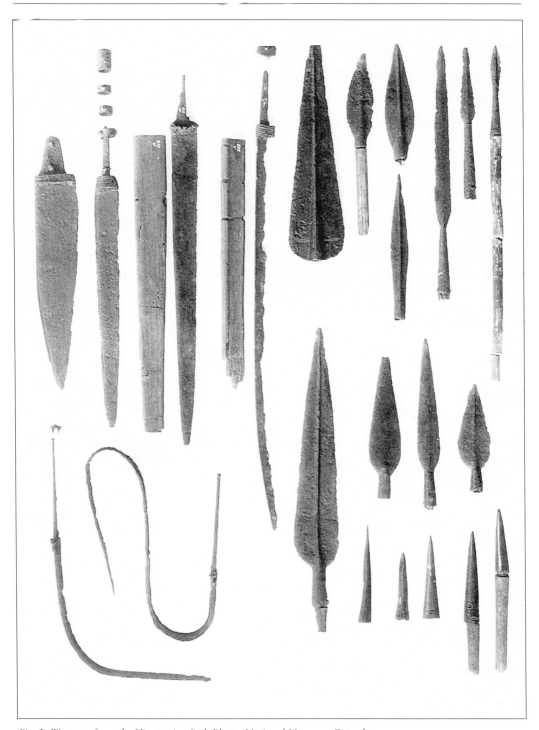

Fig. 2. Weapons from the Hjortspring find. Photo: National Museum, Copenhagen.

Table 2 Weapons of the Hjortspring sacrifice: distribution according to suggested naval and military function and rank (Randsborg 1995)

	Paddler/Fighter	Commander	Total
Crew/Fighting Unit	18 (82%)	4 (18%)	22 men per boat
Mail-coats		10+ (?)	
Swords		11	
Lances, bayonet iron head		8	
Lances, common iron head			65
– big decorated variant		1	
– common variant	64		
Javelins, iron head			64
– broad variant	30		
– narrow variant	34		
Javelins, antler/bone head	31		
Shields			63/65+
– narrow variant		11/12+ (18%)	
– broad variant	52/53+ (82%)		
Shield-handles			67/68, plus 10 unfinished spares
Fighting dogs		1+	

This allows for the reconstruction of a mobile elite fighting unit of four commanders (mail, narrow shield, sword, bayonet-lance) and eighteen (two times nine) common warriors (broad shield, one spear, one javelin – half with a broad, half with a narrow head). Half of these warrors would also have had a javelin with a small head of antler/bone (round in cross-section), perhaps for piercing mail. The age of the force was probably low, although teenagers were probably not included (because of their inadequate physical strength and stamina for full-pace paddling and line fighting). The commanders or veterans were probably in their late twenties or thirties. The bones of the dogs indicate the use of fighting hounds, possibly by the commanders.

The composition of the force reveals both uniformity and a specialisation of tasks. In particular, the lack of a veteran javelin is noteworthy. The mail, narrow manoeuvrable shield, bayonet-lance and shortsword all imply fighting at close quarters in the confusing but decisive end-phase of the battle.

This scenario is, of course, hypothetical: for instance, the veterans of the four or more boats may have formed a special unit, although this would have left the rest of the fighters without senior command. Indeed, a striking structural similarity is seen with the contemporary early Roman legion, with two tiers of common warriors, and a third of *veterani*, without javelin, but with mail. The very front Roman ranks, the lightly armed, very young scout troops, or *velites*, are missing at Hjortspring, but may be represented by the curious javelins with antler/bone heads. (Incidentally, rocks, chipped to equal size, probably for use as missiles, were also found in large numbers at Hjortspring, but again, no traditional bow and arrow.)

Beliefs

The Hjortspring find should be interpreted along traditional archaeological lines for military bog offerings of the Iron Age – as a gift to the gods following a major victory over an enemy force. The enemy equipment, in full or in part, was sacrificed in bogs and other wet places. The main references for this can be found in ancient Roman and Greek authors describing and explaining such events. In the case of Hjortspring, there was only room for a single boat, perhaps the leading one, in the tiny bog. More may lie elsewhere, or may have been used to return the defeated warriors, deeply humiliated (there is no trace of human sacrifice), perhaps to fight another day.

As to the religious dimension, the Alsian home force, or militia, after having defeated the naval invasion, sacrificed the spoils, probably to the god of war (Tyr). (Two rare, but undated, Tyr place-names are preserved just east of Hjortspring, perhaps even indicating the battlefield.) The ship is the symbol of the fertility god of Frej, encapsulating the warriors, and enabling man to travel on all surfaces. In fact, the earthly powers of fertility and the transient ones of water (Odin?) are both present in the bog, which since the Stone Age had been the traditional sanctuary of the north (Table 3).

Table 3 Suggested relationships between offerings, natural forces and (later) named deities, Bronze to Iron Ages in Denmark (etc.) (Randsborg 1995)

Sun/Sky	*Earth (Land & Sea)*	*Water*
Early Bronze Age:		
Weapons	(Female jewellery)	Skallerup model waggon
Cult axes	Ship symbols	(Web-footed birds)
The Sun Chariot		(Metal vessels)
Late Bronze Age:		
(Weapons)	Female jewellery	Metal vessels
Cult axes	Female rings	Gold cups
Shields	Ship symbols	Golden rings
Viksø helmets		Bog bodies
Lur trumpets		
Sandagergård cult house?		
Early Iron Age:		
Weapon sacrifices	Neck-rings	Bog bodies
	Other rings	Cauldrons
	Waggons	
	Bog-pots	
Later (?):		
Tyr & Tor	Nerthus/the Vanes	Odin
	(Freja, Frej, Njord)	

Other Early Iron Age sacrifices in bogs include human bodies, costly metal vessels, female neckrings, etc., fine wagons and common pots (with food) – all probably offerings to specific deities.

Barbarian and Mediterranean military forces

Traditionally, the Hjortspring find has been considered 'primitive' and 'poor' (the boat said to resemble a Bronze Age one, there being little iron, etc.), in spite of the chain-mail and the fact that several of the shortswords (those with an inward-curving edge) reflect Mediterranean types. In fact, as implied, the find is clearly a small, barbarian edition of the south European armies of the time, made up of units or 'regiments' of similarly equipped shield/spearsmen in close mutual support, using phalanx tactics to achieve a decisive result in pitched battle. Such tactics, as we shall see, were quite different from the middle-range ones of the Bronze Age.

The Hjortspring army is no doubt an amphibious elite force, to judge from its small size, magnificent boat and fine weaponry. Barbarian armies many thousands strong are, also known from the period however. These were probably made up of militia forces involving a large part of the male population, perhaps even all able men (Caesar, for instance, tells us of a barbarian 'army' of 92,000, or almost 25 per cent of the tribal population of the Helvetians, as counted by the Romans in terms of males fit for fighting).

Thus, barbarian Iron Age migrations may have come about for military reasons. The necessity to launch large forces to fight Mediterranean armies would have taken a large part of a male population away from home. The logistics would have called for additional support from the women, and a migration would have been the result – men, women, children and all. Such an army is very slow-moving, much slower than a militia force. Elite forces, by contrast, moving by foot, horse or ship, are mobile and suited to surprise attack, as well as for supporting other forces.

Although cavalry forms no part of the Hjortspring fighting force, chain-mail was originally probably a cavalry defensive weapon (slightly earlier Scandinavian rock-carvings, as well as decorations on pots from Poland, show horsemen with spear and shield). Thus, fighting at home, the 'commanders' or *veterani* might have been mounted. In fact, a local militia force fighting a Hjortspring amphibious force may have had the benefit of using cavalry for scouting, for flanking movements, and for pursuit (Spence 1993).

The enemy

Finally, the Hjortspring find also contained various other equipment, including bronze dress accessories, various vessels in bronze (?), wood and clay, wooden dishes, spoons, a spindle, a scoop (for the boat), wooden discs with handles (perhaps 'gongs', with sticks), a flute, various tools (for repair of boat and weapons), thin ropes, a cheek-piece, and not least, a series of fine, turned wooden boxes, etc. The latter reflect a technology not common in the north until a thousand years later. Surprisingly, they imitate contemporary Greek pyxides, as made in Athens in the fourth century BC, and traded, with other fine wares, across the Mediterranean, for instance through the emporium of Spina near the Po estuary and in close proximity to central Europe.

The pyxides occur as ceramic imitations in the greater Hamburg area, and only there. In Tacitus (writing *c.* AD 100), this is the ancient home of the Lombards: 'hemmed in by mighty peoples, they find safety, not in submission, but in the risks of battle'. Thus, this seems to be the region of origin of the Hjortspring amphibious force. It would have exited the Elbe, crossing the narrow land-bridge to Jutland at what would later be Hedeby, and alighted from the Sli inlet, just south of the island of Als. Possibly, the naval operation, in need of constant support (unlike Alexander's troops, for instance, which were supplied from the fleet), was only a mobile arm of a failed, much larger southern 'SeaLand' invasion. This perhaps explains the rarity of military sacrifices of the Iron Age, where raiding cannot have been uncommon.

Finally, from the fate of the Hjortspring force, we can guess the tactics necessary to counter phalanxes – possibly more of the same, probably mobility, and no doubt attacks on the lines of supply, even denying logistics to the enemy. In fact, this is a description of the successive development – in later Antiquity and the early Middle Ages – of north Germanic light mobile armies and amphibious elite forces (Adler 1993). These were highly dependent on old-fashioned lance and shield, and thus on 'Greek' phalanx fighting, right up to the time of the arrival of the Medieval cavalry and infantry.

SOCIETY

Northern Europe

Apart from the Hjortspring find, southern Scandinavia and northern Germany are almost completely devoid of military finds in the Early Iron Age (Randsborg 1995; also for the non-referenced items below). No weapons are found in the graves (all cremations), the villages and hamlets are unfortified (and made up of small farmsteads of almost equal size), no boundary walls are seen, there are no naval barriers, and so on. Still, a highly developed military organization existed in a society that belittled military prowess (as well as social stratification). Clearly, the social discourse was a very different one from that of the Bronze Age, especially the Early Bronze Age.

In the Early Bronze Age, weapons are common in both graves and sacrificial hoards of valuables, including a few cultic items like the Trundholm sun chariot and the Skallerup wagon – forerunners of the many specifically cultic objects of the following periods. In the graves, usually in prominent burial mounds, differences in personal equipment, including exotic bronze and gold, reflect competition among the elite. Settlement is scattered and made up of large farmsteads, some with wide houses up to 50 m long. Competition (and social mobility) also shows up in the weaponry, short on or devoid of defensive weapons, and dominated by various combinations of fine sword, dagger, axe, fighting lance with powerful head, and bow and arrow.

Towards the close of the Early Bronze Age, cremation gradually became the dominant rite. This did not affect the amount of grave-goods. After 1200 BC, however, the aristocratic use of mounds and burial goods as a means of competition quickly disappeared. Instead, rich sacrifices of female jewellery, some weapons (including separate finds of shields and helmets), huge cult axes, bronze vessels, gold cups, gold rings and *lurs* dominated. This leads into the sequence of Early Iron Age sacrifices, equally divided into separate categories, among which Hjortspring is be placed.

By the Late Bronze Age (around and after 1000 BC) sanctuaries and sacrifices had taken over from graves as the prime medium of investment, and no doubt served as important social foci as well. In spite of aristocratic attempts, connected with western central Europe, at restoring the old order, demonstration of social inequality was suppressed, in particular after *c.* 700 BC, when even the sacrifices get simpler. At the beginning of the Iron Age (500 BC), the settlement was dense, with complete field-systems, the individual farms being small, but with individual families in control of their own cattle, other means of production, etc.

In this north European society, towards the close of the Late Bronze Age, the bronze sword – like the earlier lance with fine bronze head – disappeared. It was supplanted by a cheaper lance or spear with an iron head. The shield, known in the Late Bronze Age in a pan-European round sheet-bronze variant, was now oval or square. Clearly, this is a reflection of the new tactics of fighting in formation appearing in the aftermath of the stepwise decline of aristocratic Bronze Age values and weaponry, leading some centuries later to the Hjortspring phalanx.

Central Europe

Much the same development is seen in central Europe, so only the salient features are highlighted here. One of these is the resurgence of aristocratic values (and sword-dominated weaponry) in the first quarter of the first millennium BC in the 'Celtic' west. In the second quarter of the first millennium BC (the local Early Iron Age), this milieu found itself at the extreme end of commercial Greek interests, thus supplying the aristocracy with the means – however short-lived and poorly understood, apart from the splendour of the artefacts – of triumphant display. Thus, a colonial western Greek bastioned city wall in mud-brick was built in the sixth century BC at the Heuneburg hillfort in south-western Germany, Near Eastern furniture with ivory fittings was imported, Archaic Greek monumental sculpture was imitated, and so on (Kimmig 1983). Indeed, a link is supposed between central Europe, the Etruscans, and Magna Graecia, the latter in some ways being the shamelessly rich 'America' of Hellenism.

In western central Europe, the sword disappeared with the advent of the strong Mediterranean impulse of the sixth century BC. It is supplanted by (double) spear and dagger – no doubt a reflection of Greek phalanx fighting.

In eastern central Europe, links were forged with northern Italy (Stary 1982). Here, double-spear (and axe) dominated fighting – again on the Mediterranean model – from about 600 BC on, with swords disappearing even earlier. Further north, in central Poland (en route to the north), pictures on cremation urns of the same period tell the same story (La Baume 1963). The dominant weapons are again two spears (usually) and an oval, now pan-European, shield – the Hjortspring one – which is sometimes called 'Celtic' (in fact, it is Italian in origin). Only the Greeks still carried round shields.

Central Poland has many traits in common with northern Europe, although it also adopts steppe features. The cultural phenotype is 'bleak' (poorly equipped cremations, rather few sacrificial hoards, but very many settlements with small house structures), there is little stress on social stratification – rather, a strong egalitarian ethos is evident.

Also from central Poland is the impressive Biskupin fortress from *c.* 700 BC, which displays features strangely and strikingly similar to the layout of the early Greek colonies in southern Italy (the earliest perhaps Syracuse of 734 BC) (Niesiołowska-Wędzka 1989; Hoepfner & Schwandner 1994). These features comprise parallel streets at equal intervals along which are house structures all of the same size and layout. There are few streets – indeed, there is only one along the inner side of the rampart, connecting the parallel ones. Such cities are known between the late eighth and the early third century BC, with Naxos and Syracuse on Sicily being the earliest, and Krane on Kephallenia in Greece possibly the last (Randsborg, forthcoming).

Thus, Biskupin, along with a few other similar complexes of the same region, may itself be a colony (perhaps from central Europe proper), adopting the structure of contemporary colonial Greek settlements, although built in wood, not in stone, and considerably smaller. At any rate, in eastern Europe, from Poland to the Mediterranean, the contemporary egalitarian discourse of Greece is very much felt, by contrast to the still aristocratic west.

Common to east and west, however, are experiments with spear-shield warfare and the many fortified settlements of the early first millennium BC – princely or not – which, with the sanctuaries, would have served as foci of local society in much the same way as did the city centre and the central sanctuaries and temples in the Greek polis of the period.

Southern Europe

In Aegean Greece, after 2000 BC (if not before), aristocratic life focused on a series of larger and smaller palaces and other centres, foci of administration, communication, even long-distance trade, production, distribution and cult (Dickinson 1994). In the 'palatial' period, for instance at Mycenae, princely tombs hold a weaponry dominated by sword and dagger, the lance playing only a secondary role.

Aristocratic Aegean Bronze Age society went through several stages, but collapsed definitively around 1200 BC, leaving only minor 'European'-style leadership, incidentally with weaponry such as long swords, similar to that of central and northern Europe. For instance, the earliest full two-piece breastplate, made famous by the Greek hoplite and the modern dragoon, is a central European invention, probably a bronze version of a leather cuirass. A fine vase of the twelfth century BC (the famous so-called 'Warrior Vase' from Mycenae) shows marching ranks of helmeted and perhaps armoured (in leather?) warriors only equipped with spear and light shield – a very early representation of what was to come. Similar light infantrymen, but with sword, are seen in contemporary Near Eastern imagery, for instance fighting Egyptians from both land and sea.

Footsoldiers occur occasionally in earlier Bronze Age imagery too, lined up behind huge shields (seemingly of hides). They may wear a boar-tusk or other helmet, carry a very long lance, and a sword or a dagger. In battle and hunting scenes alike, they are interspaced – in almost Near Eastern fashion – by lancers and bowmen without shields. Such footsoldiers are lacking in mobility, and a far cry from those on the 'Warrior Vase' and later.

In the Aegean Iron Age, grave-goods are few, and fewer still after *c.* 700 BC, with particularly few weapons (Osborne 1996). Almost only in the barbarian far north of Greece, including Macedonia, do burial customs allow a view of the weaponry. Early elite graves from Macedonia (the royal centre of Vergina), with parallels in other parts of the Mediterranean and in central Europe, hold about the same number of lances and swords (Rhomiopoulou & Kilian-Dirlmeier 1989), but only twice have the two types of weapon been found together – possibly a distinction between senior and junior warriors was made at burial.

At Vitsa in Epiros, from c. 850 BC on, the light common footsoldier with lance (and a supposed shield) as the dominant weapon is found in a cemetery holding 108 lances, nearly half in pairs, versus only 19 swords (Vokotopoulou 1986). Perhaps we can see in this a pattern of general significance, with aristocrats, in the period after 1200 BC, leading uniformly equipped spear- and shieldsmen into battle, preceding the classical heavy hoplite phalanx by several hundred years.

In other parts of southern Europe, by contrast to the Aegean, elite burials and other manifestations are not infrequent during the early first millennium BC. From Spain come stelae with pictures of aristocrats and their shield, possible helmet, sword, lance, bow and arrow, waggon, mirror, etc. (Almagro 1966). From Sardinia come figurines of warriors with helmet, greaves, perhaps pectoral, carrying shield, sword, bow and arrow, or long war-club and dagger (but no lance) (Stary 1991). In central Italy, elite graves are very common, the sword being replaced by the dagger after 700 BC, then the dagger by the axe, while the lance became ever more important, as did helmet and body armour (Stary 1979). In Etruria, the latter was often in Greek style after *c.* 650 BC. However, the Etruscans, like other Italians and Europeans, never fully traded mobility for protection. The light Greek peltast was more of a model of fighting than the prestigious, heavy hoplite with his very costly equipment (Best 1969).

Greek vase-painting in the post-palatial and especially the earliest Iron Age is almost completely devoid of images. In the later Geometric period, these reappear with representations of the life-crises of the elite, among other things. The weaponry shown in vase-painting between *c.* 850 and 700 BC is dominated by the sword, with the bow and arrow also playing a role, but lances make up only a quarter of the images (van Wees 1994). However, this may not be a full representation of actual weaponry (rather those of the elite), nor of contemporary warfare – for instance, half the scenes show fighting at sea (Ahlberg 1971), and chariots are common.

After 700 BC, by contrast, the lance makes up almost all the weapons shown in Greek painting (close to 90 per cent). Interestingly, the Iliad (composed at or shortly after 700 BC) also has the lance as the by far most quoted weapon (more than 80 per cent). Indeed, the first pictures of hoplite fighting (in full panoply) – including the famous 'Chigi Vase' made in Corinth *c.* 650 BC – is of the same period.

There are no representations in Greek art of siege warfare, which anyway did not play a large role in Greece in the Archaic and Classical periods (almost all city walls are from between *c.* 400 and 200 BC: Randsborg, forthcoming). Clear offensive superiority was not attained in this field of warfare until about 300 BC (with the new professional armies). By contrast, contemporary Near Eastern warfare, in a region dominated by cities, very much consisted of sieges, with few major pitched battles. In this respect, too, early European infantry warfare, with battles between phalanxes in the open landscape, is quite unique. On the battlefield, a measure of mobility is always a prerequisite.

Thus, shield-lance-dominated warfare in Greece ranked higher in the post-palatial Iron Age, in the hoplite version running parallel to the development of the highly competitive polis. Links between the egalitarian ideology of the polis (whatever its particular constitution) and the organisation of the citizen phalanx have already been noted. Other important links are with a strong economy that allowed for such substantial investments in military equipment.

CONCLUSIONS

The history of Europe during the late second and the first millennium BC can be viewed as a set of variations on a few central themes of social discourse. On the structural level, much the same phenomena were at work in, for instance, Denmark as in Greece at any one major period. Common cultural history – in particular archaeology – tends to mask this fact.

The reasons are: that societies had different technologies, economies, and different levels of organisation in Antiquity, especially in particular periods, and along the north–south axis; that production and distribution was mainly local and that societies had a strong desire for self-expression. Therefore, upon inspection, we find societies culturally positioned in a geographical pattern or hierarchy obscuring common bonds. A centre-periphery perspective, inspired by an economic view of the world, is therefore often more robust than the 'stage by stage' ones propagated by the 'social discourse' perspective.

Nevertheless, the rise and fall of aristocracies comply with the 'stage-and-discourse' model, as does the rise in the early first millennium BC of a Europe of 'communes' – aristocratic or other – defined by well-defined social bodies, centres, and important sanctuaries.

Finally, the changing patterns of warfare are on the one hand the result of a general shift towards lance-shield fighting (with rather cheap weapons), at work even before c. 700 BC, on the other the result of the particular Greek development towards elaboration of weaponry, both offensive and defensive, and the tactics connected with 'regimental' or phalanx fighting in the open field, which in turn had a tremendous effect on European warfare, both in the Mediterranean and beyond.

Whichever way we see it, the rise of lance-shield fighting, and thus of European infantry, was seemingly the result of the decline of aristocratic norms and lifestyles (and high productivity) at the end of the Mediterranean Bronze Age. The phalanx is concomitant with the rise of poorer but focused and highly competitive societies, in Greece as across Europe. The new weaponry and tactics no doubt meant more bloodshed. However, it also allowed for a high measure of decision in battle – a prerequisite both for outnumbered but well-organised troops, and for successful military expansion, as in the case of the Romans.

THIRTEEN

HOPLITE OBLITERATION: THE CASE OF THE TOWN OF THESPIAI

VICTOR DAVIS HANSON

THE NATURE OF HOPLITE BATTLE

In the seventh and sixth centuries BC, most decisive fighting among the Greek city-states was by heavy infantry composed of farmers, outfitted in bronze armour with thrusting spears. If a community was self-supporting through, and governed by, its surrounding private landowners, then hoplite warfare made much more sense than fortification or garrisoning passes: muster the largest, best-armed group of farmers (*pandêmei*) to protect land in the quickest, cheapest and most decisive way possible. It was far easier and more economical for farmers to defend farmland on farmland than to tax and hire landless others to guard passes endlessly – the sheer ubiquity of which in mountainous Greece ensured that they could usually be turned by enterprising invaders anyway. Raiding, ambush and plundering, of course, were still common, but the choice of military response to win or protect territory with the rise of the polis was now a civic matter, an issue to be voted on by free, landowning infantrymen themselves.

Almost all these wars of a day between rugged and impatient yeomen were infantry encounters over land, usually disputed border strips involving agrarian prestige more than prized fertility. Customarily the army of one city-state, an Argos, Thebes, or Sparta, met their adversary in daylight in formal columnar formation – the word 'phalanx' means 'rows' or 'stacks' of men – according to a recognised sequence of events.

After divination (*hiera*), a seer (*mantis*) sacrificed a ram to the god (*sphagia*). The 'general' (*stratêgos*) made a brief exhortation, and then the assembled infantry (*pezoi*, *stratia*) prepared to charge the enemy. In minutes the respective armies packed together (*sunkleisis*) to achieve a greater density (*puknotês*) of armed men (*hoplitai*, *stratiôtai*), who sought to crash together, sometimes trotting (*dromô*) the last two hundred yards between the two phalanxes (*metaichmon*). For the defenders, battle often took place on the same soil (*chôra*) they and their neighbours had worked a few days before. For the invaders, the farmhouses, orchards, vineyards and stone field walls were largely identical to their own plots (*klêroi*) back home. Once a neighbouring community had fashioned a force of armoured columns (*phalanges*) to take or hold flatland, there was very little a like-minded rival could do other than to meet the challenge in approximately the same manner.

After the meeting of phalanxes (*sunodos*), farmers, blinded by the dust and their own cumbersome helmets, stabbed away with their spears, screamed the war-cry (*Eleleu!* or *Alala!*), pushed on ahead with their shields, and failing that, grabbed, kicked and bit, desperately hoping to make some inroad into the enemy's phalanx, usually having little idea whom, if any, they had killed or wounded. Success was at first gauged by the degree of motion achieved by the pushing of the ranks – the literal thrusting of a man's shield upon the shoulders, side or back of his comrade ahead (*othismos aspidôn*). There were few feints, reserves, encircling manoeuvres or sophisticated tactics of any kind in hoplite battle before the later fifth century BC – just the frightful knowledge that a man must plough through the spears across the plain.

The first three ranks of the eight rows of the classical phalanx alone reached the enemy in the first assault with their spears (*eis doru*). When they broke, they went hand-to-hand (*es cheiras*) with swords (*xiphoi, kopides*) and their butt-spikes (*sturakes, saurôtêres*). Later tactical writers stress just how important such front-line fighters were in achieving an initial inroad. Once the phalanx ripped and stormed through the ranks of its adversary, the opponent often collapsed completely through panic and fright, perhaps not more than half an hour after the initial collision. This short duration and sudden disintegration of battle is understandable if we bear in mind that combatants were squeezed together in column, trapped in heavy bronze under the summer sun, mostly robbed of sight and hearing, in a sea of dust and blood – the captives, as the historian Thucydides reminds us, of rumour and their own fears.

Still, there were countless tasks for all infantrymen of the phalanx as it pounded the enemy. Hoplites – the name probably derives from *hopla*, the Greek word for their heavy battle gear – in the initial ranks sought targets with their spears, all the while searching for protection for their vulnerable right flanks by means of the round shields of the men at their sides. Some struggled to step over the debris of fallen equipment and the detritus of the wounded and the dead at their feet, striving always to keep their balance as they pushed and were pushed into enemy spears at their faces. All the hoplites in the killing zone kept their own 20 lb shield chest-high to cover themselves and the men on their own immediate left. Thus, all at once hoplites might feel steady pressure from the rear, dodge enemy spear points and friendly spear-butts jostling in their faces, stab and push ahead, accommodate comrades shoving from the left to find protection, seek their own cover by nudging in to friends' shields on their right, and nearly trip over wounded bodies, corpses and abandoned equipment at their feet.

Once the line cracked (*pararrêxis*), hoplites turned (*tropê*), scattered and ran (*phugê*), to prevent encirclement (*kuklôsis*) and probable annihilation (*diapthora*). But few of the victorious pressed the chase to any great distance. Heavy infantrymen made poor pursuers, especially when the defeated threw away their equipment and sprinted to the hills. And in any case, under the war practice of early city-state, warfare there was not much desire to exterminate an adversary who spoke the same language, worshipped identical gods, observed common festivals and enjoyed similar types of government by landowning citizens. Again, the primary purpose was to acquire or take back border real estate and gain prestige, not to risk time and money in annihilating a neighbouring society of like-armoured farmers over the hill.

After hoplite battle, the dead were not desecrated, but exchanged, in what Euripides called 'the custom of all the Greeks'. Greek painting and sculpture – in contrast to Near-

Eastern, Egyptian or MesoAmerican engravings, for example – reveal almost no mutilation of corpses in a wartime context. A formal trophy (*tropaion*) was erected, and the victors marched home to congratulations. The defeated begged for the remains of their comrades to be returned formally (*nekroi hupospondoi*), to be buried in a common grave on the battlefield (*poluandron*) or carried back home to a public tomb (*dêmosion sêma*). If the battle was exclusively between Greek hoplites, before the fifth century BC and by agreement (*ex homologou*), then rarely were the vanquished enslaved – quite unlike the great sieges and later wars of annihilation against non-Greeks, in which thousands were sold off as chattels once defeated.

Such fighting between city-states could be frequent but not necessarily catastrophic, once cavalry and missile men were largely excluded from any integrated role in the fighting and the infantry combatants were uniformly encased in bronze. And while it is true that Plato and other Greek thinkers felt that war was a natural state of affairs in Greece, not an aberration from accustomed tranquillity, their notion of war, *polemos*, was much different from our own. Only the Persian and Peloponnesian conflicts of the Classical Age, which inaugurate a second stage in the development of Western warfare, conjure up anything like the modern idea that fighting is intended to destroy entire armies, murder civilians, kill thousands of soldiers, and wreck culture – and so to be an uninterrupted, all-encompassing activity until ultimate victory through annihilation or capitulation is achieved. In the first two centuries of hoplite fighting (700–490 BC), it was enough, as the philosophers noted, every so often to kill a small portion of the enemy in an afternoon crash, crack his morale, and send him scurrying in defeat and shame whence he came.

The Greeks, then, for a brief time practised a quasi-ritualised warfare in which fighting was frequent but did not seem to imperil the cultural, economic and political renaissance of the Hellenic city-state – even at the height of the hoplite age, rarely did more than 10 per cent of the men who fought on a particular day die. If anything, the sheer terror of hoplite battle, the courage needed to stare at a wall of spears across the plain, and the urgency of group solidarity in the confines of the phalanx gave positive momentum to ideas of civic responsibility and egalitarianism, and formed the emotional and spiritual substructure of much of Archaic Greek sculpture, painting and literature.

COALITION WARFARE

This type of hoplite infantry battle is usually described as a decisive collision of roughly equally sized armies – a fight which Herodotus characterised as 'most irrational', yet to be waged on the 'fairest and most level plain'.[1] But in the age before the great Macedonian mercenary armies of Alexander and the Successors and the legions of Rome, we should remember that in nearly every major Classical battle, both sides were almost always composed of coalition forces, usually temporary alliances of small city-states whose militias occupied various places along their respective battle lines – mutually visible fronts that were usually not more than a mile or two long and often only a few hundred yards apart. Literally dozens of small communities – the Boiotians are a good example – might line up to form one horn of a phalanx, and themselves be joined by additional foreign contingents. Hence, even apparently homogeneous corps might be rife with tribal and class rivalries, as the experience of the Athenian and Spartan armies attests. Thus, while every ancient army was eager to arrange its particular corps to find effective matches against an enemy – Frontinus, drawing on mostly Roman examples, devoted an entire section of his *Stratagems* to 'De Acienda Ordinanda' – in the classical Greek case, the order of battle took on much greater political and cultural significance.[2]

W.K. Pritchett has published a lengthy study on the wings of these allied Greek phalanxes, reviewing both the historical descriptions of such musters and the more abstract observations of the later military writers (Pritchett 1974–94). In general, he confirms the general impression that in theory, the right wing was the place of honour – usually occupied either by those troops with the greatest military prestige, or (in the case of armies on the defence) by local militias whose native ground was the scene of the engagement. Pritchett, following Thucydides, explains the usual reasons why stronger forces were stationed on the right – to guard against the inevitable rightward drift of hoplites seeking protection for their bare right spear-side in their comrades' shields. Skilful armies, such as the Spartans, might develop this natural drift into a deliberate outflanking movement from the right side. While regional practice varied, less adept troops were stationed on the left wing, and perhaps the weakest of all corps in the middle – effectively reducing hoplite battle to a contest where an army sought to win on the right before its own inferior left collapsed.[3]

Yet in a world where the strongest wing usually fought the weakest, the overall interest of an allied army was not always the paramount consideration of local hoplite militias. Ancient historians often remark on the tension – both ethnic and political – within a coalition when respective states were allotted their particular assignments. Because of the proximity of ancient armies before battle, and the usual decision to fight during the day and in summer, hoplites could nearly always view quite clearly the troops arrayed against them. It is no exaggeration to state that at every recorded major hoplite battle, there is either disagreement before the battle over the placement of troops, or evidence in the aftermath that the fighting had inordinately affected a particular tribal or national contingent in the allied line – often with demographic, cultural and political ramifications for generations. In short, hoplite battle was never a simple and simultaneous collision between two uniform armies, and casualties were usually not shared proportionally among allied participants. Unfortunately, very little has been written about either the selective nature of Greek battle casualties or the effect on small Greek communities from hoplite fatalities. Yet the history of dozens of city-states was predicated on a few hours of hoplite fighting, and political tensions and rivalries often governed the course of the fighting itself, on both sides of the battlefield.

At Marathon (490 BC), we know that the Athenian centre nearly collapsed, and suffered disproportionate casualties. From a somewhat fuzzy account in Plutarch we are told that the Athenian tribal Antiochis and Leontis experienced the brunt of the attack, resulting in inordinate deaths among those contingents, but also enhancing the reputations of both Aristides and Themistocles, who survived the Persian onslaught. At Plataia (479 BC), the Athenians and the Spartan exchanged and then counter-exchanged their wings, hoping to pit the Athenian veterans of Marathon against the Persians, and the Peloponnesians against the Medizing Greeks – manoeuvres answered by the Persians across the plain, who themselves changed wings to nullify the Greek adaptations. The later Spartan mystique of Classical infantry prowess – what Aeschylus called 'the Dorian Spear' – arose from their magnificent charge from the Greek right wing against the Persian elite at Plataia, where ninety-one Spartiates fell – well over half the total Greek hoplite dead reported by Herodotus.[4]

Class considerations may sometimes also have played a role in both the deployments and the fighting itself. Thus, at the battle of Mantineia (418 BC) the Spartans seem to have been eager to destroy the Argive democrats opposite them, and yet were less inclined to press the fight further against the more privileged Argive 1,000, who shared their oligarchial tastes. Some scholars – following a theme of Ephorus – have argued for collusion of sorts at Mantinea between Argive and Spartan ideologues, as the two purported enemies agreed to allow their respective poorer confederates bear the brunt of the hard fighting. Within a year of the battle, 1,000 aristocratic Argives and a like number of Spartans joined together to overthrow the democracy at Argos. Whether we believe that class considerations transcended national enmity at Mantinea, it is at least true that Argive democrats suffered the most heavily in the battle. As Aristotle pointed out, those losses encouraged surviving aristocrats, basking in their successful service at Mantineia, to overthrow the constitution.[5]

At the battle of Nemea (394 BC), we once more hear of pre-battle manoeuvres as the Boiotians selfishly refused to fight until they obtained the safer assignment on the right wing, far distant from the Spartan elite. Furthermore, their subsequent massing in depth beyond the agreed sixteen-shield limit put their Athenian allies in greater danger still. And at Leuktra, Epameinondas deliberately occupied the left wing, massed his phalanx fifty men deep, and sought a head-to-head collision with the Spartan royal guard. Scholars claim an apparent novelty in that move – the beginning of the so-called 'concentration of force' – but Epameinondas may have been just as interested in sparing his Boiotian allies of the new, reconstituted confederation: these less able troops were now on the vaunted right, pitted against inferior Peloponnesian allies, and thus not in danger from the Spartans nor too concerned about the inevitable exposure of their flanks once their Theban allies massed to fifty shields. Worry over the stability of a more democratic confederacy as much as tactical consideration may have explained why Epameinondas charged from the left – in marked contrast to the usual Theban selfishness of the past.[6]

The aftermath of Leuktra also reveals the century-long repercussions of those few minutes of fighting. The Spartan 400 élite who were annihilated by the Theban mass were irreplaceable troops – with their loss, the army itself, materially and psychologically crippled, was scarcely able to face an enemy in the field. The Spartan débâcle at Leuktra led directly to the invasion the next winter by Epameinondas at the head of some 70,000 allied troops – many of them former Peloponnesian adversaries of the Boiotians. These Peloponnesians must have been grateful to have been ignored at Leuctra while the Thebans concentrated on the unpopular Spartan hegemonists.[7]

Such manoeuvring of wings before battles illustrates that not all adversaries were on opposite sides of the plain, as confederacies were plagued by national, class, tribal and ethnic rivalries, in addition to very human concerns of self-preservation in simply surviving the ordeal. Such sensitivity was understandable: armies knew that politics and culture in their small city-states might be altered for generations as a result of a single day of fighting. A city-state's infantry muster often represented roughly two-thirds of its available adult male citizenry. If a small contingent on a line should find itself in the wrong place at the wrong time and be cut off or isolated against a strong enemy onslaught, then the history of that community might be changed forever. Thus, often in Greek battle, entire contingents fled before coming to arms, in the expectation that resistance in a hopeless cause would sacrifice a generation of their city's precious hoplite soldiers.[8]

We tend to think of casualties in hoplite battles as tolerable – roughly, on average, 4–5 per cent killed among the winners, and somewhere near 15 per cent for the losers. But those statistics are averages only, and represent losses for an entire coalition – they do not reflect precise percentages for particular communities. In some cases, an entire polis's hoplite force might be nearly wiped out, regardless of the outcome of the battle or the degree of casualties overall. A good example of the ramifications of hoplite obliteration and the political considerations that led to such catastrophe is the small Boiotian town of Thespiai (Fig. 1). The Thespians' tragic experience in hoplite battle emphasises both the close connection between political and military decisions in the Greek world, and the calamitous effects of infantry warfare for generations, well beyond the immediate dead on the killing field.[9]

THE THESPIANS AT WAR

Nothing remains of Thespiai today. At the beginning of the twentieth century, French archaeologists dismantled the walls – mostly dating from Roman times – to recover dozens of inscriptions that were incorporated into the later fortifications. Thus, it is impossible archaeologically to date precisely the series of destructions the city experienced, or to ascertain the exact extent of the repeated devastations. Any modern visitor who surveys the rich countryside and the numerous small valleys of the immediate environs, the relative proximity to the Gulf of Corinth, and the access both to Attica or the Peloponnese via routes over Mt Pateras and Kithairon can understand why Thespiai grew to be the second largest and most important polis in Boiotia – and thus a constant irritant to the aspirations of its larger and more powerful neighbour, Thebes. And this rivalry between the two city-states explains much of the tragic Thespian experience in hoplite battle for nearly two centuries.[10]

We first hear of the Thespian Army during the Persian Wars, when a contingent of 700 hoplites marched north with Leonidas to stop the Persian onslaught. The force – larger than Thebes's contribution of 400 heavy infantrymen – probably comprised *all* the adult, male property-holding citizenry of Thespiai. It was an extraordinary muster that emptied the community of its hoplite class; Thespian opposition to the Persian attack was more in the spirit of Athenian and Spartan obstinacy than the submission of its immediate neighbour, Thebes.

When the pass was turned, the Thespians, along with some Thebans, chose to stay with King Leonidas and his 300 Spartans; we should assume that they were annihilated to the man. Various explanations have been adduced for their remarkable courage, ranging from the fatalistic notion that nothing remained for them in a Medized Boiotia, to a genuine belief that their gallantry might give valuable time for their own women and children to evacuate Thespiai, to the idea that a more moderate government had existed at Thespiai than elsewhere in Boiotia, and thus the doomed hoplites were fulfilling their democratic mandate to obey the will of the popular assembly to defend Greece. In any case, of the 1,400 Greeks who stayed behind with Leonidas, the Thespian dead represented 50 per cent of the total allied casualties – a remarkable percentage when we remember that they

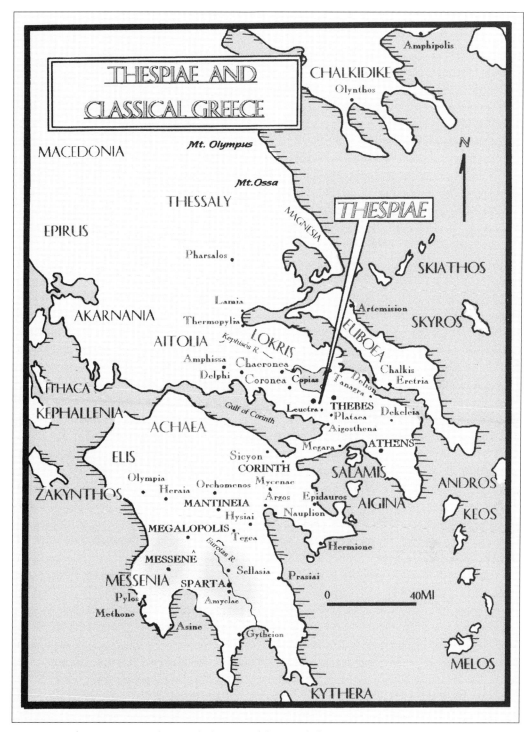

Fig. 1. Map of Ancient Greece, showing the location of the city of Thespiae.

composed only about 10 per cent of the original Greek force of 7,000 hoplites. Posterity remembers the 300 Spartans; few recall that over twice that number of Thespians died on the same day. In the aftermath of the defeat, Sparta itself was safe from Persian attack; Thespiai was in the immediate path of the invaders. Sparta lost at Thermopylai a little under 4 per cent of her land owning citizen body; Thespiai probably lost almost all of hers.

The Persians marched south, and with Theban guidance demolished the town: Thespiai's surviving population fled south to the Peloponnese. Thus, Thespiai as a material community of several generations ceased to exist once its army of hoplites was annihilated in a few hours to the north at Thermopylai. Even though Thermopylai was not technically a pitched engagement between two coalition Greek armies, its disastrous consequences to Thespiai would be similar to subsequent hoplite battle catastrophes.[11]

Events the next year at Plataia (479 BC) confirm the unfortunate consequences of the Thespians' decision to stand fast the year before at Thermopylai. Herodotus says that Themistocles made his child's tutor, Sikinnos, a citizen of Thespiai 'at a time later when the Thespians were enrolling citizens' – ostensibly to rebuild their community after the loss of the 700 at Thermopylai and the diaspora to the Peloponnese. Nevertheless, the exiled community sent its surviving male population en masse – 1,800 strong – to join the Greeks at Plataia. Interesting enough, Herodotus remarks that the Thespians came without hoplite armour (*hopla de oud' houtoi eichon*), confirming the notion that their city's hoplite yeomen and their arms and armour had been lost the year before. A rough estimate would suggest that out of 2,000–3,000 adult males in Thespiai, a third (700) qualified for hoplite service, and all had perished at Thermopylai. In essence, the decision on day three at Thermopylai to stay with the Spartans resulted in the obliteration of the city, the death of most property-owning adult males, and the temporary evacuation of the surviving population to the Peloponnese.

Again, we do not know the precise reasons why the contingent was so large or so determined to stay, or the political ideology of these 700 who perished – the author has argued elsewhere that fifth-century BC hoplites were neither aristocratic elites nor part of a democratic mass, but rather comprised the timocratic middle of the native-born resident population.[12] But the sudden demise of 700 property-owners and the appearance of 1,800 unarmoured and poorer surviving citizens at Plataia would suggest that the result of the losses of Thermopylai was to strengthen the landless, who would win respect for their service at Plataia, and go on to be elevated in order to reformulate the hoplite classes. The farms of the dead would have to be worked, and the males – whether relatives or not – who took care of the land, widows and orphans would all soon have found themselves in the hoplite census, eligible for heavy infantry service. The consequences for the community of Thespiai of the battles at Thermopylai and Plataia – destruction of the old city, empowerment of the landless, and anti-Persian service in contrast to Theban Medism – would exacerbate already uneasy relations with Thebes for the ensuing century, as Thespians fell increasingly under suspicion in their choice of foreign allies and in their own domestic politics.[13]

In theory, by 460 BC, Thespiai would have rebuilt its walls and, with new citizen musters, reconstituted its citizenship to levels approaching its status before Thermopylai. But we do not hear of the army until the battle of Delion (424 BC), when it was part of a Boiotian federated force, opposing the Athenian army under Hippokrates. Delion nicely illustrates both the political nature of hoplite deployment and the lethal consequences of those decisions for communities in years to come. The Thebans, as would become typical of later battles, in a rather self-interested manner, stacked deep and on the right, leaving their Boiotian allies on the left and centre to shorten their battle line to avoid being outflanked, and to face the more formidable Athenian troops under the Athenian general Hippokrates. It may not be accidental that the Thespians occupied the extreme left wing – the most likely place to be outflanked or demolished by the enemy's crack units. Thucydides' description suggests that a brutal collision occurred there; he says the left wing was encircled by the Athenians, and 'those Thespians who perished were cut down as they fought hand to hand'.[14]

In any case, Thucydides does not give us the precise numbers of the Theban contingent, but only some idea of the number of aggregate confederate dead – about 500 Boiotians, of whom the vast majority were Thespians and Tanagrans. Modern scholars, reviewing the epigraphical and archaeological evidence of casualty records and burials, surmise that about 300 Thespians were killed at Delion (Fig. 2), perhaps again from a militia present that day numbering 600–700, or about two-thirds of the hoplite census of roughly 1,000 land owning Thespians. We should imagine, then, that around 50 per cent of the Thespians present at the battle were killed in an hour or so of fighting, and that those losses mean that a third of *all* the small farmers at Thespiai were now dead. In short, roughly three generations after Thermopylai, once again Thespian hoplites had suffered a catastrophe – and again there were to be immediate consequences of that loss to the city.[15]

Thucydides says that a few months later, in summer 423 BC: 'The Thebans destroyed the walls of the Thespians, on the allegation of pro-Athenians sympathies. They had always wished to do this, but now they found an easy opportunity since the flower [*anthos*] of the Thespians had been annihilated in the battle against the Athenians.' Scholars have argued over the exact explanation of Thucydides' account, dividing over two possible scenarios for the dramatic Theban retaliation. Some have seen in the destruction blatant Theban tyranny: the Thebans took advantage of the Thespian losses, razed their walls, and thus assumed their voice in the Boiotian confederacy. With the absorption of Thespiai, Thebans now controlled $\frac{4}{11}$ of the Boeotarchs but only contributed $\frac{2}{11}$ of the hoplite muster. Alternatively, Robert Buck has suggested that the attack was a Boiotian – not merely a Theban enterprise – to ensure Thespian loyalty: the Thespian hoplites had been more conservative and thus greater supporters of the Boiotian confederacy; with their losses at Delion, more democratic surviving factions were liable to agitate for independence from the league, and thus the city had to be neutralised.[16]

In any case, whether the Thebans alone (as Thucydides explicitly states) destroyed the walls of Thespiai out of long-standing jealousy or the Boiotians at large committed the act from fear of democratic insurrection, there is no doubt that the events at Delion led within a few months to the destruction of the city's fortifications, and hence the end of her independence. Nine years later, the Thebans helped put down an uprising of the Thespian *dêmos* – not difficult, since the city's fortifications had long since been dismantled.[17]

However, the question remains why the Thespians hoplites were placed on the most vulnerable wing of the confederate army at Delion in 424 BC if they were known to be more sympathetic to oligarchic rule at Thebes in particular and to the Boiotian confederacy in general. The author would argue that there is little evidence that Classical hoplites ever favoured narrow oligarchy, and that it was more likely that such soldiers shared with the more radical landless democrats a desire to be independent of both the Boiotian League and Thebes. In several hoplite battles fought by the Boiotians, there is evidence that the Thespian hoplites were either exposed to the most vulnerable spot on the battle line or felt to be less than patriotic to the Theban cause – suggesting that *all* Thespians, regardless of their particular status, were always suspect to their neighbours.[18]

Thus, the Thespian hoplites were probably by design stationed on the dangerous left wing, across from Athenian strength; in addition, they were vulnerable on their flanks from the massing of the Theban right to the unusual depth of twenty-five shields. Was there a general Theban consensus that if there were to be casualties at Delion, better they be from Thespiai? Of the roughly 7,000 Boiotians present at the battle, perhaps 60 per cent of the dead were from a group that made up 10 per cent of the army. It is significant that the left wing of Thespians, Tanagrans and Orchomenians was not a natural geographical cluster that might explain these regiments' close proximity to one another on the battlefield. However, all three city-states at times showed open hostility to Thebes and

Fig. 2. Grave stele from Thespiae of Delion battle dead.

entertained pro-Athenian sympathies, perhaps explaining their deployment together against the enemy's better units, where they were expected to hang on until the Theban mass across the way cleared the field.[19]

Furthermore, Thucydides states that the 'troops [the Tanagrians and Orchomenians] stationed alongside them gave way and the Thespians were encircled in a small area'. Apparently, not all hoplites on the left wing were annihilated when the Athenians made their encirclement. More circumspect contingents withdrew, saving their own lives, but also – as was the co-dependent nature of hoplite battle – making the plight of their Thespian neighbours behind even more desperate. It seems that the traditionally independent Thespians were intentionally stationed at the most dangerous spot at Delion out of general enmity on the part of the Thebans. The town itself was targeted the next year out of national rather than factional rivalry, once it was clear that a third of the landowning males of the town were gone and its hoplite forces permanently weakened. And the subsequent democratic revolt of 414 BC was put down not because of battle losses to conservatives, but because of the simple fact that there were few heavy infantrymen left to defend the city from foreigners.[20]

The next major engagement in which Thespian hoplites played a notable role was at the Nemea river near Corinth (394 BC), where the Boiotians and Athenians met Sparta and her allies. Presumably, in the thirty years since Delion, for a second time a new generation of hoplites had brought infantry strength back up to normal levels of 700–1,000 or so, and the population was once more subject to the Boiotian confederation. Whether the walls had been rebuilt after the destruction of 423 BC, we do not know, but it is unlikely after such traumatic losses. At Nemea, the entire Boiotian confederation was placed on the favoured right wing, while the Athenians' allies took up the left horn, opposite the crack Spartans. Xenophon provides us with little real detail about the action, except to note that all the Boiotians were successful against their Peloponnesian enemies, except the Thespians, who were stationed opposite the Achaians from Pellene. He states that while other Peloponnesians fled and were pursued by Boiotians, the hoplites from Pellene and Thespiai 'kept fighting and were falling in their places' – an unusually vivid observation in an otherwise succinct description, suggesting a general slaughter at this point of the battle line on both sides. Nemea seems an almost eerie replay of Delion.

Given Xenophon's statement that of the Boiotians, only the Thespians were 'falling in their places' (*en chôra epipton*), it is natural to assume that once more several hundred hoplites were killed. There were roughly 3,000 total fatalities on the Boiotian and Athenian side at Nemea, and since the Thespians were particularly noted for the ferocity of their engagement with the men of Pellene, perhaps 10–20 per cent of that overall dead figure of – another 300–600 hoplites? – were Thespians. Once more, we should imagine that about 50 per cent of the Thespian muster present at Nemea (600–1,000?) perished, reducing the surviving hoplite class by at least a third. We know nothing about the Thespian role in the terrifying collision at Koroneia a few months later: 'a battle like none other in my time' wrote Xenophon. Despite the Thebans' elation at slamming head-on into the Spartan phalanx and wounding King Agesilaus, the confederation suffered more than 600 dead. Surely, at least a few at Koroneia were Thespians.[21]

What were the consequences of yet another catastrophic loss of landowning hoplites at the Battle of Nemea? For the next twenty-three years, until the fight at Leuktra

(371 BC) – during the more oligarchic Boiotian confederacy (394–387 BC), the Spartan occupation of Thebes (382–379 BC) and the democratic reconstitution of the confederation (379–371 BC) – Thespians were at odds with the Boiotians in general and Thebes in particular, at various times offering assistance either to Athens or Sparta, depending on the two states' respective hostility to Thebes at any given time. Once again, it is hard to determine the precise political effect at Thespiai of the loss of her hoplites at the battle of Nemea: the community had been hostile towards both the earlier oligarchic and later democratic incarnations of the Boiotian confederacy alike. It seems preferable to see Thespiai's vulnerability after 394 BC as deriving more from the simple loss of hoplites at Nemea, who might otherwise have offered stiff resistance to Theban inroads.

Indeed, Thespiai may have still remained unfortified after Delion, and apparently lacked the strength to rebuild her walls until 378 BC – and then only with aid from the Spartans. We should imagine that it took at least ten to fifteen years to reconstitute her hoplite strength after Nemea. But the frequent Spartan invasions of Boiotia (378–371 BC) after the expulsion of the Spartan garrison from the Kadmeia (379 BC) once again brought to the fore the Thespian dilemma of how to retain independence from a hostile Thebes and an unsympathetic confederacy in an unsettled land that Epameinondas rightly called the 'dancing floor' of war. As a rule at Thespiai, more democratic elements looked to Athens, more oligarchic to Sparta, but there seems to have been enmity towards Thebes in both camps, so it is unwise to see hoplite losses in battle as energising particular factions so much as simply weakening Thespiai in general.

By 373 BC Thespiai was apparently still controlled by oligarchic elements with lingering sympathies to Sparta when she was forced into a subordinate relationship with a now democratic Thebes, and for the third time in little more than a century, her walls were razed and her population forced to reside in scattered villages and farms. Indeed, for much of the prior decade she had been engaged in various skirmishes with the Boiotians, and had suffered continual losses.

The tragic consequences that followed hoplite battles were not always the results of large numbers killed in action. The Thespians learned this in 371 BC, when Epameinondas expelled their hoplites from the Boiotian Army that faced Kleombrotos and his Spartans – another indication that the presence and deployment of Thespian troops on the confederate battle line was always rife with political implications. Not allowed to fight, and without walls, Thespiai's only hope was a Theban defeat. But when Epameinondas achieved a stunning victory, the Thebans moved quickly to finish their earlier attack on Thespiai. Some time after Leuktra, her buildings that remained were razed and her population expelled from Boiotia. Given a century and more of continual destruction in the aftermath of hoplite battles, it is no wonder that the present-day remains of Classical Thespiai are essentially non-existent.[22]

CONCLUSION

In the century from 479 to 371 BC, the Thespians suffered inordinate losses in hoplite engagements, their deployment, participation, and role in battle in some way predicated on their uneasy relationship with Thebes. In the aftermath of these losses, the Thespians either had their circuit walls razed (by the Thebans in 423 and 373 BC) or their city itself destroyed outright (by the Persian and Thebans in 480 BC, and again by the Thebans after 371 BC).

The history of the Greek city-state cannot be understood without considering the histories of hoplite battles. It is no exaggeration that the fate of entire communities literally depended on where, how and against whom their landowning hoplite soldiers were deployed in particular engagements. In the past, the author has tended to think of hoplite battle as an economical solution to border disputes and political disagreements between Greek poleis. It was that. But because of the decisive and horrific nature of the conflict, and the uneasy nature of coalition armies, entire generation of farmers could be lost and their homes and families left vulnerable for decades – the experience of Classical Thespiai is an especially good example. In some sense, that city-state's entire history is the story of little more than three tragic hours of fighting at Thermopylai, Delion and Nemea. Hoplite obliteration on those days led directly to the demolition of the city itself.

Military archaeology is most often concerned with fortifications or the reconstruction of battles through personal autopsy and excavation of battlefields. But the ripples of battle go well beyond the plain of war. In the case of Thespiai, the walls and structures of the city rose and fell in accordance with the survival or extermination of her infantrymen fighting miles away.

NOTES

1. Hdt. 7.9. On the ritualised nature of classical hoplite battle, see Hanson (1989, 27–39); Connor (1988, 3–29); Lazenby (1991, 87–109); Mitchell (1996, 87–106); Ober (1996, 53–71). For ancient attitudes about the heroic nature of pitched battle, the economy of that way of fighting and the unfair, expensive, and unheroic use of walls, missiles, and finance see Dem. 9.48; Polyb. 13.3.2–4; 18.3.3; Thuc. 1.15; Arist. *Pol.* 7.1326a23–25; cf. Thuc. 3.98.4; Pl. *Leg.* 706B–C; Plut. *Mor.* 190A; 210E27; 212E; 215D; 221F6; Thuc. 4.40.2; Eur. *HF* 157–6; Eur. *Rhes.* 510–17; Thuc. 1.83.2; Thuc. 1.141–42.
2. Frontinus, *Strategems* 2.3.
3. Pritchett (1974–94, Part II, 190–207); cf. Anderson (1970, 94–110); Roloff (1903, 42–9).
4. Wings and casualties at Marathon and Plataia: Hdt. 6.111–15; 9.46–9; Lazenby (1985, 100–11); Hignett (1963, 311–41); Delbrück, (1975, 81–90). Kleidemos (FGrH 3.323.fr. 22) claimed that all the fifty-two Athenian dead at Plataia were from the tribe Aiantis. 'Dorian Spear': Aeschylus, *Persae* 817.
5. Thuc. 5.67–74; 81.2; cf. Diodorus 12.75.7; 79.6–7; 80.2–3; Aristotle *Pol.* 5.1304a25–6, who reviews the political ramifications when particular classes or individuals were responsible for a state's military success. See Gomme et al. (1970, 105–6, 149); Gillis (1963, 199–226); Kagan (1981, 132–3).
6. On the wings at Nemea: Xen. *Hell.* 4.2.16–18; Diod. 14.83; at Leuktra: Xen. *Hell.* 6.4.8–15; see Anderson (1970, 142–6, 192–220); Lazenby (1985, 135–40; 151–62). On the 'innovations' of Epameinondas, see Hanson (1988, 190–207). Just as the Boiotians were considered selfish for massing to depths greater than the standard eight shields and thus exposing the flanks of their allies, so too the Spartans, as they practised their vaunted right wing drift at Nemea and Leuktra, cared little for their own Peloponnesian league members, who would be forced either to follow the Spartan leader or to suffer a gap in their lines. It seems clear that larger armies, like the Thebans and Spartans, could more or less dictate to their allies the order of battle in a manner that served their own self-interest. At Leuktra, Epameinondas's deployment on the left was novel – the author would argue that he placed his mass opposite the Spartan elite in part in an unusual effort to spare his Boiotian allies of the newly reconstituted democratic confederation from being annihilated.
7. See Cartledge (1970, 240–1), for the sparing of the Peloponnesian allies at Leuktra.
8. At second Koroneia (394 BC), the Argives fled before contact: Xen. *Hell.* 4.3.17–18; the Athenians broke before Amphipolis without meeting the enemy: Thuc. 5.10.8; see also the so-called 'tearless battle', where the Arcadians fled before the Spartan advance: Plut. *Ages.* 33.3; Xen. *Hell.* 7.1.28–32.
9. On typical casualty rates, see Krentz (1985, 13–21).

10. On the remains of Thespiai, see Fossey (1986, 135–40); Pritchett (1985, 138–65); Bintliff & Snodgrass (1988, 57–71). For a history of the city, see in general Roesch (1965); Tomlinson & Fossey (1970, 243–63); Fiehn (1936, 37–59). On Thespiai's later revival, see Jones (1968, 223–55).

11. Thespians send 700 to Thermopylai (Hdt. 7.202); all Thespians were killed (Hdt. 7.222; 226); the Persians destroyed Thespiai, and the surviving population evacuated to Peloponnese (Hdt. 8.50). For the various reasons why the Thebans stayed at Thermopylai, see Hignett (1963, 146–8; 371–8); Lazenby (1993, 144–7). Delbrück (1975, 97) went so far as to argue that the Thespians had, in fact, been cut down in a retreat: 'That an entire city could be inhabited by such heroes – a small city like Thespiai could not possibly have had more than 700 hoplites – cannot be accepted on the strength of a legendary account'. For discussions concerning the size of the overall Greek force, see Lazenby (1985, 84–8). Many believe that the 700 comprised the entire hoplite class of Thespiai: see Hignett (1963, 117). Beloch (1912–27, Vol. 3, 1.287) argued that Thespiae had about 10,000 inhabitants in the early fourth century BC; if we divide that number by four or five we arrive at somewhere between 2,000 and 2,500 adult males, approximately half of which may have met the hoplite census. There was an epigram to the Thespian dead at Thermopylai, cf. Stephanos Byz. s.v., Thespeia; Page (1975, Philiades, No. 1). Sparta was said by Herodotus in the early fifth century BC to have had about 8,000 Spartiate males (Hdt. 7.234.2).

12. Hanson (1995b, 91–126). The tradition (Heracl. Pont. *FHG* fr. 43) that early Thespian elite citizens were excluded from manual labour suggests an elite stratum quite at odds with yeomen farmers, as, for example, exemplified by Hesiod in nearby Ascra.

13. The 1,800 unarmed at Plataia: Hdt. 9.30; Sikinnos, tutor of Themistocles: Hdt. 8.75. Thespiai proper comprised one of eleven districts (and was given additional representation for the surrounding environs) of the fifth-century BC Boiotian confederacy. Theoretically each district by the fourth century BC contributed about 1,000 hoplites to the more democratic federated Boiotian army. See Salmon (1953, 347–60); Seymour (1922, 70); Buck (1979, 157–60). But we should imagine a population increase since the early fifth century BC; thus it is wiser to see the 700 who fell at Thermopylae as the entire hoplite class of early fifth-century BC Thespiae, rather than two-thirds of a larger thousand-man army. We are told by Herodotus that at Plataia the Thespians were unarmed (i.e., without panoplies, suggesting that no hoplites were present). Thus, it is reasonable to suppose that the earlier Thermopylai muster to prevent the Persian onslaught had comprised *all*, rather than two-thirds, of the town's existing hoplite strength, and it is likely that all the surviving Thespians of military age (i.e., the 1,800) showed up at Plataia. See Larsen (1968, 119–20).

14. Thuc. 4.92–7. On the battle, see Hanson (1995a, 28–35); Hanson (1995b, 286–7); Hornblower (1996, 301–10); Kagan (1974, 283–7).

15. For the purported grave of the roughly 300 Thespians slain at Delion, the casualty list with a partial accounting of the dead, and the black limestone sepulchral stelai of some of the prominent Thespians killed, see Pritchett (1974–94, Vol. IV, 132, 141–3, 192–4); Demand (1982, 110–18). Larsen (1955, 47) felt that the Thespians 'may well have numbered 1,100–1,300 at Delium' comprising $\frac{2}{11}$ of the federal army there (i.e., $\frac{2}{11}$ of 7,000). But this figure included 'Thespiai together with Eutresis and Thisbai' (Hell. Oxy. 11.3), thus many hoplites of the Thespian muster would, in theory, have come also from the latter two communities.

16. Destruction of Thespiai: Thuc. 4. 133.1–2. Various reasons have been suggested for the attack: outright Theban aggrandisement, Roesch (1965, 41–2); Theban self-interest, Cloché (1952, 84–6); Boiotian worry over Thespian loyalty, Buck (1994, 18–19).

17. Democratic uprising of 413 fails: Thuc. 6.95.2.

18. Government in Boiotia progressed from the narrow aristocracy of the early fifth century BC to a broad-based hoplite timocracy of the latter fifth, and finally in the early fourth century BC to a democratic confederacy without a property qualification. Yet Thespiai remained under Theban suspicion throughout. This continual enmity suggests a centuries-old ethnic distrust that transcended the nature of Boiotian politics. At Thermopylai, Plataia, Delion, Nemea and Leuktra, the Thespians either suffered proportionately higher casualties than the Thebans, fought against them, or were dismissed outright from the confederate army before battle. Osborne (1987, 134–5), attempts to connect the pattern of Thespian settlement – nucleated residence versus homesites in the countryside – to the city's varying relationship with Thebes and demographic fluctuations after hoplite battles. When Thespiai fell under Theban domination and had a strong hoplite presence, small sites appeared in the countryside; during its brief periods of political independence and a diminished hoplite influence, greater numbers lived inside town.

19. Thespians, Tanagrans and Orchomenians were not a natural geographical cluster that might explain their proximity at Delion: Hornblower (1996, 299); Fossey (1986, 135ff).

20. Thucydides says that the Thespians were *kuklôthentes en oligô*: 4.96.3. On this, see Gomme et al. (1970, Vol. III, 566).

21. Nemea and Koroneia: Xen. *Hell.* 4.2.16–23; 4.3.15–21; Diod. 14.83.2; 14.84.2 (2,800 allied dead at Nemea; 600 at Koroneia); Boiotian losses at Nemea and Koroneia: Lazenby (1985, 136–8, 143, 143–4, 148). While our ancient sources refer to losses suffered by the Boiotians 'and their allies', in each case the Boiotians themselves appear to have borne the brunt of the fighting. The possibility that 3,400 of the anti-Spartan coalition of 394 BC were killed within a matter of weeks suggests an enormous blow to Boiotian confederacy at large. If even 2,000 of those battle dead belonged exclusively to the Boiotian states, then the confederacy may have lost 20 per cent of its total hoplite population (i.e, about 11,000) – which may explain why we do not hear of further major hoplite engagements until decades later (e.g., Tegyra, 375 BC; Leuktra, 371 BC). We do not, of course, have any information how such losses at Nemea and Koroneia were broken down by particular Boiotian contingents. Mantitheos claimed at Nemea that his own tribe had suffered the worst among the Athenian contingents (Lys. 16.15).

22. Sparta rebuilds the walls of Thespiai: Xen. *Hell.* 5.4.41; Spartan and Thespian alliance during the 370s BC fighting against Theban troops: Xen. *Hell.* 5.4.10–55. Dismissal of the Thespians before the Battle of Leuktra: Paus. 9.13.8; 9.14.2–4; Polyaen. *Strat.* 2.3.3. There is an unresolved controversy over the sequence of events involving the loss of the Theban walls in 373 BC and the subsequent destruction of the city proper in 371 BC, after the Battle of Leuktra. The ancient sources and modern arguments are discussed at length in Tuplin (1986, 321–41) and Buckler (1977, 76–9).

FOURTEEN

The Elusive Warrior Maiden Tradition: Bearing Weapons in Anglo-Saxon Society

Deborah J. Shepherd

Before the Anglo-Saxon kingdoms took political shape, the fifth-century AD north European immigrants in Britain lived in relatively isolated and homogeneous communities with a social organisation that is best described anthropologically as 'tribal'. Their coalition into regional polities with a hierarchical social structure was a gradual process, taking up the next two centuries (Alcock 1981; Evison 1981, 141–4). But in the fifth and sixth centuries, the burials show us: relatively small but noticeable accumulations of wealth; an emphasis on family, or descent group, structure; no evidence of class division, and a clear use of weapons as a marker of some kind of identity.

According to those, including Dumézil (1973), Lincoln and Littleton (1987), who have discussed the myths, world view and hypothetical culture and society of the Indo-Europeans, the warrior played a dominant role as protector of the Home territory against the outside Other. In this decidedly territorial role, the warrior was the guardian of boundaries. His place – and the use of the male gender here is representative of the dominant perception – at the edge of the ordered community, in the face of the unknown, put the warrior paradoxically outside his own society and among or nearer to the Other. His fearsome behaviour and ritual ethic of ferocious, heedless courage made him a less than ideal dinner guest. There are numerous and diverse cultural examples of the type including the Norse berserker, the Japanese samurai, and Crow warriors who refer to themselves as 'Crazy Dogs Wishing-to-Die' (Littleton 1987, 144). In fact, the warrior was often feared and shunned by his own people, who none the less acknowledged their need of him – or so the social reconstructions imply (Davidson 1989, 11; Littleton 1987). There are hints of why this is so. Roman authors and snatches of native poetry describe how Germanic and Celtic warriors proved – and very likely supported – themselves when there was no war to fight by raiding the farms of ordinary people, stealing, entering into sexual liaisons with or raping their daughters, and otherwise making themselves a general social nuisance against which there was no effective recourse. An example is given of the Irish *fiana*: roving bands of young men who had, at least in summertime, no fixed abode, but lived in the forest,

Fig. 1. Illustration of "Boadicca Haranguing the British Tribes" taken from an antique history. Craik, George L.; MacFarlane, Charles, et al. (1846), The Pictorial History of England, *volume 1. New York: Harper & Brothers, p. 40. (Attributed to Stothard.) This original woodcut depicts the often-told story of Boadicca who, with her daughters and like Zenobia, took over the leadership of the army after her husband died. The story as told by Tacitus describes how Boadicca sought revenge against the evil Romans who seized her land and raped her daughters.*

occupied by hunting and warrior contests (Davidson 1989, 14). These contests might include the harassment of settlements and livestock, and the occasional young female. Julius Caesar noted this problem in *The Gallic Wars* (Davidson 1989, 14). The warrior, for his part, developed his own set of ethical beliefs associated with patterns of ritual sacrifice to his own god: Odin for the Norse, Wodan for the Anglo-Saxons, Lug among the Celts and others (Davidson 1989, 14). His was truly a segregated segment of society.

Analysis of the nature of warfare in warrior society reveals, as ought to be expected, a large ritual component. Unless the level of conflict is truly high with no possibility of resolution, there are rules of behaviour that significantly contain the violence of much pre-modern warfare. Warriors of the past did not always fight to the death, but rather would fight until the dominant power was decided (Halsall 1989, 169). Champions may also have been used at times, as is exemplified in Irish legend, so that individual warriors would stand for their entire warband. Warrior cults – if similar, as they undoubtedly were, to what is known of the worship of Odin – embraced glorious and honourable death, with much ritualised morbidity and sacrificial bloodletting, but the actual life of the warrior was not nearly so lethally inclined as we may easily imagine, having been brought up with the very different notion of 'total' war. Deadly war was reserved for the most serious and irreconcilable threats, such as the assaults of the Romans that enraged the Celtic warband following the chief's widow, Boadicca, and her daughters in Britain (Fig. 1).

Prehistoric kings – if kings we may call them – had a sacred function quite different from political leadership. It may be that sacral kingship outweighed the political role in importance. The sacral king, like the shaman, served as a link between human society and the gods. The king could perform the correct ritual to make good things happen or bad things cease. If the king failed to set matters right, he could be held responsible for such devastation as flood, drought and crop failure. In such cases, his ultimate ritual role may be as the human sacrifice made in the ultimate attempt to appease the gods (Opland 1980, 32–3; Dumézil 1973, 121–2). Chinese myth of the prehistoric Shang period discusses this possibility quite clearly, and Davidson sees hints of such practices among the pre-Viking *Svear*.

From anthropological research, we find that social organisation and leadership in tribes and chiefdoms (however one may choose to define these categorical terms) is much more kin-group-oriented than in states where true political kingdoms manifest themselves. In the former, one's status and role in life depends more or less on one's lineage. In chiefdoms, statuses proliferate and inequality grows, while ascribed status – based on qualities over which the individual has little control – begins to eclipse status based on achievement. The transition is gradual, but kinship factors remain a constant in pre-state societies. It is no surprise that cemetery studies of this period reveal strong indications of family groupings. In the state, alternatives to kin-relations and obligations appear. Kin-group associations can be replaced by carefully chosen appointments of non-kin. Individuals may be chosen on merit or for their loyalty to the leader, and granted obligations, prestige and a position higher in the hierarchy than allowed to relatives, thus breaking up the power structure of the kin group.

At some point in the process of transformation from tribe to kingdom, the warrior moved from the fringes of society to its very centre, and ultimately to the top of the hierarchy. The author suggests that as unequal statuses began to be recognised, the symbols of 'territory' and 'protection', to which the warrior was central, also became symbols of power and identity. As populations grew and came into closer contact with one another, greater leadership was needed to negotiate interaction in ways more subtle than ritual warfare. The warrior became politicised. Thus, it makes sense that we observe, especially in the earliest Anglo-Saxon communities, biological signs of inbreeding due to endogamous relations (frequent cases of spina bifida, for example: Härke 1990, 36). One expects, were archaeologists to look for evidence, that by the mid-sixth century, economic exchange between communities and exogamous relations would be increasing. With this change, the warrior, whether an actual fighter or symbolic weapon-bearer, would find new duties and social obligations to perform in town and within his kin group.

The basic social unit in early Anglo-Saxon society was the family – more precisely, the descent group. Their kinship structure seems to have been relatively bilateral and collateral, emphasising a broad network of real and fictive kin relations (Hill, J.M. 1995, 41–7, 159–60). Kinship obligations were taken very seriously, and were the basis for keeping social order. Disputes might be arbitrated and settled by payments, as in Norse *tings*, but failing that, the institution of outlawry enabled the kin group to obtain society's permission to seek blood vengeance on behalf of one or more of its members who required redress of wrongs. In such circumstances, marriage alliances become a crucial political and economic tool for the consolidation of kin group power and wealth (Pfeffer 1987, 115). The needs of the kin group are valued far more than the needs of the individual. Female offspring served as a profitable means to forge advantageous alliances and recombinations of property. Although we may presume that neither women nor men exercised much personal choice in the selection of spouses, they both seem to have had clear rights of property and a way out of the marriage contract if necessary. Divorce was not so much intended as a personal privilege, but rather allowed the family the advantage of replacing an inadequate or ill-advised alliance with a more advantageous one. Since women seem to have been allowed a role in initiating divorce, it is possible to presume that women were key, though unofficial, players in Norse social and political relations. Although we cannot assume that Anglo-Saxon society resembled the Norse in every significant way, there is no evidence to indicate that they were substantially different. Burials occasionally appear to reveal women of status, and early Anglo-Saxon law (recorded later during Christian times) emphasises a concern for correcting unstable, irregular and flexible marriage customs (Rivers 1991). One implication is that Anglo-Saxon marriage, like its later Norse counterpart, did not meet the standards of permanence set by the Christians. Consequently, both Anglo-Saxon and Norse marriage institutions were radically altered by Christian conversion.

THE MAIDEN WARRIOR AND HER RELEVANCE TO ANGLO-SAXON SOCIETY

It has already been established that Anglo-Saxon society, like the Norse, could have accorded females certain socio-political rights and powers while insisting that they function for the good of the kin group as enablers of alliances. How do we get from that rather ordinary picture to the weapon-wielding female? Some ideas have been proposed and these explanations can be grouped into four categories.

The 'Surrogate Son' Theory

Carol Clover argued for instances of gender-bending in Norse society when rules of inheritance or compensation demanded a male heir or next of kin. Working primarily from literary and legal sources, Clover demonstrated that Norse women might stand in a male role in legal proceedings when an appropriate male relation was not available (Clover 1986, 46–9). This was a clear departure from the norm, because men were expected to stand in for their female relations in the event that a woman was involved in any litigation. Thus, in certain cases, women could directly receive compensation

Fig. 2. Woodcut based on an illustration found in Royal MS. 2 B. vii showing medieval ladies hunting deer. From: Craik, George L.; MacFarlane, Charles, et al. (1846), The Pictorial History of England, *volume 1. New York: Harper & Brothers, p. 626. The scene shown here shows ladies pursuing all the roles of the recreational hunter including the use of the long bow. Although certain weapons of war were not used in the hunt, virtually all hunting weapons could be called into service for battle purposes. The female on the right seems proficient at the use of the bow. Given the right context, women were rarely barred from practising with and using weapons that could be quite deadly. Likewise, the women of the upper class also could have formidable riding skills.*

payments or certain inheritances, bear occasional witness, oversee farms, command workers, etc.

No Norse story or history (nor any Anglo-Saxon literature, for that matter) depicts a woman as a warrior unless she has legendary or mythological characteristics, but Clover's detailed textual analyses demonstrate the logic of such actions to the Norse mind. Vengeance to preserve honour is absolutely necessary. Women regularly took part in demanding and provoking vengeful acts. If no offspring inherits the father's valued sword, it becomes lost to his descendants. But a daughter could accept the sword as a carrier, or surrogate son, to the next generation.

One legendary saga tells of a woman, Hervör, daughter of Angantyr, who both retrieves her father's sword from his burial mound by supernatural means, and also plays the son – a surrogate son – by adopting the clothing, manners and occupations of a male. After a time, however, she finds a husband. Until this point, she was a maiden, not yet admitted to womanhood, but rather also like one who has no gender at all and might choose which identity she would adopt. Once married, she adopts the female social role of woman and child-bearer, and must never appear or act as a male again. Now she can bear sons, and the father's inheritance will pass on as it properly should (Clover 1986, 38–41). Clover pointed out that for the Norse, such inheritances included more than objects such as weapons. Valued character traits – courage, strength of will, honour – were seen as things that must be manifested in each generation or become lost. The daughter as surrogate son could carry these traits with her (Clover 1986, 38–9). Again, a real-life warrior maiden is not demonstrated, but the logic behind such a phenomenon is compelling.

The 'Weapons as Signifiers of Rank' Theory

As advocated by Härke and others (Härke 1990), weapons buried with individuals are not necessarily, or even typically, markers of the warrior occupation, but can indicate both personal and family status. Given the importance of the kin group, family status might be a dominant factor. Some individuals buried with weapons do not appear to have been active warriors. They are too old and infirm, or too young (even infants). Some are physically handicapped by diseases such as spina bifida. Furthermore, many weapon combinations found in graves are non-functional.

The concern does not seem to have been to supply the deceased with adequate equipment for fighting. Since physiological characteristics of the skeletons suggest the division of cemeteries geographically into kin groups, the political use of weapons as rank indicators makes sense (cf. Härke 1990). We do not question weapon burials when the deceased is male, but what about weapons found with someone who appears to be a healthy, adult female? Is it beyond reason that women of high family rank – or, as might be suggested, women who are behaving as surrogate sons – could bear such rank signifiers as well?

Bettina Arnold (1991) has also demonstrated this argument in Hallstatt and La Tène contexts on the continent. She identifies the princely burial with weapons at Vix as that of a female, on the basis of a number of style traits that are otherwise linked to females (Arnold 1991, 368). The 'surrogate son' theory is in many ways the most straightforward and least remarkable of the suggestions.

The 'Gender Continuity' Theory

Carol Clover has also argued that gender and sex have different meanings in traditional Norse society than we expect (Clover 1993). In brief summary, according to meanings interpreted linguistically from Old Norse, being male or being female has a great deal to do with one's actual actions, behaviour and character. Thus, many women are depicted positively by the use of male adjectives denoting masculine courage and honour in grammatically masculine case structures, while men might be described insultingly as soft, lazy or cowardly with feminine grammatical forms. Men who grow old and can no longer carry out acts of physical aggression or defence are likewise described in feminine ways. The conclusion is that gender in Norse society was not an objective biological fact, but a much more fluid aspect of identity that could contradict and overshadow one's physical body. Commonly, females wish to be women and males wish to be men, but the best qualities of human beings are masculine, according to the Norse world view, and if a woman can exhibit these properly, she is praised and paid the compliment of being spoken of as a male.

From what social norms might such a view have originated? Thus, we find yet more logic in the actions of the maiden surrogate son. Likewise, such views make the combination of weapons with high-status women more sensible, since high status might itself be construed as a masculine characteristic. The Princess of Vix might be such a person, but is high status always a reasonable factor?

In a structural analysis of Norse myth, Margaret Clunies Ross (1994, 82) delineates three basic organisational semantic pairs of concepts (Table 1).

Table 1 Organisation Pairs from Norse Myth

nature	culture
female	male
disorder	order

Grouped in this fashion, these concepts define all the major characteristics of the Norse cosmos. Nature is unorganised, disordered, unconfined; this condition, which describes the reality of the otherworld of the primeval giants, always leads to mortality, death, and belongs to the feminine realm of biological reproduction, the creation of something from (visibly) nothing. Order is achieved by taking the natural resources of the otherworld – the alien, feminine, sexually charged giant world – and re-shaping these, giving order to them, and assigning social meaning to them. Thus, culture is achieved, and this kind of creation, creating something by *re*-forming something else, is akin to craftsmanship, and lies wholly within the sphere of the *male* realm of the Norse universe. The cosmogonic males, those highest gods known as the Æsir, abhor the natural and the disordered (the feminine), and are thus able to avoid death and maintain their immortality. Their role is to pseudo-create culture from existing materials, as opposed to the female process of the procreation of life from essentially nothing (Clunies Ross 1994, 82–4). The oppositions in Table 2 express this view.

Table 2 Oppositional Pairs from Norse Myth

feminine realm	masculine realm
biological	social
alien/other world (giants)	familiar/human and god world
dangerous	safe
death	eternal life
female procreation	male pseudo creation
supernatural forces	craftwork and skill

Several interesting points come out of this view of the myths. First, male pseudo-creation accounts for all the important acts of original creation: forming of the earth, the sun, moon and stars, the human race, etc. Second, in the beginning, there are only giants, and births are asexual in nature. Third, there are then females among the giants, and marriage of a god with one giant woman produces by sexual reproduction the brothers Ve, Vili, and Odin, who are the third generation of beings and the first generation of Æsir. After that, no more marriage alliances are permitted between giants and gods. (Clunies Ross makes a strong case that the Æsir are actually fearful of the giant world and its strong females (Clunies Ross 1994, 162–5).) The giant world is alien, the source of important natural resources for which the gods engage in theft rather than proper exchange – for social customs and behavioural ethics do not extend to the otherworld (just as they do not extend beyond home territory in the world of humans); the otherworld is therefore also the locus of danger and death, and is sexually charged.

The sexual nature of the cosmos is fundamental. Norse sexual symbolism presents a recognised pattern of antithesis (Table 3).

Table 3 Sexual antithesis in Norse myth

Female	Male
passivity	activity
inertia	energy
subordination	dominance
receptor	penetrator

Any inversion of male sexual traits by a man would reflect negatively on his morals and character generally. The Norse word *ergi* means 'unmanliness'. It does not properly refer to a bisexual or homosexual nature, but to the simple absence of manly qualities. For the Norse seem to have recognised only one gender, not two. The only real gender is the male. The loss of manly qualities leads one to the state defined negatively as the female. Thus, when in one myth Thor's hammer – a strong phallic symbol – is stolen from him while he is in the passive state of sleep, Thor becomes immediately feminised. In fact, the plot designed to recover the hammer requires Thor to disguise himself as a bride. Such symbolic dress is meant intentionally to 'hammer' home his feminised state. This story is no mere comedy, as twentieth-century commentators usually assert. Rather, Thor escapes from *ergi* because he is still able to take *action* by seizing and using his hammer at the proper moment (Clunies Ross 1994, 110–11). In fact, action and energy are qualities in Thor that overcome the feminine nature of his physical disguise. His temporarily feminine nature is strong enough, however, that the seemingly preposterous disguise actually does work.

Here is just one indication that for the Norse, mode of dress may not have been so strongly linked to biological identity as it is for us. In fact, the meaning of dress mode is culturally variable. Not until the twentieth century could a Western woman legitimately wear trousers and still maintain the social identity of an ordinary female. Moreover, in the same broad European cultural context, only Celtic males get to wear skirts, and then only during special occasions.

Sorcery presents another issue. *Seiðr* is a form of sorcery that is thought to have been handed down from woman to woman. The Æsir feared *seiðr*, and forbade its practice, except by women, on the grounds that it was dangerous to, and might invert, male virility (Clunies Ross 1994, 206–11). Only Odin among the Æsir dared to practice *seiðr* – because he desired to control its great power: the power to know the future.

Shamanism is another form of supernatural power focused on spirit communication and mediation, presumably practised more often but not exclusively by males, and strongly associated with Odin (Clunies Ross 1994, 209). Both forms involve possession by supernatural spirits. In the Norse mind, this possession seems to have been akin to sexual penetration, so that practitioners of both forms would be placed psychologically and semantically in the female role. The ethnographic record indicates that some North American and Siberian shamans might take on the dress and behaviour of women (Clunies Ross 1994, 209). Once again, feminisation of the individual becomes a product of one's *in*actions and receptivity.

The point presented here is that our knowledge of Norse society offers many indications that gender identity was treated rather differently in that society, and was not so strongly linked to *biological* form.

The 'Ritual Warfare and the Ritual Role of Women' Theory

Warfare in simpler societies is often contrived to occur according to a strict set of rules. The goal is not to destroy the enemy, but to establish dominance over them, to alleviate, even temporarily, resource stress, and to regain or achieve honour, high regard and renown. In small neighbouring societies, any physical conflict would naturally occur in the same vicinity as settlement, and would easily involve both women and children. There is no distancing of the danger or the outcome. Therefore, it is illogical that adult females would not become involved in some way, since the potential consequences are so immediate and threatening to the home.

We have ample evidence from widely dispersed cultures that women often function not only defensively, but as inciters and goaders of battle. Recent ethnographic film of the warrior Kayapo of Brazil amply demonstrates this point. For those who desire functional explanation, inciting men to battle frenzy and bringing battle to a head might serve to end the conflict before it escalates such that homes and children become victims. But there is more to this concept. Among the Norse, and many others, the woman's role is enhanced by her procreative powers over life and, by logical extension, death. The Valkyries of Norse myth not only oversee the conduct of battle, but select the warriors who will fall. These men become destined for Odin's retinue. The female Norns are supernatural powers often seen in the metaphor of weaving *men*'s fate (Fig. 3). Germanic legend also emphasises the woman's role of demanding blood revenge. Medieval authorities actually blamed women for perpetuating destructive blood feuds. We are mistaken to see this as merely a simple response to insult. It was originally the woman's *ritual* role in these societies, founded in the extended meaning of her reproductive powers, to bring battle to a head and to inspire the fighting men to their best efforts, and possibly, like the Valkyries, to bring men to their honourable and memorable deaths. (Part of the warrior's reward for a good death is that others will long remember him. Remembrance is a real and valued form of immortality.) Not infrequently did women actually accompany the warriors to the battle site. Modern video recordings of indigenous societies such as the Kayapo of Brazil demonstrate how women as a social group may define their political role and powers as callers for action.

Once the fighting has begun, it is not a great step for a woman, in the midst of the event, to use a weapon – any weapon – herself. Although such an action would require a defiance of normal gender identity and sexual symbolism as we know it, the idea, at least, is not obscure. And the situation itself would not be construed as normal, so norms of behaviour are themselves more likely to become redefined. Western society maintains numerous legends of the 'Sergeant Molly' Pitcher type. The preceding discussion of gender flexibility makes this possible breach of normal conduct seem easier. In general, actions are often taken in sacred ritual contexts (of which the context of battle is one) that are in defiance of profane norms. Correlations with modern attitudes towards soldierly devotion, protection of the 'home front' and proper behaviour in battle are not hard to find.

Fig. 3. Bracteate from south-west Germany depicting the Germanic weaving goddess. The Weaver is the determiner of fate, and as such the ruler of men's lives. As a woman may send a man into battle, she can also determine his survival. It has also often been noted that the implement known as a weaving baton is quite sword-like. In fact some swords in Norse female graves have been interpreted as old, blunt weapons reused as weaving batons – an interesting notion but a recycled sword makes a rather heavy tool for practical daily use in a tedious mundane task.

ANGLO-SAXON CEMETERY DATA

A preliminary study of cemetery reports reveals a surprising quantity of conflicting evidence regarding the biological sex of the deceased. Traditionally, archaeologists have taken for granted that certain artefact types among the grave goods could clearly and unambiguously indicate the sex of the deceased person. Weapons, in particular, indicated males: 'Virtually all individuals buried with weapons were males. The few exceptions can be explained as cases of secondary use of weapon parts [e.g., detached spearheads being used as knives or weaving swords]' (Härke 1990, 36). Certain brooch types pointed to females. Other types could be viewed in combination for a proper determination of sex, while insufficient grave goods could make an artefact-based determination impossible. For the most part, these intuitive categories have been useful, but it is time to question their full validity and determine the limitations of their use.

At some Anglo-Saxon cemeteries, a handful of graves are determined biologically to be of one sex, but the associated grave goods indicate the opposite gender. In the past, such contradictions were invariably thrown out as an error based on poor bone quality, or the assumption that the bones in question must exhibit that zone of measurement where male and female ranges overlap, yet osteologists understand these problems and take them into account:

> Making an attribution of sex on a human skeleton requires a degree of skill which is not always recognised. Not only does the observer need to know 'how' but also 'why'. Consideration needs to be given to the techniques available, to the completeness and provenance of the remains and the age at death of the individual concerned. It is only thus that the observer can hope to gauge the degree of confidence with which any single attribution of sex is made. (Henderson 1989, 77)

In those situations where the osteologist registers uncertainty – whether due to fragmentary evidence, categorically borderline traits or measurements, or immature age – a valid disputation might take place. Lifestyle considerations are also an issue: heavy physical labour may make a female appear robust and 'male', but archaeologists have also presumed to reverse secure sex determinations, such as Evison (1987, 123) regarding the Buckland cemetery, or comments by Henderson (1989, 81) with reference to Sewerby. What limitations of osteological interpretation may have been true in the past are now rapidly diminishing. Henderson (1989, 79) quotes a list of accuracy potentials for different approaches to skeletal sexing, and most rate better than 95 per cent. Combining methods improves matters further. New high-precision techniques of working with dental forms, for example, are providing more checks and increasing the certainty in the osteologist's work (Hoppa 1992). Furthermore, archaeologists are on the edge of realistic access to the revolutionary advances in DNA study. Soon, much macro-study of bones may be replaced by laboratory genetic analyses which will, among other matters, settle securely many arguments over gender identity.

Let us allow that conflicts of gender interpretation provided by skeletal versus grave good evidence are real (Brush 1988; Eisner 1991, 352; Lucy 1997). Is this, then, where we find our maiden warriors? Surprisingly, not exactly. Based on the random selection of cemeteries presented here, many – if not most – of these gender-ambiguous graves show *biologically male skeletons* buried with *female* artefact types. This fact represents an altogether different problem.

Curiously, finds of osteologically identified males buried with female objects have received virtually no attention whatsoever. Lucy (1997) comes closest to analysing the meaning of gender-ambiguous graves, but still considers only the biological females with 'male' grave goods. So, are we to conclude that Anglo-Saxon women were proverbial Amazon types, and think no more of it? That would be presumptive, though no doubt true in some cases, given normal levels of physical labour in this society. Since we now have a clearer understanding of the muddy Norse view of flexible gender, we should reconsider crossed male identities just as seriously as we may try to make the case for so-called 'maiden warriors'. There are also a smaller but striking number of biologically female graves that contain weapons. Why do these 'anomalies' happen?

The common response might be: what about gay men and lesbians in Anglo-Saxon society? There is simply no way to debate the matter of homosexuality without more information from another reliable context to explain and substantiate the hypothesis. The literary tradition does not seem to discuss this subject, so we would only be guessing that homosexuality could be expressed by cross-gender dressing, and that cross-dressing might be the appropriate cultural expression of an alternate sexual pattern of behaviour – appropriate even in formal

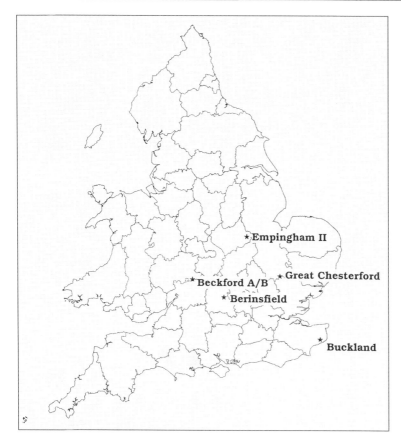

Fig. 4. Early Anglo-Saxon cemeteries mentioned in text.

burial contexts. That is not one assumption, but many. Such ideas are unsupported by current knowledge. We do not really know how homosexuality expressed itself in any Germanic society prior to Christian conversion. On the other hand, if there is cultural continuity from Germanic society to modern Western society, then we should consider the stronger cultural restrictions on male dress mentioned earlier. What social force could permit so many males, otherwise treated normally in burial and without exclusion, to adopt female dress? However, we cannot expect so much continuity. Such admittedly arguable social attitudes as a flexible notion of gender identity have surely been thickly overwritten by long-prevailing Judeo-Christian norms. We must dig very deep for our understanding.

Improved methods of sexing skeletons (better diagnostics, use of dental techniques) simply make the occurrence of gender ambiguity all the more conspicuous. It shows up more commonly than might be imagined. The following review of some burial data will report on five cemeteries containing early Anglo-Saxon inhumations (Fig. 4). Although it is possible in theory to sex remains of cremated bone, this has been attempted too rarely to include as a comparable category in this study. These five cemeteries with inhumations were chosen because: they were excavated and analysed recently by very similar standards; an osteologist made an independent analysis of the skeletal remains, and that report is separately presented; the sites are widely but randomly distributed over the Anglo-Saxon settlement area, and these are *all* the sites on which the author has so far been able to obtain information and that meet the above-mentioned criteria. This is, of course, not a statistically random sample, but there is no evidence that the data are skewed in any way.

Berinsfield

The first cemetery is Berinsfield in the Upper Thames Valley, yielding approximately 114 inhumations (Boyle et al. 1995), and weapons were found with 26 burials. As is typical, there were few swords, but numerous shields and other weapons, mostly occurring in non-functional combinations from the point of view of the requirements of the warrior. One potential case of ambiguous gender (Boyle et al. 1995, 112, grave No. 104) was found: a 'possible' male (aged 20–25 years) with a full set of feminine-gendered artefacts (including a small long brooch, beads, knife, girdle group, vessel and miscellaneous metal). The possible sex identification given here is based on a skull lacking its mandible and 'certain fragmentary long bones' (Boyle et al. 1995, 112). Using opinions expressed several decades earlier, Angela Boyle and Anne Dodd (Boyle et al. 1995, 113–15) guess that the accuracy of this sex assessment is around 80–92 per cent. It is not unreasonable that this particular skeleton identified biologically as a male is, in fact, a female. Although a number of artefacts were buried in the grave, No. 104 is not exceptionally 'wealthy' in appearance. However, grave No. 104 is the only Berinsfield burial associated with charred timbers. Only three other inhumations produced as much as small pieces of charcoal.

The human skeletons from the Berinsfield inhumations were described by Mary Harman. Preservation was found to be highly variable. Adults were sexed by relevant features of the skull and pelvic girdle, and by the general appearance and robustness of the bones (Boyle et al. 1995, 106).

Weapon burial rite at Berinsfield was discussed by Heinrich Härke, whose opinions have already been mentioned in this chapter. Härke found additional evidence at Berinsfield for the specific linkage of weapon burial rite with specific families or kin groups. He also noted that weapons were more associated with male adults, aged 20–30, and not with older males (Boyle et al. 1995, 67–9). These points, it seems, actually argue against weapons operating here as symbolic of individual rank, since in many societies greater age serves to increase rank. However, if rank is held not individually but collectively by groups (by kin groups, as Härke contends), then the attribution of weapons to males according to their age is a secondary attribute of the weapon rite. Primary is the association with specific groups.

Great Chesterford

The second cemetery is Great Chesterford in Essex, quite large, with 167 inhumations (Evison et al. 1994; the human remains are reported by Tony Waldron). Although analysis was concluded only recently, the bones were excavated in the 1950s, and not stored as discrete individuals. There has been substantial post-mortem breakage and other damage. Most but not all bones were marked with their inhumation numbers. Errors and illegibility of numbering further confounded the identification process (Evison et al. 1994, 62). Bearing these facts and conditions in mind, this cemetery produced no apparent ambiguities of burial gender identity in the finds. It is included here, however, because it was originally part of the author's study sample, and offers a contrary example while illustrating several other points about Anglo-Saxon cemeteries and their excavation.

After reconstructing individuals from Great Chesterford as well as possible, Waldron analysed the remains according to methods recommended by the Workshop of European Archaeologists in 1980 and by Krogman and Iscan in 1986 (see Evison et al. 1994, 52–66). Adults were assigned a 'definite' sex if either the pelvis or skull were present, and a 'probable' sex if other criteria such as long bone measurements were used. Most identifications were judged to be 'definite'. Only two adults were classed as 'probable' (both as males), and six were undetermined.

Weapon burials do not receive particular attention beyond a discussion of weapon types. However, grave No. 142 contained a man with spear and shield, and a horse. Another interred horse could not be directly associated with any human burial (Evison et al. 1994, 29). The other characteristic of Great Chesterford worth noting is its high incidence of juvenile and infant burials. Typically, about 20 per cent of burials in similar Anglo-Saxon cemeteries have been classed as sub-adult. Here, 51.5% (86 out of 167) of the inhumations are judged to be sub-adult (Evison et al. 1994, 31).

Beckford A (Fig. 5)

Beckford A, in Hereford and Worcester, presents us with 26 inhumations (14 males and 12 females, some sub-adult). The skeletal analysis (by Calvin Wells) was interesting in that it made particular use of dental indicators (Evison et al. 1996, 47). This is a more recently developed methodology. Wells felt that the greater robustness of the males in this cemetery (as well as at Beckford B) reflected a gender-privileged diet, as well as expected sexual dimorphism (Evison et al. 1996, 23). One individual buried in grave No. A2 presented an injury to the skull that appears to be the result of a sharp weapon blow: 'The bone report suggests that this skeleton was probably female, but the accompanying spear and shield show that it was a weapon-bearing male, and therefore more likely to incur such an injury.' The ingrained assumptions of the preceding statement are clear. Wells, in the same publication (Evison et al. 1996, 42), supplies the information that the skull hole was healed, and refutes emphatically that trephination might have been involved. He concludes that the lesion, which is found on the frontal bone, resulted from the oblique blow of a sharp instrument. Having made such a close analysis, Wells nevertheless labels this individual as 'probably female', based on 38 skull fragments, 4 teeth, 22 vertebrae, 10 fragments of pelvis and a variety of other bones (Evison et al. 1996, 42).

At Beckford A, two biological males appear with feminine grave goods or clothing in graves Nos A16 and A17. No. A16 is described by Wells as a 'fairly well-preserved' skeleton. Although muscle markings 'tend to be weak,' and stature short (5 ft 3 in), Wells saw enough evidence to deliver a definite verdict of 'male', aged 19–20 (Evison et al. 1996, 45). Evison & Hill's grave catalogue reassigns the classification of 'female' to grave No. A16 without comment, and describes two long brooches, a pin, a small number of beads, various rings that might belong to a girdle group, and a bone spindle whorl, among other objects (Evison et al. 1996, 78). This grave remains problematic.

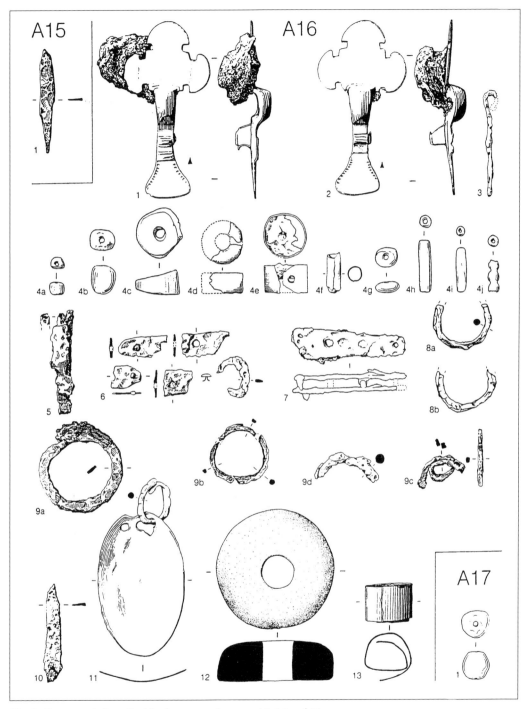

Fig. 5. Grave-goods from Beckford cemetery A, graves 15, 16 and 17.

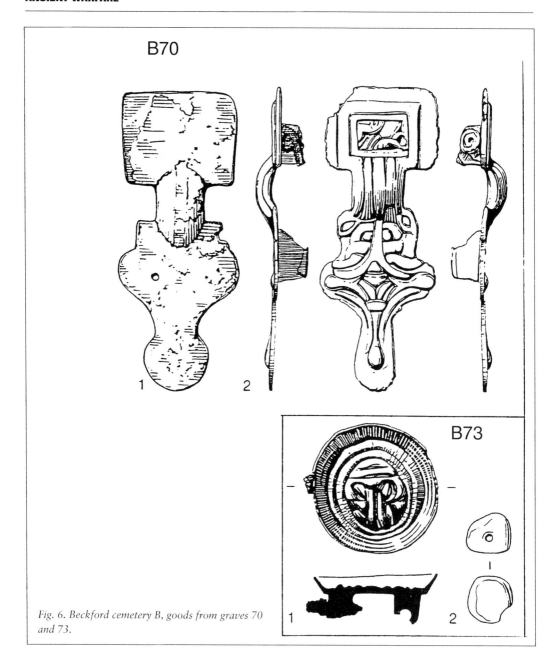

Fig. 6. Beckford cemetery B, goods from graves 70 and 73.

Grave No. A17 was much more difficult to sex. In fact, since the skeleton's age was estimated at 11–12 years, some researchers would not attempt to sex the remains at all. The assignation of 'probably male' (Evison et al. 1996, 45) may therefore be taken with a grain of salt, especially since Wells added that the skeleton was 'somewhat defective.' As before, the excavators reclassify the burial as 'female juvenile', and note that twelve amber beads, small and roughly shaped, were found at the neck (Evison et al. 1996, 78) and comprised the sole grave good inventory.

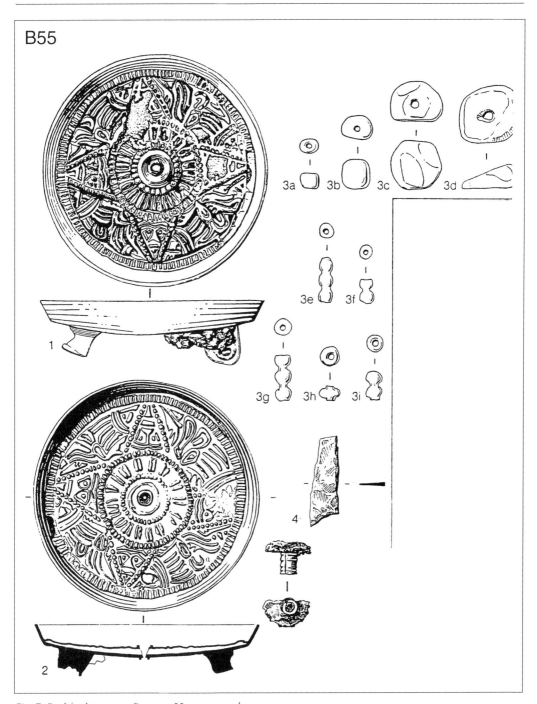

Fig. 7. Beckford cemetery B, grave 55, grave-goods.

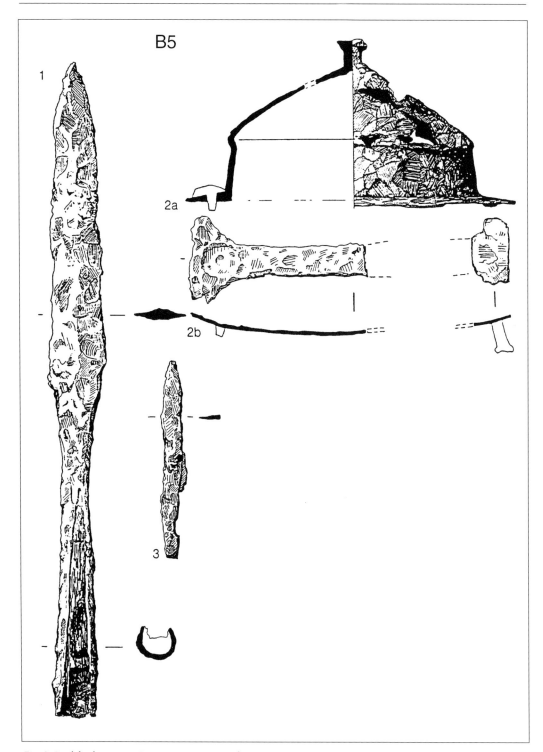

Fig. 8. Beckford cemetery B, grave 5, grave-goods.

Beckford B (Figs 6–8)

Beckford B, only 600 yards from its companion, is much larger, with 108 inhumations (Evison et al. 1996, 51–2). Notably, skeletal material at Beckford B was generally preserved much more poorly than at A. Again, analysis was made with special attention to teeth. One definite and three possible biological males were found with feminine grave goods (Nos B55, B70, B73, B75). Three possible biological females possessed masculine grave goods (Nos B5, B85, B93). Of these, No. B85 is a juvenile. In the latter group, grave No. B5 contained a spearhead and shield boss, No. B85 contained a spearhead (a knife fragment was the only other artefact), and No. B93 contained a spearhead (the only artefact). Given the possibility mentioned above that old spearheads might be adapted by women as domestic tools, graves Nos B85 and B93 do not offer enough supporting artefactual evidence to make a gender decision regardless of other assumptions.

Calvin Wells comments regarding Beckford B: 'For most of the skeletons the diagnosis of sex must remain very uncertain. Well preserved pelves or crania were non-existent and the sex had often to be inferred from limb bones and other evidence of poor quality . . . With considerable diffidence and with varying probability 28 inhumations have been presumed male, 35 female and 45 have been left unsexed' (Evison et al. 1996, 52). As at Beckford A, Wells sexed some sub-adults, with the following results: males were identified among 25 adults and 3 young adults; females were noted among 19 adults, 14 young adults, 1 adolescent, and 1 child; 10 adults, 2 young adults, 8 adolescents, and 25 children remained unsexed. Such categories require and were supplied with definitions: adults were defined as more than 25 years of age, young adults as 18–24 years, adolescents as 13–17 years, and children as under 13 years (Evison et al. 1996, 52).

Not surprisingly, given the poor bone preservation, this cemetery produced some conflicting sex-gender evidence. However, considering also the large number of burials, the cemetery certainly did not produce any greater share of these problems than is usual. Seven burials in all produced gender conflicts, but in only one of these cases, the male buried in grave No. B70, did Wells consider the sex identification to be secure. This individual was represented by forty-five pieces of cranium, including craggy mastoids, nearly all the teeth and substantial pieces of post-cranial skeleton (Evison et al. 1996, 59). The final grave description in the report, on the other hand, labels the deceased as 'female', and lists only two artefacts: a gilt bronze, square-headed brooch and another (not matching) square-headed brooch, both found at opposite shoulders. The second brooch has been lost, and is known only from a sketch made when discovered (Evison et al. 1996, 87).

Empingham II (Figs 9–10)

Empingham II, in Leicestershire, has revealed another small percentage of gender-ambiguous graves. The report on the human remains is provided by Simon Mays, who identified the inhumed remains of 150 Anglo-Saxons and one Anglo-Saxon cremation. Two burials (Nos 133 and 134) are not included in this count. Fifty-nine additional individuals were recorded in the field by Justine Bayley. May's report concentrates more on dentition than most other published osteological reports. Mays feels that dental measurements can

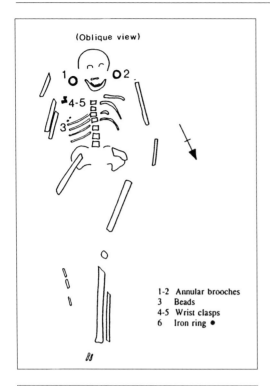

(Oblique view)

1-2 Annular brooches
3   Beads
4-5 Wrist clasps
6   Iron ring ●

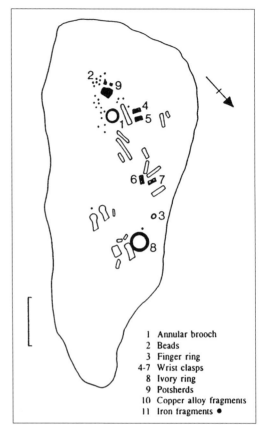

1   Annular brooch
2   Beads
3   Finger ring
4-7 Wrist clasps
8   Ivory ring
9   Potsherds
10 Copper alloy fragments
11 Iron fragments ●

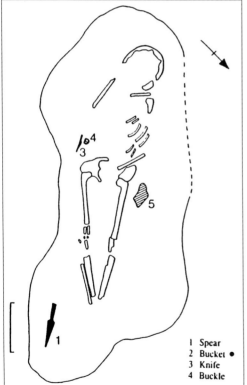

1   Spear
2   Bucket ●
3   Knife
4   Buckle

Fig. 9. Burials from the cemetery at Empingham II:
nos. 16, 46 and 75.

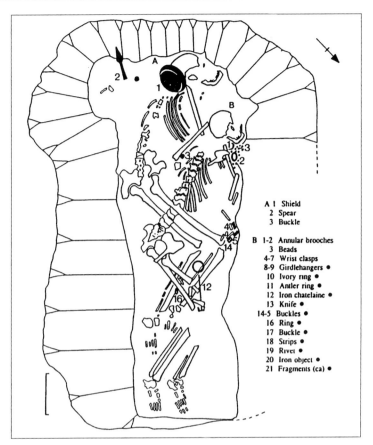

A 1 Shield
  2 Spear
  3 Buckle

B 1-2 Annular brooches
  3 Beads
  4-7 Wrist clasps
  8-9 Girdlehangers ●
  10 Ivory ring ●
  11 Antler ring ●
  12 Iron chatelaine ●
  13 Knife ●
  14-5 Buckles ●
  16 Ring ●
  17 Buckle ●
  18 Strips ●
  19 Rivet ●
  20 Iron object ●
  21 Fragments (ca) ●

Fig. 10. Burials from the cemetery at Empingham II: nos 98, 105 and 106.

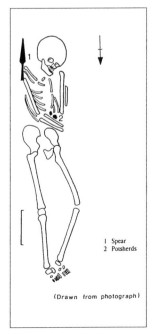

1 Spear
2 Potsherds

(Drawn from photograph)

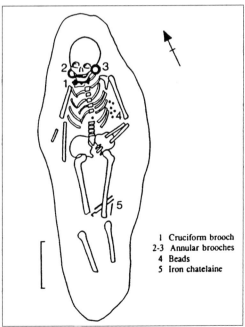

1 Cruciform brooch
2-3 Annular brooches
  4 Beads
  5 Iron chatelaine

239

help ascertain the sex of juveniles and adults who lack the usual diagnostic bones (Timby et al. 1996, 21). Dental development or attrition can also be used to estimate age. Tooth crown measurements demonstrate sexual dimorphism, and this applies, as Mays asserts, to immature as well as mature individuals (Timby et al. 1996, 21–2).

Burial No. 16A is determined by Mays to be a male, aged 35–45 years. Twenty-five teeth were recovered. The bones were described as crushed, but adequate preservation, including a pelvis, allowed for the determination of sex to be based on both skeletal and dental material. The grave goods seem typically female: two annular brooches, one on each shoulder; six beads; a single wrist clasp and a pair of wrist clasps, all by the right wrist, and an incomplete iron ring (Timby et al. 1996, 31, 101).

Despite the apparent 'femaleness' of the dress of the deceased individual in No. 16A, one can still question the arrangement of the wrist clasps and point out that men, too, could wear a smaller number of beads. For another time and place – the Hallstatt period of central Europe – Bettina Arnold has observed distinct patterns, or fashions, for the gendered arrangement of wrist clasps. Hallstatt women wore their brooches and clasps symmetrically, in matched pairs, one on each side. Males would generally wear only one bracelet, or unmatched sets (Arnold 1991, 369).

The two brooches of grave No. 16A are described as similar in decoration, perhaps a symmetrical pair. The bracelets, although consisting of a single and a pair, are treated asymmetrically. A study of Anglo-Saxon jewellery combinations, similar to Arnold's for the Hallstatt, might clear up some of this not uncommon ambiguity of gender.

Grave No. 46 at Empingham contained a male, aged 15–20 years, whose sex determination was based on dental evidence. Twenty-four teeth survived (Timby et al. 1996, 31). The remainder of the skeleton was very fragmentary. Timby et al. retain some scepticism about the male designation: 'The range of grave goods might suggest that this is a female burial and not male as deduced from the teeth' (Timby et al. 1996, 109). The grave goods consist of only one annular brooch, thirty-three beads, a copper alloy finger ring and two pairs of wrist clasps (but it is unclear how they were worn), a ring of elephant ivory and iron fragments, 'possibly part of a latch key' (Timby et al. 1996, 109). Although the use of one brooch lacks feminine symmetry on the Hallstatt model, the remainder of the grave goods follow presumed female patterns. The elephant ivory is unusual, but not unique. The pre-adult age of this individual precludes the usual skeletal methods of sexing, and the archaeologists are clearly less comfortable than Mays with a sexual determination based only on dental evidence.

Grave No. 75 is difficult and uncertain from all perspectives. Mays finds here a child, seven or eight years of age. There are associated with the remains seven permanent and seven deciduous teeth. Neither the skeletal nor dental evidence is enough in this case, and May's sex determination of 'female' is offered as uncertain (Timby et al. 1996, 32). Therefore, we should not draw any firm conclusions in this case from the grave goods assemblage, consisting of a spearhead, wooden bucket, iron knife and iron buckle (Timby et al. 1996, 115).

Likewise, grave No. 98B offered little for Mays to work with. No teeth were recovered. This individual was the second skeleton found in double grave No. 98, where two individuals were closely intertwined and lying on their sides (Timby et al. 1996, 160). Grave No. 98A was identified as a male on the basis of the eighteen teeth (Timby et al.

1996, 32). Mays also aged him as young, aged 17–25 years. He is buried with few items, but does have typical 'warrior' accoutrements of shield and spear. Mays was unable to age No. 98B beyond the designation of 'adult', and he offers the male gender determination as 'uncertain.' No. 98B is in fact associated with many objects connoting a female, from brooch and bracelet pairs to 'girdle' hangers (Timby et al. 1996, 122–3). The urge to view this burial as a young male of some status (despite his own sparse grave goods) having been buried with his wife or female slave is certainly tempting.

Grave No. 105 presents another problematic child burial, although this time the twelve permanent and ten deciduous teeth lead Mays to relative certainty about the 9- or 10-year-old child's male sex. Skeletal preservation also seems adequate although the child's age makes sexual clues derived from skeletal data circumstantial at best. The artefacts consist of an identically matched pair of annular brooches at the shoulders, a cruciform brooch with 'the head pointing downwards', twenty-two beads and other ornaments for stringing, and an iron chatelaine with three latch keys (Timby et al. 1996, 124). It would be useful to know something of the occurrence pattern of 'upside-down' cruciform brooches.

Grave No. 106 reveals to Mays an older female adolescent, aged 13–15 years, very nearly adult according to the social standards of her people. From twenty-three permanent teeth (no deciduous), Mays is confident of a female sexual identity. Grave goods, on the other hand, consisted of only a spearhead beside the head, with fragments of a wooden shaft discernible (and therefore not so likely to be a spearhead-turned-weaving baton, as some might argue) and some pottery sherds by an elbow (Timby et al. 1996, 32, 124). If we return briefly to the 'maiden warrior' scenario and the possible flexibility of a woman's gender prior to marriage, this grave could be construed as an excellent example of that particular phenomenon.

Buckland

Buckland in Dover is the largest cemetery compared to the others in this sample. With a total of 170 inhumations, Buckland has the largest number of reportedly gender-ambiguous burials (12 alleged biological males, and 8 alleged biological females buried with materials of the opposite sex), and has frequently been cited in recent articles on the 'maiden warrior' tradition (e.g., Lucy 1997). The repeated skeletal analyses are so contradictory in their results (without published explanations for changes in the gender identification of graves: see Evison 1987, 123–5) that it is best not to use this data for the construction of a sound argument concerning gender.

CONCLUSION

There are not enough suitably analysed and published cemeteries to make more than a preliminary assessment, from a distance, of gender ambiguity in Anglo-Saxon graves. Further analysis of other cemeteries is required. Future advances in the genetic sexing of bones by DNA analysis in problem cases may quickly make this entire argument and discussion moot (we can only hope), but in the meantime, archaeologists should at least consider alternative explanations and clearly record where, and especially how, artefactual indicators (the grave goods) and osteological evidence differ.

As the gender ambiguity problem found in cemeteries demonstrates, archaeologists (and historians, for that matter) have been far too cavalier in assuming that Anglo-Saxon society mirrored the sex roles and gender identities found in nineteenth- and twentieth-century Europe and America. It is now clear that a much more objective re-evaluation and interpretation of the data is needed.

Weapon-bearing may very well have had several different meanings in Anglo-Saxon society, including the representation of warrior occupation, special political or economic status or rank, the individual's functional role within the kin group, basic male identity, or other personal qualities unrelated to biological sex but denoting courage and eagerness to defend family honour or inheritance. Above all, the potential for a ritually expressed gender identity – standing in opposition to biological sexual identity – needs to be further explored. This ritual identity may be intricately bound up with other religious beliefs defining the human relationship to the spirit world. All these meanings may or may not have operated simultaneously, as a group or in some other combination. Again, a more objective view of the evidence, without contamination by *a priori* assumptions derived from later Euro-American culture history, is needed. We should focus more on the symbolic meaning of weapons, for women who might have borne weapons need not be construed as warriors.

Flexible gender continuity and surrogate behaviour are helpful concepts, but they do not address the question of why individuals may have been buried with biologically opposed gender identities. A woman who might have died while functioning as a surrogate male (this is not to say that she died fighting, but that she could have died of any cause during a period when she was fulfilling a kin-based social role and obligation) may be buried with male objects for public ritual reasons (these are her 'signifiers of *gender* rank'). We can speculate yet further, and ask the question: what is the process of feminisation? For the Norse, it was the adoption of the associated roles of married woman, child-bearer, and sexually active female. Females who had not yet taken on that status would be freer to define their own gender than we, from our own cultural standpoint, expect. It is important to remember that in Norse society, the dominant viewpoint held that only one sex existed – the male – of which the female was but a variant condition.

The explanation is not so apparent for the more obscure male case. However, we are only beginning to study the deeper meanings of shamanic behaviour in northern societies. For the males in Norse culture, the association of feminine identity with *seiðr* and shamanism suggests that certain males might function in a feminised role for ritual purposes. Here is a possible line of inquiry for interpreting the feminised male burials. Among the scant sources of evidence, we have suggestions of the actual beliefs of the early English; we feel secure in presuming that they had a similar regard for their warrior god Wodan as the Norse did for Odin. Furthermore, both shamanic and *seiðr* rituals have associations with Odin and his warrior cult following. These associations are found in the mythic project of Odin as the archetypal Norse shaman, shape-changer and bearer of mystical knowledge. The *seiðr* connections are more obscure, but are the subject of some interesting current research. Both Wodan and Odin gave power to the warrior, and later to the élite, and in a few known instances positioned at the head of the genealogies of royal dynasties. An explanation of gender inversion deriving from a ritual shamanic or related role, applied to the Anglo-Saxons as well as the Norse, makes analogical sense, but additional supporting evidence would be in order.

For all these reasons, it is not enough to focus on the concept of maiden warriors alone. We must include the other half, the apparently numerically larger half, of the equation: the individuals here described, for lack of more information, as 'feminised males'. Furthermore, if we presumptively view these individuals according to the twentieth-century categories of 'gay', 'lesbian', 'bisexual' or even 'transvestite', we would make the all too common mistake of imposing modern cultural categories on prehistoric society. Linking gender identity to sexual preference is only one kind of definition of that identity. No evidence suggests that individual sexual preferences played any part in defining gender identity in early North European society. Here, again, the author proposes the possibility of a ritual meaning for this behaviour among the Anglo-Saxons, foreshadowing the religious implications and metaphors of intercourse found in (later) Norse shamanic and *seiðr* rituals.

Therefore, gender categories must be defined in the context of the entire social system – including its economic, political, and religious aspects – in order for any proposed explanation of related behaviour to have validity. Sad to say, given the legends' popularity over the ages, stories of warrior maidens are rather likely to be a bit skewed from the reality. The Anglo-Saxon and broader Northern European context points toward the real possibility of certain ritual roles defining gendered behaviour and perhaps extending an apposite identity into the funerary sphere. But this in no way argues that the daily ordinary experience and perceptions of Anglo-Saxon or Norse women were really very much like ours, after all. In fact, the argument defines a greater fundamental difference of world view than the 'warrior maiden' explanation presumes.

ACKNOWLEDGEMENTS

None of my research, conducted for the most part at a great distance, could have been possible without the generally extremely competent, thorough analysis and publication of cemetery research in Great Britain, not to mention the patient efforts of inter-library loan staff at the University of Minnesota. I have especially benefited from assistance generously offered by C.A. Roberts of the Department of Archaeological Sciences at Bradford University, among others, who gave me access to informative materials and some current thoughts on the technical aspects of interpreting skeletal remains.

FIFTEEN

EPILOGUE: THE FUTURE STUDY OF ANCIENT WARFARE

JOHN CARMAN AND ANTHONY HARDING

This book has been about how archaeologists study war in the distant past. We have limited our focus to periods that can legitimately be called 'ancient': from prehistory to the mid-first millennium AD. We have also limited ourselves largely to warfare on the continent of Europe, because that is where most of us hail from and work, but also because it is the western style of war – developed in Europe by European peoples – that has spread across the globe to be the war of our own time. Accordingly, if we have any pretensions to saying something about war in our own time, then it is inevitably that style of war which we must address. The approach we take is similar to one adopted by students of the archaeology of more recent times: taking a subject that is pertinent today, and then looking backwards in time to understand its historical roots (Orser 1999, 281). Here, we have chosen to look at war by looking at archaeological data that we believe bears on its origins and forms millennia ago. As we enter the third millennium, it is perhaps chastening to see just how short a distance we have come from a 'barbaric' past.

In the Introduction, we set out five themes expressed as questions with which we were concerned. Here, we want to review briefly the contents of the book to see to what extent it has been possible to arrive at answers.

WHAT GENERAL LESSONS APPLICABLE TO ARCHAEOLOGY ARE TO BE LEARNT FROM A STUDY OF WARFARE IN ETHNOGRAPHIC AND HISTORICAL SITUATIONS? WHY DO SO MANY SOCIETIES ENGAGE IN WARFARE? WHAT ADVANTAGES DOES IT BRING, AND WHAT RISKS DOES IT INVOLVE?

Inevitably, all the contributors draw upon ideas about war derived from other disciplines. Archaeology alone, it would seem, is not enough. And for both Carman and Hanson – who rely heavily upon historical sources – it provides very little indeed. For the majority, however, the derivation of ideas relating to the causes of war and the conditions for it to begin is taken as natural and necessary. Some favour environmental degradation and demographic stress, leading to intensified competition for resources, in their quest for causes. Such competition, it is suggested, is more likely among farming populations than mobile groups. Here, the need to maintain territorial integrity, access to resources and group cohesion all have a part to play. Others see war as essentially ideological in origin, and the way it was carried on largely ritual in form. The notion of an 'innate' tendency in humans toward aggression is raised, for instance by Brothwell, but dismissed as an explanation for war, partly because there is a distinction drawn between aggressive tendencies and actual violence.

By contrast with this general agreement, the conditions under which war may take place are held to be more varied. While environmental degradation makes a second appearance, it is joined by other socio-political – expressly human – factors. Among these are political structures which promote war as a response to external factors. These include forms of socio-economic organisation, including specialisation, leading to the development of specific technologies suitable only for use as weapons against human enemies, and thus the rise of 'military elites'. Such military elites are generally assumed to be male: the evidence for 'warrior maidens' is seen to be at best ambiguous.

Where history and ethnography can specifically assist the archaeologist is in identifying what the archaeologist should seek as evidence of actual warfare: what warfare would 'look like' as part of the archaeological record. The accumulated evidence from ethnography and from history can tell us how to distinguish weapons from other edged and pointed tools, how to distinguish defensive sites from other kinds of structures and monuments and what kinds of social, economic and political organisations and institutions are likely to be found in societies at war or occasionally waging war. Care needs to be taken, however. While some of the contributors are able unambiguously to differentiate military organisation from other social forms, and weapons for use from ritual objects, others are less certain. 'Defensive' sites may equally be ritual monuments, and 'weapons' things for deposit with the dead or in holy places; even the locations where the actual violence of war takes place are held to have ritual-like associations and aspects. Where such objects, structures and places can be confidently identified as being related to actual warfare, the specialised weapons and 'military elites' of cultures are seen by some as the precondition for a society to be able to wage war; for others, they are an epiphenomenon – an effect of having been engaged in war. Ultimately, no common criteria for the identification of evidence for actual war can be drawn: each culture must be studied in its own terms; but this too may be a general lesson – of a kind. Some authors clearly believe that the practice of warfare by prehistoric peoples had an effect on the development of those societies, but none of those represented in this book would go so far as to maintain that warfare was a purely 'functional' practice. If raiding was common in particular periods, as has been maintained for the Neolithic and Bronze Ages of Europe, the taking of loot – whether foodstuffs, equipment or persons – might be seen as justification and advantage enough to outweigh the risks involved. Presumably, attacks would not be mounted on opponents' strongholds, fortified or not, unless the attackers were reasonably sure they could prevail. The downside – the risk – would be that they might automatically lay themselves open to just such attacks in the future, especially if the societies were ones in which revenge, the avenging of slighted honour, was important.

IN WHAT WAYS CAN ARCHAEOLOGICAL EVIDENCE BE USED TO TELL US ABOUT WARFARE IN THE PAST BEFORE (OR WITHOUT) WRITING? IS ARTEFACTUAL MATERIAL WITH WARLIKE ASSOCIATIONS (WEAPONRY, DEFENSIVE STRUCTURES) NECESSARILY TO BE SEEN AS IN ITSELF EVIDENCE FOR WARFARE? IF NOT, WHAT IS?

There is a strong focus throughout this book on the nature of material evidence for past war: to some extent, the responsibility for this lies at the door of writers such as Keeley (1996), who insist that we reassess our assumptions about what our evidence represents in terms of peaceful or warlike pasts; partly, it is an inevitable consequence of an interest in war as an explicit object of specifically archaeological study. Contributors seek evidence of the waging of war, of its causes, and of the conditions that nurture and sustain war as a human activity. What for some is clear evidence for war, for others is less so. For others again, the question of whether particular classes of object mean 'war' or not is secondary to how they played a part in the rich social functioning of a lost culture, and indeed how it is possible to separate out discrete elements of that culture. Where war is a specific concern, the focus shifts to what the available evidence can tell us about how war became part of that culture, and how war affected that culture.

To some extent, these divergent opinions are a result of uncertainty about what constitutes war, and what constitutes other forms of conflict. Until the Iron Age, considered by Randsborg and Hanson, it is impossible to interpret the evidence as indicating regularised or large-scale fighting by armies (we exclude Egypt and the Near East, largely passed over in this work, and clearly subject to quite different developmental trends). Instead, the evidence favours small-scale raiding, combat between champions, and in some instances extreme forms of personal violence – witness those sites where massacres are evident, even if their nature and causes are unclear.

An area upon which most are silent is the question of methodology. In general, the methodology applied is to compare different cultures over time and across space. The diversity of types of war – and in particular the range of different technologies and material cultures associated with war over several millennia of European history – thus become apparent. The value of this comparison is enhanced by the inclusion of examples from more recent times in North America. Short summaries of the results of specific excavations serve to emphasise the 'archaeological' nature of the approaches taken. The one contribution which specifically addresses questions of methodology does so in order to show how ideas largely derived from non-archaeological sources can be used in a programme of archaeological research into a particular body of evidence.

There is very little explicit discussion of how a 'weapon', for instance, is to be distinguished from any other kind of object it may be, or how warfare itself can actually be recognised in the archaeological record. Thus, while a sword may be found in a bog as a result of deliberate deposition, it nevertheless remains in the minds of many a functional weapon, rather than being treated as an object with strong ritual associations. To treat it as such removes it from the realm of 'true' warfare, and relocates it in the realm of religion and ritual, where combat was undertaken for specific purposes that had little to do with inter-group hostility. For most of our researchers, then, the distinction between 'war' and other parts of social life needs to be maintained. This is perhaps inevitable if the concern is to construct and develop a specific 'archaeology of warfare'; where the concern is – so far as we are able – to reconstruct a past society in its all its complex richness, or at least to gain insights into its complexity, then war is but one component in a vibrant, ever-shifting mosaic of past life.

IN WHAT WAYS WAS WARFARE A STRUCTURAL PART OF THE DEVELOPMENT OF EARLY EUROPE? HOW DID IT RELATE TO SOCIAL AND POLITICAL DEVELOPMENT – FOR INSTANCE, THE EMERGENCE OF CHIEFDOMS OR STATE-FORMATION?

Much clearly rests on the ability of archaeologists to interpret the evidence from their data sets. For some authors, the ability to separate a realm of social action called 'war' or 'warfare' from other aspects of that society is taken for granted. Thus, particular types of objects called 'weapons' can be identified and distinguished from other classes of object. The focus of so many contributors on the rise of 'military elites' in the societies they study both allows and is allowed by this ability to identify and classify objects and structures as things connected with war. However, it is also pointed out that weapon-like objects and 'defensive' structures are frequently encountered in contexts other than those related to violence: as ritual deposits or as grave goods, or as monuments which serve to identify social groups and define territory. Here, a likely difference between the distant past and our own times becomes a factor to incorporate in our understanding: our categories – the way we break our world up into manageable chunks so that we can comprehend it – may not be those that operated in other times, and seeking to impose them upon the remains from those times may impede our ability to understand how those past societies functioned. Whereas we distinguish between weapons and tools, defensive and symbolic monuments, wartime and peacetime, in past times such distinctions may not have applied. Accordingly, even such gross distinctions as 'peace' and 'war', 'civil' and 'military', may not in fact be helpful to us.

An alternative suggested by some contributors, although only hinted at by others, is to look at the effects and consequences of war. For several, the rise of specialist weapons and military elites is not a cause of war, but an effect of experiencing war. Over time, it is suggested, the tools of war began to be distinguished from the general category of tools, leading to the manufacture of objects with a combined use, then others which were predominantly to be used as weapons, and finally others exclusively for use against the human frame. Also over time, a particular form of making war became the distinctive and 'expected' manner of conducting it: the highly ritualised form of the battle, which carries symbolic and cultural meaning as well as providing a functional format in which to engage in killing. Thus, war itself creates the context within which war-like forms emerge. For the Anasazi of the south-western USA, it furthered the environmental degradation that was the condition in which war had begun, leading ultimately to the abandonment of the region and the end of the Anasazi way of life. For the city of Thespiai in Greece, the result of this process was the repeated loss of adult citizenry and even the destruction of the city itself. Both examples are a salutary reminder to us of what war itself makes.

The origins of chiefdoms and early states is not the subject of explicit study in this volume, but some of what has been written here bears on these issues, particularly in the chapters by Kristiansen and Harding. To some extent, their views recall or echo what has been written in the past by Earle and others, in that the rise of a pre-eminent warrior class, with control over the destination of imported exotica or exported raw materials, inevitably led to societies in which wealth was unevenly distributed (whether in the familiar hierarchical or the so-called heterarchical form). It is, indeed, hard to explain the prevalence of prestige weaponry other than in this way. The possible pathways to chieftainship are, however, many and various, and this is not the place to investigate them in more detail.

CAN GENERAL STATEMENTS BE MADE CROSS-CULTURALLY ABOUT ANCIENT WARFARE IN ARCHAEOLOGICAL TERMS? CAN THE STUDY OF, FOR INSTANCE, EGYPTIAN OR ROMAN WARFARE CONTRIBUTE TO THE STUDY OF PREHISTORIC OR EARLY MEDIEVAL WARFARE?

For some of our contributors, the model for prehistoric styles of warfare can be developed by studying the warfare of other ancient civilisations which have left us written or pictorial records. Similarities in weapon-types, in dress and equipment, they suggest, may also suggest similarities in organisation and fighting styles. However, others point out that although the objects may be similar, the contexts in which they were produced and used, and in which they are found today, may be very different, and do not imply other similarities. Even where it is evident that the physical form of an object has passed from one geographical region to another, the meanings it carries in one region are not those carried elsewhere: thus, the Bronze Age sword may have 'meant' one thing in central Europe, but it acquired a different meaning when taken up in contemporary Mycenaean society.

Nevertheless, comparison is a tool used widely in the various chapters in this book. Several take a long-term perspective on warfare in different parts of Europe, beginning with the first emergence of modern humans, and ending in the first millennium BC. Others prefer to compare cultures across space at a particular time, comparing the peoples of Northern Europe with their different contemporaries in central and southern Europe, for instance. Or one can compare how different peoples in different times act towards a particular class of object or place. While some degree of continuity across space or over time may be evident – and indeed argued for – each period or region can be considered to have defined a distinct culture, with its own preferences in matters of war as much as in those of other social practices. An alternative to this overt comparison is to compare how people thought and behaved in a particular period in a particular region with how people in general think and behave today, emphasising the difference between the distant past and the present. This is particularly evident where only one culture at a particular stage in its development is being considered, such as Neolithic Britain, Anglo-Saxon England or Classical Greece. In all these cases, the cross-cultural comparison is not in and of itself meaningful: it is made meaningful only in the way it is used.

WHAT CAN ARCHAEOLOGY CONTRIBUTE TO STUDIES OF WARFARE? IS A DISTINCTIVELY ARCHAEOLOGICAL CONTRIBUTION TO THE STUDY OF WARFARE A VALID OBJECTIVE?

The reliance by archaeologists for the investigation of ancient warfare upon sources of inspiration that derive from other disciplines may incline us to be pessimistic about the first of these questions: after all, we depend on anthropology and history for the models we build of what to look for as evidence of war. It could therefore be argued that the role of archaeology in the study of war is only to provide examples of practices that others have already attested in both theory and actuality. The evidence presented by the contributors is more subtle than this, however, and is *interpreted* rather than merely presented. Clearly, we all believe that archaeologists do have something to say about the study of war, and that archaeological data, archaeological method and archaeological approaches can add something to a more general understanding of war as a phenomenon. But there are differences in how we approach it. Some of us seek to study war in the distant past as a distinct object – as something quite separate from other aspects of past life. Others look to the study of war as merely part of what past cultures were like: they may have engaged in war, but they also did other things which are equally – if not more – interesting. However, perhaps here lies the common goal, if it can be said that we share one.

In general, archaeologists are specialists in particular ways of studying the past: we share a common set of techniques and methods which we apply to material we all recognise as 'archaeological' as opposed to 'historical', 'ethnographic', 'sociological', and so on. As such, we are specialists. But in terms of the pasts we study by applying those techniques and methods to that material, we are generalists, because we are interested in understanding not just particular aspects of those pasts, but as much about them as we can. We are not prey to the charge which – to paraphrase John Keegan – can be laid at the door of the specialist military – and indeed, political – historian:

> an endless repetitive examination of [wars] which . . . have [done nothing] but make the world worse; wallow[ing] in [war] for [war's] sake; and to evade any really inquisitive discussion of what [war] might be like by recourse to the . . . argument . . . that [wars are about] decision, winning or losing. (Keegan 1976, 61–2)

Archaeologists may choose to study aspects of war in the distant past, but they come to it from other directions: we are interested in, for instance, Bronze Age warfare because we are, first and foremost, interested in the Bronze Age. We are interested in particular types of objects – among them, weapons – because we are interested in the role those objects played in a past culture, what was the nature of their 'social life', and not just in how they achieved their end of killing or wounding an opponent. We are interested in ancient battlefields not because we are particularly interested in battle as such, but because through their study we can learn something of past cultures' attitudes to place and to landscape. As a by-product we may also be able to learn something about the nature of human conflict and the way it was worked out on the stage of history. But such a concern can never be divorced from a more general interest in how human cultures work. It is in this broadening interest that archaeology's specific contribution to the study of ancient warfare lies.

BIBLIOGRAPHY

Acsádi, Gy. & Nemeskéri, J. 1970 *History of Human Life Span and Mortality*, Budapest, Akadémiai Kiadó

Adams, R.M. 1966 *The Evolution of Urban Society*, Weidenfeld and Nicolson

Adler, W. 1993. *Studien zur germanischen Bewaffnung: Waffenmitgabe und Kampfesweise im Niederelbegebiet und im übrigen Freien Germanien um Christi Geburt*, Saarbrücker Beiträge zur Altertumskunde 58, Bonn, Habelt

Ahlberg, G. 1971 *Fighting on Land and Sea in Greek Geometric Art*, Skrifter utgivna av Svenska institutet i Athen, series in 4°, XVI, Lund, Gleerup

Albrethsen, S.E. & Brinch Petersen, E. 1976 'Excavation of a Mesolithic cemetery at Vedbaek, Denmark', *Acta Archaeologica* 47, pp. 1–28

Alcock, L. 1981 'Quantity or Quality: The Anglian Graves of Bernicia', in V.I. Evison. (ed.), *Angles, Saxons, and Jutes: Essays Presented to J.N.L. Myres*, Oxford, Clarendon Press, pp. 168–86

Alekshin, V.A. 1994 'Mesolithische Gräberfelder der Ukraine (chronologische, kulturelle und soziologische Aspekte der Interpretation)', *Zeitschrift für Archäologie* 28, pp. 163–89

Alexander, R.D. 1971 'The search for an evolutionary philosophy of man', *Proc. Royal Soc. Victoria* 84, pp. 99–120

Allsworth-Jones, P. 1990 'The Szeletian and the stratigraphic succession in Central Europe and adjacent areas', in P. Mellars (ed.), *The Emergence of Modern Humans*, Edinburgh, Edinburgh University Press, pp. 160–242

Almagro (Basch), M. 1966 *Las estelas decoradas del suroeste peninsular*, Madrid, Bibliotheca Praehistórica Hispana VIII

Ambrosi, A.C. 1988 *Statue Stele Lunigianesi: Il Museo nel Castello del Piagnaro*, Genova, Sagep Editrice

Anderson, D.G. 1994 *The Savannah River Chiefdoms: Political Change in the Late Prehistoric Southeast*, Tuscaloosa, University of Alabama Press

Anderson, J.K, 1970 *Military Theory and Practice in the Age of Xenophon*, Berkeley and Los Angeles, University of California Press

Andreou, S., Fotiadis, M. & Kotsakis, K. 1996 'Review of Aegean prehistory V: The Neolithic and Bronze Age of northern Greece', *American Journal of Archaeology* 100, pp. 537–97

Angel, J.L. 1974 'Patterns of fractures from Neolithic to modern times', *Antropol. Közleményei* 18, pp. 9–18

Anthony, D.W. 1986 'The "kurgan culture", Indo-European origins and the domestication of the horse: A reconsideration', *Current Anthropology* 27/4, pp. 291–313

—— 1995 'Horse, wagon and chariot: Indo-European languages and archaeology', *Antiquity* 69, pp. 554–65

Anthony, D.W. & Brown, D.R. 1990 'The origins of horseback riding', *Antiquity* 65, pp. 22–38

Archer, J. 1995 'Introduction: Male violence in perspective', in J. Archer (ed.), *Male Violence*, London, Routledge, pp. 1–20

Arhaiologia 18 1986 'I Agrosykia (Nomos Pellis)', p. 81

Arnal, J. 1976 *Les Statues-Menhirs, Hommes et Dieux*, Paris, Éditions des Hespérides

Arnold, B. 1991 'The Deposed Princess of Vix: The Need for an Engendered European Prehistory', in D. Walde and N. Willows (eds), *The Archaeology of Gender: 22nd Annual Conference of the Archaeological Association of the University of Calgary*, Calgary, Alberta, University of Calgary, pp. 366–74

Arnold, C.J. 1995 'The archaeology of inter-personal violence', *Scottish Archaeological Review* 9, pp. 71–9

—— 1997 *An Archaeology of the Early Anglo-Saxon Kingdoms* (2nd edn), London and New York, Routledge

Aslanis, I. 1990a 'Oi ohiroseis stous oikismous tou voreioelladikou horou kai i periptosi tou Diminiou', *Meletimata tou Kentrou Erevnas Ellinikis kai Romaikis Arhaiotitas* 10, Athina, Ethniko Idryma Erevnon, pp. 19–64

—— 1990b 'Befestigungsanlagen in Nordgriechenland von dem Chalkolithikum bis zum Beginn der frühen Bronzezeit', in D. Srejović and N. Tasić (eds), *Vinča and its World: International Symposium – The Danubian Region from 6000 to 3000 B.C., Belgrade, Smederevska Palanka, October 1988*, Serbian Academy of Sciences and Arts Symposia 71, Department of Historical Sciences Book 14, Beograd, Serbian Academy of Sciences and Arts, Centre for Archaeological Research, Faculty of Philosophy, pp. 183–7

—— 1993 'I halkolithiki periodos sto voreioelladiko horo: provlimata anagnorisis kai diarkeias', *Ancient Macedonia V: Papers Read at the Fifth International Symposium Held in Thessaloniki, October 10–15, 1989*, Vol. 1, Thessaloniki, Institute for Balkan Studies, pp. 133–45

—— 1995 'Die Siedlung von Dimini: Ein neues Rekonstruktionsbild', in *Settlement Patterns between the Alps and the Black Sea – 5th to 2nd Millennium B.C.*, Verona, Museo civico di storia naturale, Sezione scienze uomo 4, pp. 35–43

Avila, R.A.J. 1983 *Bronzene Lanzen- und Pfeilspitzen der griechischen Spätbronzezeit*, Prähistorische Bronzefunde, Abt. V, Band 1, Munich, Beck

Bach, A. & Bach, H. 1972 'Anthropologische Analyse des Walternienburg-Bernburger Kollektivgrabes von Schönstedt im Thüringer Becken', *Alt-Thüringen* 12, pp. 59–107

Bailey, D.W. 1997 'Impermanence and flux in the landscape of early agricultural South East Europe', in J. Chapman and P. Dolukhanov (eds), *Landscapes in Flux*, Colloquia Pontica 3, Oxford, Oxbow Books, pp. 41–58

Bamforth, D.G. 1994 'Indigenous people, indigenous violence: Precontact warfare on the North American Great Plains', *Man* NS 29, pp. 95–115

Barfield, L. 1971 *Northern Italy Before Rome*, London, Thames and Hudson

Barnard, A. & Woodburn, J. 1988 'Introduction', in T. Ingold, D. Riches and J. Woodburn (eds), *Hunters and Gatherers: Property, Power and Ideology*, Oxford, Berg, pp. 4–31

Barrett, J.C., Bradley, R. & Green, M. 1991 *Landscape, Monuments and Society: The Prehistory of Cranbourne Chase*, Cambridge, Cambridge University Press

Bates, D.G. & Lees, S.H. 1979 'The myth of population regulation', in N. Chagnon and W. Irons (eds), *Evolutionary Biology and Human Social Behaviour*, Massachusetts, Duxbury Press, pp. 273–89

Baum, N. 1991 'Sammler/Jäger oder Ackerbauern? Eine paläodontologische Untersuchung zur kulturhistorischen Stellung der Kopfbestattungen aus der Grossen-Ofnet-Höhle in Schwaben', *Archäologisches Korrespondenzblatt* 21, pp. 469–74

Behrens, H.W. 1978 'Der Kampf in der Steinzeit (ein Diskussionsbeitrag vom Aspekt des Prähistorikers)', *Mitt. der Anthropologischen Gesellschaft Wien* 108, pp. 1–7

Beková-Berounská, M. 1989 'On Eneolithic maces in Central Europe', *Praehistorica* 15–16, pp. 219–22

Beloch, K. 1912–27 *Griechische Geschichte* (2nd edn), Strasburg/Berlin

Belschner, W. 1975 'Learning and aggression', in H. Selg (ed.), *The Making of Human Aggression: A Psychological Approach*, Quartet Books, pp. 61–103

Benedict, R. 1934 *Patterns of Culture*, London, Routledge

Bennike, P. 1985 *Palaeopathology of Danish Skeletons: A Comparative Study of Demography, Disease and Injury*, Copenhagen, Akademisk Forlag

——— 1987 'Human remains from the Argus Bank', *Mesolithic Miscellany* 8/1, pp. 5–6

Berger, T.D. & Trinkaus, E. 1995 'Patterns of trauma among the Neanderthals', *J. Archaeological Science* 22, pp. 841–52

Bertemes, F. 1991 'Untersuchungen zur Funktion der Erdwerke der Michelsberger Kultur im Rahmen der kupferzeitlichen Zivilisation', in J. Lichardus (ed.), *Die Kupferzeit als historische Epoche*, Teil 1, Saarbrücker Beiträge zur Altertumskunde 55, Bonn, Habelt, pp. 441–64

Besios, M. & Pappa, M. 1990–5 'O neolithikos oikismos ston Makrygialo Pierias', *Athens Annals of Archaeology* 23–28, pp. 13–30

——— 1996 'Neolithikos oikismos Makrygialou 1993'. *To Arhaiologiko Ergo sti Makedonia kai Thraki* 7 (1993). Thessaloniki, Aristoteleio Panepistimio Thessalonikis, Ypourgeio Politismou, Ypourgeio Makedonias-Thrakis, pp. 215–22

Best, J.G.P. 1969 *Thracian Peltasts and Their Influence on Greek Warfare*, Studies of the Dutch Archaeological and Historical Society I, Groningen, Wolters-Noordhoff

Bettinger, R.L. 1991 *Hunter-Gatherers: Archaeological and Evolutionary Theory*, New York, Plenum

Bianco Peroni, V. 1970 *Die Schwerter in Italien / Le spade nell'Italia continentale*, Prähistorische Bronzefunde, Abt. IV, Band 1, Munich, Beck

Bibikov, S.N. 1953 *Poselenie Luka-Vrublevetskaya*, MIA SSSR 38, Moscow, Nauka

——— 1971 'Plotnost' naseleniya i velichina ohotnichih ugodii v paleolite Kryma', *Sovetskaya arkheologiya* 1971/4, pp. 11–22

——— 1977 'Epoha mezolita', in S.N. Bibikov (ed.), *Istoriya Ukrain'skoi RSR*, Kiev, Naukova Dumka, pp. 41–50

Bibikov, S.N. & Tolochko, P.P. 1988 'Problema paleodemografii i paleoekonomiki (arkheologicheskii aspekt issledovanii)', in S.N. Bibikov (ed.), *Problemy istoricheskoi demografii*, Kiev, Naukova Dumka, pp. 1–17

Bibikova, V.I. 1978 'Fauna iz mezoliticheskih poselenii Beloless'e i Girzhevo (Nizhnee Podnestrov'e)', in S.N. Bibikov (ed.), *Arheologicheskie issledovaniya Severo-Zapadnogo Prichernomor'ya*, Kiev, Naukova Dumka, pp. 34–9

——— 1982 'Teriofauna poseleniya Mirnoe', in V.N. Stanko (ed.), *Mirnoe: Problema mezolita stepei Severnogo Prichernomor'ya*, Kiev, Naukova Dumka, pp. 139–64

Bigelow, R. 1969 *The Dawn Warriors*, London, Hutchinson

Binford, L.R. 1973 'Interassemblage variability – the Mousterian and the 'functional' argument', in C. Renfrew (ed.), *The Explanation of Culture Change: Models in Prehistory*, London, Duckworth, pp. 227–54

Bintliff, J. & Snodgrass, A. 1988 'Mediterranean survey and the city', *Antiquity* 62, pp. 57–71

Bíró, K. 1988 'Distribution of lithic raw materials on prehistoric sites: An interim report', *Acta Archaeologica* (Budapest) 40, pp. 251–74

Blegen, C.W. 1966 *The Palace of Nestor at Pylos in Western Messenia, Vol. 1: The Buildings and their Contents*, Princeton, Princeton University Press

Bloch, M. 1977 'The disconnection between power and rank as a process: an outline of the development of kingdoms in central Madagascar', in J. Friedman and M. Rowlands (eds), *The Evolution of Social Systems*, London, Duckworth, pp. 303–40

Bocksberger, O.-J. 1978 *Le site préhistorique du Petit-Chasseur (Sion, Valais) 4: Horizon supérieur, Secteur occidental et tombes Bronze ancien*, Cahiers d'Archéologie Romande 14, Lausanne, Bibliothèque historique vaudoise

Bognár-Kutzian, I. 1972 *The Early Copper Age Tiszapolgár Culture in the Carpathian Basin*, Budapest, Akadémiai Kiadó

Bohannan, P. (ed.) 1967 *Law and Warfare: Studies in the Anthropology of Conflict*, American Museum Sourcebooks in Anthropology, Garden City, New York, The Natural History Press

Bökönyi, S. 1978 'The earliest waves of domestic horses in East Europe', *Journal of Indo-European Studies* 9, pp. 17–75

—— 1988 'The Neolithic fauna of Divostin', in A. McPherron and D. Srejović (eds), *Divostin and the Neolithic of Central Serbia*, Kragujevac, Narodni Muzej Kragujevac, pp. 419–45

Bondurant, J.V. 1965 *Conquest of Violence*, Berkeley, University of California Press

Bonsall, C. & Smith, C. 1990 'Bone and antler technology in the British Late Upper Palaeolithic and Mesolithic: The impact of accelerator dating', in P.M. Vermeersch and P. van Peer (eds), *Contributions to the Mesolithic in Europe*, Studia Praehistorica Belgica 5, Leuven, Leuven University Press, pp. 359–68

Bonsall, C., Lennon, R., McSweeney, K., Stewart, C., Harkness, D., Boroneanţ, V., Bartosiewicz, L., Payton R. & Chapman J. 1997 'Mesolithic and Early Neolithic in the Iron Gates: A palaeodietary perspective', *Journal of European Archaeology* 5/1, pp. 50–92

Bordes, F. 1981 'Vingt-cinq ans après: le complexe mousterien revisité', *Bulletin de la Societé préhistorique française* 78/3, pp. 77–87

Bordes, F. & Bourgon, M. 1951 'Le complexe mousterien', *L'Anthropologie* 55, pp. 1–23

Boroneanţ, V. 1981 'Betrachtungen über das Epipaläolithikum (Mesolithikum) in Rumänien', *Veröffentlichungen des Museums für Ur- und Frühgeschichte Potsdam* 14/15, pp. 289–94

—— 1993 'Nouvelles données sur les découvertes anthropologiques de Schela Cladovei à Drobeţa Turnu Severin (Roumanie)', *L'Anthropologie* 97, pp. 511–14

Bouville, C.P. 1995 'Les témoins (sépultures, vestiges osseaux humains) de catastrophes, massacres, épidémies', *L'Anthropologie* 99/1, pp. 120–4

Boye, W. 1896 *Fund af Egekister fra Bronzealderen i Danmark*, Copenhagen (reprinted 1986 by Aarhus, Wormianum)

Boyle, A., Dodd, A., Miles, D. & Mudd, A. 1995 *Two Oxfordshire Anglo-Saxon Cemeteries: Berinsfield and Didcot*, Oxford, Oxford University Committee for Archaeology, Oxford Archaeological Unit, Thames Valley Landscapes Monograph 8.

Braasch, O. 1995 '50 Jahre verloren', in *Luftbildarchäologie in Ost- und Mitteleuropa*, 109–22, Potsdam, Forschungen zur Archäologie im Land Brandenburg 3

Bradley R. 1998 *The Significance of Monuments: On the Shaping of Human Experience in Neolithic and Bronze Age Europe*, London and New York, Routledge

Bridgford, S. 1997 'Mightier than the pen? An edgewise look at Irish Bronze Age swords', in J. Carman (ed.), *Material Harm: Archaeological Studies of War and Violence*, Glasgow, Cruithne Press, pp. 95–115

Brinch Petersen, E., Alexandersen, V. & Meiklejohn, C. 1993 'Vedbæk, graven midt i byen', *Nationalmuseets Arbejdsmark* 1993, pp. 61–9

Broadbent, N. 1978 'Perforated stones, antlers and stone picks: Evidence for the use of the digging stick in Scandinavia and Finnland', *Tor* 17, pp. 63–106

Brooke, R. 1854 *Visits to the Fields of Battle in England of the Fifteenth Century*, (reprinted 1975, Dursley, Alan Sutton), London, John Russell Smith

Brothwell, D.R. 1964 'Further comments on the right parietal from Swanscombe; Anomalies and endocranial features', in C.D. Ovey (ed.), *The Swanscombe Skull: A Survey of Research on a Pleistocene Site*, Royal Anthropological Institute, pp. 173–4

Brown, P. 1979 'Change and the boundaries of systems in highland New Guinea: The Chimbu', in P. Burnham and R. Ellen (eds), *Social and Ecological Systems*, Academic Press, pp. 235–51

Brown, R. 1973 *Social Psychology*, Macmillan

Brown, W. 1939 *War and Peace: Essays in Psychological Analysis*, Black

Brush, K.A. 1988 'Gender and Mortuary Analysis in Pagan Anglo-Saxon Archaeology,' *Archaeological Review from Cambridge* 7 1., pp. 76–89

Buchan, J. 1928 *Montrose*, London, Thomas Nelson

Buchholz, H.-G. 1962 'Der Pfeilglatter aus dem VI. Schachtgrab von Mykene und die helladischen Pfeilspitzen', *Jahrbuch des deutschen archäologischen Instituts* 77, pp. 1–58

—— 1980 *Kriegswesen, Teil II: Angriffswaffen*, Archaeologia Homerica, Kapitel E, Göttingen, Vandenhoeck and Ruprecht

Buck, D.-W. 1979 *Die Billendorfer Gruppe* (= Veröff. des Museums für Ur- und Frühgeschichte Potsdam 13, pp. 1–219)

Buck, R. 1979 *A History of Boiotia*, Alberta, University of Alberta Press

—— 1994 *Boiotia and the Boiotian League, 432–375*, Alberta, University of Alberta Press

Buckler, J. 1977 'The Thespians at Leuktra', *Wiener Studien* 90, pp. 76–9

Burgess, C. & Colquhoun, I. 1988 *The Swords of Britain*, Prähistorische Bronzefunde, Abteilung IV, 5, Munich, Beck

Burgess, C. et al. (eds) 1988 *Enclosures and Defences in the Neolithic of Western Europe*, Oxford, British Archaeological Reports, Int. Series 403

Camps, G. 1992 'Guerre ou paix? Origines des conflits intraspécifiques humains', *Préhistoire et Anthropologie Méditerranéennes* 1, pp. 9–15

253

Carlton, E. 1977 *Ideology and Social Order*, London, Routledge

Carman, J. 1993 'The *P* is silent – as in archaeology', *Archaeological Review from Cambridge* 12.1, pp. 29–38

—— (ed.) 1997a *Material Harm: Archaeological Studies of War and Violence*, Glasgow, Cruithne Press

—— 1997b 'Introduction: approaches to violence', in Carman 1997a, pp. 1–23

—— 1999 'Bloody Meadows: The places of battle', in S. Tarlow, and S. West (eds), *The Familiar Past? Archaeologies of Later Historical Britain*, London, Routledge, pp. 233–45

Carneiro, R.L. 1970 'A theory of the origin of the state', *Science* 169, pp. 733–8

—— 1990 'Chiefdom-level warfare as exemplified in Fiji and the Cauca Valley', in J. Haas (ed.), *The Anthropology of War*, New York, Cambridge University Press, pp. 190–211

—— 1994 'War and peace: Alternating realities in human history', in S.P. Reyna and R.E. Downs (eds), *Studying War: Anthropological Perspectives*, Amsterdam, Gordon and Breach, pp. 3–28

Cartledge, P. 1970 *Agesilaos and the Crisis of Sparta*, Baltimore, John Hopkins

Case, H.J. 1969 'Neolithic explanations', *Antiquity* 43, pp. 176–86

Caspari, E. 1972 'Sexual selection in human evolution', in B. Campbell (ed.), *Sexual Selection and the Descent of Man, 1871–1971*, Chicago, Aldine, pp. 332–56

Cessford, C. 1995 'Where are the Anglo-Saxons in the Gododdin Poem?' in D. Griffiths (ed.), *Anglo-Saxon Studies in Archaeology and History* 8, Oxford, Oxford University Committee for Archaeology, pp. 95–8

Chadwick, J. 1973 *Documents in Mycenaean Greek*, Cambridge University Press (2nd edn, 1st edn 1956 by M.Ventris and J. Chadwick)

Chagnon, N.A. 1967 'Yanamamö social organisation and warfare', in M. Fried, M. Harris & R. Murphy (eds), *War: The Anthropology of Armed Conflict and Aggression*, New York, Natural History Press, pp. 109–59

—— 1968 *Yanomamö: The Fierce People*, New York, Holt, Rinehart and Winston

—— 1990 'Reproductive and somatic conflicts of interest in the genesis of violence and warfare among tribesmen', in J. Haas (ed.), *The Anthropology of War*, Cambridge University Press, pp. 77–104

Chaliand, G. 1994 *The Art of War in World History from Antiquity to the Nuclear Age*, Berkeley and Los Angeles, University of California Press

Chamla, M.-C. et al. 1970 *Les hommes épipaléolithiques de Columnata (Algérie Occidentale)*, Paris, Centre de rechercher anthropologiques préhistoriques

Chapman, J. 1981 *The Vinča Culture of South East Europe: Studies in Chronology, Economy and Society*, (2 vols), Oxford, BAR Int. Series 119

—— 1983 'Meaning and illusion in the study of burial in Balkan prehistory', in A. Poulter (ed.), *Ancient Bulgaria, Volume 1*, Nottingham, University of Nottingham Press, pp. 1–45

—— 1989a 'Demographic trends in Neothermal south-east Europe', in C. Bonsall (ed.), *The Mesolithic in Europe*, Edinburgh, John Donald, pp. 500–15

—— 1989b 'The early Balkan village', in S. Bökönyi (ed.), *Neolithic of Southeastern Europe and its Near Eastern Connections: International Conference, 1987, Szolnok-Szeged*, Varia Archaeologica Hungarica 2, Budapest, pp. 33–53

—— 1991 'The creation of social arenas in the Neolithic and Copper Age of South East Europe: The case of Varna', in P. Garwood, P. Jennings, R. Skeates & J. Toms (eds), *Sacred and Profane*, Oxford Committee for Archaeology Monograph 32, Oxford, Oxbow, pp. 152–71

—— 1993 'Social power in the Iron Gates Mesolithic', in J.C. Chapman and P. Dolukhanov (eds) *Cultural Transformations and Interactions in Eastern Europe*, Worldwide Archaeology Series 5, Aldershot, Avebury, pp. 61–106

—— 1994 'The living, the dead, and the ancestors: Time, life cycles and the mortuary domain in later European prehistory', in J. Davies (ed.), *Ritual and Remembrance: Responses to Death in Human Societies*, Sheffield, Sheffield Academic Press, pp. 40–85

—— 1995 'Social power in the early farming communities of Eastern Hungary – perspectives from the Upper Tisza region', *A Jósa András Múzeum Evkönyve* 36, pp. 79–99

—— 1996 'Enchainment, commodification and gender in the Balkan Neolithic and Copper Age', *Journal of European Archaeology* 4, pp. 203–42

—— 1998a 'The impact of modern invasions and migrations on archaeological explanation. A biographical sketch of Marija Gimbutas', in M. Díaz-Andreu and M.L.S. Sørensen (eds), *Excavating Women: A History of Women in European archaeology*, London, Routledge, pp. 295–314

—— 1998b 'Objects and places: Their value in the past', in D.W. Bailey (ed.), *The Archaeology of Value*, Oxford, British Archaeological Reports 730, pp. 106–30

—— forthcoming, *Fragmentation and social Practices in the Prehistory of South East Europe*, London, Routledge

Chapman, J. & Hamerow, H. (eds) 1996 *Migrations and Invasions in Archaeological Explanation*, Oxford, BAR Int. Series 664

Chapman, J. & Laszlovszky, J. 1994, 'The Upper Tisza Project 1993', *Archaeological Reports from Durham and Newcastle 1993*, pp. 1–7

Chernykh, E. 1978 *Gornoe delo i metallurgija v Drevnejshej Bolgarii*, Sofia, Bulgarian Academy of Sciences

Chernysh, E.K. 1982 'Eneolit pravoberezhnoi Ukrainyi Moldavii', in V.M. Masson & N.Y. Merpert (eds), *Eneolit SSSR*, Arheologiya SSSR, Moscow, Nauka, pp. 165–320

Childe, V.G. 1941 'War in primitive societies', *Sociological Review* 33, pp. 126–38

—— 1958 *The Dawn of European Civilization* (6th edition), New York, Knopf

Chochol, J. 1970 'Die anthropologische Analyse der auf dem schnurkeramischen Gräberfelde von Vikletice geborgenen Menschenreste', in M. Buchvaldek and D. Koutecký (eds), *Vikletice*, Prague, Praehistorica III, pp. 257–83

Chochorowski, I. 1993 *Ekspansja kimmeryska na terenie europy środkowej*, Krakow, Uniwersytet Jagiellonski

Clark, J.G.D. 1963 'Neolithic bows from Somerset, England, and the prehistory of archery in north-west Europe', *Proc. Prehist. Soc.* 29, pp. 50–98

Clarke, D.V., Cowie, T.G. & Foxon, A. 1985 *Symbols of Power at the Time of Stonehenge*, Edinburgh, HMSO

Cleary, S. E. 1993 'Approaches to the Differences between Late Romano-British and Early Anglo-Saxon Archaeology', in W. Filmer-Sankey (ed.), *Anglo-Saxon Studies in Archaeology and History* 6, Oxford, Oxford University Committee for Archaeology, pp. 57–64

Cloché, P. 1952 *Thèbes de Béotie*, Namur, Secrétariat des Publications

Clover, C. 1986 'Maiden Warriors and Other Sons', *Journal of English and Germanic Philology* 85/1, pp. 35–49

—— 1993 'Regardless of Sex: Men, Women, and Power in Early Northern Europe,' *Speculum* 68/2, pp. 363–87

Clunies Ross, M. 1994 *Prolonged Echoes: Old Norse Myths in Medieval Northern Society, Volume I: The Myths*, Odense, Odense University Press

Coles, J.M. 1962 'European Bronze Age shields', *Proc. Prehist. Soc.* 28, pp. 156–90

Coles, J.M. and Orme, B.J. 1984 'Ten excavations along the Sweet Track (3200 BC)', *Somerset Levels Papers* 10, pp. 5–45

Coles, J.M., Leach, P., Minnitt, S.C., Tabor, R. & Wilson, A.S. 1999 'A Later Bronze Age shield from South Cadbury, Somerset, England', *Antiquity* 73, pp. 33–48

Colson, I.B., Richards, M.B., Bailey, J.F., Sykes, B.C. & Hedges, R.E.M. 1997 'DNA Analysis of Seven Human Skeletons Excavated from the Terp of Wijnaldum', *Journal of Archaeological Science* 24, pp. 911–17

Comşa, E. 1960 'Considerations sur le rite funéraire de la civilisation de Gumelniţa', *Dacia* N.S. 4: pp. 5–30

—— 1987 'Despre virfurile de sageaţa in silex dîn arealul culturii Gumelniţa', *Cultura şi Civilizaţie la Dunarea de Jos* 3–4, pp. 21–8

—— 1991 'Les pointes de flèche en silex de l'aire culturelle Salcutsa', *Starinar* 40–1, pp. 61–5

—— 1995 *Figurinele antropomorfe dîn epoca neolitica pe teritoriul României*, Bucureşti, Edita Academiei Române

Connor, W.R. 1988 'Early Greek Warfare as Symbolic Expression', *Past and Present* 119, pp. 3–29

Constandse-Westermann, T.S. & Newell, R.R. 1984 'Mesolithic trauma: Demographical and chronological trends in Western Europe', in G.T. Haneveld & W.R.K. Perizonius (eds), *Proceedings of the 4th European Meeting of the Paleopathology Association, Middleburg – Antwerpen 1982*, Utrecht, pp. 70–6

Coombs, D. 1975 'Bronze Age weapon hoards in Britain', *Archaeologia Atlantica* 1, pp. 49–81

Corcoran, J.X.W.P. 1967 'The excavation of three chambered cairns at Loch Calder, Caithness', *Proc. Soc. Antiq. Scotland* 98, pp. 1–75

Cordell, L. 1997 *Archaeology of the Southwest* (2nd edn), New York, Academic Press

Cordier, G. 1990 'Blessures préhistoriques animales et humaines avec armes ou projectiles conservés', *Bulletin de la Société Préhistorique Française* 87, pp. 462–81

Courville, C.B. 1967 'Cranial injuries in prehistoric man', in D. Brothwell and A. Sandison (eds), *Diseases in Antiquity*, Springfield, Thomas, pp. 606–22

Cowen, J.D. 1955 'Eine Einführung in die Geschichte der bronzenen Griffzungenschwerter in Süddeutschland und den angrenzenden Gebieten', *Bericht der Römisch-Germanischen Kommission* 36, pp. 52–155

—— 1966 'The origins of the flange-hilted sword of bronze in continental Europe', *Proc. Prehist. Soc.* 32, pp. 262–312

Creasy, E. 1908 [1851] *The Fifteen Decisive Battles of the World: From Marathon to Waterloo*, London, Macmillan

Crouwel, J.H. 1981 *Chariots and Other Means of Land Transport in Bronze Age Greece*, Amsterdam, Allard Pierson Series, Vol. 3

Csalog, J. 1958 'Das Wohnhaus "E" von Szegvár-Tuzkoves und seine Funde', *Acta Archaeologica* (Budapest) 9, pp. 95–114

Cullen, T. 1995 'Mesolithic mortuary ritual at Franchthi cave, Greece', *Antiquity* 69, pp. 270–89

Cunliffe, B. 1986 *Danebury. Anatomy of an Iron Age Hillfort*, London, Batsford

Daly, M. & Wilson, M. 1995 'Evolutionary psychology of male violence', in J. Archer (ed.), *Male Violence*, London, Routledge, pp. 253–88

Danilenko, V.N. 1955 'Volochskiy epipaleolitcheskiy mogil'nik', *Sovetskaya etnografiya* 1955/3, pp. 56–61

D'Anna, A. 1977 *Les Statues-Menhirs et Stèles anthropomorphes du Midi mediterranéen*, Paris, Éditions du CNRS

Darwin, C. 1890 *The Descent of Man*, London, Murray

Davidson, H.E. 1989 'The Training of Warriors', in S.C. Hawkes (ed.), *Weapons and Warfare in Anglo-Saxon England*, Oxford, Oxbow Books, Oxford University Committee for Archaeology Monograph 21, Oxford, University Committee for Archaeology, pp. 11–23

Davies, J. 1994 'One hundred billion dead: A general theology of death', in J. Davies (ed.), *Ritual and Remembrance: Responses to Death in Human Societies*, Sheffield, Sheffield Academic Press, pp. 24–39

De Waal, F. 1989 *Peacemaking Among Primates*, Harmondsworth, Penguin

—— 1996 'Chimpanzees' adaptive potential', in R. Wrangham, W. McGrew, F. de Waal & P. Heltne (eds), *Chimpanzee Cultures*, Harvard University Press, pp. 243–60

Dean, J.S., Euler, R.C., Gumerman, G.J., Plog, F., Hevly, R.H. & Karlstrom, T.N.V. 1985 'Human behavior, demography, and paleoenvironment on the Colorado plateaus,' *American Antiquity* 50.3, pp. 537–54

Delbrück, H. 1975 *History of the Art of War, Vol. I*, English trans. of *Geschichte der Kriegskunst im Rahmen der politischen Geschichte* [Berlin 1920], Westport CT, Greenwood Press

Demand, N. 1982 *Thebes in the Fifth Century*, London, Routledge

Dickinson, O. 1994 *The Aegean Bronze Age*, Cambridge, Cambridge University Press

Dieck, A. 1965 *Die europäischen Moorleichenfunde I*, Neumünster, Wachholtz

Dimitrijević, S. 1979 'Vučedolska kultura i vučedolski kulturni kompleks', in A. Benac (ed.), *Praistorija jugoslavenskih zemalja III*, Sarajevo, Akademija Nauka i Umjetnosti Bosne i Hercegovine, pp. 267–341

Dixon, P. 1989 'Crickley Hill', in C. Burgess et al. (eds), *Enclosures and Defences in the Neolithic of Western Europe*, Oxford, British Archaeological Reports Int. Series 403, pp. 75–87

Dollard, J., Miller, N., Doob, L., Mowrer, O. & Sears, R. 1944 *Frustration and Aggression*, Paul, Trench and Trubner

Dolukhanov, P.M. 1982 'Upper Pleistocene and Holocene cultures of the Russian Plain and Caucasus: Ecology, economy and settlement pattern', *Advances in World Archaeology* 1, pp. 323–58

—— 1997 'Landscape and the Mesolithic–Neolithic transition in the Boreal East European Plain', in J. Chapman and P. Dolukhanov (eds), *Landscapes in Flux: Central and Eastern Europe in Antiquity*, Oxford, Oxbow Books, pp. 289–306

Dolukhanov, P.M. & Fonyakov, D.I., 1984 'Modelirovanie kul'turno-istoricheskih processov', in V.M. Masson (ed.), *Kompleksnye metody izucheniya istorii s drevneishih vremen do nashih dnei*, Moscow, Nauka, pp. 33–5

Dolukhanov, P.M., Kozłowski, J.K. & Kozłowski, S.K. 1980 *Multivariate Analysis of Upper Palaeolithic and Mesolithic Stone Assemblages*, Warzsawa-Kraków, Panstwówe Wydawnictwo Naukowe

Dolukhanov, P.M. & Miklyayev, A.M. 1988 'Prehistoric lacustrine lake dwellings in the north-western part of the USSR', *Fennoscandia archaeologica* 3, pp. 81–9

Doyle, P. & Bennett, M. R. 1997 'Military geography. Terrain evaluation and the Western Front 1914–1918', *Geographical Journal* 163, pp. 1–24

Drews, R. 1993 *The End of the Bronze Age: Changes in Warfare and the Catastrophe ca. 1200 BC*, Princeton University Press

Driehaus, J. 1960 *Die Altheimer Gruppe und das Jungneolithikum in Mitteleuropa*, Mainz, Verlag des Römisch-Germanischen Zentralmuseums Mainz (Kommission Habelt, Bonn)

Dumézil, G. 1973 *Gods of the Ancient Northmen*, ed. and trans. Einar Haugen, Berkeley, Los Angeles, London, University of California Press, *Publications of the UCLA Center for the Study of Comparative Folklore and Mythology* 3

Dupuy, R.E. & Dupuy, T.N. 1970 *The Encyclopaedia of Military History from 3500 BC to the Present*, London, Macdonald and Jane's

Durham, W.H. 1979 'Toward a coevolutionary theory of human biology and culture', in N. Chagnon and W. Irons (eds), *Evolutionary Biology and Human Social Behaviour*, Massachusetts, Duxbury Press, pp. 39–59

Durkheim, E. 1947 *The Elementary Forms of Religious Life*, Glencoe, Ill., The Free Press

Dvoryaninov, S.A. 1978 'O dneprovskikh mogil'nikakh kamennogo veka', in P.O. Kryschkovski (ed.), *Arkheologicheskie issledovaniya Severozapadnogo Prichernomor'ya*, Kiev, pp. 5–16

Earle, T. 1978 *Economic and Social Organisaton of a Compex Chiefdom: The Halelea Distraict, Kaua'i, Hawaii*, Museum of Anthropology, Anthropological Papers 63, Ann Arbor, University of Michigan

—— 1997 *How Chiefs Come to Power: The Political Economy in Prehistory*, Stanford University Press

Ecsedy, I. 1979 *The People of the Pit-Grave Kurgans in Eastern Hungary*, Fontes Archaeologici Hungariae. Budapest, Akadémiai Kiadó

Edmonds, M. & Thomas, J. 1987 'The archers: An everyday story of country folk', in A.G. Brown & M.R. Edmonds (eds), *Lithic Analysis and Later British Prehistory*, British Archaeological Reports 162, pp. 187–99

Ehrich, R.W. 1975 'A note on the interpretation of defensive ditches', *Zbornik Narodnog muzeja* (Beograd) 8, pp. 585–8

Eibl-Eibesfeldt, I. 1979 *The Biology of Peace and War: Men, Animals and Aggression*, London, Thames and Hudson

Eisner, W.R. 1991 'The Consequences of Gender Bias in Mortuary Analysis: A Case Study', in D. Walde and N. Willows (eds), *The Archaeology of Gender: 22nd Annual Conference of the Archaeological Association of the University of Calgary*, Calgary, Alberta, University of Calgary, pp. 352–7

Elia, R.J. 1982 'A Study of the Neolithic Architecture of Thessaly, Greece', unpub. PhD thesis, University of Boston

Ellis, L. 1984 *The Cucuteni-Tripolye Culture*, Oxford, British Archaeological Reports Int. Series 217

Ember, C. 1978 'Myths about hunter-gatherers', *Ethnology* 17, pp. 439–48

Ember, C.R. & Ember, M. 1992 'Resource unpredictability, mistrust, and war: A cross-cultural study,' *J. Conflict Resolution* 36, pp. 242–62

Endicott, K. 1988 'Property, power and conflict among the Batek of Malaysia', in T. Ingold, D. Riches & J. Woodburn (eds), *Hunters and Gatherers*, Oxford, Berg, pp. 110–27

English Heritage 1995 *Register of Historic Battlefields*, London, English Heritage

Enright, M.J. 1996 *Lady with a Mead Cup: Ritual, Prophecy and Lordship in the European Warband from La Tène to the Viking Age*, Blackrock, Co. Dublin, Four Courts Press

Eogan, G. 1965 *Catalogue of Irish Bronze Swords*, Dublin, Stationery Office

Epstein, J. & Straub, K. (eds) 1991 *Body Guards: The Cultural Politics of Gender Ambiguity*, New York and London, Routledge

Erhardt, S. 1960 'Schlagspuren, Brüche und Sprünge an den Skeletten von Langhnaj im nördlichen Quajarat, Vorderindien', *Anthropolog. Anzeiger* 24, pp. 178ff.

Escalon de Fonton, M. 1964 'Naissance de la guerre en Occident aux temps préhistoriques', *Archeologia* (Paris) 1, pp. 30–4

Evans, A. 1935 *The Palace of Minos at Knossos, vol. IV*, London, Macmillan

Evans, J. D. & Renfrew, C. 1968 *Excavations at Saliagos near Antiparos*, British School of Archaeology at Athens Supplement 5, London, Thames and Hudson

Evison, V.I. (ed.) 1981 *Angles, Saxons and Jutes: Essays Presented to J.N.L. Myres*, Oxford, Clarendon Press

Evison, V.I. 1987 *Dover: The Buckland Anglo-Saxon Cemetery*, Archaeological Report 3, London, Historic Buildings and Monuments Commission for England

Evison, V.I. et al. 1994 *An Anglo-Saxon Cemetery at Great Chesterford, Essex*, CBA Research Report 91,York, Council for British Archaeology

Evison, V.I. et al. 1996 *Two Anglo-Saxon Cemeteries at Beckford, Hereford and Worcester*, CBA Research Report 103, York, Council for British Archaeology

Farruggia, J.-P., Guichard, Y. & Hachem, L. 1996 'Les ensembles funéraires rubanés de Menneville "Derrière le village" (Aisne)', *Revue archéologique de l'Est*, 14ᵉ supplément, Université de Bourgogne, Dijon, pp. 119–74

Ferguson, J. 1977 *War and Peace in the World's Religions*, Sheldon Press

Ferguson, R.B. 1984 'Introduction: Studying war,' in R.B. Ferguson (ed.), *Warfare, Culture and Environment*, Orlando, Academic Press, pp. 1–81

—— 1990 'Explaining war', in J. Haas (ed.), *The Anthropology of War*, Cambridge University Press, pp. 26–55

—— 1994 'A savage encounter: Western contact and the Yanomami war complex', in R.B. Ferguson and N. Whitehead (eds), *War in the Tribal Zone: Expanding States and Indigenous Warfare*, Santa Fe, School of American Research Press, pp. 199–227

—— 1997 Review of *War Before Civilization* by Lawrence Keeley, *American Anthropologist* 99/2, pp. 424–5

Ferguson, R.B. & Whitehead, N. (eds) 1994 *War in the Tribal Zone: Expanding States and Indigenous Warfare*, Santa Fe, School of American Research Press

Ferrill, A. 1985 *The Origins of War: From the Stone Age to Alexander the Great*, London, Thames and Hudson

Feustel, R. & Ullrich, H. 1965 'Totenhütten der neolithischen Walternienburger Gruppe', *Alt-Thüringen* 7, pp. 105–202

Fiehn, C. 1936 'Thespeia', in A. Pauly, G. Wissowa & W. Kroll, *Real-Encyclopädie der klassischen Altertumswissenschaft*, Berlin, pp. 37–59

Filer, J.M. 1997 'Ancient Egypt and Nubia as a source of information for cranial injuries', in J. Carman (ed.), *Material Harm: Archaeological Studies of War and Violence*, Glasgow, Cruithne Press, pp. 47–74

Fischer, A. 1987 'The Argus site', *Mesolithic Miscellany* 8/1, pp. 1–4

—— 1989 'Hunting with flint-tipped arrows: Results and experiences from practical experiments', in C. Bonsall (ed.) *The Mesolithic in Europe*, Edinburgh, John Donald, pp. 29–39

Fisher, G. 1995 'Kingdom and Community in Early Anglo-Saxon Eastern England', in L.A. Beck (ed.), *Regional Approaches to Mortuary Analysis*, New York, Plenum Press, pp. 147–66

Fishman, J.A. 1977 'Language and ethnicity', in H. Giles (ed.), *Language, Ethnicity and Intergroup Relations*, Academic Press, pp. 15–57

Fitzpatrick, A.P. et al. 1997 *Archaeological Excavations on the Route of the A27 Westhampnett Bypass, West Sussex, 1992. Volume 2: The Late Iron Age, Romano-British, and Anglo-Saxon Cemeteries*, Wessex Archaeology Report 12, Salisbury, Trust for Wessex Archaeology

Foard, G. 1995 *Naseby: The Decisive Campaign*, Whitstable, Pryor Publications

Foltiny, S. 1980 'Schwert, Dolch und Messer', in H-G. Buchholz (ed.), *Kriegswesen, Teil II: Angriffswaffen*, Archaeologia Homerica, Kapitel E, Göttingen, Vandenhoeck and Ruprecht, pp. 231–74

Fossey, J. 1986 *Topography and Population of Ancient Boiotia*, Chicago, Ares Press

Frayer, D. 1997 'Ofnet: Evidence for a Mesolithic massacre', in D. Martin and L. Frayer (eds), *Troubled Times: Violence and Warfare in the Past*, Amsterdam, Gordon and Breach, pp. 181–216

Fried, M.H. 1967 *The Evolution of Political Society: An Essay in Political Anthropology*, New York, Random House

Fried, M., Harris, M. & Murphy, R. (eds) 1967 *War: The Anthropology of Armed Conflict and Aggression*, New York, Natural History Press

Frodi, M., Macauley, J., & Thome, P. 1977 'Are women always less aggressive than men? A review of the experimental literature', *Psychological Bulletin* 84, pp. 634–60

Fromm, E. 1973 *The Anatomy of Human Destructiveness*, Harmondsworth, Penguin

Fuller, J.F.C. 1970 *The Decisive Battles of the Western World and Their Effect Upon History* (2 vols), ed. J. Terraine, London, Paladin

Gallis, K. 1996 'Central and western Thessaly', in G.A. Papathanassopoulos (ed.), *Neolithic Culture in Greece*, Athens, Nicholas P. Goulandris Foundation, Museum of Cycladic Art, pp. 61–6

Garlan, Y. 1975 *War in the Ancient World: A Social History*, London, Chatto and Windus

Gilchrist, R. & Morris, R. 1993 'Monasteries as Settlements: Religion, Society, and Economy, AD 600–1050', in M. Carver (ed.), *In Search of Cult*, Woodbridge, Boydell Press, pp. 113–18

Gillis, D. 1963 'Collusion at Mantineia,' *RIL* 97, pp. 199–226

Gilman, A. 1995 'Prehistoric European chiefdoms: Rethinking 'Germanic' societies', in T.D. Price and G. Feinman (eds), *Foundations of Social Inequality*, New York, Plenum Press, pp. 235–51

Gimbutas, M. 1978 'The first wave of steppe pastoralists into Copper Age Europe', *Journal of Indo-European Studies* V/4 , pp. 277–338

—— 1979 'The three waves of the Kurgan people into Old Europe, 4500–2500 BC', *Archives suisses d'anthropologie générale* 43/2, pp. 113–37

—— 1980 'The Kurgan Wave 2 (*c.* 3400–3200 BC): Into Europe and the following transformations of culture', *Journal of Indo-European Studies* 8, pp. 273–315

—— 1989 *The Language of the Goddess*, London, Thames and Hudson

—— 1991 *The Civilisation of the Goddess*, San Francisco, Harper

Giner, S. 1975 *Sociology*, Robertson

Gladilin, V.N. 1976 *Problemy rannego paleolita Vostochnoi Evropy*, Kiev, Naukova Dumka

Gladykowska-Rzeczycka, J. 1989 *Schorzenia ludności prahistorycznej na ziemiach polskich*, Gdańsk, Muzeum archeologiczne w Gdansku

Godwin, H. 1975 *History of the British Flora: A Factual Basis for Phytogeography* (2nd edn), Cambridge, Cambridge University Press

Gokhman, I.I. 1966a 'Iskopaemye neoantropy', in V.V. Bunak (ed.), *Iskopaemye gominidy i proishozhdenie cheloveka*, Moscow, Transactions of the Institute of Ethnography, Vol. 92

—— 1966b *Naselenie Ukrainy v epohu mezolita i neolita / The Ukrainian Population in the Mesolithic and Neolithic*, Moscow, Nauka

Goldberg, N.J. & Fidlow, F.J. 1984 'A quantitative analysis of Roman military operations in Britain, *circa* 43 to 238', in R.B. Ferguson (ed.), *Warfare, Culture and Environment*, Orlando, Academic Press, pp. 359–85

Gomme, A., Andrewes, A. & Dover, K. 1970 *A Historical Commentary on Thucydides*, Oxford, The Clarendon Press

Goodall, J. 1990 *Through a Window*, Harmondsworth, Penguin

Goody, J. 1971 *Technology, Tradition and the State in Africa*, Oxford, Oxford University Press

Goody, J. & Tambiah, J. 1973 *Bridewealth and Dowry*, Cambridge, Cambridge University Press

Gordon, D.H. 1953 'Swords, rapiers and horse-riders', *Antiquity* 27, pp. 67–78

Grammenos, D.V. 1996 'Neolithic settlements in Macedonia and Thrace', in G.A. Papathanassopoulos (ed.), *Neolithic Culture in Greece*, Athens, Nicholas P. Goulandris Foundation, Museum of Cycladic Art. pp. 41–5

Gramsch, B. & Kloss, K. 1989 'Excavations near Friesack, an Early Mesolithic marshland site in the northern plain of Central Europe', in C. Bonsall (ed.), *The Mesolithic in Europe*, Edinburgh, John Donald, pp. 313–24

Gräslund, B. 1967 'The Herzsprung shield type and its origin', *Acta Archaeologica* 38, pp. 59–71

Gray, C.H. 1997 *Postmodern War: The New Politics of Conflict*, London, Routledge

Green, H.S. 1980 *The Flint Arrowheads of the British Isles*, Oxford, British Archaeological Report 75

Greenfield, H. 1986 *The Palaeoecology of the Central Balkans (Serbia): A Zooarchaeological Perspective on the Late Neolithic and Bronze Age 4000–1000 BC*, BAR Int. Series 304, Oxford, British Archaeological Reports

Grigor'ev, G.P. 1968 *Nachalo verhnego paleolita i proiskozhdenie* Homo sapiens *v Evrope*, Leningrad, Nauka

—— 1993 'The Kostenki-Avdeevo archaeological culture and the Winnendorf-Kostenki-Avdeečo cultural unity', in O. Soffer & N.D. Praslov (eds), *From Kostenki to Clovis: Upper Palaeolithic – Palaeo-Indian Adaptations*, New York and London, Plenum Press, pp. 51–66

Grimm, H. 1976 'Paläopathologische Befunde an Menschenresten aus dem Neolithikum in der DDR als Hinweise auf Lebenslauf und Bevölkerungsgeschichte', *Ausgrabungen und Funde* 21, pp. 268–77

Groebel, J. & Hinde, R.A. 1989 'A multi-level approach to the problems of aggression and war', in J. Groebel and R.A. Hinde (eds), *Aggression and War: Their Biological and Social Bases*, Cambridge, Cambridge University Press, pp. 223–9

Guidi, A. & Piperno, M. 1992 *Italia Preistorica*, Rome-Bari, Editori Laterza (Manuali Laterza 34)

Gulliver, H. 1966 *The Family Herds*, London, Routledge

Gumerman, G.J. (ed.) 1988 *The Anasazi in a Changing Environment*, Cambridge, Cambridge University Press

Gurina, N.N. 1956 *Oleneostrovskii mogil'nik*, Leningrad, Nauka

Haas, J. 1982 *The Evolution of the Prehistoric State*, New York, Columbia University Press

—— 1989 'The evolution of the Kayenta regional system', in S. Upham, K. Lightfoot & R. Jewett (eds), *The Sociopolitical Structure of Prehistoric Southwestern Societies*, Boulder CO, Westview Press, pp. 491–508

—— (ed.) 1990a *The Anthropology of War*, New York and Cambridge, Cambridge University Press

—— 1990b 'Warfare and the evolution of tribal polities in the prehistoric Southwest', in J. Haas (ed.), *The Anthropology of War*, New York and Cambridge, Cambridge University Press, pp. 171–89

Haas, J. & Creamer, W. 1993 *Stress and Warfare Among the Kayenta Anasazi of the Thirteenth Century A.D.*, Chicago, Museum of Natural History, Fieldiana, Anthropology, new series 21

—— 1996 'The role of warfare in the Pueblo III Period,' in M. Adler (ed.), *The Pueblo III Period in the Northern Southwest*, Tucson, University of Arizona Press

—— 1997 'Warfare among the Pueblos: Myth, history and ethnography', *Ethnohistory* 44, pp. 235–61

Hagberg, U.E. 1988 'The bronze shields from Fröslunda near Lake Vänern, West Sweden', in B. Hardh, L. Larsson, D. Olausson & R. Petré (eds), *Trade and Exchange in Prehistory: Studies in Honour of Berta Stjernquist*, Acta Archaeologica Lundensia, series in 8°, 16, Lund, Historiska Museum, pp. 119–26

Hallpike, C.R. 1977 *Bloodshed and Vengeance in the Papuan Mountains*, Oxford, Clarendon Press

Halsall, G. 1989 'Anthropology and the Study of Pre-Conquest Warfare and Society: The Ritual War in Anglo-Saxon England', in S.C. Hawkes (ed.), *Weapons and Warfare in Anglo-Saxon England*, Oxford University Committee for Archaeology Monograph 21, Oxford, Oxbow Books, pp. 155–77

Halstead P. 1993 '*Spondylus* shell ornaments from Late Neolithic Dimini, Greece: specialized manufacture or unequal accumulation?' *Antiquity* 67. pp. 603–9

—— 1994 'The north-south divide: Regional paths to complexity in prehistoric Greece', in C. Mathers and S. Stoddart (eds), *Development and Decline in the Mediterranean Bronze Age*, Sheffield Archaeological Monographs 8, Sheffield, J.R. Collins, pp. 195–219

—— 1995 'From sharing to hoarding: the Neolithic foundations of Aegean Bronze Age society?', in R. Laffineur & W.-D. Niemeier (eds), *Politeia: Society and State in the Aegean Bronze Age. Proceedings of the 5th International Aegean Conference/5e Rencontre égéenne internationale, University of Heidelberg, Archäologisches Institut, 10–13 April 1994*, Aegeum 12, Annales d'archéologie égéene de l'Université de Liège et UT-PASP, Université de Liège, Histoire de l'art et archéologie de la Grèce antique/University of Texas at Austin, Program in Aegean Scripts and Prehistory, pp. 11–22

Hamburg, D.A. 1991 'An evolutionary perspective on human aggression', in P. Bateson (ed.), *The Development and Integration of Behaviour*, Cambridge, Cambridge University Press, pp. 419–57

Hamilton, W.D. 1975 'Innate social aptitudes of man: An approach from evolutionary genetics', in R. Fox (ed.), *Biosocial Anthropology*, Malaby Press, pp. 133–55

Hanáková, H. & Vyhnánek, L. 1981 'Paläopathologische Befunde aus dem Gebiet der Tschechoslowakei', *Sborník Národního muzea* 37B.1, pp. 1–76, Taf. I–XIII

Hanson, V.D. 1988 'Epameinondas, the Battle of Leuctra, and the "Revolution" in Greek Battle Tactics', *Classical Antiquity* 7.2., pp. 190–207

—— 1989 *The Western Way of War: Infantry Battle in Classical Greece*, Oxford, Oxford University Press

—— (ed.) 1991 *Hoplites: The Classical Greek Battle Experience*, London, Routledge

——1995a 'Delium', *Quarterly Journal of Military History* 8.1, pp. 28–35

—— 1995b *The Other Greeks: The Agrarian Roots of Western Civilization*, New York, The Free Press

Haraway, D. 1985 'A manifesto for cyborgs: Science, technology and socialist feminism for the 1980s', *Socialist Review* 80, pp. 95–107

Harding, A.F. 1984 *The Mycenaeans and Europe*, London, Academic Press

—— 1995 *Die Schwerter im ehemaligen Jugoslawien*, Prähistorische Bronzefunde, Abt. IV, 14, Stuttgart, Franz Steiner

—— 1996 'Reformation in Barbarian Europe, 1300–600 BC', in B. Cunliffe, (ed.), *The Oxford Illustrated Prehistory of Europe*, Oxford, Oxford University Press, pp. 304–35

—— 1997 'Wie gross waren die Gruppenverbände der bronzezeitlichen Welt?', in C. Becker et al. (eds), *Beiträge zur prähistorischen Archäologie zwischen Nord- und Südeuropa: Festschrift für Bernhard Hänsel*, Internationale Archäologie, Studia Honoraria 1, Espelkamp, Verlag Marie Leidorf, pp. 443–51

Härke, H. 1990 '"Warrior Graves"? The Background of the Anglo-Saxon Weapon Burial Rite' *Past and Present* 126, pp. 22–43

—— 1992 'Changing Symbols in a Changing Society: The Anglo-Saxon Weapon Burial Rite in the Seventh Century', in M.O.H. Carver (ed.), *The Age of Sutton Hoo*, Woodbridge, The Boydell Press, pp. 149–65

Harmon, M., Molleson, T.I. & Price, J.L. 1981 'Burials, Bodies and Beheadings in Romano-British and Anglo-Saxon Cemeteries,' *Bulletin British Museum Nat. Hist. Geol.* 35.3., pp. 145–88

Harris, M. 1978 *Cannibals and Kings: The Origins of Cultures*, Glasgow, Fontana

Häusler, A. 1990 'Die ältesten Befestigungsanlagen im Südwesten des europäischen Teiles der UdSSR', *Jahresschrift für mitteldeutsche Vorgeschichte* 73, pp. 87–92

Hedges, R.E.M., Housley, R.A., Bronk, C.R. & van Klinken, G.J. 1991 'Radiocarbon dates from the Oxford AMS system', *Archaeometry* 33, pp. 121–34

Hencken, H. 1950 'Herzsprung shields and Greek trade', *American J. Archaeology* 54, pp. 295–309

Henderson, J. 1989 'Pagan Saxon cemeteries: a study of the problem of sexing by gravegoods and bones', in C.A. Roberts, F. Lee and J. Bintliff (eds), *Burial Archaeology: Current Research, Methods and Developments*, Oxford, British Archaeological Report 211, pp. 77–83.

Henry, J. 1966 *Culture Against Man*, Tavistock Publications

Hernandez Perez, M.S. 1987 'Arte rupestre en pais valenciano', in *Arte rupestre en España*, Revista de Arqueologia, num. spécial pp. 78–95

Herrmann, J. 1982 'Militärische Demokratie und die Übergangsperiode zur Klassengesellschaft', *Ethnographisch-Archäologische Zeitschrift* 23, pp. 11–31

Heurtley, W.A. 1939 *Prehistoric Macedonia: An Archaeological Reconnaissance of Greek Macedonia (West of Struma) in the Neolithic, Bronze and Early Iron Ages*, Cambridge, Cambridge University Press

Hignett, C. 1963 *Xerxes' Invasion of Greece*, Oxford, Clarendon Press

Hill, D. 1964 'Aggression and mental illness', in J.D. Carthy and F.J. Ebling (eds), *The Natural History of Aggression*, New York, Academic Press, pp. 91–9

Hill, J.D. 1995 'How should we understand Iron Age societies and hillforts ? A contextual study from southern Britain', in J.D. Hill and C.G. Cumberpatch (eds), *Different Iron Ages: Studies on the Iron Age in Temperate Europe*, BAR Int. Series 602, Oxford, Tempus Reparatum, pp. 45–66

Hill, J.M. 1995 *The Cultural World in Beowulf*, Toronto, University of Toronto Press

Hinde, R.A. 1974 *Biological Bases of Human Social Behaviour*, New York, McGraw-Hill

Hines, J. 1989 'The Military Context of the *adventus Saxonum*: Some Continental Evidence', in S. C. Hawkes (ed.), *Weapons and Warfare in Anglo-Saxon England*, Oxford University Committee for Archaeology Monograph 21, Oxford, Oxbow Books, pp. 25–48

Höckmann, O. 1980a 'Lanze und Speer', in H-G. Buchholz (ed.), *Kriegswesen, Teil II: Angriffswaffen*, Archaeologia Homerica, Kapitel E, Göttingen, Vandenhoeck and Ruprecht, pp. 275–319

—— 1980b 'Lanze und Speer im spätminoischen und mykenischen Griechenland', *Jahrbuch des Römisch-Germanischen Zentralmuseums Mainz* 27, pp. 13–158

—— 1990 'Frühneolithische Einhegungen in Europa', *Jahresschrift für mitteldeutsche Vorgeschichte* 73, pp. 57–86

Hodder, I. 1982 *Symbols in Action*, Cambridge, Cambridge University Press

—— 1990 *The Domestication of Europe*, Oxford, Blackwell

Hoepfner, W. & Schwandner, E.-L. 1994 *Haus und Stadt im klassischen Griechenland: Wohnen in der klassischen Polis I*, Munich, Deutscher Kunstverlag

Hoffmann, J., Ireland, T. & Widom, C. 1995 'Traditional socialisation theories of violence', in J. Archer (ed.), *Male Violence*, London, Routledge, pp. 289–303

Hogbin, H.I. 1963 *Kinship and Marriage in a New Guinea Village*, Athlone Press

Hood M.S.F. 1981–2 *Excavations in Chios, 1938–1955: Prehistoric Emporio and Ayio Gala*, Vols 1–2, British School of Archaeology at Athens Supplements 15–16, London, Thames and Hudson

Hopf, M. 1975 'Pflanzenfunde aus dem Tell Goljamo Delchevo', in H. Todorova, St. Ivanov, V. Vasilev, M. Hopf, H. Quitta & G. Kohl, *Selishnata mogila pri Goljamo Delchevo*, Sofia, Bulgarian Academy of Sciences, pp. 303–24

Hoppa, R.D. 1992 'Evaluating Human Skeletal Growth: An Anglo-Saxon Example', *International Journal of Osteoarchaeology* 2, pp. 275–88

Hornblower, S. 1996 *A Commentary on Thucydides*, Vol. II Oxford, Clarendon Press

Horowitz, D.L. 1985 *Ethnic Groups in Conflict*, Berkeley, University of California Press

Hourmouziadis, G.H. 1979 *To neolithiko Dimini: Prospatheia gia mia nea prosengisi tou neolithikou ilikou*, Volos, Etaireia Thessalikon Erevnon, reprinted 1994, Thessaloniki, Vanias

—— 1980 'Eisagogi sto neolithiko tropo paragogis I', *Anthropologika* 1, pp. 118–29

—— 1981 'Eisagogi sto neolithiko tropo paragogis II', *Anthropologika* 2, pp. 39–54

Housley, R.A., Gamble, C.S., Street, M. & Pettitt, P. 1997 'Radiocarbon evidence for the late glacial human recolonisation of Northern Europe', *Proc. Prehist. Soc.* 63, pp. 25–57

Hovland, C. & Sears, S. 1940 'Minor studies of aggression: VI correlations of lynchings with economic indices', *J. Psychology* 9, pp. 301–10

Hrala, J., Sedláček, Z. & Vávra, M. 1992 'Velim: A hilltop site of the Middle Bronze Age in Bohemia. Report on the excavations 1984–90', *Památky Archeologické* 83, pp. 288–308

Hrysostomou, P. 1992 'O neolithikos oikismos ton Giannitson B', *To Arhaiologiko Ergo sti Makedonia kai Thraki* 3 (1989). Thessaloniki, Aristoteleio Panepistimio, Thessalonikis Ypourgeio Politismou, Ypourgeio Makedonias-Thrakis, pp. 119–34

Hrysostomou, P. & Hrysostomou, P. 1993 'Neolithikes erevnes sta Giannitsa kai stin periohi tous', *To Arhaiologiko Ergo sti Makedonia kai Thraki* 4 (1990), Thessaloniki, Aristoteleio Panepistimio Thessalonikis, Ypourgeio Politismou, Ypourgeio Makedonias-Thrakis, pp. 169–177

Hrysostomou, P. & Hrysostomou, V. 1994 'Oi neolithikes erevnes stin poli kai tin eparhia Giannitson kata to 1991', *To Arhaiologiko Ergo sti Makedonia kai Thraki* 5 (1991). Thessaloniki, Aristoteleio Panepistimio Thessalonikis, Ypourgeio Politismou, Ypourgeio Makedonias-Thrakis, pp. 111–25

—— 1996 'O neolithikos oikismos Giannitson B: Nea anaskafika dedomena (1992–1993)', *To Arhaiologiko Ergo sti Makedonia kai Thraki* 7 (1993). Thessaloniki, Aristoteleio Panepistimio Thessalonikis, Ypourgeio Politismou, Ypourgeio Makedonias-Thrakis, pp. 135–42

Ivanov, I. 1991 'Der Bestattungsritus in der chalkolithischen Nekropole von Varna mit einem Katalog der wichtigsten Gräbern', in J. Lichardus (ed.), *Die Kupferzeit als historische Epoche*, Saarbrücker Beiträge zur Altertumskunde 55, Saarbrücken, Saarland Museum, pp. 125–50

Ivanov, S. & Vasilev, V. 1975 'Untersuchungen des Tierknochenmaterials aus dem prähistorischen Tell bei Goljamo Delchevo', in H. Todorova, S. Ivanov, V. Vasilev, M. Hopf, H. Quitta & G. Kohl, *Selishnata mogila pri Goljamo Delchevo*, Sofia, Bulgarian Academy of Sciences, pp. 245–302

Jacob-Friesen, G. 1967 *Bronzezeitliche Lanzenspitzen Norddeutschlands und Skandinaviens*, Veröff. der urgeschichtlichen Sammlungen des Landesmuseums zu Hannover 17, Hildesheim, August Lax

Jacobi, U., Selg, H. & Belschner, W. 1975 'The aggressive instinct', in H. Selg (ed.), *The Making of Human Aggression: A Psychological Approach*, Quartet Books, pp. 41–58

Jacobs, K. 1992 'Human population differentiation in the peri-Baltic Mesolithic: The odontometrics of Oleneostrovskii mogilnik (Karelia)', *Human Evolution* 7, pp. 33–48

—— 1993 'Human postcranial variation in the Ukrainian Mesolithic-Neolithic', *Current Anthropology* 34, pp. 311–24

Jakobsson, M. 1997 'Burial Layout, Society and Sacred Geography: A Viking Age Example from Jämtland', *Current Swedish Archaeology* 5, pp. 79–98

Jochens, J. 1996 *Old Norse Images of Women*, Philadelphia, University of Pennsylvania Press

Jockenhövel, A. 1990 'Bronzezeitliche Burgenbau in Mitteleuropa: Untersuchungen zur Struktur frühmetallzeitlicher Gesellschaften', in *Orientalisch-ägäische Einflüsse in der europäischen Bronzezeit*, Römisch-Germanisches Zentralmuseum Mainz, Monographien 15, pp. 209–28

—— 1991 'Räumliche Mobilität von Personen in der mittleren Bronzezeit des westlichen Mitteleuropa', *Germania* 69, pp. 49–62

John, E. 1992 'The Point of Woden', in W. Filmer-Sankey et al. (eds), *Anglo-Saxon Studies in Archaeology and History* 5, Oxford, Oxford University Committee for Archaeology, pp. 127–34

Johnson, A.W. & Earle, T.K. 1987 *The Evolution of Human Societies: From Foraging Group to Agrarian State*, Stanford, Stanford University Press

Jolly, A. 1972 *The Evolution of Primate Behaviour*, London, Macmillan

Jones, C. 1968 'A Leading Family of Roman Thespiae', *Harvard Studies in Classical Philology* 74, pp. 223–55

Jones, S. 1980 'Institutions of violence', in J. Chafas & R. Lewin (eds), *Not Work Alone: A cross-cultural View of Activities Superfluous to Survival*, London, Temple Smith, pp. 98–111

—— 1996 'Discourses of identity in the interpretation of the past', in P. Graves-Brown, S. Jones & G. Gamble (eds), *Cultural Identity and Archaeology: The Construction of European Communities*, London, Routledge, pp. 62–80

Jungwirth, J. 1977 'Die Bevölkerung Österreichs im Neolithikum', in *Festschrift 75 Jahre Anthropol. Staatssammlung München*, pp. 233–56

Kabo, V.R. 1986 *Pervobytnaya dozemledel'cheskaya obshchina*, Moscow, Nauka

Kagan, D. 1974 *The Archidamian War*, Ithaca NY, Cornell University Press

—— 1981 *The Peace of Nicias and the Sicilian Expedition*, Ithaca NY, Cornell University Press

Kaufmann, D. 1990a 'Ausgrabungen im Bereich linienbandkeramischer Erdwerke bei Eisleben, Kr. Wanzleben', *Jahresschrift für mitteldeutsche Vorgeschichte* 73, pp. 15–28

—— (ed.) 1990b 'Befestigte neolithische und äneolithische Siedlungen und Plätze in Mitteleuropa', *Jahresschrift für mitteldeutsche Vorgeschichte* 73, pp. 1–531

Keegan, J. 1976 *The Face of Battle*, London, Hutchinson

—— 1993 *A History of Warfare*, London, Hutchinson

Keeley, L.H. 1992 'The introduction of agriculture to the western North European plain', in A.B. Gebauer & T.D. Price (eds), *Transitions to Agriculture in Prehistory*, Madison, Prehistory Press, pp. 81–95

—— 1996 *War Before Civilization: The Myth of the Peaceful Savage*, Oxford and New York, Oxford University Press

Keeley, L.H. & Cahen, D. 1989 'Early Neolithic forts and villages in NE Belgium: A preliminary report', *J. Field Archaeology* 16, pp. 157–76

Kesisoglou M., Mirtsou, E. & Srtatis, I. 1996 'Meleti deigmaton kerameikis apo to Mandalo: Proimi epohi tou halkou', in I. Stratis, M. Babelidis, K. Kotsakis, G. Tsokas & E. Tsoukala (eds), *Archaeometrical and Archaeological Research in Macedonia and Thrace: Proceedings of the 2nd Symposium of the Hellenic Archaeometrical Society, Thessaloniki, 26–28 March 1993*, Thessaloniki, pp. 161–8

Kilian-Dirlmeier, I. 1993 *Die Schwerter in Griechenland (ausserhalb der Peloponnes), Bulgarien und Albanien*, Prähistorische Bronzefunde Abt. IV, Band 12, Stuttgart, Franz Steiner

Kilikoglou, V., Bassiakos, Y., Grimanis, A.P., Souvatzis, K., Pilali-Papasteriou, A. & Papaefthimiou-Papanthimou, A. 1996 'Carpathian obsidian in Macedonia, Greece', *Journal of Archaeological Science* 23, pp. 343–9

Kimmig, W. 1983 *Die Heuneburg an der oberen Donau*, Führer zu archäologischen Denkmälern in Baden-Württemberg 1 (2nd edn), Stuttgart, Theiss

Kirch, P. 1984 *The Evolution of the Polynesian Chiefdoms*, Cambridge, Cambridge University Press

—— 1991 'Chiefship and competitive involution: The Marquesas Islands of eastern Polynesia', in T. Earle (ed.), *Chiefdoms: Power, Economy and Ideology*, Cambridge, Cambridge University Press, pp. 119–45

Klíma, B. 1987 'Mladopaleolitický trojhrob v Dolních Věstonicích', *Archeologické rozhledy* 39, pp. 241–54, 353–7

Koenig, G.G. 1982 'Schamane und Schmied, Medicus und Monch: Ein Überblick zur Archäologie der merowingerzeitlichen Medizin im südlichen Mitteleuropa', *Helvetia Archaeologica* 13, plt. 52, pp. 75–154

Kokkinidou, D. 1989 'The Neolithic and Bronze Ages in Central-Western Macedonia: A Study of the Period from the Mid Sixth to the End of the Second Millennium B.C. in the Area between the Rivers Axios and Aliakmon in Northern Greece', unpublished PhD thesis, University of Birmingham

—— 1990 *I proistoria sto horo tou nomou Pellas: Katoikisi kai fisiko perivallon sti neolithiki kai tin epohi tou halkou*, Edessa

—— 1995 'I Edessa kai i evriteri periohi tis kata ti diarkeia tis neolithikis kai tis epohis tou halkou', in *Praktika A Panelliniou Epistomonikou Simposiou 'I Edessa kai i periohi tis: Istoria kai politismos', Edessa, 4, 5 kai 6 Dekemvriou 1992*, Edessa, Dimos Edessas, pp. 51–68

Kokkinidou, D. & Trantalidou, K. 1991 'Neolithic and Bronze Age settlement in western Macedonia', *Annual of the British School of Archaeology at Athens* 86, pp. 93–106

Kopytoff, I. 1986 'The cultural biography of things: Commoditization as process', in A. Appadurai (ed.), *The Social Life of Things*, Cambridge: Cambridge University Press, pp. 64–91

Korfmann, M. 1972 *Schleuder und Bogen in Südwestasien*, Bonn, Habelt

Kotsakis, K. 1987 'Apokatastasi passalopikton oikimaton me ti voitheia ilektronikou ipologisti stin anaskafi Mandalou D. Makedonias', in *Eilapini: Tomos timitikos gia ton kathigiti Nikolao Platona*, Herakleion, Vikelaia Vivliothiki, Dimos Herakleiou, pp. 117–27

—— 1996 'The coastal settlements of Thessaly', in G.A. Papathanassopoulos (ed.), *Neolithic Culture in Greece*, Athens, Nicholas P. Goulandris Foundation, Museum of Cycladic Art, pp. 49–57

Kotsakis, K., Papaefthimiou-Papanthimou, A., Pilali-Papasteriou, A., Savopoulou, T., Maniatis, Y. & Kromer, B. 1989 'Carbon 14 dates from Mandalo, W. Macedonia', in Y. Maniatis (ed.), *Archaeometry: Proceedings of the 25th International Symposium, Athens, 19–23 May 1986*, Amsterdam, Elsevier, pp. 679–85

Kozłowski, J.K. & Kozłowski, S.K. 1982 'Lithic industries from the multi-layer Mesolithic site Vlasac in Yugoslavia', in J.K. Kozłowski (ed.), *Origin of the Chipped Stone Industries of the Early Farming Cultures in the Balkans*, Krakow, Jagiellonian University, pp. 11–109

—— 1983 'Chipped stone industries from Lepenski Vir', *Preistoria Alpina* 19, pp. 259–94

Kozłowski, S.K. 1989 'Nemrik 9, a PPN Site in Northern Iraq', *Paléorient* 15/1, pp. 25–31

Krentz, P. 1985 'Casualties in Hoplite Battles', *Greek, Roman, and Byzantine Studies* 26, pp. 13–21

Kristiansen, K. 1984a 'Krieger und Häuptlinge in der Bronzezeit Dänemarks: Ein Beitrag zur Geschichte des bronzezeitlichen Schwertes', *Jahrbuch des Römisch-Germanisches Zentralmuseums Mainz* 31, pp. 187–208

——— 1984b 'Ideology and material culture: An archaeological perspective', in M. Spriggs (ed.), *Marxist Perspectives in Archaeology*, Cambridge, Cambridge University Press, pp. 72–100

——— 1987a 'From stone to bronze: The evolution of social complexity in Northern Europe 2300–1200 BC', in E.M. Brumfiel & T. Earle (eds), *Specialization, Exchange, and Complex Societies*, Cambridge, Cambridge University Press, pp. 30–51

——— 1987b 'Center and periphery in Bronze Age Scandinavia', in M. Rowlands, M.T. Larsen & K. Kristiansen (eds), *Centre and Periphery in the Ancient World*, Cambridge, Cambridge University Press, pp. 74–85

——— 1989 'Prehistoric migrations: The case of the Single Grave and Corded Ware Cultures', *J. Danish Archaeology* 8, pp. 211–25

——— 1991 'Chiefdoms, states and systems of social evolution', in T.K. Earle (ed.), *Chiefdoms: Economy, Power and Ideology*, Cambridge, Cambridge University Press, pp. 16–43

——— 1998a *Europe before History*, Cambridge, Cambridge University Press

——— 1998b 'The construction of a Bronze Age landscape: Cosmology, economy and social organisation in Thy, northwest Jutland', in B. Hänsel (ed.), *Mensch und Umwelt in der Bronzezeit Europas*, Kiel, Oetker-Voges Verlag, pp. 281–91

——— forthcoming, 'Swords and sword fighters in Bronze Age Hungary: A use-wear analysis'

Kristiansen, K. & Rowlands, M. 1998 *Social Transformations in Archaeology: Global and Local Perspectives*, London and New York, Routledge

Kunkel, O. 1955 *Die Jungfernhöhle bei Tiefenellern: eine neolithische Kultstätte auf dem fränkischen Jura bei Bamberg*, Munich, Beck

Kunter, M. 1981 'Frakturen und Verletzungen des vor- und frühgeschichtlichen Menschen', *Archäologie und Naturwissenschaften* 2, pp. 221–46

Kurtz, D.V. 1978 'The legitimation of the Aztec states', in H. Claessen & P. Skalnik (eds), *The Early State*, The Hague, Mouton, pp. 169–89

La Baume, W. 1963 *Die Pommerellischen Gesichtsurnen*, Römisch-Germanisches Zentralmuseum zu Mainz, Kataloge vor- und frühgeschichtlicher Altertümer 17

Laffin, J. 1995 *Brassey's Battles: 3,500 Years of Conflict, Campaigns and Wars from A–Z*, London, Brassey's

Larsen, J. 1955 'The Boeotian Confederacy and Fifth-century Oligarchic Theory', *Transactions of the American Philological Association* 86

Larsen, J.A.O. 1968 *Greek Federal States: Their Institutions and History*, Oxford, Clarendon Press

Larsson, L. 1984 'The Skateholm Project. A late Mesolithic settlement and cemetery complex at a southern Swedish bay', *Meddelanden från Lunds historiske museum*, 1983–4, n.s. 5, 5–38

László, A. 1993 'Le sud-est de la Transylvanie dans le néolithique tardif et le chalcolithique: Nouvelles données et considérations', in P. Georgieva (ed.), *The Fourth Millennium B.C.*, Sofia, New Bulgarian University Press, pp. 62–76

Lawrence, A.W. 1979 *Greek Aims in Fortification*, Oxford, Clarendon Press

Lazarovici, Gh. 1976 *Iklod*, Cluj-Napoca, Muzeul de Istorie

——— 1990 'Über neo- bis äneoneolithische Befestigungen aus Rumänien', *Jahresschrift für mitteldeutsche Vorgeschichte* 73, pp. 93–118

Lazenby, J. 1985 *The Spartan Army*, Warminister, Aris and Philips

——— 1991 'The Killing Zone' in V.D. Hanson (ed.), *Hoplites: The Classical Greek Battle Experience*, London, Routledge, pp. 87–109

——— 1993 *The Defence of Greece*, Warminister, Aris and Philips

Le Bon, G. 1916 *The Psychology of the Great War*, London, Unwin

Levick, B. 1997 'New Anglo-Saxon Helmet Discovered in Northamptonshire', *Angelcynn: Anglo-Saxon Living History 400–900 AD*, 17 May, 1997, http://www.hrofi.demon. co.uk/angelcyn/helmet.html

Lewis, I.M. 1985 *Social Anthropology in Perspective*, Cambridge, Cambridge University Press

Lichardus, J. 1988 'Der westpontische Raum und die Anfänge der kupferzeitlichen Zivilisation', in A. Fol & J. Lichardus (eds), *Macht, Herrschaft und Gold*, Saarbrücken, Moderne Galerie des Saarland Museums, pp. 79–130

Liddell, D.M. 1929–32 [1930] 'Report on the excavations at Hembury Fort, Devon, 1930', *Proc. Devon Archaeol. Explor. Soc.* 1, pp. 40–63

——— 1929–32 [1931] 'Report on the excavations at Hembury, Devon, 1931: Second season', *Proc. Devon Archaeol. Explor. Soc.* 1, pp. 90–119

——— 1929–32 [1932] 'Report on the excavation at Hembury Fort: Third season, 1932', *Proc. Devon Archaeol. Explor. Soc.* 1, pp. 162–90

——— 1933–36 [1935] 'Report on the excavations at Hembury Fort: fourth and fifth seasons, 1934–35', *Proc. Devon Archaeol. Explor. Soc.* 2, pp. 135–75

Lies, H. 1963 'Ein Gefäss der Linienbandkeramik mit reliefierten Gesichtsdarstellungen von Barleben, Kr. Wolmirstedt', *Ausgrabungen und Funde* 8, pp. 9–16

Linger, D.T. 1992 *Dangerous Encounters: Meanings of Violence in a Brazilian City*, Stanford CA, Stanford University Press

Littleton, C.S. 1987 'War and Warriors,' in M. Eliade (ed.), *Encyclopedia of Religion*, Vol. 15, New York, Macmillan, pp. 339–49

Lloyd, A.B (ed.) 1996 *Battle in Antiquity*, London, Duckworth

Lonsdale, K. 1951 'Foreword', in A.G. Enock, *This War Business*, Bodley Head, p. 15

Lorenz, K. 1966 *On Aggression*, London, Methuen

Lorimer, H.L. 1950 *Homer and the Monuments*, London, Macmillan

Loudon, J.B. 1972 'Teasing and socialization on Tristan de Cunha', in P. Mayer (ed.), *Socialization: The Approach from Social Anthropology*, Tavistock, pp. 293–332

Louwe Kooijmans, L.P. 1998 'Bronzezeitlichen Bauern in und um die niederländische Delta-Niederung', in B. Hänsel (ed.), *Mensch und Umwelt in der Bronzezeit Europas*, Kiel, Oetker-Voges Verlag, pp. 327–39

Loze, I.A. 1979 *Pozdnii neolit i rannyaya bronza Lubanskoi ravniny*, Riga, Zinatne

Lubell, D., Jackes, M. & Meiklejohn, C. 1985 'Archaeology and human biology of the Mesolithic–Neolithic transition in southern Portugal: A preliminary report', in C. Bonsall (ed.), *The Mesolithic in Europe*, Edinburgh, John Donald, pp. 632–40

Lucy, S.J. 1997 'Housewives, Warriors and Slaves? Sex and Gender in Anglo-Saxon Burials', in J. Moore & E. Scott (eds), *Invisible People and Processes: Writing Gender and Childhood into European Archaeology*, London and New York, Leicester University Press, pp. 150–68

Lüning, J. 1988 'Zur Verbreitung und Datierung bandkeramischer Erdwerke', *Archäologisches Korrespondenzblatt* 18, pp. 155–8

Lyneis, M.M. 1988 'Antler and bone artifacts from Divostin', in A. McPherron & D. Srejović (eds), *Divostin and the Neolithic of Central Serbia*, Kragujevac, Narodni Muzej Kragujevac, pp. 301–24

Lyons, H.A. 1972 'Depressive illness and aggression in Belfast', *British Medical Journal* 1, pp. 342–5

Maccoby, E. & Jacklin, C. 1980 'Sex differences in aggression: A rejoinder and reprise', *Child Development* 51, pp. 964–80

Maier, N.R.F. 1949 *Frustration: The Study of Behaviour Without a Goal*, New York, McGraw-Hill

Makkay, J. 1978 'A Szegvár-Tüzkovesi újkökori férfiszobor és a "Föld és Ég elválasztásának" ösi mítosza', *Archaeológiai Értesitö* 105, pp. 164–83

—— 1982 'The earliest use of helmets in south-east Europe', *Acta Archaeologica* (Budapest) 34, pp. 3–22

—— 1984 *Early Stamp Seals in South-East Europe*, Budapest, Akadémiai Kiadö

Mallory, J.P. 1977 'The chronology of the early Kurgan tradition, Part Two', *Journal of Indo-European Studies* 5, pp. 339–68

—— 1989 *In Search of the Indo-Europeans: Language, Archaeology and Myth*, London, Thames and Hudson

Maniatis Y. & Kromer, B. 1990 'Radiocarbon dating of the Neolithic-Bronze Age site of Mandalo, W. Macedonia', *Radiocarbon* 32, pp. 149–53

Manolakkakis, L. 1996 'Production lithique et émergence de la hiérarchie sociale: l'industrie lithique de l'énéolithique en Bulgarie, première moitié du IVe millenaire.', *Bull. Soc. Préhist. Française* 93.1, pp. 119–23

Marazov, I. 1988 'Tod und Mythos: Überlegungen zu Varna', in A. Fol & J. Lichardus (eds), *Macht, Herrschaft und Gold*, Saarbrücken, Moderne Galerie des Saarlands Museums, pp. 67–78

Marx, K. & Engels, F. 1985 *The German Ideology* (ed. C.J. Arthur), London, Lawrence and Wishart

Masson, V.M. & Merpert, N.Ya. 1982 *Eneolit SSSR* (Arkheologiya SSSR), Moscow, Nauka

Matthäus, H. & Schumacher-Matthäus, G. 1986 'Zyprische Hortfunde: Kult und Metallhandwerk in der späten Bronzezeit', in O-H. Frey, H. Roth & C. Dobiat (eds), *Gedenkschrift für Gero von Merhart*, Marburger Studien zur Vor- und Frühgeschichte 7, Marburg, Hitzeroth, pp. 129–91

Matuschik, I. 1991 'Grabenwerke des Spätneolithikums in Süddeutschland', *Fundberichte aus Baden-Württemberg* 16, pp. 27–55

Mayer-Gross, W., Slater, E. & Roth, M. 1977 *Clinical Psychiatry*, Tindall

McCauley, C. 1990 'Conference overview', in J. Haas (ed.), *The Anthropology of War*, Cambridge, Cambridge University Press, pp. 1–25

McGeehan-Liritizis, V. 1996 *The Role and Development of Metallurgy in the Late Neolithic and Early Bronze Age of Greece*, Studies in Mediterranean Archaeology and Literature Pocket Book 122, Jonsered, Paul Åström

Mellars, P.A. 1986 'A new chronology for the French Mousterian Period', *Nature* 322, pp. 410–11

Mercer, R. 1970 'Metal arrowheads in the European Bronze and Early Iron Ages', *Proc. Prehist. Soc.* 36, pp. 171–213

—— 1980 *Hambledon Hill: A Neolithic Landscape*, Edinburgh, Edinburgh University Press

—— 1981 *Excavations at Carn Brea, Illogan, Cornwall 1970–73: A Neolithic Fortified Complex of the Third Millennium bc* (= *Cornish Archaeology* 20)

—— forthcoming 'The excavation of the Neolithic enclosure complex at Helman Tor, Lostwithiel, Cornwall', *Cornish Archaeology* 35

Mercer, R.J. & Healy, F.M. forthcoming *The Excavation of the Neolithic Enclosure Complex of Hambledon Hill, Dorset, England*, London, English Heritage

Merpert, N.Y. 1961 'Eneolit stepnoi polosy evropskoi chasti USSR', in J. Böhm & S. de Laet (eds), *L'Europe à la fin de l'âge du pierre*, Prague, Éditions de l'Academie Tschechoslovaque des Sciences, pp. 161–92

—— 1968 *Drevneishaya istoriya naseleniya stepnoi polosy Vostochnoi Evropy*, Moscow, Nauka

Milner, G.R. 1995 'An osteological perspective on ancient warfare', in L.A. Beck (ed.) *Regional Approaches to Mortuary Analysis*, New York, Plenum, pp. 221–44

—— 1998 'Archaeological evidence for Prehistoric and Early Historic intergroup conflict in eastern North America', in P.Y. Bullock (ed.) *Deciphering Anasazi Violence; with regional comparisons to Mesoamerican and Woodland cultures*, Santa Fe NM, HRM Books, pp. 69–91

Milojčić, V. 1955 'Einige mitteleuropäische "Fremdlinge" auf Kreta', *Jahrbuch des römisch-germanischen Zentralmuseums Mainz* 2, pp. 153–69

Mirchev, M. 1961 'Tri pogrebeniya ot eneolitnata epoha', *Izvestiya Naroden Muzei Varna* 12, pp. 117–25

Mitchell, S. 1996 'Hoplite Warfare in Ancient Greece' in A. Lloyd (ed.), *Battle in Antiquity*, London, Duckworth, pp. 87–106

Mohr, A. 1971 'Häufigkeit und Lokalisation von Frakturen und Verletzungen am Skelett vor- und frühgeschichtlichen Menschengruppen', *Ethnographisch-Archäologische Zeitschrift* 12, pp. 139–42

Monah, D. 1997 *Plastica antropomorfna a culturii Cucuteni-Tripolie*, Piatra Neamţ, Centrul de Cercetăre a culturii Cucuteni

Monah, D. & Cucos, S. 1985 *Aşezarile culturii Cucuteni din România*, Iaşi, Junimea

Monks, S. J. 1997 'Conflict and competition in Spanish prehistory: the role of warfare in societal development from the late fourth to third millennium BC', *Journal of Mediterranean Archaeology* 10/1, pp. 3–32

—— 1998 'The role of conflict and competition in the development of prehistoric Western Mediterranean societies from the late fourth to early second millennium BC', unpublished PhD thesis, University of Reading

Montagu, A. 1976 *The Nature of Human Aggression*, Oxford, Oxford University Press

—— (ed.) 1978 *Learning Non-aggression: The Experience of Non-literate Societies*, Oxford, Oxford University Press

Montgomery of Alamein, Field Marshall Viscount, 1968 *A History of Warfare*, London, Collins

Movsha, T.G. 1985 'Pozdnii etap tripol'skoi kul'tury', in I.I. Artemenko (ed.), *Arheologiya Ukrainskoi SSR*, Vol. 1, Kiev, Naukova Dumka, pp. 223–62

Moyer, K.E. 1976 *The Psychobiology of Aggression*, New York, Harper and Row

Mozsolics, A. 1975 'Bronzkori kardok folyókból', *Archaeológiai Értesitó* 102, pp. 3–24

Müller-Karpe, H. 1968 *Handbuch der Vorgeschichte II*, Munich, Beck

Murphy, R.F. 1957 'Intergroup hostility and social cohesion', *American Anthropologist* 59, pp. 1,018–35

Nandris, J. 1968 'Lepenski Vir', *Science Journal* 1, pp. 64–70

Needham, S.P. 1979 'Two recent British shield finds and their continental parallels', *Proc. Prehist. Soc.* 45, pp. 111–34

Neeley, M.P. & Clark, G.A. 1990 'Measuring social complexity in the European Mesolithic', in P.M. Vermeersch & P. van Peer (eds), *Contributions to the Mesolithic in Europe*, Leuven, Leuven University Press, pp. 127–37

Nelson, S. M. 1997 *Gender in Archaeology: Analyzing Power and Prestige*, Walnut Creek, AltaMira Press

Němec, I. et al. 1986 *Dědictví Řeči*, Prague, Panorama

Němejcová-Pavúková, V. 1995 *Svodín, Band I. Zwei Kreisgrabenanlagen der Lengyel-Kultur*, Bratislava, Katedra archeologie Filozofickej fakulty Univerzity Komenského

Němejcová-Pavúková, V. et al. 1997 *Kreisgrabenanlage der Lengyel-Kultur Ružindol-Borová*, Bratislava, Katedra archeologie Filozofickej fakulty University Komenského

Nemeskéri, J. 1969 'Populacija Lepenskog Vira', in D. Srejović (ed.), *Lepenski Vir: Nova praistorijska kultura u Podunavlju*, Beograd, Srpska kniževna zadruga, pp. 239–62

—— 1974 'Outline on the anthropological finds of a neolithic site', in M. Gimbutas (ed.), *Obre I and II*, Sarajevo, Wissenschaftliche Mitteilungen des Bosnisch-Hercegowinisch Landesmuseums Band VI/Heft A, pp. 37–46

—— 1978 'Demographic structure of the Vlasac population', in D. Srejović & Z. Letica (eds), *Vlasac: Mezolitsko naselje u Djerdapu*, Tom II, Beograd, Srpska Akademija Nauka i Umetnosti, pp. 97–133

Nemeskéri, J. & Lengyel, I. 1976 'Neolithic skeletal finds', in M. Gimbutas (ed.), *Neolithic Macedonia, Monumenta Archaeologica* 1, Los Angeles, University of California Press, pp. 375–410

Neugebauer, J.W. et al. 1983 'Die doppelte mittelneolithische Kreisgrabenanlage von Friebritz, NÖ', *Fundberichte aus Österreich* 22, pp. 87–112

Neumann, H. 1981 'Jutish Burials in the Roman Iron Age', in V.I. Evison (ed.), *Angles, Saxons, and Jutes: Essays Presented to J.N.L. Myres*, Oxford, Clarendon Press, pp. 1–10

Neustupný, E. 1983 *Demografie pravěkých pohřebišt'*, Prague, Archaeological Institute

—— 1995 'The significance of facts', *J. European Archaeology* 3/1, pp. 189–212

—— (ed.) 1998 *Space in Prehistoric Bohemia*, Prague, Archaeological Institute, Czech Academy of Sciences

Nevizansky, G. 1985 'Sozial-ökonomische Verhältnisse in der Polgár-Kultur auf Grund der Gräberfeldanalyse', *Slovenská Archeológia* 32.2, pp. 263–310

Newell, R.R., Constandse-Westermann, T.S. & Meiklejohn, C. 1979 'The skeletal remains of Mesolithic man in Western Europe: An evaluative catalogue', *J. Human Evolution* 8/1, pp. 1–228

Newman, P. 1981 *The Battle of Marston Moor*, Strettington, Anthony Bird Publications

Nicolăescu-Plopşor, D. 1976 'Deux cas de morts violents dans l'Epipaleólithique final de Schela Cladovei', *Annuaire Roumain d'Anthropologie* 13, pp. 3–5

Niesiołowska-Wędzka, A. 1989 *Procesy urbanizacyjne w kulturze łużyckiej w świetle oddzialywań kultur południowych*, Polskie Badania Archeologiczne 29, Wrocław, Polski Akademia Nauk

Nikolaidou M. 1997 'Ornament production and use at Sitagroi, northeast Greece: Symbolic and social implications of an Early Bronze Age technology', in R. Laffineur & P.P. Bentacourt (eds), *Techni: Craftsmen, Craftswomen and Craftsmaship in the Aegean Bronze Age. Proceedings of the 6th International Aegean Conference/6e Rencontre égéenne internationale, Philadelphia, Temple University, 18–21 April 1996*, Aegaeum 16, Annales d'archéologie égéenne de l'Université de Liège et UT-PASP, Université de Liège, Histoire de l'art et archéologie de la Grèce antique, University of Texas at Austin, Program in Aegean Scripts and Prehistory, pp. 177–96

Nikolaidou, M. & Kokkinidou, D. 1997 'The symbolism of violence in palatial societies of the late Bronze Age Aegean, a gender approach', in J. Carman (ed.), *Material Harm: Archaeological Studies of War and Violence*, Glasgow, Cruithne Press, pp. 174–97

Nobis, G. 1986 'Zur Fauna der frühneolithische Siedlung Ovcharovo–Gorata, Bez. Targovishte NO Bulgarien', *Bonner Zoologische Beiträge* 37/1, pp. 1–22

Nosworthy, B. 1992 *The Anatomy of Victory: Battle tactics 1681–1763*, New York, Hippocrene Books

—— 1995 *Battle Tactics of Napoleon and His Enemies*, London, Constable

Nuzhnyj, D. 1989 'L'utilisation des microlithes géometriques et non géometriques comme armatures de projectiles', *Bulletin de la Société Préhistorique Française* 86, pp. 88–96

Ober, J. 1991 'Hoplites and obstacles', in V.D. Hanson (ed.), *Hoplites: The Classical Greek Battle Experience*, London, Routledge, pp. 173–96

—— 1996 'The Rules of War in Classical Greece', in J. Ober, *The Athenian Revolution: Essays on Ancient Greek Democracy and Political Theory*, Princeton, Princeton University Press, pp. 53–71

Oldroyd, D.R. 1980 *Darwinian Impacts*, Milton Keynes, Open University Press

Oosterbeek, L. 1997 'War in the Chalcolithic? The meaning of the West Mediterranean hillforts', in J. Carman (ed.), *Material Harm: Archaeological Studies of War and Violence*, Glasgow, Cruithne Press, pp. 116–32

Opland, J. 1980 *Anglo-Saxon Oral Poetry: A Study of the Traditions*, New Haven, Yale University Press

Orschiedt, J. 1997 'Die Jungfernhöhle bei Tiefenellern: neue Interpretation der menschlichen Skelettreste', *Bericht Hist. Verein Bamberg* 133, pp. 185–97

—— 1998 'Ergebnisse einer neuen Untersuchung der spätmesolithischen Kopfbestattungen aus Süddeutschland', *Urgeschichtliche Materialhefte* 12, pp. 147–60

Orser, C.E. 1999 'Negotiating our "familiar" pasts', in S. Tarlow & S. West, (eds), *The Familiar Past? Archaeologies of Later Historical Britain*, London, Routledge, pp. 273–86

Osborne, R. 1987 *Classical Landscape with Figures*, London, Sheridan House

—— 1996 *Greece in the Making, 1200–479 BC*, London, Routledge

O'Shea, J.M. 1996 *Villagers of the Maros: A Portrait of an Early Bronze Age Society*, New York and London, Plenum Press

O'Shea, J. & Zvelebil, M. 1984 'Oleneostrovski Mogilnik: Reconstructing social and economic organization of prehistoric foragers in northern Russia', *J. Anthropological Archaeology* 3, pp. 1–40

Osgood, R. 1998 *Warfare in the Late Bronze Age of North Europe*, Oxford, British Archaeological Reports International Series 694

Oshibkina, S.V. 1982 'Mezoliticheskii mogil'nik "Popovo" na r. Kineme', *Sovetskaya arkheologiya* 1982/3, pp. 122–38

—— 1983 *Mezolit basseina Suhony i Vostochnogo Prionez'ya*, Moscow, Nauka

Otterbein, K.F. 1967a 'An analysis of Iroquois military tactics', in P. Bohannan (ed.), *Law and Warfare: Studies in the Anthropology of Conflict*, American Museum Sourcebooks in Anthropology, Garden City, New York, The Natural History Press, pp. 345–49

—— 1967b 'The evolution of Zulu warfare', in P. Bohannan (ed.), *Law and Warfare: Studies in the Anthropology of Conflict*, American Museum Sourcebooks in Anthropology, Garden City, New York, The Natural History Press, pp. 351–7

Page, D. 1975 *Epigrammata Graeca*, Oxford, Clarendon Press

Papaefthimiou-Papanthimou, A. 1987 'Tria neolithika eidolia apo to Mandalo tis Makedonias', in *Eilapini: Tomos timitikos gia ton kathigiti Nikolao Platona*, Herakleion, Vikelaia Vivliothiki, Dimos Herakleiou, pp. 171–7

Papaefthimiou-Papanthimou, A. & Pilali-Papasteriou, A. 1990a 'Anaskafes sto Mandalo', *To Arhaiologiko Ergo sti Makedonia kai Thraki* 1 (1987), Thessaloniki, Aristoteleio Panepistimio Thessalonikis, Ypourgeio Politismou, Ypourgeio Makedonias-Thrakis, pp. 173–80

—— 1990b 'I anaskafiki erevna sto Mandalo, 1987–1990, *Egnatia: Epetirida tou Istorikou kai Arhaiologikou Tmimatos tou Aristoteleiou Panepistimiou Thessalonikis* 2, pp. 411–21

—— 1991 'Anaskafi sto Mandalo', *To Arhaiologiko Ergo sti Makedonia kai Thraki* 2 (1988), Thessaloniki, Aristoteleio Panepistimio Thessalonikis, Ypourgeio Politismou, Ypourgeio Makedonias-Thrakis, pp. 127–35

—— 1993 'O proistorikos oikismos sto Mandalo: Nea stoiheia stin proistoria tis Makedonias', *Ancient Macedonia V: Papers Read at the Fifth International Symposium Held in Thessaloniki, October 10–15, 1989*, Vol. 2. Thessaloniki, Institute for Balkan Studies, pp. 1207–16

Papathanassopoulos, G.A. (ed.) 1996 *Neolithic Culture in Greece*, Athens, Nicholas P. Goulandris Foundation, Museum of Cycladic Art

Pare, C.F.E. 1992 *Wagons and Wagon-graves of the Early Iron Age in Central Europe*, Oxford University Committee for Archaeology Monograph 35

Pariente, A. 1991 'Chronique de fouilles et découvertes archéologiques en Grèce en 1990', *Bulletin de Correspondance Hellénique* 115, pp. 835–957

Pashkevich, G.A. 1982 'Paleobotanicheskaya harakteristika poseleniya Mirnoe', in V.A. Stanko (ed.), *Mirnoe: Problema mezolita stepei Severnogo Prichernomor'ya*, Kiev, Naukova Dumka, pp. 132–8

—— 1997 'Early farming in the Ukraine', in J. Chapman & P. Dolukhanov (eds), *Landscapes in Flux: Central and Eastern Europe in Antiquity*, Oxford, Oxbow Books, pp. 263–74

Passingham, R. 1982 *The Human Primate*, Oxford, Freeman

Patay, P. 1984 *Die Kupferzeitliche Meissel, Beile und Äxte in Ungarn*, Prähistorische Bronzefunde IX/15, Munich, C.H. Beck

—— 1990 'Die kupferzeitliche Siedlung von Tiszaluc-Sarkad', *Jahresschrift für Mitteldeutsche Vorgeschichte* 73, pp. 131–6

Patokova, E.F. 1979 *Usatovskoe poselenie i mogil'niki*, Kiev, Naukova Dumka

Paunescu, Al. 1970 *Evoluţia unelţelor şi armelor de piatră cioplтă descoperite pe teritoriul României*, Bucureşti, Editura Academiei Republicii Socialiste România

—— 1987 'Les industries lithiques du Néolithique ancien de la Roumanie et quelques considerations sur l'inventaire lithique des cultures du Néolithique moyen de cette contrée', in J.K. Kozłowski & S. K. Kozłowski (eds), *Chipped Stone Industries of the Early Farming Cultures in Europe*, Kraków, Jagiellonian University, pp. 75–94

Pavúk, J. 1991 'Lengyel-culture fortified settlements in Slovakia', *Antiquity* 65, pp. 348–57

Pavúk, J. & Bátora, J. 1995 *Siedlung und Gräber der Ludanice-Gruppe in Jelšovce*, Nitra, Archaeological Institute of Slovak Academy of Sciences

Penrose, L.S. 1952 *On the Objective Study of Crowd Behaviour*, Lewis

Péquart, S.-J. & Péquart, M. 1931 'Sur une vertèbre humaine mésolithique percée d'une flèche', in *Congrés de l'Association française pour l'avancement des sciences*, Nancy, pp. 321–4

Peregrine, P. 1992 *Mississippian Evolution: A World-system Perspective*, Monographs in World Archaeology 9, Madison WI, Prehistory Press

—— 1993 'An archaeological correlate of war', *North American Archaeologist* 14.2, pp. 139–51

Perrett, B. 1992 *The Battle Book: Crucial Conflicts in History from 1469 BC to the Present*, London, Arms and Armour Press

Petrasch, J. 1991 'Mittelneolithische Kreisgraben in Mitteleuropa', *Bericht der Römisch-Germanischen Kommission* 71, pp. 407–564

Pétrequin, A.-M. & Pétrequin, P. 1990 'Flèches de chasse, flèches de guerre: le cas des Danis d'Irian Jaya (Indonésie)', *Bulletin de la Société Préhistorique Française* 87, pl. 10–12, pp. 484–511

Petty, G. & Petty, S. 1993 'A geological reconstruction of the site of the Battle of Maldon', in J. Cooper (ed.), *The Battle of Maldon: Fiction and Fact*, London and Rio Grande, The Hambledon Press, pp. 159–69

Pfeffer, G. 1987 'The Vocabulary of Anglo-Saxon Kinship,' *L'Homme* 27.3., pp. 113–28

Piggott, S. 1954 *The Neolithic Cultures of the British Isles*, Cambridge, Cambridge University Press

—— 1962 *The West Kennet Long Barrow Excavations 1955–56*, Ministry of Works Archaeological Reports 4, London, HMSO

—— 1983 *The Earliest Wheeled Transport: From the Atlantic Coast to the Caspian Sea*, London, Thames and Hudson

Pilali-Papasteriou, A. & Papaefthimiou-Papanthimou, A. 1989 'Nees anaskafikes erevnes sto Mandalo D. Makedonias, 1985–1986', *Egnatia: Epetirida tou Istorikou kai Arhaiologikou Tmimatos tou Aristoteleiou Panepistimiou Thessalonikis* 1, pp. 17–28

Pilali-Papasteriou, A., Papaefthimiou-Papanthimou, A., Kotsakis, K. & Savopoulou, T. 1986 'Neos proistorikos oikismos sto Mandalo Ditikis Makedonias', *Ancient Macedonia IV: Papers Read at the Fourth International Symposium Held in Thessaloniki, September 21–25, 1983*, Thessaloniki, Institute for Balkan Studies. pp. 451–65

Plesl, E. 1961 *Lužická kultura v severozápadních Čechách*, Prague, Czech Academy of Sciences

Plog, F. 1984 'Exchange, tribes, and alliances: The Northern Southwest', *American Archaeology* 4, pp. 217–23

Plog, S. 1997 *Ancient Peoples of the American Southwest*, London, Thames and Hudson

Podborský, V. 1988 *Těšetice-Kyjovice 4: Rondel osady lidu s moravskou malovanou keramikou*, Brno, Univ. J.E. Purkyně, Filosofická fakulta

Praslov, N.D. 1984 'Rannii paleolit Russkoi ravniny i Kryma', in P.I. Boriskovsky (ed.), *Paleolit SSSR* (Arkheologiya SSSR), Moscow, Nauka, pp. 94–134

Prestwich, M. 1996 *Armies and Warfare in the Middle Ages: The English experience*, London and New Haven CT, Yale University Press

Price, B. 1984 'Competition, productive intensification, and ranked society: Speculations from evolutionary theory', in R.B. Ferguson (ed.), *Warfare, Culture and Environment*, Orlando FL, Academic Press, pp. 209–40

Price, T.D. 1985 'Affluent foragers of Mesolithic southern Scandinavia', in T.D. Price and J.A. Brown (eds) *Prehistoric Hunter-Gatherers: The Emergence of Complexity*, Orlando FL and London, Academic Press, pp. 341–63

Price, T.D. & Feinman, G. (eds) 1995 *Foundations of Social Inequality*, New York, Plenum Press

Priebe, H. 1938 *Die Westgruppe der Kugelamphoren*, Halle, Gebauer-Schwetschke

Pritchett, W.K, 1974–94 *The Greek State at War*, Vols I–V, Berkeley and Los Angeles, University of California Press

—— 1985 *Studies in Ancient Greek Topography*, Part V, Berkeley and Los Angeles, University of California Press

Pryor, F.M. 1976 'A Neolithic multiple burial from Fengate, Peterborough', *Antiquity* 50, pp. 223–33

—— 1984 *Excavations at Fengate, Peterborough, England: The Fourth Report*, Toronto, Royal Ontario Museum Archaeological Monograph 7 (Northants. Archaeol. Soc. Monograph 2)

Pyke G. & Yiouni, P. 1996 *Nea Nikomedeia I: The Excavation of an Early Neolithic Village in Northern Greece, 1961–1964. The Excavation and the Ceramic Assemblage*, British School at Athens Supplement 25, London

Radosavljević-Krunić, S. 1986 'Résultats de l'étude anthropologique des squelettes provenant du site Ajmana', *Djerdapske Sveske* III, pp. 51–8

Radovanović, I. 1981 *Ranoholocenska kremena industrija sa lokaliteta Padina u Djerdap*, Beograd, Arheološki Institut SAN

—— 1994 'A review of formal disposal areas in the Mesolithic of Europe', *Starinar* 44, pp. 93–102

—— 1996 *The Iron Gates Mesolithic*, Ann Arbor MI: International Monographs in Prehistory

Raduntcheva, A. 1976 *Vinica – eneolitno selishte i nekropol*, Sofia, Bulgarian Academy of Sciences

Randsborg, K. 1995 *Hjortspring: Warfare and Sacrifice in Early Europe*, Aarhus, Aarhus University Press

—— (ed.) forthcoming, *Kephallenia – Archaeology and History: The Greek Cities*, Acta Archaeologica Supplementum, Copenhagen

Rausing, G. 1967 *The Bow: Some Notes on its Origin and Development*, Acta Archaeological Lundensia, series in 8°, 6, Lund, Gleerup/Bonn, Habelt

—— 1991 'The chariots of the petroglyphs', in K. Jennbert, L. Larsson, R. Petré & B. Wyszomirska-Werbart (eds), *Regions and Reflections: In Honour of Märta Strömberg*, Lund, Acta Archaeologica Lundensia, Series in 8°, 20, pp. 153–62

Redmond, E.M. 1994 *Tribal and Chiefly Warfare in South America*, Ann Arbor: Museum of Anthropology, University of Michigan

Renfrew, C. 1969 'The autonomy of the south-east European Copper Age', *Proc. Prehist. Soc.* 35, pp. 12–47

—— 1972 *The Emergence of Civilisation: The Cyclades and the Aegean in the Third Millennium B.C.*, London, Methuen

—— 1973 *Before Civilization: The Radiocarbon Revolution and Prehistoric Europe*, London, Jonathan Cape

—— 1986 'Varna and the emergence of wealth', in A. Appadurai (ed.), *The Social Life of Things*, Cambridge, Cambridge University Press, pp. 141–68

Renfrew, C. & Cherry, J.F. (eds) 1986 *Peer-polity Interaction and Socio-political Change*, Cambridge, Cambridge University Press

Reynolds, T. 1990 'The Middle-Upper Palaeolithic transition in southwestern France: Interpreting the lithic evidence', in P. Mellars (ed.), *The Emergence of Modern Humans*, Ithaca NY, Cornell University Press, pp. 262–75

Rhomiopoulou, K. & Kilian-Dirlmeier, I. 1989 'Neue Funde aus der eisenzeitlichen Hügelnekropole von Vergina, Griechisch Makedonien', *Prähistorische Zeitschrift* 64/1, pp. 86–151

Richards, J.D. 1984 'Funerary Symbolism in Anglo-Saxon England: Further Social Dimensions of Mortuary Practices,' *Scottish Archaeological Review* 3.1, pp. 42–55

Ridley, C. & Wardle, K.A. 1979 'Rescue excavations at Servia, 1971–73: A preliminary report', *Annual of the British School of Archaeology at Athens* 74, pp. 185–230

Rigaud, J.-P. & Simek, J.F. 1998 'Interpreting spatial patterning at the Grotte XV', in E.M.L. Kroll & T.D Price (eds), *The Interpreting of Archaelogical Spatial Patterning*, New York and London, Plenum Press, pp. 199–220

Rivers, T.J.1991 'Adultery in Early Anglo-Saxon Society: Æthelberht 31 in Comparison with Continental Germanic Law,' in M. Lapidge (ed.), *Anglo-Saxon England* 20, Cambridge, Cambridge University Press, pp. 19–25

Rivers, W.H.R. 1924 *Instinct and the Unconscious*, Cambridge, Cambridge University Press

Robbins, L.H. & Lynch, B.M. 1978 'New evidence on the use of microliths from the Lake Turkana Basin, East Africa', *Current Anthropology* 19, pp. 619–20

Rodwell, W. 1993a 'The battle of *Assundun* and its Memorial Church: A reappraisal', in J. Cooper (ed.), *The Battle of Maldon: Fiction and Fact*, London and Rio Grande, The Hambledon Press, pp. 127–58

—— 1993b 'The Role of the Church in the Development of Roman and Early Anglo-Saxon London', in M. Carver (ed.), *In Search of Cult*, Woodbridge, Boydell Press, pp. 91–8

Roesch, P. 1965 *Thespies et la confédération béotienne*, Paris, Éditions E. de Bocard

Rolland, N. 1990 'Middle Palaeolithic socio-economic formations in Western Eurasia: An exploratory survey', in P. Mellars (ed.), *The Emergence of Modern Humans*, Ithaca NY, Cornell University Press, pp. 347–88

Roloff, G. 1903 *Probleme aus der griechischen Kriegsgeschichte*, Berlin, E. Ebering

Roman, P. 1977 *The Late Copper Age Coţofeni Culture of South-East Europe*, Oxford, BAR Int. Series 32

Roper, M.K. 1969 'A survey of the evidence for intrahuman killing in the Pleistocene', *Current Anthropology* 10, pp. 427–59

Rosenberg, G. 1937 *Hjortspringfundet*, Nordiske Fortidsminder III/1, Copenhagen, Gyldendal

Rowlands, M. 1980 'Kinship, alliance and exchange in the European Bronze Age', in J. Barrett & R. Bradley (eds), *Settlement and Society in the British Later Bronze Age*, Oxford, British Archaeological Reports 83, pp. 15–55

Rutter, J.B. 1998 *The Prehistoric Archaeology of the Aegean*, http://devlab.cs.dartmouth. edu/history/bronze_age

Ryan, D.J. 1977 'The Paleopathology and Paleoepidemiology of the Kayenta Anasazi Indians in Northeastern Arizona', unpublished PhD thesis, Tempe AZ University

Sallé, A. 1990 'Les mystères de l'archéologie', *Archaeologia* (Paris) 263, pp. 34–40

Salmon, P. 1953 'L'Armée fédérale des Béotiens', *L'Antiquité classique* 22, pp. 347–60

Sandars, N.K. 1961 'The first Aegean swords and their ancestry', *American J. Archaeology* 65, pp. 17–29

—— 1985 *The Sea Peoples: Warriors of the Ancient Mediterranean* (2nd edn), London, Thames and Hudson

Sanderson, S.K. 1992 *Social Evolutionism: A Critical History*, Oxford, Blackwell

Sauter, M.-R. 1976 *Switzerland from Earliest Times to the Roman Conquest*, London, Thames and Hudson

Savvaidis P., Doukas, G. & Bandellas, L. 1988 'Apotiposi anaskafon me geodetikes methodous: Efarmogi stin anaskafi Mandalou Giannitson', *Arhaiologia* 28, pp. 55–6

Schauer, P. 1971 *Die Schwerter in Süddeutschland, Österreich und der Schweiz I*, Prähistorische Bronzefunde Abt. IV, Band 2, Munich, Beck

—— 1979 'Eine urnenfelderzeitliche Kampfweise', *Archäologisches Korrespondenzblatt* 9, pp. 69–80

—— 1984 'Überregionale Gemeinsamkeiten bei Waffengräbern der ausgehenden Bronzezeit und älteren Urnenfelderzeit des Voralpenraumes', *Jahrbuch des Römisch-Germanischen Zentralmuseums Mainz* 31, pp. 209–35

—— 1990 'Schutz- und Angriffswaffen bronzezeitlicher Krieger im Spiegel ausgewählter Grabfunde Mitteleuropas', in *Beiträge zur Geschichte und Kultur der mitteleuropäischen Bronzezeit*, Berlin-Nitra, Archeologický Ústav Slovenskej Akadémie Vied/Akademie der Wissenschaften der DDR, pp. 381–410

Schiffer, M.B. 1977 *Behavioral Archaeology*, New York, Seminar Books

Schmidgen-Hager, E. 1992 'Das bandkeramische Erdwerk von Heilbronn-Neckargartach', *Fundberichte aus Baden-Württemberg* 17/1, pp. 173–291

Schmidt, H. 1932 *Cucuteni in der oberen Moldau, Rumänien*, Berlin/Leipzig

Schmidt, S. 1993 'Kriege bei rezenten Wildbeutern und Nicht-Wildbeutern', *Archäologische Informationen* 16/2, pp. 189–99

Schneirla, T.C. 1973 'Instinct and aggression', in A. Montagu (ed.), *Man and Aggression*, Oxford University Press, pp. 144–9

Schwidetsky, I. 1971–2 'Menschliche Skelettreste von Vinča', *Glasnik Antropološkog Društva Jugoslavije* 8–9, pp. 101–12

Scott, D.D., Fox, R.A., Connor, M.A. & Harmon, D. 1989 *Archaeological Perspectives on the Battle of the Little Big Horn*, Norman O and London, University of Oklahoma Press

Scott, E. 1997 'Introduction: On the Incompleteness of Archaeological Narratives', in J. Moore & E. Scott (eds), *Invisible People and Processes: Writing Gender and Childhood into European Archaeology*, London and New York, Leicester University Press, pp. 1–12

Scull, C. 1993 'Archaeology, Early Anglo-Saxon Society and the Origins of Anglo-Saxon Kingdoms', in W. Filmer-Sankey (ed.), *Anglo-Saxon Studies in Archaeology and History* 6, Oxford, Oxford University Committee for Archaeology, pp. 65–82

Séfériadès, M. 1995 '*Spondylus gaederopus*: the earliest European long-distance exchange system', *Poročilo o raziskovanju paleolitika, neolitika in eneolitika v Sloveniji* 22, pp. 233–56

Selkirk, A.R. 1971 'Ascot-under-Wychwood', *Current Archaeology* 3, pp. 24, 7–10

Seymour, P. 1922 'Note on the Boiotian League', *Classical Review* 36, p. 70

Shackleton, N. & Renfrew, C. 1970 'Neolithic trade routes re-aligned by oxygen isotope analysis', *Nature* 228, pp. 1062–5

Shennan, S.J. 1982 'Ideology, change and European Early Bronze Age', in I. Hodder (ed.), *Symbolic and Structural Archaeology*, Cammbridge, Cambridge University Press, pp. 155–61

Sheridan, A. 1992 'Two Scottish firsts – The Rotten Bottom longbow', *PAST* 14, p. 6

Sherratt, A. 1982 'Mobile resources: Settlement and exchange in early agricultural Europe', in C. Renfrew & S. Shennan (eds), *Ranking, Resource and Exchange*, Cambridge, Cambridge University Press, pp. 13–26, reprinted in A. Sherratt 1997, *Economy and Society in Prehistoric Europe: Changing Perspectives*, Princeton, Princeton University Press, pp. 252–69

—— 1987 'Neolithic exchange systems in Central Europe', in G. de G. Sieveking & M.N. Newcomer (eds), *The Human Uses of Flint and Chert*, Brighton, Harvester Press, pp. 193–204

—— 1996 'The transformation of early agrarian Europe: The Later Neolithic and Copper Ages', in B. Cunliffe (ed.), *The Oxford Illustrated Prehistory of Europe*, Oxford, Oxford University Press, pp. 167–201

Simek, J.F. & Price, H.A. 1990 'Chronological change in Perigord lithic assemblages', in P. Mellars (ed.), *The Emergence of Modern Humans*, Ithaca NY, Cornell University Press, pp. 243–61

Sinitsyn, A.A., Praslov, N.D., Svezhentsev, Yu.S. & Sulerzhitskii, L.D. 1997 'Radiouglerodnaya hronologiya verhnego paleolita Vostochnoi Evropy', in A.A. Sinitsyn & N.D. Praslov (eds), *Radiouglerodnaya hronologiya verhnego paleolita Vostochnoi Evropy i Severnoi Azii: Problemy i perspektivy*, St Petersburg, Institut istorii materialnoi kultury RAN

Smith, B.D. 1989 'Origins of agriculture in Eastern North America', *Science* 246, pp. 1566–71

Smith, M.O. 1995 'Scalping in the Archaic period: Evidence from the Western Tennessee Valley', *Southeastern Archaeology* 14, pp. 60–8

Snodgrass, A.1964 *Early Greek Armour and Weapons from the Bronze Age to 600BC*, Edinburgh, Edinburgh University Press

—— 1971 'The first European body-armour', in J. Boardman, M.A. Brown & T.G.E. Powell (eds), *The European Community in Later Prehistory: Studies in Honour of C.F.C. Hawkes*, London, Routledge and Kegan Paul, pp. 31–50

Sofaer Derevenski, J. 1997 'Age and gender at the site of Tiszapolgár-Basatanya, Hungary', *Antiquity* 71, pp. 875–89

Soffer, O. 1985 *The Upper Palaeolithic of the Russian Plain*, Orlando FL, Academic Press

—— 1993 'Upper Palaeolithic adaptations in Central and Eastern Europe and man–mammoth interactions', in O. Soffer & N.D. Praslov (eds), *From Kostenki to Clovis: Upper Palaeolithic – Palaeo-Indian Adaptations*, New York and London, Plenum Press, pp. 31–50

Spatz, H. 1998 'Krisen, Gewalt, Tod – zum Ende der ersten Ackerbauernkultur Mitteleuropas', in A. Häusser (ed.), *Krieg oder Frieden? Herxheim vor 7000 Jahren. Katalog zur Sonderausstellung*, Herxheim, Landesamt für Denkmalpflege Speyer, pp. 10–19

Spence, I.G. 1993 *The Cavalry of Classical Greece: A Social and Military History*, Oxford, Clarendon Press

Spriggs. M. (ed.) 1984 *Marxist Perspectives in Archaeology*, Cambridge, Cambridge University Press

Sprockhoff, E. 1930 *Zur Handelsgeschichte der germanischen Bronzezeit*, Vorgeschichtliche Forschungen 7, Berlin, de Gruyter

Srejović, D. 1969 *Lepenski Vir: Nova praistorijska kultura u Podunavlju*, Beograd, Srpska kniževna zadruga

—— (ed.) 1988 *The Neolithic in Serbia*, Beograd, University of Belgrade

—— 1989 'The Mesolithic of Serbia and Montenegro', in C. Bonsall (ed.), *The Mesolithic in Europe*, Edinburgh, John Donald, pp. 481–91

Srejović, D. & Babović, Lj. 1984 *Umetnost Lepenskog Vira*, Beograd, Jugoslavia

Stanev, P. 1982 'Stratigrafiya i periodizacija na neolitnite objekti i kulturi po basejna na reka Jantra', *Godishnik na Muzeite ot Severna Bulgariya* 8, pp. 1–15

Stanko, V.N. 1982 *Mirnoe: Problema mezolita stepei Severnogo Prichernomor'ya*, Kiev, Naukova Dumka

—— 1997a 'Landscape dynamics and Mesolithic settlement in the North Pontic Steppe', in J. Chapman & P. Dolukhanov (eds), *Landscapes in Flux: Central and Eastern Europe in Antiquity*, Oxford, Oxbow Books, pp. 253–62

—— (ed.) 1997b *Davnya istoriya Ukrainy*, Vol. 1, Kiev, Naukova Dumka

Stary, F.P. 1979 'Foreign Elements in Etruscan Arms and Armour: 8th to 3rd centuries BC', *Proc. Prehist. Soc.* 45, pp. 179–206

—— 1982 'Zur hallstattzeitlichen Beilbewaffnung des circum-alpinen Raumes', *Bericht der Römisch-Germanischen Kommission* 63, pp. 17–104

—— 1991 'Arms and Armour of the Nuragic Warrior-Statuettes', in B.S. Frizell (ed.), *Arte militare e architettura Nuragica: Nuragic Architecture in its Military, Territorial and Socio-Economic Context*, Proc. First International Colloquium on Nuragic Architecture, Skrifter utgivna av Svenska institutet i Rom, series in 4°, XLVIII, pp. 119–42

Steuer, H. 1989 'Erdwerke', in *Reallexikon der Germanischen Altertumskunde*, Band 7, Berlin, de Gruyter, pp. 443–75

Stewart, T.D. 1959 'The restored Shanidar I skull', *Smithsonian Report for 1958*, pp. 473–80

Stig Sørensen, M.L. 1997 'Reading dress: The construction of social categories and identities in Bronze Age Europe', *J. European Archaeology* 5/1, pp. 93–114

Stolyar, A.D. 1959 'Pervyi Vasil'evskii mezoliticheskii mogil'nik', *Arkheologicheskii Sbornik Gosudarstvennogo Ermitazha* 1, pp. 78–165

Strassburg, J. 1997 'Inter the Mesolithic – Unearth Social Histories: Vexing Androcentric Sexing through Strøby Egede,' *Current Swedish Archaeology* 5, 155–78

Streuver, S. & Holton, F.A. 1979 *Koster: Americans in Search of the Prehistoric Past*, New York, Anchor Press

Tainter, J.A. 1990 *The Collapse of Complex Societies*, Cambridge, Cambridge University Press

Tasić, N. 1979 'Bubanj-Salcuṭa-Krivodol kompleks', in A. Benac (ed.), *Praistorija jugoslavenskih zemalja III*, Sarajevo, Akademija Nauka i Umjetnosti Bosne i Hercegovine, pp. 87–113

Telegin, D.Ya. 1961 'Vasylevs'kii tretii nekropol' v Nadporozzi', *Arkheologiya* (Kiev) 13, pp. 3–19

—— 1973 *Seredn'o stohiv'ka kul'tura epokhy midi*, Kiev, Naukova

—— 1977 'Ob absolujutnom vozraste jamnok kul'tury i nekotorye voprosy khronologii eneolita Juga Ukrainy', *Sovetskaya Arkheologija* 2, pp. 5–19

—— 1982 *Mezolitichni pam'yatki Ukrainy*, Kiev, Naukova Dumka

Teschler-Nicola, M. et al. 1995 'Traumatische Veränderungen an den linearbandkeramischen Skelettresten aus dem Erdwerk von Asparn/Schletz, NÖ', in *Aktuelle Fragen des frühen und mittleren Neolithikums in Mitteleuropa*, Poysdorf

Theocharis, D.R. 'The Neolithic civilization: A brief survey', in D.R. Theocharis (ed.), *Neolithic Greece*, Athens, National Bank of Greece, pp. 17–128

Thomas, J. 1991 *Rethinking the Neolithic*, Cambridge, Cambridge University Press

—— 1996 *Time, Culture and Identity: An Interpretative Archaeology*, London, Routledge

Thrane, H. 1975 *Europæisker forbindelser: Bidrag til studiet af fremmede forbindelser i Danmarks yngre broncealder (periode IV–V)*, Copenhagen, Nationalmuseets Skrifter Arkæologisk-Historisk række 16

—— 1990 'The Mycenaean fascination: A northerner's view', in *Orientalisch-ägäische Einflüsse in der europäischen Bronzezeit*, Mainz, Römisch-Germanisches Zentralmuseum, Monographien 15, pp. 165–79

Timby, J.R. et al. 1993 'Sancton I Anglo-Saxon Cemetery: Excavations Carried out between 1976 and 1980,' *Archaeological Journal* 150, pp. 243–365

—— 1996 *The Anglo-Saxon Cemetery at Empingham II, Rutland: Excavations Carried out between 1974 and 1975*, Oxbow Monograph 70, Oxford, Oxbow Books and Oakville CT, David Brown Book Co.

Tinbergen, N. 1976 'Ethology in a changing world', in P.P.G. Bateson & R.A. Hinde (eds), *Growing Points in Ethology*, Cambridge, Cambridge University Press, pp. 507–27

Todorova, H. 1975 'Arheologichesko prouchvane na selishnata mogila i nekropola pri Goljamo Delchevo, Varnensko', in H. Todorova, S. Ivanov, V. Vasilev, M. Hopf, H. Quitta & G. Kohl (eds), *Selishnata mogila pri Goljamo Delchevo*, Sofia, Bulgarian Academy of Sciences, pp. 5–243

—— 1981 *Die Kupferzeitliche Äxte und Beile in Bulgarien*, Prähistorische Bronzefunde IX/14, Munich C.H. Beck

—— 1982 'Kupferzeitliche Siedlungen in Nordostbulgarien', *Materialien zur allgemeinen und vergleichenden Archäologie* 14, Munich

—— 1983 'Arheologicheskie issledovanije praistoricheskih objektov v raione s. Ovcharovo, Targovishtskogo okrug', in H. Todorova, V. Vasilev, Z. Yanushevitsch, M. Kovacheva & P. Vulev (eds), *Ovcharovo*, Sofia, Bulgarian Academy of Sciences, pp. 5–105

Tomlinson, R. & Fossey, J. 1970 'Ancient Remains on Mount Mavrouni, South Boiotia', *Annual of the British School at Athens* 65, pp. 243–63

Touchais, G. 1986 'Chronique de fouilles et découvertes archéologiques en Grèce en 1985', *Bulletin de Correspondance Hellénique* 110, pp. 671–761

Toynbee, A.J. 1951 *A Study of History*, Oxford, Oxford University Press

Trbuhović, V. & Vasiljević, M. 1973/4 "Obrovci" – poseban tip neolitskih naselja u zapadnoj Srbiji', *Starinar* 24/25, pp. 157–62

Treherne, P. 1995 'The warrior's beauty: The masculine body and self-identity in Bronze Age Europe', *J. European Archaeology* 3.1, pp. 105–44

Tringham, R. 1972 'Territorial demarcation of prehistoric settlements', in P.J. Ucko, G.W. Dimbleby & R. Tringham (eds), *Man, Settlement and Urbanism*, London, Duckworth, pp. 463–76

Tringham, R. & Krstić, D. 1990 'Conclusion: Selevac in the wider context of European prehistory', in R. Tringham & D. Krstić (eds), *Selevac: A Neolithic Village in Yugoslavia*, Monumenta Archaeologica 15, Los Angeles, University of California Press, pp. 567–617

Tringham, R. & Stevanović, M. 1990 'The nonceramic uses of clay', in R. Tringham & D. Krstić (eds), *Selevac: A Neolithic Village in Yugoslavia*, Monumenta Archaeologica 15, Los Angeles, University of California Press, pp. 323–96

Trinkaus, E. 1983 *The Shanidar Neanderthals*, Orlando FL, Academic Press

Trnka, G. 1991 *Studien zu mittelneolithischen Kreisgrabenanlagen*, Vienna, Verlag der Österreichischen Akademie der Wissenschaften

Trogmayer, O. 1990 'Der Gott mit Axt: Gedanken zu einem neuen Statuettenfund Statuette V', in P. Raczky. (ed.), *Alltag und Religion: Jungsteinzeit in Ost-Ungarn*, Frankfurt-am-Main, Museum für Vor- und Frühgeschichte, pp. 66–9

Tsokas, G.N., Rocca, A.C. & Papazachos, B.C. 1986 'Magnetic prospecting at the prehistoric site of the village of Mandalo in northern Greece', in Y. Liritzis & T. Hackens (eds), *First South European Conference on Archaeometry, Delphi 1984*, Strasburg, Council of Europe, pp. 159–67

Tsountas, H. 1908 *Ai proistorikai akropoleis Diminiou kai Sesklou*, Athens, P.D. Sakellariou

Tuplin, C., 1986 'The Fate of Thespiae During the Theban Hegemony', *Athenaeum* 64, pp. 321–41

Turney-High, H. 1949 (2nd edn 1971) *Primitive War: Its Practice and Concepts*, Columbia, University of South Carolina Press

Turner, A.K. 1995 'Genetic and hormonal influences on male violence', in J. Archer (ed.), *Male Violence*, Routledge, pp. 233–52

Turner, C.G. 1989 'Teec Nos Pos: more possible cannibalism in Northeastern Arizona', *The Kiva* 54, pp. 147–52

—— 1993 'Cannibalism in Chaco Canyon: The Charnel Pit excavated in 1926 at Small House Ruin by F.H.H. Roberts, Jr.', *American Journal of Physical Anthropology* 91, pp. 421–39

Turner, C.G. & Turner, J.A. 1992 'The first claim for cannibalism in the Southwest: Walter Hough's 1901 discovery at Canyon Butte Ruin 3, Northeastern Arizona,' *American Antiquity* 57, pp. 661–82

—— 1995 'Cannibalism in the Prehistoric American Southwest: Incidence, taphonomy, explanation, and suggestions for standardized world definitions', *Anthropological Science* 103/1, pp. 1–22

Tylor, E.B. 1881 *Anthropology*, London, Macmillan

Ullrich, H. 1971 'Skelette und trepanierte Schädel der Kugelamphorenleute aus Ketzin, Kr. Nauen', *Veröffentlichungen des Museums für Ur- und Frühgeschichte Potsdam* 6, pp. 37–55

—— 1982 'Artificial injuries on Upper Palaeolithic human fossils found in Czechoslovakia', in V.V. Novotný (ed.) *2nd Anthropological Congress of Aleš Hrdlička*, Prague, Universitas Carolina Pragensis, pp. 451–4

Unverzagt, W. & Herrmann, J. 1958 'Das slawische Brandgräberfeld von Prutzke, Kr. Eberswalde', *Ausgrabungen und Funde* 3, pp. 107–10

Vajsov, I. 1993 'Die frühesten Metalldolchen Südost- und Mitteleuropas', *Prähistorische Zeitschrift* 68, pp. 103–45

Valamoti, S. 1989 'The Plant Remains from the Late Neolithic–Early Bronze Age Site of Mandalo, Macedonia, Greece', unpublished MSc thesis, University of Sheffield

—— 1995 'Georgika proionta apo to neolithiko oikismo Giannitsa B: prokatarktiki prosengisi meso ton arhaiovotanikon dedomenon', *To Arhailogiko Ergo sti Makedonia kai Thraki* 6, 1992, Thessaloniki, Aristoteleio Panepistimio Thessalonikis, Ypourgeio Politismou, Ypourgeio Makedonias-Thrakis, pp. 177–84

Van Wees, H. 1994 'The Homeric Way of War: The Iliad and the Hoplite Phalanx (I) and (II)', *Greece and Rome* (2nd Ser.) 41/1 and 2, pp. 1–18, 132–55

Van West, C.R. 1994 *Modelling Prehistoric Agricultural Productivity in Southwestern Colorado: A GIS Approach*, Pullman WA, Washington State University Department of Anthropology Reports of Investigations 67

Vasić, M.M. 1902 'Die neolithische Station Jablanica bei Medžuluzje in Serbien', *Archiv für Anthropologie* 27, pp. 517–82

—— 1911 'Gradac, preistorisko nalazište latenskog doba', *Glasnik Srpske Kraljevinske Akademie* 85, pp. 97–134

Vasilev, V.K. 1985 'Izledvaniya na faunata ot selishna mogila Ovcharovo', *Interdisciplinarni Izledvaniya* 13, pp. 11–199

Vávra, M. 1990 'Die Höhensiedlungen der Lengyel-Kultur in Böhmen', *Jahresschrift für mitteldeutsche Vorgeschichte* 73, pp. 183–9

Vayda, A.P. 1961 'Expansion and warfare among swidden agriculturalists', *American Anthropologist* 63, pp. 346–58

—— 1974 'Warfare in ecological perspective', *Annual Review of Ecology and Systematics* 5, pp. 21–31

Veit, U. 1993 'Burials within settlements of the Linienbandkeramik und Stichbandkeramik cultures of Central Europe', *J. European Archaeology* 1, pp. 107–40

Vencl, S. 1960 'Kamenné nástroje prvních zemědělců střední Europě – Les instruments lithiques des premiers agriculteurs en Europe Centrale', *Acta Musei Nationalis Pragae* 14 A, pl. 1–2, pp. 1–116

—— 1979 'Počátky zbraní – The origins of weapons', *Archeologické rozhledy* 31, pp. 640–94

—— 1980 'K poznání méně nápadných artefaktů', *Archeologické rozhledy* 32, pp. 521–37

—— 1983 'K problematice fortifikací v archeologii – Fortifications and their problems in archaeology', *Archeologické rozhledy* 34, pp. 284–315

—— 1984a *Otázky poznání vojenství v archeologii – Problems Relating to the Knowledge of Warfare in Archaeology*, Prague, Archeologické studijní materiály 14, Archaeological Institute

—— 1984b 'War and warfare in archaeology', *J. Anthropological Archaeology* 3, pp. 116–32

—— 1984c 'Stopy zranění zbraněmi jako archeologický pramen poznání vojenství – Traces of injuries by weapons as archaeological evidence of warfare', *Archeologické rozhledy* 36, pp. 528–45

—— 1991 'Interprétation des blessures causées par les armes au Mésolithique', *L'Anthropologie* 95/1, pp. 219–28

Videiko, M.Y. 1994 'Tripolye – "pastoral" contacts, facts and character of interactions, 4800–3200 BC', *Baltic-Pontic Studies* 2, pp. 29–71

Vokotopoulou, I. 1986 *Vitsa: Ta nekrotapheia mias molossikis komis*, Dimosievmata tou archaiologikou deltiou 33, Athens, tameio archaiologikon poron kai apallotrioseon

Völling, T. 1990 'Funditores im römischen Heer', *Saalburg-Jahrbuch* 45, pp. 24–58

Von Clausewitz, C. 1976 [1832] *On War* (ed. and trans. M. Howard and P. Paret), Princeton NJ, Princeton University Press

Von Soden, W. 1994 *The Ancient Orient*, Michigan, Eerdmans

Von Treitschke, H. 1916 *Politics*, Constable

Voytek, B. 1990. 'The use of stone resources', in R. Tringham & D. Krstić (eds), *Selevac: A Neolithic Village in Yugoslavia*, Monumenta Archaeologica 15, Los Angeles, University of California Press, pp. 437–94

Vulpe, A. 1975 *Die Äxte und Beile in Rumanien*, Prähistorische Bronzefunde II, Munich, C.H. Beck

Vutiropulos, N. 1991 'The sling in the Aegean Bronze Age', *Antiquity* 65, pp. 279–86

Wahl, J. & Höhn, B. 1988 'Eine Mehrfachbestattung der Michelsberger Kultur aus Heidelberg-Handschuhsheim, Rhein-Neckar-Kreis', *Fundberichte aus Baden-Württemberg* 13, pp. 123–98

Wahl, J. & König, H. 1987 'Anthropologisch-traumalogische Untersuchung der menschlichen Skelettreste aus dem bandkeramischen Massengrab bei Talheim, Kreis Heilbronn', *Fundberichte aus Baden-Württemberg* 12, pp. 65–193

Wakely, J. 1997 'Identification and analysis of violent and non-violent head injuries in osteo-archaeological material', in J. Carman (ed.), *Material Harm: Archaeological Studies of War and Violence*, Glasgow, Cruithne Press, pp. 24–46

Warry, J. 1980 *Warfare in the Classical World: An illustrated Encyclopedia of Weapons, Warriors and Warfare in the Ancient Civilizations of Greece and Rome*, Salamander

Wechler, K.-P. 1994 'Zur Chronologie der Tripolje-Cucuteni-Kultur aufgrund ^{14}C Datierungen', *Zeitschrift für Archäologie* 28, pp. 7–21

Weidenreich, F. 1943 'The skull of Sinanthropus pekinensis', *Palaeontologica Sinica* N.S. 10, pp. 1–484

Weigley, R.F. 1991 *The Age of Battles: The Quest for Decisive Warfare from Breitenfeld to Waterloo*, Bloomington and Indianapolis, Indiana University Press

Weisfeld, G. 1995 'Aggression and dominance in the social world of boys', in J. Archer (ed.), *Male Violence*, London, Routledge, pp. 42–69

Wells, H.G. 1936 *The Anatomy of Frustration*, Cresset

Wels-Weyrauch, U. 1989 'Mittelbronzezeitliche Frauentrachten in Süddeutschland (Beziehungen zur Hagenauer Gruppierung)', in *Dynamique du bronze moyen en Europe occidentale*, Paris, Éditions du CTHS, pp. 117–34

Wendorf, F. 1968 'Site 117: A Nubian Final Palaeolithic graveyard near Jebel Sahaba, Sudan', in F. Wendorf (ed.), *The Prehistory of Nubia II*, Dallas, Southern Methodist University Press, pp. 954–95

Wendorf, F., Schild, R. & Close, A.E. (eds) 1986 *The Prehistory of Wadi Kubbaniya*, Vol. 1, Dallas, Southern Methodist University Press

Wenham, S.J. 1989 'Anatomical Interpretations of Anglo-Saxon Weapon Injuries', in S.C. Hawkes (ed.), *Weapons and Warfare in Anglo-Saxon England*, Oxford University Committee for Archaeology Monograph 21, Oxford, Oxbow Books, pp. 123–39

Wheeler, R.E.M. 1943 *Maiden Castle*, London, Report of the Research Committee of the Society of Antiquaries 12

White, T.D. 1992 *Prehistoric Cannibalism at Mancos 5MTUMR-2346*, Princeton University Press

Whitehouse, R. 1993 'Tools the Manmaker: The cultural construction of gender in Italian prehistory', *The Accordia Research Papers* 3, pp. 41–53

Whittle, A.W.R. 1977 *The Earlier Neolithic of S. England and its Continental Background*, Oxford, British Archaeological Reports Suppl. Series 35

—— 1988 *Problems in Neolithic Archaeology*, Cambridge, Cambridge University Press

—— 1996 *Europe in the Neolithic: The Creation of New Worlds*, Cambridge, Cambridge University Press

Wilcox, D.R. & Haas, J. 1994 'The Scream of the Butterfly: Competition and Conflict in the Prehistoric Southwest' in G.J. Gumerman (ed.), *Themes in Southwestern Prehistory*, Santa Fe, School of American Research Press, pp. 211–38

Wilkinson, J.G. 1878 *The Manners and Customs of the Ancient Egyptians*, London. Murray

Willroth, K.-H. 1997 'Prunkbeil oder Stosswaffe, Pfriem oder Tätowierstift, Tüllengerät oder Treibstachel? Anmerkungen zu einigen Metallobjekten der älteren nordischen Bronzezeit', in C. Becker et al. (eds), *Beiträge zur prähistorischen Archäologie zwischen Nord- und Südeuropa: Festschrift für Bernhard Hänsel*, Internationale Archäologie, *Studia Honoraria* 1, Espelkamp, Verlag Marie Leidorf, pp. 469–95

Wilson, E.O. 1971 'Competitive and aggressive behaviour', in J. Eisenberg & W. Dillon (eds), *Man and Beast: Comparative Social Behaviour*, Washington, Smithsonian Institution, pp. 181–217

—— 1978 *On Human Nature*, Harvard University Press

Windl, H. 1994 'Zehn Jahre Grabung Schletz, VB Mistelbach, NÖ', *Archäologie Österreichs* 5/1, pp. 11–18

—— 1995 'Schletz – das Ende einer linearbandkeramischen Siedlung?', in *Aktuelle Fragen des frühen und mittleren Neolithikums in Mitteleuropa*, Poysdorf

—— 1996 'Archäologie einer Katastrophe und deren Vorgeschichte', in H. Windl & M. Teschler-Nicola, *Rätsel um Gewalt und Tod vor 7000 Jahren – Eine Spurensicherung*, in *Ausstellungskatalog Museum für Urgeschichte Asparn a.d. Zaya*, pp. 7–29

Winghart, S. 1993 'Überlegungen zur Bauweise hölzerner Speichenräder der Bronze-und Urnenfelderzeit', *Acta Praehistorica et Archaeologica* 25, pp. 153–67

Woodcock, G. 1974 *Gandhi*, London, Fontana

Wright, Q. 1942 *A Study of War*, Vol. 1, Chicago, University of Chicago Press

Wüstemann, H. 1974 'Zur Sozialstruktur im Seddiner Kulturgebiet', *Zeitschrift für Archäologie* 8, pp. 67–107

—— 1978 'Zur Sozialentwicklung während der Bronzezeit im Norden der DDR', in W. Coblenz & F. Horst (eds), *Mitteleuropäische Bronzezeit: Beiträge zur Archäologie und Geschichte*, Berlin, Akademie-Verlag, pp. 195–209

Yates, A.J. 1962 *Frustration and Conflict*, London, Methuen

Yorke, B. 1993 'Fact or Fiction? The Written Evidence for the Fifth and Sixth Centuries AD', in W. Filmer-Sankey (ed.), *Anglo-Saxon Studies in Archaeology and History* 6, Oxford, Oxford University Committee for Archaeology, pp. 45–50

Zachos, K. 1996 'Metal jewellery', in G.A. Papathanassopoulos (ed.), *Neolithic Culture in Greece*, Athens: Nicholas P. Goulandris Foundation, Museum of Cycladic Art, pp. 166–7

Zaitseva, G.I. & Timofeyev, V.I. 1997 'Radiouglerodnye daty pamjatnikov mezolita-eneolita yuga evropeiskoi Rossii i Sibiri', in G.I. Zaitseva, V.A. Dergachev & V.M. Masson (eds), *Arheologiya i Radiouglerod* 2, St Petersburg, pp. 109–16

Zalai-Gáll, I. 1990 'A neolitikus korarokrendszerek kutatása a Dél-Dunántúlon', *Archaeológiai Értesitö* 117, pp. 3–23

Zápotocký, M. 1992 *Streitäxte des mitteleuropäischen Äneolithikums*, Weinheim, VCH, Acta Humaniora

Zbenovich, V.G. 1976 *Pozdnetripol'skie plemena Severnogo Prichernomor'ya*, Kiev, Naukova Dumka

Žeravica, Z. 1993 *Äxte und Beile aus Dalmatien und andere Teilen Kroatien, Montenegro, Bosnien und Herzegovina*, Prähistorische Bronzefunde IX/18, Stuttgart, F. Steiner

Zhilin, M. 1998 'Technology of the manufacture of Mesolithic bone arrowheads on the Upper Volga', *European Journal of Archaeology* 1/2, pp. 149–76

Zimmerman, L. 1997 'The Crow Creek Massacre: archaeology and prehistoric plains warfare in contemporary perspective', in J. Carman (ed.), *Material Harm: Archaological studies of war and violence*, Glasgow, Cruithne Press, pp. 75–94

Živanović, S. 1976 'The masticatory apparatus of the Mesolithic Padina population', *Zbornik Radova Antropološkog Društva Jugoslavije* 3, pp. 79–96

—— 1986 'Restes des ossements humains à Velesnica', *Djerdapske Sveske* III, pp. 286–8

Zoffmann, Zs. K. 1972 'Anthropological analysis of the cemetery at Zengövárkony and the Neolithic Lengyel culture in south west Hungary', *A János Pannonius Múzeum Évkönyve* XIV–XV, pp. 63–74

Zotović, M. 1972 'Dosadašnji saznava o arheološkoj prošlosti užickog kraja', *Užicki Zbornik* 1, pp. 5–18

INDEX